THE DEMOCRATIC CONTRADICTIONS
OF MULTICULTURALISM

METROPOLITAN COLLEGE OF NY
LIBRARY, 12TH FLOOR
431 CANAL STREET
NEW YORK, NY 10013

THE DEMOCRATIC CONTRADICTIONS
OF MULTICULTURALISM

Jens-Martin Eriksen & Frederik Stjernfelt

Copyright © 2012 Jens-Martin Eriksen and Frederik Stjernfelt

All rights reserved. No portion of this book may be reproduced or transmitted in any form by any means, electronic, mechanical, photocopying, recording, or otherwise, without permission in writing from the publisher. For information on getting permission for reprints or excerpts, contact telos@telospress.com.

Printed in the United States of America
16 15 14 13 12   1 2 3 4 5

Originally published in Danish as *Adskillelsens politik: Multikulturalisme—ideologi og virkelighed* by Lindhardt & Ringhof. Copyright © 2008 Jens-Martin Eriksen and Frederik Stjernfelt.

ISBN: 978-0-914386-46-9

Library of Congress Cataloging-in-Publication Data

Eriksen, Jens-Martin.
 [Adskillelsens politik. English]
 The democratic contradictions of multiculturalism / Jens-Martin Eriksen & Frederik Stjernfelt.
      p. cm.
 Includes bibliographical references and index.
 ISBN 978-0-914386-46-9
 1. Multiculturalism. 2. Social groups. I. Stjernfelt, Frederik. II. Title.
 HM1271.E7513 2011
 320.56'1--dc23
                                    2011036875

Telos Press Publishing
431 East 12th Street
New York, NY 10009

www.telospress.com

Contents

Preface	vii
Introduction: Multiculturalism: Soft and Hard	1

Malaysia

Malaysia and Its Road to Multiculturalism	13
Chirita's Anger and Patience	16
The Challenges of Multiculturalism	23
Human Rights and Islam: Two Different Worlds	30
An Alliance with Liberal Muslims Is Indispensable	39
There Is a Way for Us to Live That Is Pleasing to God	50
The Ban on Apostasy Is Meant to Control Muslims	60
The Problem Appears If You Do Not Have Any Religion	64
Ethnopolitical Communitarianism and the Public Sphere	72
We Could Not Have Imagined This in Our Worst Nightmares!	78
Postscript	97

The Broken Cup: From Culturalism to Multiculturalism

The Roots of Culturalism	103
From Anthropology to Politics: Anthropologists against the UN	116
Culturalism: From Idea to Unconscious Presupposition	122
The Argument of Culturalism Dissected	130
Left- and Right-Wing Culturalism: UNESCO and Lévi-Strauss	139
Finkielkraut and UNESCO Culturalism	147
From Culturalism to Multiculturalism	152
From Communitarianism to Campus Radicalism	160
Multiculturalism and Recognition: Charles Taylor	164
Liberal Multiculturalism as Political Philosophy: Will Kymlicka	171
Does Liberalism Need Multiculturalism?	183
Kymlicka in the Liberal Field of Gravity	193
The Chips from the Cup	198

Protection against Defamation: A Multicultural Group Right?

Muhammad and Fogh Caricatures: A Comparative Analysis	201
The Religious Pressure against Freedom of Speech	221

Political Columns

Culturalism: Culture as Political Ideology	237
Islamophobia	243
Free Speech and "Those in Power"	247
Culture as a Refuge	249
The Other	251
Xenophobia and Xenophilia: Two Kinds of Difference Worship	253
Secularism is Fundamentalist!	258
Fifty-five Questions to the New Norm	260
Enlightenment Versus Culturalism	263
Republicanism and Culturalism	269
Who Is Entitled To Disagree?	272
Two Levels of Values	274
Freedom of Speech: Freedom from Whom?	277
Islamic Rights	280
Apostasy	283
Asian Values	288
Christianity as the Mother of Enlightenment: A Culturalist Myth	290
The Invasion of the Word Snatchers: Culturalist Newspeak	294
Tolerance and Respect Are Not the Same Thing	297
Diversity as a Good	301
Monoculturalism in Plural	304
Revealed by the Veil	306
Spokesmen for a Culture	310
The Dynamics of Extremism	313
The Disneyland of Culture	323
Appendix: The Religious Pressure against Free Speech: A Chronology	325
Bibliography	381
Endnotes	391
Name Index	415

Preface

For financial support thanks are due to the Literature Section of the Danish Art Council, as well as to the Author Account of the Danish Writers Union. Thanks also to the Center for Semiotics, Aarhus University, for good working conditions.

Furthermore, we are grateful to the following for different sorts of contributions or help during work: Lars Erslev Andersen, Peer Bundgaard, Hans Hauge, Thomas Hoffmann, Lasse Horne Kjældgaard, John Michael Krois, Sune Lægaard, Mehdi Mozaffari, Morten Ebbe Juul Nielsen, Kirsten Marie Raahauge, Agnete Stjernfelt, Søren Ulrik Thomsen. A special thanks to Tom Griffiths and Neil Forsyth. Shorter sections of this book have appeared in earlier versions in the newspapers *Information* and *Weekendavisen*, the journals *Kritik, Lettre Internationale, Classicisme et Lumières*, the websites *Eurozine, Sign and Sight, Open Democracy*, as well as the books *Skabt til vækst* and Eriksen's travelogue *Timernes Bro*.

Eriksen is mainly responsible for section I, Stjernfelt for sections II and III whilst the introduction and section IV is by both of us. Quotes from non-English literature have been translated by the authors.

Jens-Martin Eriksen and Frederik Stjernfelt

METROPOLITAN COLLEGE OF NY
LIBRARY, 12TH FLOOR
431 CANAL STREET
NEW YORK, NY 10013

Introduction
Multiculturalism: Soft and Hard

Although multiculturalism has become a familiar concept in newspaper debates, political discussions, sociology, political science and other public and academic discourses, the term "multiculturalism" is often confusing and imprecise. It is frequently used to describe a condition, which already exists in Western Europe, the United States, and elsewhere, because of the actual presence of various cultural and religious groups and immigrants in these countries, but there is little elaboration of how these diverse cultures coexist in reality. The concept of multiculturalism also has another meaning which points toward a development in a not too distant future whose challenge we must be prepared to meet. Multiculturalism is something in the making, which will be realized rather than something already existing in our societies. Both usages are *descriptive*. But neither offers a substantive description of social coexistence, its various experiences, nor even which cultures constitute the supposed multitude, nor how these should co-exist.

A third way to use the concept of multiculturalism is *normative*. Here the meaning does not point to an existing or a coming condition, but rather to a set of changes in politics and ways of thinking necessary in order to meet the challenge of various cultural groups living together according to rules and ideals that each envisions as morally right. Here the use of multiculturalism sets up a declaration of intent, but the ambiguity of the concept persists as it remains unclear precisely what set of political changes this normative use of the concept implies.

Whether multiculturalism is understood as a definition of an already existing condition, a coming development or a declaration of political intent, the concept implies a historically determined condition in which political decisions are already fixed. It presents itself as a historical imperative; that is, a concept we are morally compelled to seek, simply because it represents an inexorable tendency in human history which will be realized no matter what, much like liberal democracy or human rights. To question the normativity of multiculturalism often meets much political resistance. Given such pressure, our only choice is to embrace multiculturalism and its often-unclear demands. Rather than blindly following such imperatives, we should seek out a better, more substantive understanding of multiculturalism, both in its descriptive and normative definitions.

In what we tentatively could call the individualist or the "soft" version of multiculturalism, it is perceived as a system where the individual can choose to live in whatever way she or he wishes. One can worship whatever god one wants to, or no god at all, one can live according to whatever cultural, sexual or gender preference one desires without discrimination from society. One can dress in whatever way one finds attractive or culturally right or individually expressive. In this meaning the concept seems to define the rights and freedoms of the individual. This diversity of cultural expression might appear hurtful, provocative or insulting to some with different cultural and religious norms, but others will have to accept that. For in this individualist or "soft" meaning of the concept, multiculturalism is defined by the rights of individuals to express their cultural identities. Moreover, the realization of the diversity of cultures in society implies that all individuals can demand their rights and express themselves freely as long as the freedom of others is not restricted.

There is also, however, another definition of multiculturalism contrary to the one which emphasizes individual human rights and freedom. In this version, a community may legally and socially enforce its own mores and traditions, whatever it holds sacred. In the most extreme form of this version of multiculturalism, the community may even mobilize its own police force and legal system in order to demand, to some extent or another, the conformity of individuals. This version of multiculturalism underlining collective rights we could define as the "hard" version.

The majority, at least in Western Europe, would perhaps not find many problems in the first, "soft" version of multiculturalism. But the second, the "hard" version, would appear a dubious project to many, despite the persistent fact that neither soft nor hard versions of the concept are employed with any kind of regular precision—particularly not when promoting "multicultural society" as an ideal. Multiculturalism is such a volatile concept, however, that it is crucial which version is promoted. Since most societies and academic institutions eschew both extreme "soft" and "hard" versions, the question arises whether a variant somewhere between the two extremes could function as a political ideal.

What initially looks like a semantic problem about ambiguity and precision related to the term is in fact a political problem. What variants of multiculturalism are compatible with Western political standards such as rule of law, liberal democracy, human rights? It is the hypothesis of this book that a proper understanding of the democratic contradictions of multiculturalism requires a plural perspective, arguing from both existing multiculturalism, from conceptual clarification, and from political discussion. This is why this book examines this crucial question from three perspectives: an empirical perspective, a theoretical perspective and finally from a political perspective.

The first part of the book is an empirical study of multiculturalism in Malaysia, one of the leading countries in the world concerning realization of the "hard" version of multiculturalism. In interviews and discussions with intellectuals, human rights activists, lawyers, clerics, editors, and journalists we will examine the problems in this political structure.

The second part of the book maps out important trends in the history of ideas which have led to the articulation of the conception of culture upon which the term multiculturalism is based. In this perception, culture is seen as the decisive determinative for human life, while economy, politics, society and other aspects of life are merely side effects of the more basic level. But how was this concept developed? How has it spread through academia, media and politics? Where are the problems in this concept of culture?

The third and the fourth part of the book examines aspects of multiculturalism and multicultural discourse from a political perspective. The third part treats, as a case-study, the discussion about privileged rights for religions in order to prevent insult. Here we examine the cartoon crisis in Denmark and the international attempts at legislating against "defamation of religions."

The fourth part of the book is a cluster of small, polemical essays addressing the problems with multicultural discourse and rhetoric and where we pose the most decisive questions that are rarely addressed: which variants of multiculturalism are compatible with basic liberal and democratic standards—and which are not?

A recurrent term in this book is what we call "culturalism." Despite the fact that the question of culture was introduced into political vocabulary in World War II, there have not been many principled discussions dealing with the conflict between cultural dogmas and universal ideas about individual freedom. Nor have there been many studies examining the problems of real, existing multiculturalism. Nor have the political complications of the concepts that maintain that individuals are wholly determined by their culture been scrutinized. This is the point of view we describe in this book as "culturalism," and according to which collective rights and community rights take precedence over individual rights.

Surprisingly, we find this culturalism represented both on the right and on the left of the political spectrum. In the left version, it is propagated under the term of multiculturalism, much too often accepting any value, dogma, or rule as long as it can be justified with religion or culture. On the right, we find culturalism in the form of nationalism, a repressive ideology against anything that fails to conform to the national culture. This philosophical identity between the two forms of culturalism—right and left, conservative and liberal—is ignored in both academia and in the general public debate, most probably because they are political opponents. This book points to the fact that, although the right and left are adversaries, they are nevertheless homologous adversaries. They remain generally uncritical defenders of territorial nationalism or cultural-religious particularism, respectively. Culturalism is the term that captures this common tendency; in both cases, culture becomes a political ideology.

The focal point of this book is the democratic contradictions of one of these culturalisms: multiculturalism. That is why we open up the examination with a journey to Malaysia, a country which has implemented a "hard" version of multiculturalism. What is it really? What does it specifically imply? What are the implications of a multicultural political concept and what kind of compromises must be made to accept the multicultural dream?

In the West, multiculturalism is little more than a popular collective dream, a blurred vision. But in Malaysia, a society with different dynamics, multiculturalism is real. This postcolonial country, with a new complexity of culture and ethnicity, represents a stage in the history of diversity at which the West has not yet arrived. That might be the best reason to listen to voices there and reflect over their anger, emotions and experience, of which we have but little so far.

We have picked Malaysia for this empirical part of the book because it is an example of an ethnic and cultural mixed society and because it is a unique experiment with separate legislation for different religious groups (a development which is also, to a lesser extent, in the process of being realized in the UK). But it is important to keep in mind a proviso: there is no single "reality of multiculturalism" as something once and for all established, a definitive pattern for all real variants of multiculturalism. Rather, different local movements can be investigated and studied in the field to gather information on the structure of multiculturalist tendencies.

Multiculturalism, such as we have defined it in this introduction comprises softer and harder versions. Among the harder versions, with different degrees of separate legislation, can be counted the experiments in Canada, the USA, the UK, Australia, and—to the greatest degree—in Malaysia. We have chosen Malaysia as the case-study for this book for several reasons. The other countries mentioned are—no matter what the geographical and social differences between them—Western countries with mostly Western populations and culture, which have introduced special legislation to accommodate immigrant or aboriginal minorities only to a limited degree. In contrast, Malaysia is, as Stephen Gan, the oppositional editor-in-chief of the internet journal *Malaysiakini*, says, not without national pride, "something unique in the whole world."

It is a country which, until decolonization in 1957, was exposed to the reality created by its geographical location and the long history of colonialism—a multiethnic nation of people with different languages, different religions, and different ethnic backgrounds (once called "races"). In this unique situation around the "Merdeka" (independence and freedom), it was necessary to articulate a constitution and shape a nation on which all groups in society could agree and could recognize as their own. This became the draft constitution of the Lord Reid Commission for the Malaysian Federation, which only later—during the 1980s—developed into a "hard" version of multiculturalism as we have defined it: different people, different religions and cultures, different legislations in one and the same political territory.

Official Malaysian tourist organizations paint multiculturalism in rosy colors: "Multiculturalism has not only made Malaysia a gastronomical paradise, it has also made Malaysia home to hundreds of colorful festivals." From some of the informants we meet, however, it appears that it is a system which is still in a dynamic process where cultural and religious differences are permanently being deepened in a legislation process tending towards ongoing segregation, a process in which liberal democracy and human rights clash with religious bigotry.

The question, then, is what can we learn from our observations under such circumstances and to what extent are we entitled to claim that the conclusions are valid for assessing multiculturalism as such? This is the place for certain provisos. This is a hard multiculturalism, which nonetheless takes place in an officially democratic context of free and fair elections within a parliamentary system and develops in a largely Muslim country with large non-Muslim minorities, with a strong Islamic influence and a nationalistic—if not chauvinistic—policy by the Malays at the expense of the two large minorities of Chinese and Indians. These facts imply, of course, that Malaysia's experiment with multiculturalism cannot serve, in detail, as a model (positive or negative) for Western countries, not least because the demographic and religious composition differs so much; the Malaysian case cannot serve as any simplified idolization or criticism of multiculturalism.

As a case-study, however, Malaysia may indeed serve to provide empirical substance to the concept of multiculturalism. Nationalism and religion are only in principle distinct, in reality they are often mixed in diverging and powerful currents and emotions—most conspicuously in Malaysia. Sometimes a development within the Malaysian multiculturalist formula comes out of nationalism, in other cases out of religion, in still other cases a mixture of the two. Here, conceptual clarification must be added to the concrete descriptions of single cases in this multiculturalist journey, which has been a major source of insight for us. We hope the reader will be able to learn something from these experiences with a unique case of cultural meetings and political clashes.

The historical backgrounds of multiculturalism have much too rarely been charted. A major strand of the development of multiculturalism stems from the anthropological concept of culture and its dissemination as a political concept among Western middle classes, and, more specifically, in the United Nations. From there, it took root first of all in former British colonies like Canada, the USA, Australia, Malaysia, and later spread to European countries like the UK and Germany. The anthropological concept of culture is the root of culturalism. Early American anthropological doctrine claims that man is a cultural being through and through, that the beliefs and behaviors of the individual are determined by the culture he or she belongs to, and that once "enculturated" it is impossible to adopt the position of cultures other than one's own. In order to understand the intricacies of multiculturalism, it is important to appreciate that this theory of culture was originally conceived to be progressive. Early anthropology resolutely acted against racist assumptions in the social sciences, the idea that culturally specific features of different groups had a biological origin.

This is why culturalist theory is immediately coupled with a doctrine of anthropological incomparability: it is deemed impossible to pass judgment on the practices of other cultures, and their institutions, practices, and conceptions may differ in any conceivable manner. The upshot of such a culturalism, however, would seem to be the immediate incompatibility, enmity, hostility and war between cultures. This is why it is strange but understandable that anthropological culturalism hastens to add the conclusion that all cultures possess equal dignity and thus merit the same degree of tolerance and respect. The noble intention in this idea is clear: to break with earlier theories of evolutionary scale of different human races. Fair as it may seem, however, this culturalist doctrine entails some dark sides overlooked. One corollary is that even the most cruel and anti-democratic practices must be accepted, once they acquire the noble status of being "cultural" rather than political. Thus, many of the tensions in actual multiculturalism originate in anthropological culturalism. This book dissects the democratic tensions in the conceptions of culturalism in a philosophical section, pinpointing the internal contradictions already inherent in the bundle of different claims characterizing culturalism in its early, anthropological version.

On the practical level, these contradictions give rise to an immanent tension between culturalism and democratic principles: if a "culture" favors beliefs and behaviors which clash with the rule of law, democracy and human rights, which should yield? This tension appeared in an important and prophetic clash in 1947 between the American anthropologists and the UN committee writing the UN Human Rights declaration, led by Eleanor Roosevelt. Already, the incompatibility between culturalism and individual rights had begun to appear. The section of this book tracing the connection between culturalism and multiculturalism explores its further development in UNESCO up to present-day Canada's formation of the most articulate theoretical version of multiculturalism, with representatives such as Charles Taylor and Will Kymlicka. Their philosophical doctrines (Taylor's Hegelian-based multiculturalism, with its emphasis on common morality, and Kymlicka's more Kantian-flavored version, with the weight on liberal rights) are analyzed with the result that both eventually end up willing to sell out important democratic principles in order to compromise with culturalism.

A concrete example of such compromises can be seen in the famous case of the Danish cartoons of Muhammad. An analysis of the central drawing of Muhammad-with-a-bomb-in-the-turban finds that it is normal, international cartoon practice to draw the originator of a doctrine as a symbol of that doctrine; such cartoons deal with the doctrine of Islam rather than aiming at Muslims as persons. In the same vein, equipping politicians or thinkers with bombs, grenades or other weapons to convey their violent intent is just as common a device in cartoon drawing. Despite the normalcy of such drawings, many of the arguments against them (in Muslim countries as in the West) rest on a multiculturalist assumption that certain groups are entitled not to be offended, to have religious belief protected, to attack people taken to offend them, etc. The Cartoon Crisis thus offers a conspicuous example of the clash between basic, universal human rights claimed for all individuals, such as free speech, and the group rights claims of hard multiculturalism.

The empirical examples—Malaysia and the Cartoon Crisis—as well as the historical and theoretical charting of multiculturalism make possible a series of conclusions which are presented in a more pointed style in an array of columns addressing central issues in the ongoing debate. "Islamophobia," "respect and tolerance," "Asian values," and many other catchwords may now be analyzed in a new and refreshing fashion. The bottom line of the investigation is the importance of embracing the basic principles of liberal democracy. To give in on issues like group rights, split legislation, legal pluralism, protection against "defamation," differentiated rights according to gender, religion, ethnicity, culture, etc. is to give up on equal rights and liberties so basic for a dynamic democracy. Celebrating difference and group rights identities will inevitably lead us to place religious and ethnic authorities at a higher level than universal values. Against the inherent conservatism of all culturalisms, the basis of democracy is individual freedom granted by human rights.

Thus, the overall argument of the book takes us from the Malaysian case study, via the history and structure of culturalism, through a discussion of present day theoretical and practical multiculturalism to a conclusion by means of a set of pinpointed arguments.

Malaysia

Malaysia and Its Road to Multiculturalism

Most democratic critics will not refuse multiculturalism in its softer versions, recognizing that a country like Malaysia has the historical and geographical destiny of having a population mixed from several parts of Asia. It is evident that no group is in a position to demand that the other groups should disappear or make themselves invisible in an exhaustive assimilation to the former's culture and religion. Rather, the central issue of the political fight is the meeting between individual rights and the rights of cultures and religions, where the borderlines should be established between multiculturalism and liberal democracy. On that level, it resembles the ongoing political struggle in the West between religious culturalisms and nationalisms, and liberal democracy. Detailed studies of the Malaysian case may help open our eyes to the global context of which we are a part, and to the real front line that lies in our own terrain, between patriotic nationalists, religious nationalists and culturalists on the one hand and proponents of liberal, secular democracy and the rule of law on the other.

The geographical location and the biogeography of the country contribute, to a large extent, to understanding why it faced the challenge of uniting the different groups in one free nation with a democratic constitution in 1957. An important part of the identity of the original Malayan people is Islam, which came to the Malay peninsula during the 15th century with Arab merchants and missionaries. Not much later, the Portuguese and the Chinese found their way to the country and founded trade stations, especially on the west coast of the peninsula, at Penang and the Malacca Straits. These stations became the basis for the spice trade with Europe and the country became a central focus for the growing overseas trade between China, India, and Europe.

The expansion of the European empires led to armed conflicts where changing parties fought for the protection, or expansion, of their rights to markets and to position themselves in overseas trade. Singapore's strategic trade location at the southern tip of the peninsula played an important role. In this period, before the English finally assumed control of the whole peninsula, the Dutch and the French joined the Portuguese in the fight for imperial territories. At the beginning of 19th century, Britain controlled the Malacca Straits, and during the ensuing 30 years they expanded their control to the Crown Colonies of Penang, Malacca, and Singapore. In the early 20th century, large parts of the country were integrated under British control with the federal Malayan states.

During the 19th and 20th centuries, demography is drastically altered because of the introduction of the country into the global economy led by the British Empire. Until the development of the Stannium mines on the west side of the peninsula, the country was, by and large, a monoethnic country, in which the Malay population was occupied in subsistence agriculture, producing mainly for their own consumption. (Later in this book, an interview with Benjamin Dawson will elaborate on the development of juridical and political conditions during this period.) The development of mining and the resultant shortage of labor for the industry prompted mining corporations, both the powerful Chinese corporations and the British, to import Chinese workers from Southern China. The second industrial breakthrough affecting demography was the introduction of caoutchouc rubber production during the last decades of the 19th century. This led to the bringing in of what would later become the third in number of Malaysia's populations; Indian workers from Ceylon and Southern India. The expansion of the car industry in the US in the early decades of the 20th century created an immense demand for rubber in the world market and a corresponding demand for workers on the Malayan plantations. From having been an ethnically homogeneous country with basically one religion and one language, Malaya changed dramatically during the British period of overseas trading. Today, the 27 million population is made up of approximately 65% ethnic Malays, 26% Chinese, and 8% Indians; less than 1% belong to the pre-Malayan, animist native tribes of Orang Asli.

On top of imperial policies and demographical changes, the political struggles leading up to independence from Great Britain in 1957 also shaped the preconditions for Malaysian multiculturalism. When the negotiations about the country's independence began after the end of World War II, there was no unanimous agreement upon which state to create. It was the Chinese (led by the strong, Malayan-Chinese Communist Party) who formed the resistance movement against Japanese occupation during the war, and they played an important post-war role when the British returned in 1945. This contributed to the creation of high expectations in the large Chinese minority about what kind of state should be established. Neither the Chinese nor the Indians had any idea that they had immigrated into an ethnically Malayan country with Malays in power. Rather, from their perspective, they had immigrated into a part of the British Empire, or, to the Indians, from one part of that Empire to the other. This gave rise to a natural political expectation within these groups of an independent state where non-Malays would be awarded citizenship and full rights on a par with others—but also an expectation of being able to keep separate education systems, culture, and history in each group, so that all such cultures assumed the same status. The multicultural perspective also formed part of the first proposal for a constitution, which was sketched by the British in the early negotiations of Malaysian independence in 1946. Such expectations, however, provoked the establishment of organized Malay nationalism with the large Muslim Malay party UMNO (United Malays National Organization, which is now in power) in protest against the British proposal. The Malays did not want to share the country with the ethnic minorities—the "new guests," as was the standing name for both Chinese and Indians. To the Malay nationalists, on the contrary, the objective was to define the country as a nation belonging to the Malays where their culture, language, and religion had an absolute priority.

In 1955, the British Lord Reid Commission reached a compromise between representatives for the nationalists and the two minorities. This proposal became the foundation for the 1957 Constitution, according to which all "new guests" were given full citizenships as Malaysian citizens—but also that the official national language of the state is the Malay language Bahasa, that the official religion of the country is Islam, and the Malays have a certain priority in the appointment to official positions. The country got a two-chamber parliamentary system like that of Great Britain, and an electoral system with majority election in districts electing one candidate each, all to be topped off by constitutional monarchs (sultans with representative functions). In 1963, Singapore and the Borneo areas of Sarawak and British Northern Borneo joined the Malayan Federation to form Malaysia. In 1965, Singapore was expelled from the state because of fears of Chinese domination and the early years of the new state were dominated by armed conflict with Indonesia.

In 1969, however, ethnic violence broke out in Kuala Lumpur. Part of the ensuing reconstruction consisted in the establishment of Barisan

National (the National Front), which took the shape of an expansion of the alliances of the governing Malay Nationalist Party to include representatives of the Chinese and Indian minorities on a stable basis. This coalition has held power in Malaysia ever since then, and grants a remarkable number of privileges to the Prime Minister appointed by the UMNO. He may veto the candidacy of any person from the other parties of the coalition running for election, and in this way governs not only his own party but also those of the alliance partners. Thus, it is in his power to prevent any questions being raised against the legitimacy of the policy of privileges entailed by NEP (the New Economical Policy), which was introduced at the same time. NEP will be discussed below in this section. Another remarkable aspect of the power of the Prime Minister is the Internal Security Act (ISA)—also discussed later. This legislation gives the Prime Minister—*in casu* his Minister of the Interior—the right to arrest and hold any citizen for up to a period of two years without being produced before a judge. If the authorities deem it necessary, this suspension of *habeas corpus* may continue for another two years. In the argument for this ability of the Minister of the Interior to imprison citizens without a sentence, the law states that it is motivated if the Minister "... is satisfied that the detention of any person is necessary with a view to preventing him from acting in any manner prejudicial to the security of Malaysia or any part thereof or to the maintenance of essential services therein or the economic life thereof, he may make an order (hereinafter referred to as a detention order) directing that that person be detained for any period not exceeding two years." (Section 8 Internal Security Act)

Chirita's Anger and Patience
Among Indians, a minority in the ethnic state

"People live like sheep in this country, just look at them!" Chirita turns away from the table in front of the restaurant and points to the market, which is open late at night. People walk from one makeshift stall to another, which sell all kinds of goods: pirate CDs and DVDs from China, carpets, meat, vegetables, shoes, and shirts. There seems to be a movement of people in both directions of the market street. Some customers are searching curiously for something, others negotiating prices under the naked light bulbs outside the tent covers, but the picturesque view does not interest my hostess this evening.

She is filled with impatience and anger, quite unlike when I met her in Europe six months ago. Either something has happened in the meantime, or perhaps you are inclined to speak more nicely about your country when you are abroad. This evening in the Bangsar area of Kuala Lumpur, in front of the Indian restaurant, her usual devout patriotism is not apparent. Indeed, one could easily get the impression that Malaysia is not her country at all, despite the fact that she was born and raised here. She is truly Malaysian, although it seems as if she hasn't gotten used to it, or perhaps she is just incensed over something, which might be difficult to express to me. I have really tried to portray a positive attitude to politics in Malaysia since we met late in the afternoon and began to discuss my project about interviews on multiculturalism, but I immediately understood she felt a lot of anger toward her country.

She claims people in Malaysia are only concerned with eating and being led like a bunch of sheep. There is no public culture, no newspapers of interest at all, no independent news media, no interest in art and literature. The political parties—and in particular the governing Muslim party—manipulates all newspapers and TV stations and radio. She opens a newspaper on the table where we sit. The content refers chiefly to traffic accidents, sport, sensation, crime, and reports of the Prime Minister Abdullah, who opened a bazaar and a charity show, where a large group of small schoolgirls greeted him with flowers. In return he tells them what a great future Malaysia has if people will protect their virtue and their religious values against the vices of this modern world (alcohol, sex and rock music), all of which lead to debauchery.

Chirita is about to suffocate on her paratha bread over what she views as nationalist and political kitsch. It would be funny if it weren't so sad and real, she says.

But isn't there any way to escape all the charity bazaars, the moralist homilies, the flowers for the Prime Minister and sports news if you really try? She cannot be the only one suffering from idiosyncratic nausea in this country—Muslim or not Muslim? The Indians make up 8% of the population, the Chinese 26%. These two groups, which generally reject the dominant national ideology of self-denial and abstention, could together form a basis for a secular culture in the news media in public

17

debate, in public life. I helplessly try to encourage Chirita, but all is in vain. Although she points to a website, *Malaysiakini*, with a critical and intellectual approach, the rest is sheer political conformity with complete denial of the political reality of the population at large. But then again, these efforts from *Malaysiakini* don't lead to anything; they don't have any impact at all. No matter how much this website attempts to expose the dominant political ideology and its dirty laundry, Chirita asserts that it doesn't make people wake up to reality and fight the corruption and the discrimination, the segregation and the racism in the constitution, the religious hysteria and the moralist nonsense. What Malaysia needs is authenticity and truth, but a single channel like *Malaysiakini* is not enough to fight for that.

The opposition media itself tends to be part of the national lie, of the hypocrisy and the pretense that this country is supposed to be democratic; the very fact that it is published on the net is a contribution to the illusion that there really exists a free press. But *Malaysiakini* is the only one, and it is reserved for a middle class with intellectual capacity and access to the net. The site is part of the repressive tolerance and it doesn't threaten anybody, no matter what is written.

People don't care; they just want to eat. "And the Muslims eat the most. But we Indians, we eat too." It's all in order to forget. It is your only pleasure. You eat to forget, that is the privilege of the wealthy middle classes. They can afford to eat as much as they want. She adds that I am not to take all this as a sign of her bitterness, just her anger.

She might give the impression of being a young writer, a rebel in any Western country who is suffocating under the pressure of conformism and looking for her own position in a cynical and hypocritical society. But she isn't. She is in her late forties, mother to two sons, has been working in public relations for years and has published a couple of books of fiction. We meet this night in Bangsar market, in front of an Indian restaurant where she wants to present to me the Indian contribution to the gastronomic variety of Malaysian cuisine. I can't help noticing that in spite of the sarcasm, the laughter and the beers, she feels something has been stolen from her in her life. What might it be? She has just had her manuscript refused by the publishers as they couldn't see its "commercial potential." That's the supposedly laconic judgment in a populist culture. But this is only the pretext for her anger now, not the real reason.

She leans over the table towards me. I must understand, all the wealth I see here in Kuala Lumpur is of a superficial character. Only money counts here, no true democracy, no human rights, and Malaysia is the only country in the world with racism as a principle in the constitution.

Some hours before, the same evening about 7:00 PM I had arrived by taxi at the quiet road in the suburb where Chirita lives with her family. I had left from my hotel in downtown Kuala Lumpur, the luxurious Radius with a view to the Petronas Towers, the Twin Towers of Kuala Lumpur, which rise towards the sky in steel and glass, resembling the Sagrada Familia in Barcelona—but on a monstrous scale.

The hotel where I'm staying has a swimming pool on the 12th floor, sauna and massage and fitness facilities, and a 24 hour deli in the basement, a shopping mall and a bar in which to quench your thirst after a hot day. It was maybe meant to be a nice and relaxing place to enjoy a beer, but it is always strangely empty and somber, with an odor of rat poison. Every evening a fat Thai lady performs her horrible songs accompanied by a man with a music box that seems to be playing several instruments at the same time—drums, guitar, and organ. After 8:00 PM this dreadful retreat is filled with foreigners, all businessmen, who are sitting around crying into their beer glasses while looking at the singer. I have been there a couple of times, sticking to the home brew of Carlsberg, and every time the crying men take a look at me—as if I was already dead! Merriness and laughter seem to be unknown sentiments in these regions.

There is something confusing about the suburbs of Kuala Lumpur and the taxi drivers have a hard time finding any address. Maybe they have never been away from downtown, but after half an hour's futile drive in the neighborhood, we manage to find the road where Chirita lives: a nice, quiet place with kids playing and women chatting in the street.

When I arrive at the house I see a man inside who apparently doesn't expect any visitors. I enter the driveway on foot and ring the bell. To begin with I hear only some odd guttural sounds, and then Chirita's laughter. She opens the door and we embrace. Strange to see each other here after a year, when we met for only a couple of weeks at a writer's retreat in Switzerland.

The man from the window is just behind her. She introduces us to each other. He is her son. He gazes at me with his big eyes as if I am the biggest surprise he has ever seen, but I notice he also has the same gaze when looking at his mother. When walking around in the living room, he moves strangely, abruptly, mechanically, as if he were a kid or locked up in a world of his own. He is obviously mentally handicapped, but Chirita doesn't bother to mention it. I will have to manage in her home and find out how to deal with it. I take it as a question of dignity: you don't point to your own scars right away.

Her sister is there to help to cook, as the son has to eat punctually at every meal-time. Her husband will be home in an hour or so. I also meet her younger son, a student waiting for a scholarship to Germany. The sister brings me a beer and I wait in the living room with the disabled son while they prepare his meal in the kitchen. I look around, my first time in a private home here in this country.

Everything is nice and peaceful and beautiful outside, in the outskirts of the city on the border of the rainforest. This Indian home is austerely furnished, just a sofa and some religious and family pictures on the walls and, as everywhere, the inevitable Sony TV. I drop onto the sofa to relax with my beer. And the disabled son walks restlessly, like a shadow, from one room to another. He approaches me and mechanically picks up some peanuts from a bowl to swallow them instantly, shells and all. It makes him cough horribly. He is trying to rip away my beer glass, possibly to mimic a toast with me, and he wants me to help him pour the beer into his mouth. I give him just a sip, trying to help him out of his condition, but the bitter taste of the beer seems to annoy him. I am a bit insecure whether this treatment is the correct one and call for Chirita. She just laughs, shaking her head and leads the son out to the kitchen. He is like a little baby, she explains; he cannot chew and he is of course not allowed to touch beer.

Her husband arrives at the same moment, impeccably dressed in a business suit, and we shake hands. A moment later, he returns from upstairs in shirt and the sarong every Indian wears. The situation is relaxed and we are seated around the table for the dinner. The husband is feeding his disabled son. I am sitting next to him while he is doing so; he feeds him the vermicelli Chirita has prepared. I like the natural way they take for granted that I understand the table protocol.

I only drink a little bit of beer and enjoy a little of every dish, saving my appetite for when I dine with Chirita later, at the market at midnight.

Chirita's husband feeds his disabled son while looking at me as one of the political pilgrims who often arrive here. Or maybe he thinks that Malaysia really hasn't got anything particular to offer? He is bitter because of the discrimination he and his family suffer.

It is not a racial discrimination but a cultural one. He suggests that I must never forget to mention apartheid when writing about multiculturalism. These two concepts are indivisible. You cannot define multiculturalism without mentioning apartheid as ingrained within it. I will have to understand that. He has had this discussion hundreds of times before, I feel. All my objections might just be lines in an already written script for the discussion. I try, nevertheless, to go on. Couldn't he try to understand the privileges afforded to the Muslims as sort of "affirmative action," like in the US?

He is patient with me. I must understand that I am at a dinner with Indians: a besieged minority in a Muslim country, as they see it themselves. In contrast, "affirmative action" in the US was a law initiated to help minorities out of a socially unacceptable situation. But here in Malaysia the privileges granted because of discrimination are reserved for the majority. That would be the same as if the US were to implement "affirmative action" for the white majority without any indication of when the law was going to be abolished. That is the way justice works here in Malaysia.

At least for the sake of argument I try to object. I mention Bosnia, about which I have written two travel books. Like Malaysia today, it was a society with three ethnic groups, a demographic key more or less identical to the one here, with a Muslim majority of approximately half of the population and with two big minorities of Orthodox Christians and Catholic Christians, like the minorities of Chinese and Indians in this country. In the multicultural experience in Europe, the state quite simply disappeared in bloodshed and the only thing left today is an international construction under the name of Bosnia, fully dependent on foreign economic subvention, advice and security. Might that indicate that, in spite of all the drawbacks, a sort of model for multiculturalism has been found here in Malaysia? At least there is peace, security, prosperity and stability.

But he is not impressed at all. Because here is here and not other places. Injustice is done here in his life, in his family's life—in the discriminatory system called multiculturalism here in Malaysia. It's time to leave the table in order to find a new one at the market, for Chirita and me.

We are seated in front of the Indian restaurant at the night market. Chirita is not good at hiding her feelings but, as she doesn't really know what I think, she is perhaps hesitant to be more explicit, out of a sense of decorum. I get the impression she feels that she and her family must suffer for another fashionable *Weltanschauung*, which is worshipped not only here but among naïve and fanatical Westerners. The minorities in the ethnic multicultural states have fallen victims to yet another secular religion of the West, and they stand no chance of any kind of attention, in spite of the violations of human rights. As we speak, it is as if she discovers how much anger she has in her, both against the system and against Western ignorance.

She recounts aspects of the ethnic violence in 1969 in a popular neighborhood here in Kuala Lumpur, between Indians and Chinese on one side and Muslims on the other. Her friend was an eyewitness and saw how the police (that is, the Muslim police) let armed Muslims pass, despite the fact that there is the death penalty for possession of weapons. This tells her that the minority lives at the mercy of the majority, but without rights.

I understand. But nobody seems to suffer from poverty here. Wherever you walk in the city you get the impression that you might as well be in New York or Paris. There are buildings, virtual shopping quarters where you get lost as a tourist in these insane labyrinths which seem to be endless, populated with frantic consumers and idle teenagers with nowhere to go. They just seem to spend what looks like eternity in these indoor business streets, day after day, so they will eventually have nothing to fear on the last day of the world. Until then people will be able to find whatever brand they want, because this looks like anywhere else: Kaufhaus des Westens in Berlin, Les Galeries Lafayette in Paris, Bloomingdale's in New York. But Voltaire and Montesquieu don't seem to have arrived yet. Or maybe they have left again, reassured that they were not welcome here?

The Challenges of Multiculturalism
—on *The Malay Dilemma* by Mohammad bin Mahathir

In 1969, Malaysia exploded into interethnic violence in the capital, Kuala Lumpur. The violence provided the opportunity for the Muslim Mohammad bin Mahathir, whose career was in ruins, to rise to the occasion and reflect in a serious and thorough way on the possibilities of a common political life between different ethnic groups. Independent Malaysia faced a new situation with vast problems after British colonial rule. The old Muslim population of Malays now constituted little more than half the total population, while the rest were of different race, ethnicity, culture, language and religion. Still, after Mahathir assumed power, and after his authorship of the book about multicultural society, *The Malay Dilemma,* the country succeeded in developing into a rich society with security and stability. What is the price for this multiculturalism? I made a plan for the following days to meet the people behind *Malaysiakini*, the critical opposition net magazine that Chirita mentioned, in order to learn more. But let us begin with a theoretical perspective and then bin Mahathir's ideas in his early multiculturalism classic.

In his critical book on multiculturalism from 2001, *Community: Seeking Safety in an Insecure World*, the British-Polish sociologist Zygmunt Bauman points to the fact that if society lacks a common culture, a common normative basis, it will split up into enclaves, refuges, particular cultures which only care for themselves and leave the social, political, and cultural community behind. Society as such disappears and gives way to myriads of small societies. This is Bauman's description of a tendency within multiculturalism which he—unlike many other Western intellectuals—conceives of as a negative development. It destroys and atomizes society, propagating a tribal way of thinking where general political problems are left to the single groups. Individuals are not only socially ghettoized, but also individually and culturally ghettoized, so that they become reduced to their ethnicities, veritable hostages of their cultural, ethnic groups. Social problems become, so to speak, privatized, culturalized. An economically privileged middle class may flee social problems by living in unmixed neighbourhoods. They ensure their children's futures and security by sending them to private, ethnically insular schools with no immigrants, which may weigh heavily on finances. In this way, it is possible to ignore the problems of the rest of society.

Mahathir already confronts some of the same issues in his 1970 book, *The Malay Dilemma*. Written after the 1969 revolts with ethnic violence in Malaysia, the book forms a reflection on the reasons for this Malaysian catastrophe. Society no longer had any cultural cohesion. Malays (Muslims), Chinese, and Indians still lived as neighbors, and they met in professional business contexts and maybe even in social contexts. But, as Mahathir adds, when they went home, they sought a refuge, which is specifically ethnic and cultural, and—we may add—religious. "Home" in this context was a place where no one from the other groups would appear and, even if they did, where their norms would appear strange and in conflict with the local norms of such a closed community. Here, we are led to believe, is another space, a field where another discourse may find its evident unfolding without any moderation and protest from "the other strangers" in society. This may very well be described as a richness of diversity or manifold in society, but it is not a difference between individuals. On the contrary, it is a segregation which already exists before the individual is able to shape his personal experience of values, a cultural separation into which individuals are born and where they are raised as segregated from the other groups.

Such a diagnosis would be negative from the pen of Bauman, but not so from Mahathir, who wrote in 1970 about an already existing reality. As the editor-in-chief of *Malaysiakini*, Steven Gan, exclaims during my conversation with him: let us be specific when talking about the challenges of multiculturalism. The issue is Islam and the hegemonic dogma of this religion vis-à-vis other religious and ethnic groups in this national context. You cannot ignore that.

Mahathir writes that the expansion of Islam as the religion of the Malays meant that a barrier was erected against apostasy and against marriage between the different ethnic groups. Before Islam arrived on the Malayan peninsula, before Muslim missionaries arrived, Malays were free to intermarry. Islam, however, prohibited such marriages unless specific rules were observed, such as the conversion of the spouse to Islam. Mahathir claims this also meant that all that deviated from the established Islamic order was deemed suspect, and was rejected. The author does not judge whether or not this is to be taken as a positive feature of the historical development in Malaysia, but as the book is primarily written for his own ethnic group, (which should supposedly elect him, writing as a powerless politician at a nadir in his career), it must be assumed to be an observation for critical scrutiny. In any case, it is an observation that is relevant in the Western context as a central aspect of the confrontation between Islamic currents and other cultures—in Europe between Islamic movements on the one hand, and secularism or Christianity on the other.

In this context, it must be discussed whether these aspects of Islam form a normative basis of a society which is conducive to diversity and trust. A premise for such a discussion, of course, is that there is a shared assumption that there are indeed parallels between Mahathir's 1970 description of Malaysia and the situation in the West today—and that human rights are assumed to be part of a shared normative basis.

Mahathir writes that ethnic equity and equality are founded on certain values—and values differ, depending on the standards and norms, which a given ethnic society accepts. Here it can be asked to what extent it is necessary for a society to possess a *common* set of basic values, which formally and culturally regulate the behavioral patterns of the single ethnic groups. If we should not merely speak about tolerating—accepting, not necessarily respecting—the behavior and ideas of other ethnic groups, but also, in some sense, of recognizing these ways of acting and thinking, is it not necessary to reflect deeply on what such a mutual recognition entails? Does a harmony between groups—and thus a harmony between the individuals of a society—not require that they have a common normative ground, a common minimum set of principles which all must obey, respect and refer to as something given, from which ways of thinking and acting may be judged?

How can one draw the outline of such a normative basis? Can one demand of all ethnic and cultural groups the unconditional acceptance of human rights, no matter whether they clash with the religious or ideological dogma of those groups? Can it be expected that, in such cases, they will be willing to go against their own allegedly holy writings or practices? These are, of course, the most basic issues, which must be solved before judgment can be passed on dogmas and values of a multicultural society. Are you willing to recognize the universalism of the human rights, which demand that all individuals of a society are ascribed the same rights, independently of their ethnic or religious origin or their gender?

It is striking the extent to which bin Mahathir's and Bauman's observations agree—the former writing in an Asian context 40 years ago, the latter in a European context 30 years later. This might indicate that their observations do in fact address general features and problems in multicultural societies.

Mahathir addresses the "ghetto" as a phenomenon or, more generally, the ghettoization of societies in the context of ethnic equality. He writes that economic and social discrimination is just as efficient and humiliating as juridical discrimination. In a European context, much confusion reigns around this issue. Some conceive of the ghetto as a characteristic feature in a multicultural society. Some, like parts of the European left, have even glorified this as a sign of the diversity of multicultural society, based on the idea that, in just the same way that individuals of a society are different, the ethnic groups of a society are also different and would want to plan their life accordingly and settle and live within the confines of their own ethnic group. Others, however, see this is as a sort of naivety to be overcome. Both Bauman and Mahathir go against the ghetto, because ethnic segregation first and foremost suppresses individuals, restrains their possibilities, reduces them to their ethnic characteristics. And is it not the case that such a segregation, which is nominally ethnic only, also entails social, cultural, and educational segregation? Does it not have the same effects as a formalized apartheid law?

Mahathir addresses an issue in multicultural society in Malaysia which, to some extent, is comparable to contemporary issues in the West. He writes that blacks in the USA towards the end of the 1960s are more integrated in society as a whole than are the different ethnic groups in Malaysia. Blacks in the USA are Christians, with the same religious norms as white Christians, and they speak the same language. In Malaysia, you find not only different ethnic groups, but also different religions and different languages in addition to some of the economic and educational differences, which follow from ethnic partitions.

With the current demographic developments in the West, especially in parts of Europe, where the number of immigrants and their descendants grow and tend to live in segregated ghettos in European metropolises, ever larger groups will live separated from the rest of society, economically, socially, and culturally. This individual and social segregation from the surrounding society has already provoked frustrations, giving rise to destructive behavior both in immigrant groups and groups from the larger society—for instance in Copenhagen or the Paris suburbs. However, the frustrations have not yet reached the scale of Kuala Lumpur 1969.

Mahathir attempts to articulate which aspects should be taken as fundamental for the creation of a national community—what is often called the "cohesion" of a society. He claims that one single ethnic group with common language, culture, and religion, living on a specific territory, is the basic prerequisite for creating what he defines as a "national unity."

In regards to multicultural society, the issue is the factors of ethnicity, language, culture, and religion, and it is necessary to investigate critically which of them must count as primary—as indispensable and basic for any community—and which of them may be seen as secondary, derived factors, depending upon the assumption that some kind of national community forms a *sine qua non* for a harmonious multiculturalism to be possible. What does a political community require and which aspects are secondary and may be left as special features of the single cultural group?

Mahathir writes that the largest and first multicultural society we know of is, of course, the USA. Here we know that the first immigrants from Europe, who formed the nation out of the first thirteen colonies, were all of British descent. After independence, however, waves of many other different Europeans followed, along with Chinese, Russians, and many more—the upshot was an ethnically, culturally, and religiously mixed society. But this mix enjoys an unbreakable unity because the English language remained predominant and was taken as a prerequisite for citizenship, as well as for functioning in society more broadly. Nowhere was there an insistence on equality between English and later immigrant languages, and we know that in most cases, original languages withered among immigrants after only one generation. Mahathir points to the fact of language being an indispensable part of culture; this was what made possible the creation of a national community and an American culture on the basis of a mixture of a distinct Anglo-Saxon culture and different features of non-British origin. On top of that came a system of education, which was exclusively based on the English language and with a central curriculum about the history of the new nation. These factors have, according to the author, not only created the new national community, but also fostered a respect for the symbols incarnating that community, such as the Constitution, the history of the nation, etc.

Thus, Mahathir points to the fact that "loyalty" forms the decisive test for whether such a multicultural community—a community across ethnic and religious distinctions—may include everybody without exception as true Americans and not second-rate citizens or immigrants, who are only there for economical reasons. Here, Mahathir refers to the ability and will of Americans to show solidarity with, and loyalty towards, their new multicultural nation, against the ethnic communities from which they or their ancestors originate, in situations of crisis or even war. This ability to identify with one's multicultural society, this national community among several ethnic groups, against the society from which you or your ancestors come—that is, to Mahathir, the real test of whether multicultural community is true or whether it remains superficial and only coheres because of opportunistic, economic interests.

The question is what the creation of such a multicultural community requires from the different ethnic cultures—not least whether it is possible for individuals to change and invest their loyalty in the project of constructing a community across ethnicity, religion, and culture. What is it you must change in yourself and in your culture in order to form part of this new synthesis? What must you give up, which other loyalties must be discarded, and to what extent must you change your worldview?

Mahathir describes the early immigration to Malaya, long before the British came and opened up for Chinese and Indian mass immigration. The first Chinese and Indian tradesmen, who settled at the Malacca Straits, gradually assumed the Malay culture and its language and gave up their original customs. Yet, they kept their own religion, without this leading to any conflicts between them and the original or "definitive people," the Malays.

Such a historical claim raises the question whether creating a harmonious version of multiculturalism in the liberal democracies of our day merely requires that immigrants assume the language and culture of their new homeland. What degree of assimilation is required also remains unclear. Mahathir mentions, as a positive trait of those merchants who settled in the Muslim society, that they assimilated with regard to language and culture—but not religion. Could one say a similar structure should hold for Muslim immigrants in the West, that they should assimilate to such a degree that only their religion remains to separate them from the larger society? Which compromises should Muslims, in that case, be ready to accept?

When Mahathir coins the notion of the "definitive people" in his description of multicultural society, he refers to the people who originally defined the country as a state with a government in power, forming a national unity ruling the country. In his book, of course, this refers to the Muslim Malays—but his argument is easily transferred directly to the single national states in Europe.

When it comes to education systems in multicultural society, he points out that, in addition to teaching and promoting knowledge and skills, it is also the role of that system to raise the pupils to become citizens of that state in which they live — to give them knowledge about, and a feeling of belonging to, a national community. Here, the role of education is to tell the pupils that they now belong to the "definitive people," they form part of the history of that people; here, according to Mahathir, begins the process of socialization, which should enable individuals to feel a part of the new multicultural community.

This multicultural community, however, is also exclusive, for it is only constituted by "the definitive people" and nobody else. To belong to this community, it is necessary to identify with the "definitive people." The teaching of cultural issues should thus communicate the claim that the nation belongs to "the definitive people." Identification with this people must be complete and without any reservations on the part of the immigrants and their descendants, they cannot identify with other communities, their former homelands or other national communities. Mahathir writes: "To identify with the definitive people is to accept its history, its geography, its literature, its language and its culture, and to reject all other relations of belonging."

This may sound fairly bombastic to Western ears. To what extent will these definitions have any relevance for European immigrant societies today, and to what degree? Mahathir was writing on a general level in these definitions, and in the context of 1969, when the new Malaysian state was threatened by ethnic violence and disintegration. These theoretical deliberations on multiculturalism throw an interesting light upon the further development of Malaysian multiculturalism in the 40 years since then, where certain religious issues do indeed seem untouchable.

It is striking that Mahathir does not mention religion as a field about which to compromise. One should not, according to him, relativize one's religion to any degree in order to belong to one's new community. But implicitly, it is hard to escape the fact that the practice of a religion which has rules for how one may behave with individuals not part of that religion, for which connections one may entertain with them, for how to celebrate the dogma of one's faith and the details of cult and worship must also entertain certain compromises with the new community. Maybe Mahathir did not see that because of the viewpoint of his own faith. Let us be specific. As the journalist Steven Gan says: We must talk about Islam.

Human Rights and Islam: Two Different Worlds

Interview with Indian editor of the web-based weekly *Malaysiakini*, K. Kabilan, Kuala Lumpur, Malaysia

It's my impression that the press in this country is totally uncritical towards the political establishment, indeed it seems as if politics has been censored from the newspapers. You only find gossip, sport, crime, sensationalism of any sort and absolutely toothless journalism when it's about politicians and political subjects. So tell me, what are you trying to build with your website project Malaysiakini?

We are trying to be a watchdog when it comes to the political establishment in this country. It's quite right as you put it that the press in Malaysia is not critical—not at all!—when it comes to the politicians and the government, quite simply because the press is owned by the government. Directly or indirectly. All media: TV stations, radio channels and the printed press are controlled by the governing Islamic party in this country or by other parties. Nobody writes critically because people have seen what has happened to others who have tried to criticize some politicians; when people have been too curious they have been sacked immediately. Therefore, the rest are very cautious. Journalism here means repeating what the politicians have to say to the journalists. That's it. That is why we have taken this initiative to build up *Malaysiakini*. We want to ask questions, quite simply, and that is the reason why we have become so popular. Our attitude is critical and that makes the politicians uneasy. But the only way they can put obstacles for us and harass us is by excluding us from press conferences etc. and in this way withhold from us information which we need. That is their reaction to a critical voice in the media. But we get around this arrogance and obtain the information we need. We write about the marginalized parts of this society and we give voice to the opposition when it's digging up something dubious about misconduct in the government.

I notice that you exclusively publish on the internet. Is that due to the problems you could face with a printed issue of your publication?

Exactly! It is very difficult to obtain a permission to publish printed matter in this country. You need such permission according to the law. The prime minister has said directly to the parliament that if you allow *Malaysiakini* to be distributed in a printed form it will create chaos in the country. Therefore, we will never get such permission, not even if we applied again and again. But he also added that *Malaysiakini* does an excellent performance on their website so do let them continue in this way. And in this he has a point when you consider that only 20% of the population in this country has access to the internet. But we do fine with this form of publication as we don't have to worry about any kind of permit of any sort—and the government has promised not to censor the internet, and it has kept this promise so far. The only way the authorities bother us is by boycott. No admittance to interviews, conferences, no comments from anybody, no access to police reports etc. But that's all.

Does Malaysiakini have any political tendency? Is it close to any of the three groups in this country; Indians, Chinese or Muslim Malays?

No, I think our readers are from all the three races. We are not dependent on—or associated with—a particular ethnic group. But when you have said that you also need to add that speaking of a marginalized group you implicitly speak about the Indians. When you speak about freedom of religion in this country you necessarily have to deal with the Muslims here because they have no freedom to leave their religion. According to the law of the land here, they have to follow Islam from the day they are born. They cannot choose themselves. The law doesn't give room for that possibility. Therefore, you cannot deal with the subject of freedom of religion without dealing with Muslims and Islam, that's obvious.

Now we seem to approach crucial issues within the context of multiculturalism. From conversations I have had here with an Indian family, I got the clear impression that they were very annoyed by what they see as racism, as an inseparable part of multiculturalism, at least the way it is practiced here. They claim that racism is officially approved of by the state with multiculturalism built into the constitution. They mention various privileges you are granted if you belong to Islam. Couldn't you interpret this in a more positive way by looking at it as a sort of affirmative action to help this country's original population out of poverty and let them get the benefits of more education—like we know affirmative action from the United States?

I admit there is something of affirmative action to it, that's right. But the case is that now these privileges have been granted to a special group for a longer period than it was initially planned. It's added to our constitution that Malays (Muslims) shall be granted special privileges and rights. And the reason for this is that at the time of independence from Great Britain this group was without many resources. The Malays were backward, to put it bluntly. They were not involved with other jobs than agriculture on a small scale and fishing, and they had no influence nor played any part in business and administration or as intellectuals. At that time, these measures giving special rights and privileges were reasonable in order to bring the Malays to level with the two other groups in society.

But when we move approximately forty years ahead to now, then these privileges are still applied. In spite of the fact that Malays play a role like anybody else, they still enjoy these privileges. That is the main question in this society. And when we speak of privileges we speak of possibilities for special loans guaranteed by the state, privileges in education, in jobs—but only if you are a Muslim. Moreover, Muslims get a special rate when buying real estate and apartments due to subventions from the state. It's also an obligation for any bigger firm to have a Malay in front. Everybody calculates with this, it's the only way you can get on. And a minimum of 30% of the employees have to be Malays. That's accepted by anybody. And 30% of the stocks have to be owned by Malays. You simply have to have a Malay leading any kind of business here—everybody has realized that. It's to guarantee that things will function, that you can obtain the necessary permits for this and that. And it's also the precondition if you want to talk yourself out of any sort of problem you might face with the authorities, the police etc. That is broadly accepted. But of course the rules provoke discontent—among the minorities. But nevertheless, it is difficult to see how we can get rid of this situation, as it is the majority who are in power. But the minority is discontent, very discontent, particularly when speaking on a confidential level. Anger has accumulated which you cannot express openly. But there is no way out of this situation. Approximately 60% of the voters here are Muslim Malays.

I read in the book The Malay Dilemma *by former Prime Minister Mohammad bin Mahathir that the state in this country must protect what he defines as community rights—and not to the same extent individual rights. It's an interpretation I also find in the book* Malaysia—State and Civil Society in Transition *by the Indian professor in political studies, Vidhu Verma, who also analyzes Mahathir's later political writings. According to Mahathir, this priority is due to the fact that community rights traditionally are more respected here in Asia, contrary to the West where individual rights are more respected. If we now interpret these duties and obligations Muslims also have—the ban on apostasy, obedience to a regulated lifestyle etc.—isn't that a reflection of what Mahathir writes about giving priority to community rights? These rules are there to protect the community against individuals who will rebel against tradition or quite simply leave the community of Islam?*

Regarding the Muslims, they have a special system, *sharia*, which is not applied to the other groups in society. As the leading body for this system there is the National Islamic Council. This council has an executive power as they have a religious police under their authority whose job it is to take care that Muslims abide by the religious rules of conduct—but this police force has jurisdiction only over Muslims, not individuals from other groups.

Muslims must obey the rules for Ramadan etc., not drink alcohol, not be in a place where alcohol is served, not participate in gambling, not be in what they call a "close proximity" situation with another individual, meaning no hugs, no kissing etc. in public places. These police patrol parks and check restaurants and bars to enforce the law. Sometimes they arrest people who are brought to the sharia court for breaking the rules of conduct and they are often fined from 300 to 500 ringgit (100 to 167 US dollars) for what is called public indecency—seen from a religious point of view. All these misdemeanours are punished with fines. But when we talk about apostasy then it's very serious. According to the Koran, people can be punished with death for such a crime, though not in this country. But according the laws here you are forbidden to leave your religion—again we only talk about Muslims, of course.

Simply put, you cannot leave Islam. It's not even something that you can imagine people will want to do. Although there was a case some years ago with some peasants in fact, who left Islam. Then the sharia court gave them a reprimand and told them it was wrong and sent them to some sort of re-education. They basically had to learn how to behave as good Muslims. It helped. But people know how to control themselves mostly because of the social pressure. You don't step outside. Here at *Malaysiakini* we have the intention of running stories about this subject of apostasy. You can talk about Muslims as they are according to the law—and how they are in reality. About the latter they have to keep silent.

When we look at this zealous determination with which religious rules are enforced here, couldn't it be seen as a way to control Muslims and, in this way, to also control power from the point of view of the political and religious leadership of the Muslim parties? If people lose loyalty toward religion and ethnicity and religion are torn apart, so it is not any longer a given fact that a Muslim party will obtain massive support from the majority of the population, then the ethnic-religious parties will lose power.

You might have a point there, but I don't think that's the reason why you have these religious rules. But on the other hand, of course the rules are exploited in the power play in politics. They are there to make sure the political elite can stay in power.

I am familiar with the fact that mixed marriages are only possible if the non-Muslim partner converts to Islam before—otherwise the marriage is not legal. Do you indeed find mixed marriages in this country? And is there any conversion to Islam in this way?

Yes, there are cases of this. And conversion to Islam from Chinese and Indians do happen in this way, for personal reasons. But mixed marriages are not very common in this country. People don't marry out, but rather stay inside their own ethnic group, in other words their religious group. In general, people stay within their group. Take a look in the countryside and you will notice that people live segregated: the Chinese live in their communities, the Indians in theirs—and the Muslims in their communities. And take a look at Kuala Lumpur. It is not something that happens just by chance. When you have a new project here in town for people from outside, some blocks are simply reserved for Muslims who will then live segregated in their own neighborhood. The same with the other two groups. You cannot just move in where you want to.

It also happens because you can more efficiently control a group when you have it located in the same space, when you look at this from the point of view of politics of power. That's a fact. In this way, you also make sure that business will only take place within the ethnic community—not between individuals from different communities. But this politics is not conducive to national integration between the three communities.

But maybe there is something ambivalent with the concept of integration in terms of various meanings? The ethnic elite could be said to have an interest in segregation because it ensures loyalty from the voters and thereby safeguards the interests of power. On the other hand it appears as if there are always some rules to be respected when Muslims live in a context with other communities. My question is then: is this idea about separate rules and obligations for Muslims that are in contradiction with liberal democracy and human rights inseparable from Islam? And are these rules inseparable from the very idea of multiculturalism where communities are supposed to live side by side—but not mixed?

I don't think that the various communities will be happy if people mix too much. They want segregation and they want individuals to stick to their own kind and live according to the norms of the community. To ask them to throw all this overboard, these differences, so we can have a greater community in Malaysia, a more integrated community between individuals will not function in this country.

According to Mahathir, the religious council, the religious police, sharia etc. are also there to control the individuals and protect the community. He writes that community rights are more respected here than in the West. Therefore, you cannot apply the human rights inflexibly here because they are developed in another social context in Europe. They can better be applied in ethnic and culturally homogenous societies where there is an identity between ethnicity, religion and culture—and therefore there will not be any confrontations between different groups because all share something and belong to the same big community. They are all individuals in a group.

My question is: Confrontation is a risk when you have a multicultural society with institutionalized cultures with their own institutions, jurisdictions etc. So how can you respect human rights and at the same time promote multiculturalism?

There is no balance between the two—human rights or multiculturalism—it's either or. And here in Malaysia we still have to fight for respect, for human rights. But everything must give way to Islam. That is the bottom line. All the time. You must give the Muslims what they demand. They are the majority. When it comes to the community rights of others, they must also give in to the Muslim community rights. That's a fact. For instance, if you have a non-Muslim neighborhood, they will have to accept the loudspeakers calling to prayer from the mosque, any hour day and night.

There is also something else I am thinking about. As you are probably aware, there is a tension in Europe between the secular and Christian parts of society on one side and the Muslim communities on the other. And the interesting angle is here, when you look at these contradictions between two sets of values, that it can be seen as the Muslim communities' attempt to protect themselves with the same means as are here formalized in the legal system in Malaysia: apostasy is not permitted, mixed marriages can only take place when the non-Muslim part converts, but it's better if they don't take place at all. Do you see some tendencies in Muslim culture and religion, which make it difficult to co-exist with other cultures in the same society without collective protection of their religious values? This may be done with a formalized legal system, a religious police etc., as here in Malaysia, or non-formalized as in Muslim communities in Europe with social pressure and physical threats. For it seems as if the Muslim communities in Europe do the same to protect the faith and the culture as the Malaysian state does here with the formalized, repression of internal opposition to culture and religion. And therefore you could maybe see this protection of collective rights in Islam as something general, and not something special for Malaysia. It is quite simply a tendency, which is a characteristic of Muslim culture. Do you think this is a correct reflection?

Yes, this is absolutely correct! But I don't know why it is like that. If you ask Muslims in this country, they will tell you that they just obey the law of the Prophet. He has told them what to do and then they do it. And that you cannot question. If you break the law anyway you will face a prison sentence. And moreover you will never get an answer to the question: why?

Quite simply it is not a question, which is open to discussion because the Koran is read literally, so there is no room for interpretation. The case is very simple. You describe this relation between Muslim culture and all other cultures very correctly; it's a universal phenomenon.

Let's take a look at the dynamics when you have a divided multicultural society. What happens in a society like this where the parties are organized along ethnic and religious lines? You have a party for the Chinese, a party for the Indians and two parties for Muslims. Doesn't it mean that you "take politics out of politics," so to speak? You reduce the parliamentary election to a census. Isn't that the consequence? People simply support the political organization claiming to represent their ethnic and religious community.

In a society with no political division in terms of culture and ethnicity, you will instead follow your ethical and economical preferences. What party is doing the right thing from my personal point of view and what party is promoting interests that I am dependent on? That's the questions you will ask in a liberal democracy with no organized cultural division. And whether the party you support is lead by Chinese or Indians or Malays is really not important. But what happens to the political dynamics when you have a multicultural political structure?

I think that the fact that we have ethnically organized parties is the reason why we don't have any integration in this country. We have been talking about changing the political structure with ethnic/religious parties for the last decade and instead organize national, multiethnic parties. But nothing has happened. None of the present parties seems to be interested. There is no prospect that there will be any change in that direction. The governing Muslim party controls completely the Muslim community in this country.

That also means that you can never be sure when our Prime Minister Abdullah talks about the rights of Muslims or the rights of society; party and state tends to be mixed up. There is no hope in terms of integration on the political level. And things are going from bad to worse. People tend to segregate more and more, the races tend to segregate. For instance you never see a Muslim in a Chinese restaurant any more—and that's of course because pork is served.

The religious values are strongly promoted. It started in the nineties. Muslim women began wearing the veil again and the politicians don't speak up against this. They need this identity politics as part of their power play. And if anybody else speaks up against it—be they Indian or Chinese—then you will hear Muslim politicians warn them to stop it: it will only lead to ethnic tension.

It seems as if ethnicity and ethnic culture are the primary identification denominators before you are Malaysian or anything else?

That's true. The question is then how you relate to that politically as a fact you can't do anything about. Many people emigrate from this country, all of them non-Muslims. They have quite simply given up. They can't stand it any longer. And that might be due to political, economic or strictly personal reasons. Demographically, it means that the Muslim percentage is growing while the Chinese and the Indians are becoming fewer. Particularly the Indians are emigrating. In the longer term, they will be fewer than the community of guest workers from Indonesia. And we are talking about brain drain: it's the most successful who emigrate from here.

An Alliance with Liberal Muslims Is Indispensable

Interview with Editor-in-chief Steven Gan, *Malaysiakini*, Kuala Lumpur

From your outlook here in a multicultural society where Muslims, Hindus, Buddhists and Christians live together, what is the reason for the miserable relation between the Muslim world and the West?

You will first have to take a look at things the way Muslims do in order to understand the situation. Take the conflict in the Middle East for instance. The way to perceive this conflict between Israel and the Muslims is reasonably balanced in, say, Scandinavia and the rest of Europe, but unfortunately not in the US. The Muslims cannot understand why the West is so focused on who in the Muslim world are in possession of nuclear weapons, for instance Iran, when nobody talks about Israel. This country is clearly in possession of nuclear weapons, but that fact is ignored in the West, nobody talks about it. But the Muslims here in Asia—well in all societies—clearly realize that the West, in particular US, applies a double standard to Israel and the Muslim countries. The consciousness of this double standard from the point of view of particularly the US has been growing in recent years, and the pressure on Muslim countries after 9/11 and after the invasion of Iraq has dramatized this aspect for Muslims all over the world. Before it was just one theme among others, but now it is paramount. They feel injustice is done to them. These are the global questions you cannot ignore any place—the double standard in relation to Israel and the Muslims from the US—and that aspect plays a decisive role for the relation between Muslims and others here in Malaysia, but of course also in Europe, where the Muslim minority is growing.

This is a fact you will have to face unless you really want this condition of a threatening clash between the civilisations, as described by Samuel P. Huntington. Maybe the situation will even deteriorate if we don't solve the conflict and the US not only back Israel exclusively. And in relation to the struggle against terrorism, it's also crucial to solve the Middle East conflict. It is important, too, that the Muslim countries become democratic in order to stop extremism and tame it. Here, I would like to use Malaysia as a model, where even the fundamentalist PAS party respects the rules of democracy. They don't like them, but they accept their defeat and then run for another election. In this way we are lucky here in this country, but, unfortunately that is not the case with fundamentalists in other Muslim countries. These are the aspects which are decisive to deal with in order to make the situation between the West and Islam less dramatic.

But isn't the problem with fundamentalists that they just pose as democrats in order to gain power and in the very same moment they actually get it, they discard all rules of democracy and human rights?

If that was the truth here, then PAS would never be elected for anything! But we must also remember that democracy is not just the naked procedure of the election process every 4 or 5 years, but also a degree of transparency in society. I am thinking of the fight against corruption, the abuse of power by the authorities and so on. And when we witness the fiasco of free elections and democratic experiments it is often due to the fact that the country has not been able to implement the democratic procedures in the way the state and society is functioning. If democracy is just about changing one team of autocrats with another in a rigged election or a coup d'état, it is all the same. Nothing of this has anything to do with democracy.

It is basically about the structures in society and being able to prevent corruption and abuse of power—this is the basic character of democracy. And here in Malaysia it is important for us at *Malaysiakini* to be able to control the authorities, to be sure that the election commission is independent, that the anti-corruption unit inside the police is independent and efficient, and that the courts of law are independent etc. Just take a look at the case against Abdullah Ibrahim, the former leader of UMNO, who lost an internal struggle in the party and was accused of homosexuality at the High Court—that was a complete travesty of Justice! So it's about securing civil society, making it strong, and being sure we have independent media, that the structures are functioning and procedures are transparent. And it's my opinion that we are on the right path here in Malaysia.

Let us return to the miserable relation between Islam and the West and in particular the relation between Islam and human rights. Isn't it quite simply a problem that Muslim leaders—maybe to a lesser degree in this country, but at least in other places in the world—have so many difficulties respecting human rights, and that this fact is poisoning the relations with other groups when you have a society with a plurality of cultures?

I don't think this is a big problem here in Malaysia. We have a big minority of approximately 40 to 45% of non-Muslims, so you will have to negotiate with them when it comes to human rights, women's rights etc. You cannot ignore them. In a mixed society like this you will have to deal with others and pay attention to rules other than Islam. You cannot demand that women should be banned from working out and stay at home, that they should not be granted any rights when it comes to divorce etc., and you cannot argue that women should not be treated fair and equal in society, you have to pay attention to the multicultural aspect. Other points of view than the Islamic have to be respected as well.

What about the rules that do not derive from a state authority but are enforced by a community—rules and customs in Muslim culture that are antagonistic to human rights? Doesn't that create a tension in a mixed society like this? Maybe that's a problem the human right organizations haven't paid attention to, as they are focused on human rights violations from governments, not from cultures, from communities against individuals. But a tension between a culture and human rights may very well be a problem?

In a society like this, I don't think lack of respect for human rights is only a problem in the Muslim community. It is also a problem in the other communities—the Chinese and the Indian. And speaking about the powers that be, politicians from no matter what ethnic group, nobody is interested in losing their power and they are prepared to use any means, even to abuse the laws, to stay in office. And with little transparency in this country and a totally lame press, which is only repeating what the politicians want it to write, this is an imminent problem. The people in power control everything in this country; there is no free media to check them. And all the NGOs are very weak. This unbalanced relation between the power and the civil society will inevitably lead to abuse, so, from that perspective, the question of Islam is irrelevant. This is a general problem. That's the way it is in this country. There is, generally speaking, a lack of respect for human rights. But, when that is said, it is of course right to point to the fact that Muslim politicians are out of touch with the development in the modern world when it comes to human rights; these are the cold and hard facts you of course will have to face.

But when you speak of non-transparency, a lame press and the lack of a critical civil society, aren't all these problems due to the fact that, in this country, you have ethnically organized parties where you, so to speak, take politics out politics in the name of ethnic loyalty? People just follow the ethnic elites like cattle?

Yes. That is correct! That is one of the reasons why Malaysia cannot make real progress when it comes to human rights and the development of democracy—the reason is exactly because the parties are ethnically based. But to change that will really be difficult because an ethnic party only represents one community and nobody else. You represent only Muslims, Chinese or Indians. Nobody else. You only have to take care of your own group, to protect its interests. Nobody pays attention to the common interest of people in society. And you are never held responsible for this ignorance.

But isn't that one of the biggest problems in an institutionalized form of multiculturalism, as you have implemented it here in Malaysia, where the parties are defined ethnically in relation to society and citizens? It generates a sort of tribal thinking, and you may ask yourself where the Malaysian identity is: where is the national identity?

Now, I think Malaysia is quite unique in the world because we have the system we have and we have the mixed society we have and there are few other countries that have the problems we have in the first place. Here, we are speaking of a society with a vast minority, which cannot be compared to any country in Western Europe, for instance. You are all mono-ethnic societies in Europe with few cases of minorities, and never more than ten percent of the population.

No, that's true, but the reason I ask you on this matter is that we in Europe are on the move toward mixed societies as you know them in Asia and in particular in Malaysia with a constitutionally-based system of multiculturalism. But tell me: will you always, in a society like this, first of all identify yourself with your ethnic group before you will see yourself as a part of nation? Is that the way it is in an ethnically and culturally mixed society? Do you always organize yourself along ethnic lines?

No, it does not necessarily need to be like that. And in spite of what we saw in Bosnia and in spite of tendencies around the world, I still believe in progress, in the possibilities of democracy if we are able to have transparency and independence in the institutions. Then another society that is not ethnically divided stands a chance. But until we are able to consolidate democracy, this ethnic aspect will unfortunately still be strong. And in this situation we can only do our duty and perform our work: fight for democracy and for human rights and for the right to agree to disagree. We ought to be able to live together, and it should not end like it did in Europe in the nineties when people killed each other because they belonged to different ethnic groups. This is indeed very important. But we must also be able to discuss more openly and not immediately shut down all discussions just because they involve a critical look at the relations between the ethnic groups. Here, people immediately think of what happened in 1969 and everybody is scared that any conflict will escalate to a situation like that. But it doesn't need to be like this. We must be open, discuss everything, but always keep an eye to the democratic rules, even when we deeply disagree: Chinese, Indians and Muslims. That, by the way, is tolerance, isn't it?

But isn't the heart of the matter that all political leaders first of all must come to terms with the fact that the human rights necessarily must be the normative basis for this society, and that they must have priority over all particular sets of rules, customs and ideas of any ethnic or religious origin? Isn't that quite simply Alpha and Omega, in order to have a real spirit of community in a nation?

Hey, listen. Let's be specific! When speaking about this I think the biggest problem is Islam. You can't run away from that.

That's what I am trying to talk about.

I think we must encourage liberal Muslims and give them our support, even here in Malaysia they are victimized by extremists. Whenever they write in *Malaysiakini* they are singled out and someone demands a fatwa pronounced against them. That's why we must support them so they will be able to express themselves. In this way, we can tell Muslims and others that there are also Muslims who think in a liberal way and are different from the fundamentalists, and that fact does not necessarily mean that they are apostates or that they advocate apostasy. At least that's the way we here on *Malaysiakini* find a way to fight for democracy. All the other media, the ethnically based newspapers, don't write about such an issue, as it is too sensitive to touch. Of course we are attacked for being anti-Islam etc., but what we want is quite simply to open the possibility for debate.

I have noticed that all your articles are signed with pseudonyms. Is that due to the fact that it is too dangerous to speak out when you have a dissenting opinion on topics related to Islam—maybe not so much in relation to the authorities but in relation to extremists in the community?

All articles are signed with pseudonyms and that is not only when they touch issues as Islam—also when they touch corruption etc.—and that is due to the fact that the respect for human rights is very low in this country. There is a fear of speaking out here in Malaysia. People are afraid to be arrested because of The Internal Security Act. You can be put into custody for up to two years, without any specific indictment, and this custody might be prolonged endlessly. The ISA is of course the mother of all laws, so to speak, here in Malaysia. For instance, one of our columnists, a Muslim, was held in custody for two years. He had been involved in student politics and in another form of political activity and in an alternative theatre group etc.—he is a sort of freethinker, film director, and socialist. But the authorities don't need to specify their indictment; they just have to claim that he is a threat to national security. That's it. Then they can put him in custody and there is nowhere you can appeal against that in the judicial system. There are no legal procedures. The case is closed.

That's of course why people are scared. But here at *Malaysiakini*, we journalists always sign our articles with our own names. In this way we signal that we are not afraid, that we stand up for what we write, and the authorities can always accuse us and then we will know to defend ourselves. But, of course, this puts an enormous pressure on us, because despite the fact that there is no censorship on the net we have to pay attention to the laws of this country, but the very way we publish implies that we are more free than other media in Malaysia. We don't have to submit an application to publish every year. The others—no matter if it's a newspaper, radio or TV station—have to apply over and over to have their permit for publication renewed. And if you don't succeed then you are dead and no longer in circulation in the news stream. So, in this way, you create a self-censorship in order to avoid this situation happening. You can also, as a news medium, be warned when you have submitted your application, and it's obvious what impact such a warning will have for your further work.

That's why all media in this country is so lame, but we don't have to deal with that problem of application here on *Malaysiakini*, but again, then there are other laws we have to pay attention to, of course (for instance a law which prohibits you from exposing state secrets), but as there is a situation with lack of transparency in every matter in this country, any kind of document can very well be considered a state secret, which puts us in a dilemma.

But in January 2003, we were in conflict with another law as the authorities confiscated our computers because we had published a letter against the legal discrimination which exists in Malaysia. So we just have to be sure all the time, that if we have to go to court we will always be able to defend our stories. That is the precaution we must take. And nothing came out of the case I just mentioned. The authorities might have concluded that they did not have anything serious they could hold against us in court.

I saw an interesting story in the Chinese newspaper, The Star, *the other day where they told about how the religious police had arrested some young Muslim people and brought them in and harassed them and humiliated them. One of the aspects of the story was about sexual harassment of some girls they had brought in from a discothèque. The reason they were brought in was that they were in a place where alcohol was served and, moreover, that they were indecently dressed, according to the religious police. But isn't that an unusual story to read in a newspaper, where you are told what obviously has happened when Muslims—according to our point of view—are harassed by the religious police? And moreover, it's a flagrant criticism of the religious police.*

No, that is not unusual anymore, because *The Star* has had to compete with *Malaysiakini* in recent years and therefore they have to write some relevant and interesting stories and not just about traffic accidents and sports and communiqués from the government. In the growing competition, they will simply have to find stories that the readers find interesting, otherwise there is nothing to read in the paper. But as long as they just criticise the low ranking officers in the religious police, it isn't dangerous. The criticism in the article you mention is not targeting the system but the specific harassment from some officers inside the police who don't hold any other responsibility than being police officers.

I know what I am talking about because I have myself worked on the Chinese newspaper, *The Star*. The journalists there are professionals and they know what a good story is and how to write it, also in case they have to go court. And they also know there are sensitive issues that you just don't touch at all.

Could you define these issues you are not allowed to touch when you write for the public?

Generally speaking: race, religion and language. Particularly, a Muslim must not under any circumstances question the way the system works and advocate reform and support people's right to think and act freely. That is banned. You mentioned the religious police. A Muslim is not allowed to question the existence of that police. And, indeed, that has never happened!

Let's see what your former Prime Minister Mohammad bin Mahathir has to say in relation to this. He has said that this society will only be able to function if every ethnic group has its own rules for living. And here Muslims bring themselves in focus because of the flagrant breaches of the human rights in sharia law. But the logic is that it is not up to either Indians or Chinese to tell Muslims how to live; that seems to be the logic of multiculturalism with legal pluralism as here in Malaysia, but isn't this legal pluralism a necessity?

No, I don't think so. And that's an issue we try to put on the agenda again and again, but there is much resistance against that from the government. They warn us all the time, in a very dramatic way, by pointing to the perspective that hell would break out if we all were to follow *Malaysiakini*'s suggestion. Here, everybody thinks of the violence in 1969. And many people support the government in this case, then again, we don't really know, as we cannot debate this openly. But for sure, law and order and stability have a high priority, as Malaysia has been a very stable country for the last 40-50 years, with the exception of the incidents in 1969. With the economic development and the growing prosperity people know they have a lot to lose, so that also generates a sort of conservative view on the risk of debating a change in the system. Not many dare to try to change the system as it is now. We have a middle class who support the government, human rights abuses or not. The middle class first of all wants stability, and the government knows how to play that card. It points to Indonesia, for instance, after Suharto, where members of the Chinese community were raped and murdered, and their property was burned down and their homes were pillaged.

What do you think of Mahathir's criticism of human rights: that they are thought up for European countries for mono ethnic societies and they don't work for multi ethnic societies in Asia? Universal human rights don't pay attention to the special dynamics in multi ethnic and multi cultural societies where Islam exists with other religions. You will need a tool to protect the Muslim communities from defection.

I am familiar with the fact that Mahathir used many opportunities to criticize human rights and to defend what he defined as "Asian values" when he was in office, but this point of view does not have much resonance anymore, and few propagate it nowadays. The people who are still critical of human rights will really have to tell us what it is that make them so unhappy. In this way, the discussion has changed from the time when Mahathir was in power.

Let us talk about freedom of religion because, in a wider sense it touches on the right to criticize the religious establishment in Islam, and it also deals with the possibility of mixed marriages etc. As we know, anybody who intends to marry a Muslim must convert, and it is not allowed for the Muslim to do so. There are many more implications of the restrictions on the freedom of religion for Muslims in sharia law of course. One of the arguments for the ban on apostasy is that it protects the religious community from defection. This is clearly a breach of a basic and very important human right, as articulated in the UN declaration. The law in this country is, on that point, antagonistic to the UN declaration. Is this ban also supported by the Muslims in this country?

Yes, because the ban on apostasy is stated in sharia, and therefore you cannot ignore it, they will say.

But how can you find a sustainable way to live together with Muslims when you do not have common rules for the community—human rights?

I am not in a position to tell them to change their mind because I am Chinese and if I say anything about that I will be accused of being Islamophobic and anti-Muslim. Whatever I say will not have any positive meaning whatsoever. I will only give someone a chance to attack me, that is all. There is only one way to move things and to encourage people to change their minds in relation to these rules that are hostile to the human rights, and that is to help and support liberal Muslims and Muslim intellectuals. You will really have to defend them whenever they stand up against violations of the human rights and whenever they are attacked for it. And that happens here in Malaysia. These intellectuals write in *Malaysiakini* and they are really attacked and we defend them. In this way, we keep the discussion of human rights going.

From what you say I get the impression that things are moving all the time, in spite of the repression of human rights.

Yes, that is correct, but I don't have any clear idea of how we shall proceed. I am a liberal, I believe in freedom of religion, and I live in a Muslim country among a majority of Muslims who have another opinion on these matters of what multiculturalism should mean, and I must therefore conclude that the only way out of this situation is that, as a non-Muslim, I must support my liberal Muslim friends. This is what you can do. Only a Muslim can change the minds of other Muslims. If you are not a Muslim, they will never listen to you, only be filled with hatred. They will say that you don't know the Koran. It is also important to get support from the Muslim clerics, as they enjoy much support from ordinary Muslims. These people have a profound understanding of the religion and that is a fact which earns them a lot of respect, but unfortunately very few clerics are liberal. On the contrary, they are very often very conservative. Well, they seem to be the biggest problem in a multicultural society. But this way I have described for a change is the only one. It is not an easy way, but it is the only one. In the end, Islam will have to begin to reform. The Muslims cannot continue to live according to a law that was made 750 years after Jesus Christ. But as a non-Muslim, you will have to create an alliance with Muslims in the fight for human rights; otherwise, you will end up as being a part of the hatred that is generated among the ethnic groups.

There Is a Way for Us to Live That Is Pleasing to God

Interview with Dr. Yaacob bin Yussoff, Sultan Ismail Petra International College, Kota Bharu, Kelantan, Malaysia.

According to its constitution from 1957, Malaysia is both defined as a multicultural country and as a Muslim country. How is that to be understood? Is Malaysia a truly Muslim country?

Islam has been the foundation for the state here long before the British arrived and introduced the Western system, which considers the religious domain as something that does not concern politics and administration. With the independence in 1957, we drew up our own constitution, but even in that religion is defined as something that exclusively concerns the individual human being's relation to God, not as "a way of living." But in the Koran, Islam is described as "a way of living." That includes the individual human being's relation to God, but also the relation that should exist between people in a society. That is the reason why PAS is against the secular constitution, because Islam has never been fully implemented in this country. The divine law is not implemented. In this respect, PAS is different from the Muslim national governing party, UMNO.

When we talk about multiculturalism and the state, I see it in this way that you cannot describe Islam as a matter of the individual's relation to God. It is also a way of living. Islam has this broader meaning. But that does not mean that there is no room for other religions. Here in Kelantan, which is governed by PAS, you will find both Hindu and Buddhist temples, Christian churches etc. Everybody can live in harmony with each other. PAS would put it like that: it's best in this way and it should be like this over all in Malaysia. It makes this aspect come true in Islam, that it is not only a faith but also a way of living.

Please explain specifically the difference between living under a secular law and living under sharia law.

There are many aspects of life that are not described in the Koran, but for those there are, you must follow the directions. Concerning economy, politics etc., then non-Muslims will also have to do that. But concerning religion and rituals etc., everybody else of course has their own rights and will have to follow their own customs. Now, I know that somebody would object and say that you cannot mix religion and politics, but Islam is politics, Islam comprises politics.

Do I understand you right: politics are only a part of Islam along with other aspects?

Yes, but the rituals are the most important part. And politics must relate to the principles of Islam. For instance, the political leader in a Muslim country must be a faithful person and abide by the rules for praying. Otherwise he cannot be a leader. All in all, the religious dimension must be the precondition, the foundation for everything such as economy, politics, social questions, culture, education etc. That's the way it is here in Kelantan under the government of PAS. But in other parts of Malaysia, where UMNO is in power, it is not like that. There, Islam is seen as exclusively a religion and not like here—as a way of living. There is the difference between UMNO and PAS. PAS would also add to this that you are not in accordance with the Koran in Malaysia when you, instead of implementing hudud—the criminal law of sharia—govern the country according to a secular criminal law. We would happily implement the hudud law here in Kelantan (the criminal law according to sharia) but that we cannot do because of the federal government in Kuala Lumpur. Hudud would be in conflict with the federal, secular law. Then you will have to ask yourself if the federal government really wants Islam.

Let me ask you about something else. The concept of tolerance seems to be central to the discussion of multiculturalism everywhere. But it's apparently a term whose exact meaning does not always seems to be clear. So, let's define tolerance in a Muslim context. Is it fair to say that you, as a Muslim, respect non-Muslims, but you don't respect non-Muslim dogmas, you only tolerate them? You tolerate the fact that there is another way to live other than the one prescribed in the Koran, and as a politician and as a religious leader you want to give room for that way to live? Or am I wrong?

In principle, tolerance does not exist. Islam must stay Islam, and if you are a Muslim you will have to follow Islam's prescriptions. But you will also have to be together with other kinds of people who are not Muslims, for instance in connection with business, your work etc. In that context, you will have to show tolerance. You must appreciate their way of living. Actually, the Koran says: Muslims who hurt other people of another faith commit a sin against God. You must show tolerance towards others as long as they really follow their own religious dogmas. But the problem is that some non-Muslims don't follow their own dogmas and teachings. That goes for Muslims as well, of course.

What about persons who don't profess any religion at all and who do not follow any religious dogmas?

That you cannot tolerate. In these cases you will have to punish, counsel or correct them. Or you will have to make sure that their own religious authorities will take care of that, if they don't follow their own religion. You will have to make sure that these authorities will do the same as the Muslim authorities do in this country when it comes to Muslims who don't behave as they should do.

I understand that, in an Islamic context, you fully respect other religious people and the way they profess their religion, but what about these secular people who don't profess any religion at all and who might have some ideas that could insult others? Take an example with the cartoons published in the country where I come from. The people behind the publication would say that the very publication of the cartoons was just a way for them to practice their ideas, even if these ideas happened to be insulting to Muslims. But these people also insult each other in the same way, and that's also a part of their ideas that you can behave in that way. How will you explain to them that they can't publish the cartoons of the Prophet?

I believe in the idea of a civilized dialogue. You have some artists who want to do these cartoons. But first we must pay attention to the concept of dialogue. As Muslims, we ask whether you can do this or that, might it hurt or insult anybody? A respect for the civilized dialogue will give the answer. These people who have made the cartoons should have asked before if they really should have done it. The same counts for the Muslims, if they want to do something that is related to Christianity, and then they will have to ask first. It is a question of tolerance. You can't just say: "This is my right!"

It is true that people are born free, not to be slaves of anybody, but we also live under the law of God. That is also the way it is here in Malaysia. If Chinese or Muslims want to do something, then they will have to ask the competent authorities first not to insult anybody. You ask first before you act. This is the definition of a civilized dialogue. We can't have a *religious* dialogue; the Christians believe in the Trinity, Muslims believe in one God and others believe in something else. There is no basis for a religious dialogue, but we must have a civilized dialogue about how to live together.

But the problem is that these people who made these cartoons and published them believe that they can do so. Now, I will present their point of view for you, Dr. Yousoff, so you can contradict it. These people believe we should live together with verbal polemic, discussions, exchange of opinions, and insult each other's dogmas. This is their vision of a civilized dialogue. And if you, Dr. Yousoff, will make fun of them, ridicule them, insult their ideas, then they will be happy too. These people don't live according to religious prescriptions; they might not even profess any religion or believe in God. They also claim that it is not their intention to insult Muslims as persons, but at the same time they do claim it's their right to make fun of ideas, to draw the cartoons for instance. To them, religion is just an idea, like a political idea is. Everything is open to insult and critique. And if you, Dr. Yousoff, will tell them that they can't do the cartoons, they will answer you that you restrict their freedom. How will you explain to these people that it is wrong anyway to publish the cartoons?

I know that there are people in this world who don't explicitly believe in God, who don't profess a religion, but on the other hand, I also think that, deep in their hearts, they believe in a supreme being who is more powerful than Man. There must be a faith within them, and they must also have an idea of the good in this world we inhabit together. They must rely on that condition that we share something together, that there are also religious people here, there are Christians, and there are Muslims etc, and we must be considerate towards each other. And then they will have to ask themselves if they really have the right to insult others, for what is a right in the first place? These questions they will have to give some consideration. They will have to ask themselves what is best for a civilized dialogue between humans. They must respect other people's feelings. They can't just follow their own impulse and think of themselves.

I understand from what you say that these people can do whatever they want to, but in this case they will have to pay attention to what you, as a Muslim, will consider as blasphemy.

Yes, that's correct.

Then these people who made the cartoons will say that they don't make any distinction between political ideas and religious ideas. For them all ideas are human made. During the cartoon crisis in Denmark, a Saudi academic paid a visit to Copenhagen. On this occasion he stated that he would not accept that these cartoonists insulted his "holy ideas," meaning Islam. But these people will then answer to that: because you say Islam is holy it doesn't mean that Islam is holy for them. They are secularists and for them Islam is a human idea which they will claim the right to criticize. They will claim the right to criticize all ideas no matter how the people who defend these ideas will define them. For these secularists, all ideas are equal, and all ideas may be targeted for ridicule and insult. How will you, Dr. Yousoff, explain to these people that they are all wrong? But first we must agree that we can all criticize political ideas, otherwise there wouldn't be democracy. So, how will you make these people make a distinction between religious ideas and political ideas?

For me, it's very simple: sincere people, good people, intelligent people want to appreciate others, and if these other people really say that their holy dignity is being hurt, then sincere people can't ignore that. They should not offend what is of importance to the others' dignity, and they know in advance what will hurt this dignity. Therefore, they cannot, as sincere and good people, choose to hurt others. If they intentionally choose to hurt others knowing what impact their action will have, then they are not human. They must understand that there are people who can't live if you hurt their religion. Everybody must understand that there is something that is holy for others which you cannot disgrace. That is also true of Christianity, of course. You must appreciate, and not hurt and insult. That, in fact, is tolerance.

But how will you then explain to these people who did the cartoons how to make a distinction between political ideas and religious ideas?

It is very simple. Politics and religion are connected. Regarding Muslims they will always have to support a politics, which follows Islam, And likewise for the Christians: they will have to support a politics following Christianity. Religion must always regulate the political domain. In this way, you can see the importance of religion. But these people you talk about are very problematic because they have no ideas about God or religion. That's why they will all the time make troubles for themselves and for others; it's their own fault. But for normal people, there will always be a God to obey. I can't say why these people we are talking about are rejecting God. Maybe they have been rejected themselves in life, who knows? But you can't have unlimited freedom in life. For what actually is freedom? What does it mean? It means you must obey religion. I would say: religion is a necessary guideline, which we cannot do without. But these people we talk about have gone beyond the boundaries for human behavior and have turned bestial, for when you reject God you turn bestial. It's very far away from Islam and it's very far away from Christianity. It's a variant of Darwinism, everybody's struggle against everybody, social Darwinism without moral and universal ethics, which in Europe has led to racism, to apartheid etc. Both Islam and Christianity are universal religions and talk about a human brotherhood; we are all God's creatures. But many people in the West reject God. That also counts for these people we talk about who have insulted the prophet. But they have a secret agenda, which is more sinister than their talk about freedom. We cannot accept that these people tell us there is no God. For the consequence of what they say is that they make a god out of themselves. They worship their own vices (their sexual vices, for instance), so they worship a god anyway, but it is a false god and that can't be accepted by normal people.

Let us draw our attention towards another aspect of the co-habitation of various cultures and religions in a society. How will you define the vision of multiculturalism as a Muslim scholar? Could you imagine it as a society with families, the members of which will worship different gods, will belong to different religions and cultures where, for example, you find a family with a Muslim father, a Hindu mother and both Muslim and Hindu children? That means integration of the various religions and cultures in the family.

That has happened in Indonesia! But I don't believe in this vision, for it is not a real marriage, a true life together. People who are married in this way are only married in a physical sense. But marriage is also spiritual. It comprises many more aspects than the physical and sexual and is much more complex. You also have to share the religious dimension. Of course, there are many things to be shared outside the religion, but this is not sufficient for a life together in a marriage; it's too superficial. When souls are united they must share the religion, otherwise it's not a true marriage and can only create problems for the persons involved, also in the hereafter. It will end up in idolatry, in worshipping the human they have in common in this life, but the soul is the most supreme in human life.

Is that the reason why conversion to Islam is compulsory when a non-Muslim marries a Muslim so they can share this spiritual dimension you underline?

Yes. Life is not restricted to this world here on Earth. We must also think of the hereafter; we must prepare ourselves so we will be able to continue our life together after death. This is basic in order to understand the nature of marriage. You will always have to consider that you must be able to share the religion. You must be able to live in spiritual harmony. There is a way for us to live that is pleasing to God, but it's only pleasing to God because it's best for us in this way.

I have another question about co-habitation of cultures and religions in a society: it concerns Muslims who live outside the Muslim world, for instance in Europe or the United States. In one of the biggest immigration societies in the world, in United States there is a so-called intermarriage, for example in Jewish and Latino communities. People marry persons who are not from their own community or religion, but Muslims don't do that. They stay in the Muslim community because the person they marry must either be a Muslim or he or she will have to convert to Islam first.

Does this rule of compulsory conversion exist to protect the ban on apostasy? If the conversion didn't take place, you could maybe imagine the Muslim person in a marriage convert to the religion of the other, or simply lose his or her religion, and then the children would maybe be raised outside Islam. Will you explain how important the ban on apostasy is in Islam? Why does it exist? Is it there to protect the Muslim community?

First of all, I don't think it will lead to anything good if individuals mix in the way you describe it. I think it will lead you astray from religion. You will have to limit the bond between people of various religions to other spheres of life. Reserve it for business, work etc. Christians should marry Christians, Muslims should marry Muslims etc. It is best like that.

In other words you envision multiculturalism as a society where the cultures and religions live side by side, but the individuals live segregated along religious lines? The individuals ought to stay inside their culture and religion and not mix with anybody else in society?

Yes. That's the way it is here in Malaysia and that's also the way it ought to be. It is the beauty of life when it is like that. It realizes the plurality of life. We already share so many things in life as humans, in business, in sport etc., but in one domain it ought to be different. There, the individuals from different religions should not mix. Islam is Islam. Christianity is Christianity. If people mixed in families, then the unique in both religions would wither away.

But what if individuals mixed with each other? What if Muslims also intermarried and mixed with other individuals from other groups? How do you envision an integrated, multicultural society like that?

I think everything in culture and religion would lose value. It sounds like a vision for an open society, but the dignity would be gone in that vision, the spiritual dimension would be gone. I, for my part, will try to protect the unique in my religion, and I hope everybody else will do the same regarding their own religion. God has created the world like this; we are different with our different customs. This difference is our dignity. But we also have something in common. But there is a borderline between the unique and the common. We must preserve it in that way. It's the most beautiful. This is the way for us to live that is pleasing to God.

I mentioned the ban on apostasy in Islam. Will you explain why it exists? Why is it forbidden to Muslims to leave their religion? We know there are people here in Malaysia who have tried to leave Islam or to convert to another religion but have been told by the authorities that it was not possible. So what is the meaning of this ban?

As Muslims, we have been told how to live by God and the model for that was the prophet Muhammad. When he died, others showed the model. And because we belong to God, all his commands must be followed. The ban on apostasy is very clear and explicit and you cannot compromise. It will only lead to chaos. And as a Muslim you are obliged to take care that those who want to leave Islam will not be in distress when they arrive in the hereafter. Therefore, you are obliged to kill them or in another way help them so they will not be in distress. And if someone really insists on leaving Islam, you definitely will have to kill them in order to save their souls so they will not have the opportunity to commit a sin against God in this life here on earth.

In an Islamic state, the authorities will have to take care of that obligation and kill those who want to leave Islam, but it is only in order to save a person so he will have a good life in the hereafter. And it is quite simply the responsibility of the state to fulfill that obligation. You must take care that those who leave Islam will not risk worshiping other gods, but there are those who don't understand that principle. But Islam attaches great importance of looking upon our life from the perspective of the hereafter.

We must all the time keep an eye on what the consequences of our acts will have for the hereafter, that's a significant aspect of Islam, which will decide many of the problems you will face as a human being. You must think of the perspective of the hereafter. That counts for all aspects of life, even the small details. You must trust the justice of God because he will reward you. You must rely on God and his eternal justice. It also goes for the punishments you will have to face if you have committed a crime. By being punished, you will atone for your crime and thereby be liberated from your sin in the hereafter. In the worst case, you must accept your death in order to be happy in the hereafter. You must receive the punishment in this life to be happy in the hereafter. In this way, everything has a deeper meaning. That is what I have read in the Koran.

Explain to me the meaning of punishment in sharia. It is there to prepare the sinner for the life in the hereafter. The meaning of punishment is not retribution or vengeance but purification, if I have understood you right, but how can Muslims who live in non-Muslim countries, say in Europe or the United States, live without sharia punishment? There is no sharia law there.

It is a very interesting question, indeed! The punishment you will receive in these countries for a crime will not purify you and prepare you for the hereafter, because it is not a punishment which has been delivered from a sharia court but from a secular court. It is only through the punishment from a sharia court that you will receive this purification from God.

So what are the Muslims supposed to do in these countries where there is no sharia law?

Now, the law must always come from the State, but when Muslims are a minority, they could establish sharia court within the frameworks of their congregations. That is, of course, in co-operation with the authorities, which is obvious. But the sharia law is there to guarantee the dignity of the Muslims, to guarantee the sublime in Islam and to guarantee the happiness for the Muslims in the hereafter. That is the meaning of sharia law.

The Ban on Apostasy Is Meant to Control Muslims

Interview with Dr. Abdul Hakim bin Abdullah, Institute for Islamic Contemporary Studies, University of Terengganu, Malaysia.

Let us talk about what importance Islamic law, sharia, has for Muslims. In the discussion about multiculturalism and Islam in the West, there is an idea among well-intentioned liberal people of a simplified Islam—a wish for a, so to speak, user-friendly Islam, in which perhaps less attention is paid to the status that sharia actually has in the religion. Would you clarify what sharia means in Islam?

Let us first of all make it clear what Islam actually means. The word 'Islam' has references to "submission" and "peace." It means that Islam is there to bring peace to us through the submission to God. This submission takes place by following sharia law. In sharia there are three aspects to pay attention to: the relation between humans, the relation between man and God, and the relation between man and his environment. These are the three relations that Islamic law is meant to regulate. More specifically, the relation between humans is the social, political and economic relations in society. The relation between man and God concerns the submission to God and the worshipping of God. And the relation between man and his environment concerns responsibility towards nature.

The reason why I ask you what importance sharia has for Muslims is that here in Malaysia you have a plural legal system based on common law for all citizens and also a specific law, sharia, which is applied to Muslims only. How does this system function?

Islam recognizes freedom and human rights for all citizens. Islam doesn't compel anybody to convert to Islam. Religion is a question of man's free choice, no compulsion in religion. But if anybody wants to convert to Islam he must first consider it seriously. You will have to ask yourself if you really want to resign to Islam. You will have to choose with your heart. In the multicultural society there is a place for all religions, but sharia is exclusively applied to Muslims. Other religions have their right to practice their own rules and apply their own laws.

Some non-Muslims have this idea that you can take away something from Islam, that you can take away the law, and consider Islam only a faith. But isn't that a misconception?

You must first of all make it clear whether or not the particular aspect is fundamental or not to Islam. If it is fundamental you cannot just take it away. But some aspects are historically conditioned and they change over time, dress codes, for instance. The Arabs have some rules, and here we have some others, but of course you have basic rules for men and women respectively. But the fundamental aspects are the prayer, the Ramadan, the faith, the Koran. When we talk about dress codes, there are different rules applied to women. For instance, hijab is historically conditioned; there are no rules about that in the Koran. Various scholars hold an opinion on that subject, but there is no final truth. But for women to cover the hair, that is fundamental.

How would you consider the ban on apostasy? Is that fundamental or could you interpret it in one way or another?

The ban on apostasy is meant to control Muslims. Muslims cannot leave Islam; that is fundamental and not open for negotiation. That is also one of the reasons why conversion to Islam should be considered seriously. You will have to make up your mind whether you are serious or not, for when you have resigned to Islam as a religion there is no way back because if you try to get out of Islam you will be punished. The ban on apostasy is there to control the Muslim community. You can also put it in another way: it is a protection of the Muslim community against apostasy. There are no different interpretations or different ideas within Islam on the ban on apostasy. It is quite simply a ban from which you cannot deviate. There is no doubt about it.

What about those people who are born into Islam and who have never been asked to accept the religion? Does the ban on apostasy also apply to them?

Yes. The ban is there to protect the Muslim community.

How should people be punished if they try to leave Islam?

First of all, a religious leader should counsel the person and help him or her consider the situation, and this leader should try to influence the person not to leave Islam. A religious leader should try to counsel three times before a person can be punished for trying to leave Islam and not listening to the advice. This is a regular procedure, according to the Koran. That's the way you do it.

But what if the person doesn't want to listen and still intends to leave Islam? What is the procedure then? I talked to another Muslim scholar who explained to me that capital punishment should be applied for such a crime, according to the Koran.

But we don't practice hudud (penal legislation according to the Koran) in this country. That is only done in Saudi Arabia and Iran. So nobody is being punished in this way in this country.

Let us then take a look at the consequences of this ban on apostasy for the Muslim communities outside the Muslim world.
    For instance, in the United States there is an intermarriage of Jews and Latinos; you marry someone else from another community or from another faith—non-Jews or non-Catholics—then it's maybe not certain what the religious identity of the family will be, but this is not true for the Muslims. They don't intermarry because if someone is to marry a Muslim they must convert. Is that one of the impacts of the ban on apostasy that the religion does not suffer from defection in this way?

When you marry someone from another faith, then the religion will disappear. But, true, that situation does not exist for Muslims because they have a good understanding of Islam.

Is it fundamental that if someone marries a Muslim they must convert first?

Yes. That is not open for negotiation. There are not two opinions about that. However, it happens once in a while that a Muslim marries a non-Muslim. But according to the Koran it is not legal.

Do you marry outside your religious community in this country?

Yes. My mother, for instance, was a Buddhist, and then she converted to Islam in order to marry my father.

But do you also see conversions the other way around? Do you see someone leaving Islam to marry a Hindu, a Buddhist or a Christian?

I think there have been two or three cases of that, yes. In one of the cases it was a Muslim woman who married a Christian man. But since we have passed sharia law, the marriage was abolished by the authorities.

How is apostasy handled in this country?

We don't literally follow sharia law in this area. People are fined, but not punished with a prison sentence.

Could you imagine a multicultural society where the individuals would mix in the families? Where a Muslim would marry a Hindu or a Christian, and there would be individuals of different faiths within the families? Is that a version of multiculturalism which you would find appealing?

Mixed marriages, in the way you describe them, are not the only way to have a society in harmony. We have another opinion of how to create harmony through respect for each other in the multicultural society. Although a Muslim does not marry a Hindu, he will respect the Hindu as a human being with rights. And that is true for all religious people. Everybody deserves respect. The mutual respect between the different religions will guarantee the harmony in the multicultural society. Muslims here in this country understand what is fundamental and what is not fundamental in Islam, and when it comes to something not fundamental you will always be able to find a compromise.

But now there is this vision of multiculturalism according to which the individuals mix across faith and community and where you will then find the diversity of culture and faith in the families. What do you think of that vision of multiculturalism? Isn't it unrealistic, since it is not compatible with fundamental aspects in Islam?

The ambition is to create harmony in society, but mixing religions in the families the way you describe it, is not the only way to strive for harmony. We Muslims believe that religions should protect their identity and at the same time show respect and tolerance towards other religions. If individuals from different religions marry, it will only lead to the disappearance of religions, and no good Muslim will accept that. Only Muslims who have not understood Islam at all will accept that vision of multiculturalism, for, over time, the differences between the religions will vanish in such a society you describe. The very religions will disappear.

The Problem Appears If You Do Not Have Any Religion

Interview with director Yap Swee Seng, SUARAM—*Suara Rakyat Malaysia* ("The Voice of the Malaysian People")

After the Islamist part of my journey in the northern states of Kelantan and Terrenganu, I return to Kuala Lumpur to meet Yap Swee Seng, the Chinese director of the human rights organization, SUARAM. I take a taxi to the suburb where the organization has an office in a commercial street. In the cab I get into a conversation with the Chinese driver who is curious about where I come from. When I tell him, he seems quite astonished. To him, Denmark is synonymous with the country where the caricatures of the Prophet were drawn. I figure out that he belongs to a minority of Chinese Muslims. He tells me that he has not converted to Islam; his family has always been Muslim ever since they emigrated from China.

There was some trouble, he tells me with a smile, and he says that you cannot go around and insult others in that way. I have understood that. He doesn't forget to add that there was never any sign of violence in relation to the protests against Denmark. He emphasizes that they are peaceful people in Malaysia. I assure him that I am glad to hear this on my journey to discuss multiculturalism, Islam and human rights.

In its latest human rights report, SUARAM described some cases of conflict between religious organizations and the authorities on the one side and dissident sects and individuals on the other. A conversation with Seng will possibly clarify the consequences of the rules that my Islamic partners have described when they maintain that it is religious communities' obligation to enforce regulations and to correct the behavior of rebellious members of the congregations. In the report there appear to be no examples of rebellions in the Hindu or Buddhist communities. The problem is only visible in the case of Muslim dissidents versus the authorities, as they are obliged and entitled to enforce sharia law on Muslim citizens. I ask director Seng:

You write in your human rights report for 2005 that the government has declared Sunni Islam the "only true" direction for Islam, and that other interpretations of the religion are prohibited. Where do you find that statement? In the constitution of Malaysia or in the sharia law for Muslims in this country?

It's not something which is written anywhere in any law, but it's quite simply the praxis of the government! It implies that any deviation from Sunni Islam will be treated in a negative way, and this negative way may vary in sanctions from prohibition against publication and distribution of written material to custody according to the Internal Security Act. We have experienced Shia Muslims being put in jail according to that law. There has also been a case in the state of Terengganu where the Department for Religious Affairs has cracked down on the freethinker Ayah Pin and his congregation.

Could you elaborate a little about Ayah Pin and his congregation?

He is a person who claims to be a sort of messiah, but, according to him, he is still a Muslim. He has propagated his own version of Islam, which he calls "Sky Kingdom." But the problem is that if you are a Malay, like him, and you are born in this country, then it is stated in the constitution that you are a Muslim, and Islam in this country is Sunni Islam. So if you deviate from that you will run into trouble with the authorities. Nevertheless, Ayah Pin propagated his own teachings and he also claimed he could perform miracles, that he could cure people, for example. At the same time, he showed an open attitude to religions other than Islam and people from various faiths began to attend the meetings in his community (Indian Hindus, for example), but it was considered a deviant sect by the authorities.

Did he take any initiative other than professing his faith in his community? Did he publish books or anything else? Did he become politically active or did he instigate any political initiative?

No, he organized this community, which was absolutely peaceful and where he held speeches and his followers gathered around him. No violence and no demonstrations. The same can be said about another deviationist sect called Al Arqam. It was also a peaceful Islamic sect that met in a community and was, in its interpretation of the religion, very conservative. But they were peaceful and just lived together in their communities where they professed their faith according to certain rules regarding dress code, for example. But it was something they kept to themselves. In the meanwhile they received more and more sympathizers—also among government officials. Maybe that was what frightened the government. So in the end the authorities closed down the communities and threw the leader in prison in accordance with the Internal Security Act, where he can be held in custody without time limit. Last year [2005], he was released, but lives under surveillance from the police.

Did Al Arqam practise a form of political Islam?

No, not really. They just practiced their own way of living.

I read in your human rights report that the community of Sky Kingdom worshipped an enormous teapot, which was destroyed by the authorities when they closed down the community. It's also said in your report that a crowd of people—civilians—helped the police when they forced their way into the premises of the community.

Yes, that's true. Both the police and the civilian crowd forced their way into the community, but still they didn't catch the leader Ayah Pin. He had been warned and had gone underground.

Can you tell me what justification the authorities had for cracking down on deviant sects in Islam? For we are only talking about different sects within Islam, not about other religions. What is the motivation for the authorities for maintaining this discipline among Muslims?

I believe it's due to the race politics here in Malaysia. Because this country is very racially divided (for example, political life is divided along racial lines) and for the government party UMNO it is very important to maintain the support from the Muslims, and Islam is regarded a tool for that purpose. With Islam they can unite and control the Malays. I reckon that UMNO has concluded that if you allow various sects inside the religion it can cause disintegration where you lose the control. You already have the fundamentalist party, PAS, which is still a Sunni Islam party. I think it is a troubling perspective for the government, if more Muslim parties pop up.

Isn't there any contestation of this racially divided political life from the Chinese and the Indians in this country?

Yes, but the opposition in this country is very weak. It doesn't have any impact, and awareness about race-dividing policy in this country is very low. It is due to having the same policy since independence fifty years ago. Well, even before independence we were racially divided. People only think in terms of race and find it quite natural to support their own leaders in government, so they in turn can support their respective race group and promote their interests. That's the way the system works.

But isn't this policy, NEP (New Economic Policy), which grants some economic and other privileges to Malays, contested by the Chinese and the Indians?

It has been contested once in a while, but the government has refused to change anything about it. People who have protested have also been put in custody according to the Sedition Act. Quite simply, you cannot question these privileges, which are mentioned in the law. Neither can you question the status of Islam, the status of the Sultans etc. It is statutory, so it cannot be challenged. The same with Bahasa—the Malay language. You cannot question its prominence and, if you do you, you will be accused and put in custody indefinitely. The argument is that the authorities need to prevent the kind of racial riots that we had in 1969. Therefore, everything must be done to preserve the racial policy and status quo, with the argument of maintaining law and order. But it's the political elites who create this racial division with the political system we have and at the same time they tell their respective communities that they are the true heroes to fight for the ethnic interest of their community and to promote their interest in the face of the other groups in the government.

Hasn't there ever been any discussion about organizing political life in another way, as in a liberal democracy, around ethical, economic and social interests and not according to religious affiliation and ethnic origin?

There have been tentative efforts, but they have never been successful. This whole society is racially divided and it is difficult for people to ignore their racial origin. In Malaysia, we have had politicians who have tried to organize parties open to members of different races, but they have never had any success at all. The first president of UMNO tried in the fifties to open up the party for Chinese and Indians, but that was obstructed by other Malays in the party. After that, he left the party and formed another, which flopped totally in the following election.

So you have to be both Malay and Muslim to be a member of the majority party UMNO here in Malaysia?

Yes, both Malay and Muslim.

But tell me, the privileges mentioned in NEP—are they only privileges for Malays or are they for all Muslims, also the few Indians and Chinese who are of Muslim faith?

In the constitution it is defined that you are Malay if (1) you are a Muslim, (2) you speak Bahasa, and (3) you live according to the Malay culture. So it doesn't matter if you are of Indian or Chinese origin.

But everybody has to learn Bahasa here in this country, and everybody can speak it, so doesn't it follow that these privileges are religiously defined? They are only for Muslims?

You fulfill the conditions to be a Bumiputra (son of the soil), if you can meet these three requirements. That's the way it is—theoretically. But in practice it is completely different, because both Indian and Chinese Muslims are excluded from these privileges. The decisive aspect is racial, but the Malays in UMNO have some problems because it is not so simple. For instance, former Prime Minister Mohammad Mathathir has a partial Indian background and our present Prime Minister (2006) Abdullah has a partial Chinese background as some of his family originates from the island of Hainan. You also find a tiny minority of Muslims of Thai origin in the Northern part of the country.

You mentioned the repression of sects in Islam, people who propagate a deviant version from Sunni Islam. But what about people who propagate atheism, who are quite simply against religion as such?

If we talk about something which is anti-Islam, the authorities will repress it. But we are touching a sensitive area now. To be Muslim is the best, that's for sure, but it's also OK if one belongs to one of the old religious communities, like Hinduism, Buddhism or Christianity. The problem appears if you do not have any religion. That's the worst.

How come?

Because the perception is that you have to have a religious community to lead you and to correct you if you make any mistakes or if you happen to insult somebody. It is very precarious not to have any religion here in Malaysia. It also has a historical explanation. It is due to the communist resistance movement, which was formed here during the Japanese occupation during World War ll. Later, after the war, this movement continued as a revolutionary army against the British, and after independence in 1957 the communists of this movement continued their struggle against the government, and the communists said that religion was opium for the people. The British (and, later, the government) understood how to use that slogan against the communists by pointing to the fact that they were godless and that they were against Islam. Therefore, neither socialism nor communism has any appeal whatsoever to Malays today.

The communist revolutionary movement continued up until the seventies, when it was finally crushed by the military. And the anti-socialist attitude that this caused has the consequence that we don't have any legal communist or socialist parties here in Malaysia today, and neither do we have free trade unions that can organize nationally and negotiate working conditions and salary. The whole leftwing was crushed once and for all by the military, and the idea of the antagonism between socialism and Islam was created. The idea of social class is also dangerous for the establishment in this country. This idea about class could jeopardize the political system. It could make the poor Malays realize that they have more in common with the poor Chinese and the poor Indians than with the rich Muslim Malays. All the poor are repressed and controlled by the apparatus of state.

Of what character are the trade unions in this country? Are they so-called apolitical? Are they controlled by the government? Are they defined by religion and ethnic origin?

The trade unions have had a hard time here. Many of the leaders were put in prison in the sixties and seventies because they were accused of affiliations with the communist and Marxist circles that conspired against the government. During the seventies and the eighties, the government then formalised a lot of restrictions, which destroyed the trade unions and made it impossible to register them with the authorities. For instance, now you can only form a trade union, which organizes the workers in a given factory and is called a "house union," but you are not allowed to organize these "house unions" on a national scale. In this way, you can prevent the trade unions from organizing their potential force, which they could do otherwise. Moreover many of the leaders have been corrupted by the government through the eighties and nineties by being offered political appointments.

Haven't there been recent attempts to organize the workers?

Attempts are going on all the time. Recently the Socialist Party of Malaysia tried to organize homeless people, plantation workers and students. They have applied to have their party registered for eight years but their applications have been dismissed by the government because, according to the Ministry of Home Affairs, they are a threat to the internal security in Malaysia. But they never release any specific reason, just this formulation.

Does the Socialist party exist as a secret organization?

No, they organize demonstrations all the time, even though it's illegal to do so. But everything is illegal in Malaysia. Sometimes they are arrested, at other times nothing happens, but the Socialist Party simply carries on as though it's legal and ignores the prohibition on the party. They continually try to take legal steps in order to get registered.

In your human rights report for 2005, you mention an initiative from a group of lawyers, the so called "interfaith" initiative, the intention of which was to bring different groups together from various religious communities. The purpose was to advise and discuss with the government new initiatives on religious affairs. Will you tell me about that?

The idea was to form a board to advise the government on religious tolerance and human rights. They would also deal with conflicts between the religious communities. It started with the consultation of several NGOs, also Muslim NGOs. After that, Muslim NGOs claimed that these lawyers had a secret agenda with their interfaith initiative. One of the NGOs who made the accusation was the youth faction of the government party, UMNO. They claimed that an interfaith commission would endanger the status of Islam in the country, promote freedom of religion and promote Muslims' right to leave Islam. Therefore, they withdrew from the initiative. They also began to attack the initiative and physically threaten those involved.

When the initiative finally came up with a proposal for the government, the Prime Minister dismissed the very idea of such a commission. This is the background for why we still have these problems described in our report. For instance, we mention a case where a man had converted to Islam but his wife had not. They were then divorced and he claimed the custody of his children by maintaining that they are Muslims as he is. These cases are complicated, but it is because of cases like this that many NGOs have joined in the so-called Article 11 initiative, named after Article 11 of our constitution, which speaks of freedom of religion. The initiative has organized a number of meetings to provide information about the law and to discuss the consequences in reality.

These meetings have been physically attacked by Muslim groups and demonstrations have been organized against them by UMNO's youth, by Jamaah Islah Malaysia, and others. PAS has also protested against them. The Article 11 initiative has been accused of promoting apostasy disguised as promotion of religious freedom. It has even been accused of endangering the status of Islam. The same has been said in relation to the case of Lina Joy, a woman who has converted from Islam to Christianity, and whom the sharia court now will force into re-education. This can go on for years, and such a form of re-education is, in fact, imprisonment, but she refuses to acknowledge the decision as she claims not to be a Muslim anymore and therefore outside the jurisdiction of the sharia court. Nevertheless, this is challenged by the sharia court as it maintains that its very existence is justified to prevent a case like hers. They are afraid that if they give in to such a case it will create a precedent and Islam will lose believers who will convert to other religions. It's a prominent case here in Malaysia, which has not yet been finally concluded.

Ethnopolitical Communitarianism and the Public Sphere

Interview with Professor Norani Othman, Sisters-in-Islam

One of the critical writers I have noticed in various human rights activist and academic journals and books, who opposes the growing Islamization of public life, is Professor of Sociology, Norani Othman. She is a member of the pro-human rights and pro-democracy network, Sisters-in-Islam. The unique point in their criticism of Islamization is the fact that they seek a normative basis through an interpretive reading of the Koran.

Another aspect Norani Othman pays attention to is the transformation of the public sphere under multiculturalism—or the damage done to the public sphere as an accessible space for everybody, any citizen, for democratic discussion.

In the book Muslim Women and the Challenge of Islamic Extremism, *which you have edited and which is published by Sisters-in-Islam, you write about the regressive utopian project the Islamists try to carry into effect in this country. As we know, it's the fundamentalists in PAS in the State of Kelantan who have passed a number of spectacular laws covering behavior and decorum in the public sphere, all of them concerned with gender segregation and surveillance of citizens. They have passed laws regulating dress code for women, considering it a matter of government policy. They have passed laws dealing with gender segregation in relation to public meetings of any sort, and other cultural arrangements, other laws securing differentiated cash registers for men and women in supermarkets, they have closed down hairdressing salons which they considered to offer "unisex" hair styles for men and women, they have closed down cinemas to prevent what they consider inappropriate behavior between individuals who couldn't be supervised in the darkness. All in all, rules and laws which could be classified as "petty segregation." You perceive this policy as an effect of a fundamentalist reading of the Koran, I understand?*

Yes, and also something which is based on a historical interpretation of sharia which is now practiced in certain places, but without any contextualization of the sources the interpretation builds on, and without any attention paid to the fact that over a thousand years have passed since these rules were written down. The fundamentalists don't do any comparative, critical reading of the Koran in relation to other principles of, say, justice, in the Koran.

You write in the aforementioned book that Islamism stages itself as a teaching of authenticity and this is to be understood in a post-colonial context characterized by collective loss of identity. The Islamists try to get rid of the occidental and alienating influence by searching for what they consider to be their historical roots, and this strategy is implemented in the Islamist politics of identity. But isn't it also fair to say that not only the Islamists but also the leftwing in the West has been mobilized for this understanding? The leftwing has imperceptibly reached a position where it tries to understand non-Western authenticity as something, which must reject universal ideas about human rights at any price, with the motivation that these ideas are Western and local. The leftwing is therefore receptive to recognizing of the Islamists politics of authenticity —their regressive utopianism—with the justification that it is without stains of Western, colonial influence. On the contrary it is an expression of the authentic, repressed "other" whom you cannot command to understand your Western human rights, and the Islamists understand very well how to play the part that they are offered in this post-modern scenography.

This is one plausible perspective, but we in Sisters-in-Islam are not first of all trying to search for inspiration for a universal-based humanism and human rights thinking in Western ideas, but in the sources we find in the Koran. We will maintain that Islam is a religion for all times and for all people, and it is characterized by human compassion. Therefore, you cannot put this restrictive interpretation on the holy scripture and understand everything undigested and *en masse* which is described in a Middle East context in the 9th century or before, way back to the time of the Prophet. We must develop a historical sensibility in our reading of the sources, in the intention, the meaning of the texts. The Prophet himself never claimed to be a messiah as Jesus did, or to be a son of God, or to be both divine and human, but his duty was to receive and to communicate the divine message in the human world while he lived here.

I think the universal aspect in his message first of all is expressed in the fact that all men are considered equal and Islam is for everybody, no matter what race and nationality. The value of the words you preach, as you have interpreted them from the Koran depends on the deeds you perform yourself. The value of the words depends on the extent to which you have understood them yourself by living in accordance with them. You must treat others as you want to be treated yourself, so if you don't want anybody to insult your religion, if you want your dignity to be respected, then you must not insult others' religion and what other peoples respect. I think you will realize if you read in the Koran—in particular the verses, which were revealed during the time in Mecca, in the first 23 years of the time of revelation—that they are very universal in their principles. They speak of justice, of equality, of ethics, about abolishment of slavery and repression, and about helping the poor. This you must accept and be able to interpret and discuss, but the fundamentalists today read the laws on prohibitions and punishment literally and out of context.

Is it true that the fundamentalist approach and interpretation are something relatively new?

No, this is wrong and a simplified way to understand the phenomenon. By studying Islamic jurisprudence, you will see that at a certain period it is dominated by men. But in Basra, for instance, when the Islamic Empire was spread all over the Arabic world, you would also find female scholars. This is a tradition, which has been repressed, but now we see again female scholars working on religious exegesis. But approximately one thousand years have gone since the female scholars interpreted in Basra. Moreover, in the classical Muslim jurisprudence, there are several schools—if we also include the Shia schools in Muslim jurisprudence—which speak about the integrity of a people in relation to religion. So you see, already here we witness a "metabolism," so to speak, as the sources are interpreted rather than read literally. So you cannot say that things are as simple as the fundamentalists do. But this tradition for interpretation has nevertheless been repressed today.

You write in the work I just mentioned that a growing Islamization has taken place here due to the codification and implementation of sharia law. This in turn has led to a higher degree of alienation between Muslims and the two other groups in this country—the Chinese and the Indians—and also led to a higher degree of segregation. Moreover, it has led to—and that might be the most radical aspect, from the point of view of the Malays—a growing distance to the historical Malay culture, stemming from the period before this country became Muslim, before the Malay people adopted Islam as their religion. Now these traditions are considered suspiciously un-Islamic simply because they are pre-Islamic. This observation you make in your article makes me think of V.S. Naipaul's travelogue, Beyond Belief— Islamic Excursions among the converted Peoples. *He characterizes this tendency you describe as a relentless cultural imperialism, as the historical Arabic Islam causes these converted peoples to lose their own history. It then provokes a conflict between national identity and religious identity. How do you see this interpretation?*

I agree. This obsession with veils and gender segregation is indeed a form of cultural imperialism. It's something which is imported from a patriarchal, Saudi Arabian context. It is strange in all respects—historically, but also in other ways. Here, in a tropical country, it is very impractical to hide oneself in a tent disguised as clothing. There are indeed many, many other cultural differences where we do not interpret sexuality and sexual symbols in ways of dressing and in language in the same way as in Arabic culture. What has followed with the narrow-minded, literal reading of the Koran is a perception of our traditional clothing here in Malaysia as not being sufficiently virtuous. Instead, we have been asked to hide ourselves in a tent. In this way, our cultural identity disappears. On the other side, whenever you lose your identity, you will lose your moral integrity because you no longer have any moral autonomy. I hold the opinion that moral values must derive from individual autonomy.

Traditionally, Malaysian Muslim women used to wear what looks like Western summer dresses, and it has never provoked any kind of sexual obsession. It has been considered quite normal here. I have never understood Arabic men who fall over women because they see a piece of naked skin, an ankle, and who claim that the woman should be covered from head to toe, almost like the Victorians perceived it. But all these trends are culturally specific. The men here, the Malays, usually don't have this extreme sensitivity towards female bodies that are not covered, this profound sexual obsession with women, but now Islamist Malays have adopted this obsession. One of the impacts of Islamization is that the female body is exclusively seen as a sexual object. This is very alien to the Malay culture, which has never been so patriarchal. Neither has it been extravagant, but simply prudent, moderate.

So isn't it a duty of Sisters-in-Islam to try to underline this distinction between cultural heritage and tradition on one side, and religion on the other side?

Of course. What we need is a reformation, and that—exactly that—is the sad history of the relation between Islam and the modern world. It is the history of the defeat of our forefathers who, in the meeting between the Islamic heartland and Western influence, have not been able to renew Islam. With colonialism, other problems arrived too, and because they lost power and influence, they turned to an obsession with rituals, culture and sharia. Everything else was taken from them. Therefore, I think the great battle for us now is how to initiate a cultural and social reform of Islam. That is the project. I think an intellectual reform must come first, however, a new theological, interpretive approach to the Koran, a critical alertness, a critical examination when studying the sources. This is our task as intellectuals.

Let me then point to a more structural problem in multiculturalism in this country which might put obstacles in the way of reform, democratization and promotion of human rights. In his book From Majapahit to Putrajaya, *the scholar Farish A. Noor describes multiculturalism in this country as "ethno-political communitarianism," as he draws attention to the destruction of the public sphere as a forum for common reasoning and for debate of common interests, and to where any citizen—as citizen, as citoyen—has a right to intervene and speak out about all matters in society. Instead society has been split into different religious and ethnic spheres governed by sectarian rules. That is what he calls "ethno-political communitarianism."*

Non-Muslims may not speak out about Islam and Islamism as these are subjects that are not of their concern. They don't belong to the Muslim community; they may not even speak out in spite of the fact that the sharia rules have consequences for society as a whole. The general welfare and human rights—interests and rights all citizens have in common—are no longer valid references in the social discussion, but the normative basis for judging the validity of an argument is now a sectarian religious exegesis of the holy script. Multiculturalism is the end of liberal democratic society. And the point, according to Farish A. Noor, is that it is due to a structural impact of the multicultural system, of ethno-political communitarianism—because of this the foundations of liberal democracy will necessarily be eroded.

Yes. This is absolutely correct. And to counter that development, Sisters-in-Islam approached other groups outside the Muslim parties, when the

Islamists in Kelantan wanted to pass the hudud laws, the sharia-based penal system. We did not want to go to the Muslim parties, but to the Chinese and the Indians. We approached the non-Muslims, and we explained to them that they should ignore the Sedition Law and the fact that they were not themselves Muslims; they should not simply accept this, but should instead protest as citizens of Malaysia—as *citoyens*. They should protest against the Islamists and we should protest, but we neither should do it as Muslims, but as citizens, and as women against the patriarchal sharia laws which they wanted to pass. These laws would, for instance, make it impossible to prove a case of rape.

We told the non-Muslims that they should stand up and protest loud and clear against these laws and not accept the segregation into two different nations. We have been divided enough in history. You get the notion that this is like it was in the time of the Weimar republic; if nobody speaks out, if nobody fight Islamism, then we all know what is going to happen to us. We must speak up as citizens.

But this is a very sensitive subject you are touching upon. In one of my first interviews here with the editor-in-chief of Malaysiakini, *Steven Gan, he pointed out to me that it was important that he not criticize Islamist initiatives because of his Chinese background , that he leave that to other Muslims, otherwise he would be accused of Islamophobia, no matter how well-founded his criticism would be.*

This is his point of view, but gradually this kind of reasoning is changing. For instance, the Chinese party in the government coalition is very open in its criticism, and more and more non-Muslims stand up against the Islamist project. The public sphere is important for the democratic process.

We Could Not Have Imagined This in Our Worst Nightmares!

Interview with Benjamin Dawson, lawyer, council for the defense of Lina Joy

My intention was to hear more about a specific case of apostasy—Lina Joy's story—and what had motivated her to take such a serious step as submitting an application to change her name and alter her registration as a Muslim on her national identification card. The case of Lina Joy has been widely reported in the Malaysian press and is still going on in the court when I begin my series of interviews with her lawyer, Benjamin Dawson, in Kuala Lumpur. For that reason, we cannot explicitly go into this case, as his duty is to protect his client against any kind of unforeseen publicity related to the interview and coverage in the foreign media.

I understand that Lina Joy is very affected by the attention that her case has attracted—the persecution from the authorities and condemnations from Muslim organizations—so, by way of introduction to our conversations on human rights and apostasy in general, we chose to touch on a wide range of related subjects: the decolonization and the legal inheritance from the British, the radical change in the demography in Malaya (as the country was then called) during the time of the British Empire, the genesis and the development of the sharia laws in Malaysia after Independence in 1957, and the origins of the multi-legal system.

Will you briefly describe the relation between the common law and religious laws during British rule in Malaya?

Before the British came here, to what was then the States of Malaya, it was the Sultans who held the political power, and they also administered the laws for their subjects. The British brought British law with them, but they also respected the local laws—the so-called Adat laws—which regulated domestic relations, heritage, etc. These were local laws the British didn't want to interfere with, but colonization also changed demography in this country. There was a huge immigration of subjects from other parts of the British Empire, from India and also from China. But, of course, the Adat laws only applied to the Muslim native population. For all others, British common law applied, and common law was also applied to all citizens where the Adat law didn't apply. The administration of the Adat laws was eventually taken over by the clerical authorities and the Sultans were reduced to a sort of constitutional monarchy, as we know it from contemporary Europe. In this way, local laws were mixed with religious laws and now called Kadi laws.

When we come to the time of Independence in 1957, how did the British influence the Constitution and the legal system?

At that time, the British had been here for more than hundred years, and the bureaucracy, the legal system and British law covered all of Malaya, which was part of the British Empire. Our educational system was also British. When a constitution was to be drawn up, legal experts were brought together from all over British Commonwealth—from Pakistan and from Australia for instance—to form a text under the leadership of the British judge, Lord Reid. There were hearings involving various people in society before a text was put together, and the result was in accord with British law and normal legal principles, human rights etc.

But the Constitution paid attention to the local conditions and the special positions of the Muslim Malays, regarding their religious customs and their domestic legal system. Already at this point there was a special position regarding the religious majority in family law. In all other domains, however, the common law is applied, but the privileged position for the Malays as the native people—or, as Mahathir later coined it "the definitive people"—was not mentioned anywhere, but as the Constitution was drawn up the question of granting citizenship to immigrants became a theme, and in order to do so, as a quid pro quo, the Malays' position as the native people was recognized. It was something that was added to the Constitution and something everybody agreed on.

When did you adopt a fully multi-legal system with sharia law and common law in this country?

First of all, we must make clear that there is no religiously defined penal code. In this domain, you have only common law. Islamic penal code, or hudud, has never been applied here in Malaya during colonialism or in independent Malaysia. The legal system from the time of British colonialism continued after independence. It was not before the eighties that the government established sharia courts whose jurisdiction was to be applied to Muslims in certain domains. This is the introduction of a parallel legal system on state basis, as the former Kadi laws were administered locally. It's from this point on that the Islamization of the country seriously accelerates; it is related to this reorganization and codification of sharia law in all Malaysia.

You will then observe that Muslims who have had their case heard with the sharia court approach the secular court in order to get different treatment because they are not satisfied with the sharia court. The reason might be that they find the ruling unreasonable. Although the sharia system has developed to some extent, it is still backward in jurisprudence, when compared with common law systems. For instance, you have generally accepted rules for appeal, fair play etc. Everywhere, but the codified local Kadi laws, which were inherited in the sharia laws, are characterized by many accidental elements. That led to a lot of complaints and some pressure on the common courts from people who wanted different rulings.

I am not sure that was the only reason, but it was at least one of the reasons for the Parliament to pass a law that stated that once the sharia court had made a ruling it was no longer possible for the common court to alter it. The rulings from the sharia courts now became definitive. That law was passed in 1988. Here, it is also clearly underlined that the sharia court can only rule over persons who profess Islam as their religion. It is this primary condition that specifies the jurisdiction of the sharia court. It was never clearly formalized before; it was an inheritance from local laws and rulings administered by clerical authorities. But to make sure that the rulings of the sharia were now definitive, it was specified that this system was only applied to Muslims.

There is also another condition regarding the jurisdiction of sharia courts. They can only try cases related to laws, which are passed on the state level, and the states' legislative powers are limited. For instance they cannot pass laws related to the criminal law—that is an area where decisions can only be taken at a federal level—and the penal code is the same for any citizen in this country, no matter what faith or ethnicity. Neither can the states pass corporation laws. There are many more examples, but laws for domestic relations can be passed at state level, and in this way the sharia courts can regulate Muslims' way of living. There is a general agreement that because sharia is an integral part of Islam it cannot be separated from the faith.

In this way we have a multi-legal parallel system with two set of laws here in Malaysia and in some ways they can function happily together, but lately there have been some problems. We have ended up in a situation where a decision has to be made whether one system or the other is right. For instance, there may be a situation where a man and a woman marry and at the time neither of them is Muslim, but some years later the man might convert to Islam. What happens then, in the case of divorce, who has jurisdiction to decide what happens to the children: the common court or the sharia court?

My answer is that it's the common court, for how could the sharia court have jurisdiction over citizens who are not Muslim? But in more and more cases, we see that it's the sharia court that is granted jurisdiction even where one party is not a Muslim. The Muslim can then get a ruling from a court, but the non-Muslim is not covered by any court. In such a case it is a clear conflict between two different legal systems. We must admit that the sharia courts are granted jurisdiction which in fact belong to the common courts.[1] We must also admit that the judges in the common courts are not courageous enough to fight this tendency in our country.

May I point to one aspect of what you just said? You mentioned the expression "persons who profess Islam," but how do you define that?

I don't think there ought to be any controversy over what the sentence "persons who profess Islam"—or for that matter any other religion—is supposed to mean. To profess your religion is to declare and confirm your religion, or declare and confirm no religion at all. You can open any English dictionary and you will find that definition is right. But the interesting point is that in the Malaysian constitution the formulation "is professing" is mentioned, and that can only mean a continual declaration and confirmation of the religion. It would mean, concerning myself for instance, that I was professing Hinduism fifteen years ago, but I am not professing Hinduism anymore as my religion. So today, I would say that I am no longer a Hindu.

The constitution nevertheless mentions "professing" at least five times when it refers to persons under the jurisdiction of the sharia courts. I mean, you ask me an important question regarding the problems we are up against when it comes to the jurisdiction of the sharia courts. For instance, in cases of apostasy, where persons want to leave Islam. This I consider a fundamental constitutional right as it's mentioned in article 11, that persons are free to choose what religion they want to profess, but again we observe that the sharia court is granted the right to rule in these cases and to ban apostasy. So, again, we have a clash between two legal systems.

What domains are covered by the Sharia courts?

Law of domestic relations, non-commercial domains, law of wills and succession, law of parental authority, matrimonial law and so on. It also covers domains regarding the dealing between the genders, prohibition of alcohol for Muslims, rules for obedience of fasting and attention to rules of holidays and prayers etc. But after the addendum to the constitution in 1988 concerning the definitive status of the decisions of the sharia courts, then it also covers cases of apostasy.

In many of these cases the penalty for violation is described in the Islamic penal code—hudud—but, as it is not applied in this country the punishment is mostly a fine when it's not too serious.

Let's take a look at a specific difference between common law and sharia law: what about matrimonial law? Where are the significant differences?

Take will of succession, for example. When a Muslim dies, all his property will have to be inherited by another Muslim, but if it's not a Muslim, then he can testament his property to anybody, regardless of faith. This a Muslim cannot do. This is a religious ruling that is not to be altered. Another question is matrimonial law. A Muslim man is allowed to have four wives although he has to have permission from the wife or wives he is already married to, but a non-Muslim cannot marry more than one wife, otherwise it would be seen as bigamy and considered illegal. Concerning custody of children, there is a problem with having two legal systems. Let's imagine one partner in a marriage converts to Islam while they are married; the Muslim partner will always be granted custody of the children in case of divorce because the non-Muslim partner will not be able to raise the children in a correct Muslim way and a Muslim always has the right to have his children raised in a Muslim way.

If a man converts to Islam during marriage, will his children then from that moment of conversion be under the jurisdiction of the sharia courts?

That's a good question. You will find some rules somewhere, in certain states of Malaysia, where a minor is considered a Muslim if just one of the parents is a Muslim. And it doesn't matter whether it's the mother or the father who has converted to Islam, the minors will then be considered Muslims as well. Moreover, the other partner (the non-Muslim partner of the marriage) will lose all his or her rights in the common law in a divorce—for instance, rights to custody of the children. Because the Muslim partner is covered by sharia law, the children are also now covered by sharia law. The non-Muslim partner is left helpless and without any legal protection. The common courts can't do anything, as it is outside their jurisdiction.

Then the consequence of conversion of one partner in a marriage to Islam is that the other partner is left without any legal protection whatsoever in case of divorce?

Yes, but this is not a dilemma which is comprehensible to those in Malaysia who pass the laws.

Let us focus for a moment on this basic contradiction between the constitution and human rights on one hand and sharia law on the other. The UN Declaration of Human Rights, article 18, speaks about the right to change religion, but in sharia there is a ban on apostasy. It is difficult to see how there can be a compromise here.

I think Muslim scholars disagree on the subject of apostasy, and that goes centuries back. They are divided on the question of whether Muslims have the right or not to leave Islam, but it is my impression that those who administer sharia law—from Pakistan to Saudi Arabia and Africa—all claim that it's a sin, that it's prohibited to leave Islam. It's the prevailing interpretation everywhere. But the question is of growing importance here in Malaysia. It's due to the problem of jurisdiction that we are talking about: which court has the jurisdiction to decide whether an individual is permitted to leave Islam—the sharia court or the Common court? Another question is Article 11 in our constitution, which guarantees freedom of religion. Does that article also cover people who are born into Islam? And it's really a problem for Muslims who consider the sharia more important than our constitution. How are we to treat this paradox in this country? If these Muslims said the constitution was more important than sharia law, it would amount to them saying that a human law is more important than a divine law.

That leads us to take a look at the implications that the ban on apostasy has for social relations—and for that matter in all societies where Islam coexists with other religions and secularism, de facto multicultural societies. My question is: isn't it the ban on apostasy that always leads to confrontation between Islam and other cultures and religions? It seems as if there is a huge identity crisis in this country on this question of the right to apostasy.

Unfortunately, for that question, the Malay parties—the Muslim parties—have paramount influence in this country, and the government party UMNO has a slogan that Malays will always remain Muslims. The identity for them is first the race—the nativity of this country—then Islam, and then the country Malaysia, all of us. This is their understanding of national identity, and it's now ingrained in every mind, in every Malay in this country, that there cannot exist a Malay who is not a Muslim too. It's an understanding so firmly established that the constitution put it like this: a Malay is a person who professes Malay culture and Islam as his culture.

At present, I have a case concerning a Malay who has converted from Islam to Christianity and now wants this step to be recognized. She wants her identity card altered so she is no longer registered as a Muslim, but as a Christian. However the judges in the sharia court claim—pointing to the definition I have just referred to—that a Malay is defined as a person who professes Islam. And this woman is a Malay, and so far the court has denied her the right to leave Islam.

For my part, I claim that this definition in the constitution is relevant in relation to whether or not you will qualify to be granted the privileges the Malays enjoy in this country. The definition doesn't say anything about whether or not you may leave Islam, but Article 11 speaks about freedom of religion, and that article covers all citizens. But if you ask people, nine out of ten seem to hold the opinion—according to what the media write on this issue—that Malays cannot leave Islam. A Malay is once and for all a Muslim. But you cannot pass legislation on people's choices for professing religion; you just cannot do that today. You cannot pass legislation on faith, at least that's the point of view of lawyers and that's also my point of view. We claim the country should be built on the rule of law and not on religious dogmas, but it seems as if it's a losing game for us.

I have had conversations with two Muslim scholars on this subject, the ban on apostasy, and I have heard two versions of how to relate to it as a Muslim. Perhaps unsurprisingly, I have heard from a PAS supporter at a University in the State of Kelantan that the death penalty should be handed down in cases of apostasy. Another scholar from Kuala Terengganu holds the opinion that you should first try to re-educate people and hand out fines to them. I have been informed by Muslim scholars that the original meaning of apostasy concerns those who backstabbed the vulnerable Islamic community in the times of the prophet and thereby acted as traitors to their kin, and that that definition, of course, cannot be applied to those people today who just want to leave Islam. But tell me, what is your opinion of the general attitude among Muslims in this country on this subject?

People are divided, but the dominant opinion is—and has been for centuries—that Islam doesn't recognize that any person can leave the religion. They seem to refer to the punishment described in the Koran for such a crime; during the early period of Islam, the punishment was death unless you regretted and repented your sin. Our country is not a theocratic country governed by sharia law, however, and we have a constitutional guarantee for all people—and that includes Muslim too, as I see it—for the freedom of religion. I conclude that if a person wants to leave his religion then the religious authorities have no jurisdiction over that person any more, for you cannot force anybody to stay within a religion. You might get different answers from Muslims scholars about how apostasy should be punished, but whatever they might think, in my opinion they have no authority whatsoever what should be ruled, as a person is free to leave his or her religion according to our constitution. In some cases, the apostate has been fined or sent to re-education; in other cases nothing has happened, but the apostate has just been denied the possibility of leaving Islam.

I read in the SUARAM Human Rights Report about a case of four persons (Malays) in the State of Kelantan who wanted to convert from Islam to another religion. The sharia court denied them this right and sentenced them to twenty months imprisonment. In August 1998, they renounced Islam in front of a civil servant nevertheless, and then the sharia court sentenced them for contempt of court, as they did not show up at the re-education lessons to which they were sentenced earlier as an addendum to their prison sentence. They were then sentenced to 3 years in prison in a re-education camp. They tried to appeal this sentence to the Supreme Court, but that was refused in 2004. Then they had no more legal possibilities. Therefore, the ban on apostasy seems to be a very serious matter and it appears as if punishment can be prolonged endlessly. Will you comment on that?

I think this trial has been staged to show people that if you want to leave Islam you will never get away with it. They want every sensible person to realize that if you understand Islam and appreciate your life in the hereafter you should not try to leave Islam. It appears to be one of the dogmas of Islam that the community has an obligation to ensure that the members of the congregation don't leave Islam. The religious duty is then translated and formalized in the form of a punishment with this re-education, where religious teachers will warn you not to stray away from the right path. And I don't think they will ever give up.

In a democratic context nowadays you cannot overrule human rights in order to promote your religion or your political faith, but nevertheless it's what we see is being done in the case I just referred to from the State of Kelantan. These people don't seem to have any more legal possibilities. What is your comment on this?

Let me try to answer your question to this paradox in two ways. First of all I want to state on a general level that I cannot imagine you can pass legislation covering the regulation of faith—for we are talking about freedom of religion today. And to whom does the right to believe belong? I cannot imagine that the right to faith is not inalienable for the individual. Here, I talk from the point of view of a universalism. However, there is also another point of view. The Islamic standpoint does not necessarily pay attention to the individual, for Muslim rights must be seen in a context: what is good for the community? In this way, they understand that in this case the community knows best what is good for the individual, and when it comes to a conflict between a community right and an individual right, then the community right overrules the individual right. When you have a rule within Islam that if you defect then you will burn in Hell or there will be a regular mass defection from the religion that will undermine the Muslim community, then the community right will overrule the individual right. We are talking about two different ways to look upon the world. The first one is individually-based through human rights; the second one is based upon community rights.

Which point of view will have to give in?

That depends on what legislation you find in a given country, and when it comes to a specific subject, what law should then be applied in this country? To me, it appears to be Article 11 in the constitution, covering freedom of religion. Moreover, the Constitution is the supreme law—but that is not acceptable to certain groups; we have witnessed that on several occasions when someone wanted to leave Islam.

In what way does the ban on apostasy work when it prevents two individuals of different confessions from marrying each other and having a family?

Let's imagine a Muslim boy meets a Hindu girl, and then the two of them can't marry before she has converted to Islam. That's always the condition that the non-Muslim partner converts before the marriage can be legitimate, so therefore you will never see mixed marriages. No Muslim is permitted to convert. When two young people really want to marry, then the non-Muslim partner just converts out of necessity, but this can cause serious problems later in case of divorce because if the former non-Muslim partner wants to convert back to his or her original religion, then comes the ban on apostasy in Islam. It is prohibited.

To what extent do you think the ban on apostasy is necessary for Muslims? For secular people, the problem could be solved if you could join the sharia jurisdiction voluntarily, as any kind of association, and the law could be administered in this context for the congregation. You could live according to rules as in any other association. Why do you think that sharia needs the state as law enforcer? The sharia court needs the authorities to enforce its jurisdiction, to enforce its sentences. But why?

For Muslims, the sharia law and the sharia court must be there because of the strong feeling of religious duty underlining the obedience of the commandments in the Koran, both privately and in public, and there must be an authority to ensure that this really happens. Otherwise the Islamic way of living will not be followed. That is the reason why there is no distinction between state and religion as you know it in the West. I really cannot imagine how you would be able to abolish the sharia courts when you want the Islamic dogmas to be followed and to rule people's lives.

Let us talk about a person who, during his time in government, promoted sharia law to its prominent position: Mohammad bin Mahathir. He wrote The Malay Dilemma, *a book of tremendous political importance. But to me, when reading the book, he is writing as a nationalist rather than as a Muslim, and not at all as an Islamist. As we know, he coins the concept of "the definitive people" when he defends the privileges of the Malays and when he wants to underline what part of history—the Malays' history—is decisive and what group this country belongs to as a native people.*

That's true. When he wrote the book in 1970, there was not any religious theme on the agenda and, globally, Islam was not a theme at all. Independence was the paramount theme in third world countries and the focus was on economy. Human rights were not an important theme either. At that time, we were just getting used to sharing political power in this country—it was just thirteen years after independence—so the nationalist leaders did everything they could to seize the political power within their ethnic group. You are quite right, Dr. Mahathir's cause at that time was the social and the political position of the Malays; no religious theme was on the agenda. Indeed, religion hadn't been on the agenda before the Iranian revolution. Since then people discovered how secular leaders in Muslim countries were either corrupt or authoritarian. Therefore, Islam became a powerful tool to topple these leaders.

But what do you think of the concept he uses in the book: the definitive people? By that he means the people who have had the power in the country, who have defined the country with respect to their culture and history, who have formed governments; here in Malaysia, it is of course the Malays. It is on the basis of this definition that he supports the idea of privileges for the Malays, because they did not have the same position as the Chinese and the Indians at the time of independence. What do you think of this motivation for "affirmative action," if we chose to define these measures as such with reference to the politics in, for instance, the United States?

I would not call it a sound argument because discrimination based on ethnicity and race will raise a form of wrath and anger in parts of society who do not enjoy these privileges; they have been created at the expense of these other groups. You should instead set up programs based on the criterion of poverty. That is something everybody can agree should be rectified, and is a place where you can support the individual in education and the fight against poverty. Ethnic criteria for discrimination only divide and corrupt society, and it's not sufficient that it is all set up to serve a noble cause. Take an example: a wealthy Malay kid with bad marks is privileged compared with a poor Indian kid with good marks for a desirable place at the university. It only creates anger and frustration. And it doesn't create equality in society.

When were these laws passed concerning privileges for the Malays?

The Constitution already mentions the prominent position of the Malays when it comes to allocation of public jobs etc., but that's in a very general way. After the riots in 1969, the government decided to pass the so-called "New Economic Policy," and since then there has been a flow of regulations and laws all concerned with promoting the position of the Malays. We are talking about initiatives that go much further than what the Constitution indicates. For instance, in any company 30% of the stocks must be given to Malays. How these people are found is not clear.

When you say "given" I understand it as "allocated." Malays will be given the priority to buy no less than 30% of a new company. I presume that's on normal market conditions?

When it comes to allocation of stocks for Malays then the government imposes on any company a minimum of 30% of stocks allocated for Malays and, in order to avoid unknown or unfriendly stockholders getting access to the board, the non-Malays offer stocks to a friendly group of Malays which they pick up themselves and sell to for a favorable price. The final result is that the Malay group gets the stocks at a price under the market.

When we talk about privileges, how would you describe the way it's handled when Muslims buy real estate at a more favorable price compared to non-Muslims?

Let's imagine a new housing project where the developer has to meet the condition that a certain proportion of the houses has to be sold to Muslims and that they should be able to buy the houses for a price 5 to 15% below the average for the other houses. This percentage is different from State to State. It is quite simply part of the budget that some houses must be sold under market price.

So it means that the other buyers have to pay for that subvention?

Yes. It's clearly not the developer who will pay for the loss of proceeds of the sale. That must be calculated in the total budget.

How are privileges regulated and administered in other areas?

For instance, at the universities 60% of the places are reserved for Muslim Malays and it doesn't matter whether they are all qualified or not—or, for that matter, if others are more qualified than the Malays with less good marks. The precise quotas vary from subject to subject, but you will find ethnic quotas all over. Also, with regard to scholarships and paid expenses for study, most of them are granted to Malays. It's not a subject that is written openly about in the media.

What do you think of the concept "the definitive people" in the first place? Doesn't it sound problematic to you? Mahathir demands quite dramatically that immigrants or descendants of immigrants will have to recognize the history and the language of the definitive people as their own. You have an Indian-Chinese background. How do you feel when you hear these proclamations? Do they insult you?

I'll have to understand what context the book is written in. It was just after the riots in 1969, where the situation was very overheated, and there was a fear among the Malays that they were about to lose control of this country. So I think he wrote out of the fear that the immigrants—if I may use that word—that the non-Malays would take over the country. Mahathir writes that we—the Malays—are the most important people. The history, the language and the country are ours and we must not lose it to someone else. His book was a sort of a political program in order to bring the Malays together.

He writes that one should look to the United States which he describes as the greatest immigrant country in the world, the greatest multicultural society, with the concept of the melting pot where all cultures meet and are mixed together. It appears as if he sees that as an ideal—though with reservations. As a Muslim, he must recognize that there are many aspects which must be kept apart and not mixed with other cultures. But how do you perceive his concept of the definitive people and that you, as an immigrant or descendant of immigrants, will have to adopt this country's history, the native language Bahasa etc.? An immigrant never has to convert to another religion, he always underlines that point, but in spite of that, isn't there anything which insults you or just makes you unhappy in what he writes?

Of course it doesn't make me happy! On the other hand: obviously the Malays have their place here in Malaysia, but hardliners like Mahathir emphasize that the country belongs to the Malays. And when the Chinese and the Indians arrive, then it is still the Malays who create the rules and the others will have to obey, they must adopt and respect our culture—that is, the Malay culture.

It's more or less the same demands that Muslim immigrants are met with in a more and more self-conscious Europe today, no matter whether they come from Pakistan or the Middle East, and no matter if they are themselves immigrants or descendants of immigrants in first, second or third generation. Where is the problem with this approach when people still have the opportunity to worship according to their religion?

Let me explain it in this way: if you enter any kind of cultural show or cultural festival in this country then there will be an Indian show, a Chinese show and a Malay show. You might define the show itself as a Malaysian show, where different aspects flourish and are expressed. It is this very combination which embodies the Malaysian culture. It is something else to put on an exclusively Malay show and call it the only expression of Malaysia. I myself prefer the first version, the expression of all the elements, the collection of cultures, the diversity of ethnic cultures that actually live in this country.

This is your point of view: the melting pot of cultures can only work to a certain point? You would rather talk about (to continue the metaphor) a mosaic of ethnic cultures?

You are quite right. A true melting pot where all elements are mixed in one culture will never be realized. There must never be only one dominant culture and no room for others. Look at the United States: there you will see the ethnic cultures live separated to a certain degree with their particular expression, but is there one and only one American culture?

It appears as if all this misery is due to the fact that we are used to thinking in terms of national culture and not ethnic culture. We think of Indian culture as something necessarily from India and not from elsewhere where people of Indian origin live, but maybe that is very backward. With migration from countries and continents, the perception of what a culture is must change. Therefore, Indian can be many things: Indian culture in Malaysia and Pakistani culture in Europe for instance. On the other hand, we must also have a minimum program, to which the local cultures must adopt everywhere: human rights, women's rights, democracy, and a secular public sphere; there is no room for divine laws and you cannot lock people up in their religion. Faith can only be received in freedom, otherwise you give way to communities where human rights are not respected. But in the paramount version of multiculturalism, it is difficult to make that distinction between local, particularistic rights and universal rights for everybody everywhere with no compromise. It seems as if non-democratic aspects tend to enjoy respect from multiculturalists if they can be traced to and identified with a culture. I am trying to spell out the meaning of the metaphors melting pot and mosaic, and how they relate. What do you think of it?

I fully agree with you, and in fact that is what this case I have taken about an apostate is all about. This is what Lina Joy's case is all about. It's about a Muslim woman who has converted to Christianity and thereby claims her constitutional right. According to what you have just said, I conclude that it is also her unalienable right to do so. But it's a problem that is not evident in this country of ours. What kind of ideology are we in the process of developing here in Malaysia? We wouldn't have imagined just twenty years ago, even in our worst nightmares, that you could not convert from one religion to another. Because then we could, and people converted as they pleased without problems. It was not a problem before the codification of sharia law under Mohammad bin Mahathir.

How would you understand the meaning of freedom of expression the way Muslims perceive it? I am interested because we have had this cartoon crisis in Denmark, this conflict between freedom of expression which is implicitly critical of a religious doctrine and the feelings of insult of Muslims. For an immediate understanding, it could be seen as if there were an internal contradiction between two human rights: the freedom of expression and the freedom of religion. From the conversations I have had in this country with Islamists and Muslims I have the impression that they don't understand that freedom of expression might have the consequence that an expression could insult other people's feelings. I have then tried to explain that in human rights there is no such protection against insulted feelings.

To be absolutely clear: if an atheist says a lot of negative things about Jesus Christ on Trafalgar Square in London, then I would say that he claimed his freedom of expression in England. Devout Christians would just have to accept that as a consequence of free speech. We can all have different opinions of who Jesus Christ is and what he means to us, but I would never condemn or accuse anybody for exposing my God to ridicule.

I think that in a European context and most probably also in an American context, the support for freedom of expression and trust in the culture of freedom of expression is so strong that it cannot be questioned. But, generally speaking, Muslims will all overreact in a different way from us. Christians will never take to the streets and act violently if someone insults their religious feelings. They will be hurt and insulted but they will never react in a violent way. Usually, we don't react with the same passion as the Muslims do. They feel insulted to an extent where they are prepared to act if something unfortunate is said about their prophet.

When it comes to people of a faith other than Islam who are insulted and hurt, then it's never a serious theme in the media. For instance, a Christian would say that you should not mock and expose Jesus Christ to ridicule. It will insult me, but I will not react against those who mock and expose Jesus Christ to ridicule. That's not the way it is with certain Muslim groups who very often simply see it as their religious duty to defend their religion with violence. This violence is more than just an emotional reaction. It's a religious duty to prevent insult to Islam. You don't find this doctrine in other religions, not in Hinduism, Buddhism, or Christianity. A few Christian fundamentalists might possibly react violently, but as it's a doctrine in Islam, where the thought of freedom of expression has difficulty being accepted.

But is this defense of religious doctrines not possible through public debate in an open society?

When it comes to religion, then there are problems. At the moment we have a strange case here in Malaysia where Christian Bibles and other books have been confiscated by the authorities because the Muslim word for God—Allah—appears in those books, and the opinion of the authorities is that this word should be reserved for the Muslim God. They say it would bring too much confusion if Christians also use this word for god. The State interferes with censorship against freedom of religion. What I am going to call my god and how I express myself is covered by basic human rights.

A more concrete example is a Christian priest who appealed to the court to overrule the Ministry of the Interior's confiscation of some books for Sunday schools and Bibles for the Malaysian speaking Christians on Borneo in the Eastern part of Malaysia who are not Muslims. When the Bible was to be translated to their language, Bahasa, then the word Allah was used for God and that's what was bothering the Ministry of the Interior. It's prohibited to call your god Allah unless it's the Muslim god you refer to. That's what the Ministry of the Interior has stated with a reference to the Internal Security Act! It might sound surprising to you, but that's the way it is. You can hardly believe it.

But isn't that yet another example of how sharia rules disseminate into society when the state changes its character and sharia is codified for a group who is forcibly covered by its jurisdiction? The state undergoes a destructive metamorphosis and laws are legitimated by religious exegesis.

It's true. Sharia disseminates into society and far beyond the realm of law of domestic relations etc., and eventually sharia laws will cover not only Muslims. But to end this story about the appropriate word for God I would like to add—for the sake of argument—that the word Allah was also applied by the Arabian Christians for their god, long before the prophet was born! But the Muslim community here is so rigid that they don't want to face how other people think. They just pass a lot of laws and rules which are utterly nonsensical.

But tell me then: how do these Christians solve their problem when they are not allowed to call their god "God" in their own language?

They use the word "Dohan," which means "Lord," but they are not allowed to say "God."

Postscript

Some months after my interview with Benjamin Dawson I read in *Le Monde*, June 3, 2007, that the Malaysian Supreme Court had ruled in the case of Lina Joy. Her right to change religion has been denied by the court. Her counsel, Benjamin Dawson, issued the following public statement after the decision of the court:

> The Federal Court's majority decision in the Lina Joy case has dire implications to religious freedom in Malaysia. In its sweep, the case has dealt a mortal blow to the fundamental right to freedom of conscience and belief for all Malaysian citizens, which is enshrined in Article 11 of the Federal Constitution. It is therefore a case, which has seriously undermined our constitutional scheme that was settled 50 years ago by our founding fathers and which underpins our unique constitutional history [...].

The Lina Joy Case: The Facts

Azlina Binti Jailani was baptized into the Christian faith on May 11, 1998. She wanted a change of name to reflect her new status.

For this purpose, she applied to the National Registration Department (NRD) to change her name on her identity card (ID) to Lina Joy. On October 20, 1999, she succeeded.

The real objective, however, failed. This was because the NRD, while allowing the change of name, inserted "Islam" as her religion on the ID.

In January 2000, Lina applied to the NRD for deletion of "Islam" on her ID. Her application was rejected by the NRD. They insisted that she must first produce a certificate or order from the Islamic Religious Authority or the Sharia Court, certifying that she was no longer a Muslim [...]

Lina challenged the NRD's policy in court. She contended, first, that there was no such requirement in the NRD Regulations, and secondly, that the NRD's policy is unconstitutional.

On May 30, 2007, the Federal Court by a majority of 2 to 1 rejected Lina's appeal. It sanctioned the NRD's policy.

The majority judgment held: "*Islam is not only a collection of dogmas and rituals, but it is also a complete way of life which covers all human activities, private or public, legal, political, economic, social, cultural, moral or judicial. According to Article 11(1), 74(2) and item 1 in list 2 of Schedule 9 of the Federal Constitution, it is evident that Islam covers inter alia, the Islamic law. Therefore, as submitted by the learned counsel from the Malaysian Muslim Lawyers Association, who are holding a watching brief, if a Muslim wishes to leave the religion of Islam, he actually uses his right under the context of the sharia law, which has its own jurisprudence on the issue of apostasy. If a person professes and practices Islam, it would definitely mean that he must comply with the Islamic law which has prescribed the way to embrace Islam and converting out of Islam.*"

In short, the majority judgment held that a Muslim who wishes to renounce Islam must go to the sharia court and obtain an apostatisation order.

Leaving aside the correctness of the majority decision, what are the implication and realities for a person who goes to the sharia court for an apostatisation order?

To begin with, the person will be hard pressed to find a lawyer. Not every lawyer can appear in the sharia court. Only a lawyer who has qualification in sharia law and is registered to practice as a sharia lawyer in a particular state can appear before the sharia court of that particular state. There are only a handful of non-Muslims with such qualification, and, invariably, Muslim sharia lawyers are reluctant to take up such cases. The person will have to fend for himself/herself. This happened very recently in the Ayah Pin case in Terengganu; no Muslim lawyer in Terengganu was willing to act for the "Muslim," who was regarded as a deviant.

The suggestion that a person who wishes to renounce Islam should approach the sharia court—an institution created under the Islamic Enactment and whose foremost objective is the promotion, advancement and administration of Islamic affairs—is rather surreal. In reality, the prospect of obtaining an apostatisation order is illusory given the general belief that apostatisation is a sin and that the Muslim community has an obligation to prevent its adherents from falling into sin. There is a strong abhorrence in the Muslim community against someone who apostasizes. […]

The majority judgment in the Lina Joy case has treated the apostasy issue as an Islamic question *simpliciter* rather than a constitutional matter. In doing so, the constitutional guarantee of freedom of religion is denied and the civil court's jurisdiction on a purely constitutional issue has been abrogated.

METROPOLITAN COLLEGE OF NY
LIBRARY, 12TH FLOOR
431 CANAL STREET
NEW YORK, NY 10013

The Broken Cup:
From Culturalism to Multiculturalism

The Roots of Culturalism

"Multiculturalism" is a concept which is used variously as a liberal principle of individual freedom of religion, thought and expression, or as the idea that single cultures have the right to self-government, including law, courts and punishments, as is the case in Malaysian multiculturalism. In a Western context, it is very often unclear which use of the concept is intended in individual assertions using the word, and it is not unusual to encounter ideas lying close to Malaysian multiculturalism—as, for example, when the Anglican Archbishop Rowan Williams claimed (in the spring of 2008) that Muslim Britons should have their own sharia laws in some domains.[2] But how has this "hard" version of multiculturalism been able to gain ground in the West, not only among Muslims and Christians, but also among liberals and the left wing? One of the roots of this development lies in a particular version of the anthropological concept of culture.

During the interwar period, "culture" became a central concept in American anthropology in that sense of the word where it makes sense to talk about a singular "culture" as an autonomous object separated from other cultures; it is a variant of this concept of culture which results in "multiculturalism."

The background to this development is already present in the foundation of American anthropology which is, to a large extent, the work of one man: Franz Boas. He founded the first American anthropology department (at Columbia University) and laid the foundations for a new tradition in anthropology which went against the ethnocentric tradition of placing the white "race" on the top of an evolutionary tree and other "races" on lower branches of that tree. The race concept current around 1900 was a mess of biology and culture. Very often, the concept groups human beings by common features without further investigation of the origin of those features. At other times, in so-called "scientific racism," it is presupposed that those features have biological roots.

Among Boas's great merits is the fact that he goes against this pseudo-scientific race concept and makes the important distinction between biological and cultural variation.[3] Thus, he participates in the separation of physical anthropology and cultural anthropology as distinct sub-disciplines. He continues to maintain that "race" may have a biological relevance; however, he considers this relevance to be rather small. He distinguishes the issue of culture from biological determination, observing that children from all "races" may be socialized into other cultural groups. Alongside Bronislaw Malinowski in England and the "structure functionalism" of British anthropology, he made empirical fieldwork central to anthropology. American anthropology was constructed by his many disciples.

Anthropological cultural relativism is founded in Boas's *The Mind of Primitive Man* (1911). Even though Boas did not explicitly develop a concept of culture, this became, to a large extent, a task for the generation of his disciples. In his philosophical family tree, the German tradition has a considerable weight: Kant and especially the founder of nationalism, Johann Gottfried von Herder, with his insistence on the special features and the organic character of the single nation.[4] Wilhelm von Humboldt, Wilhelm Dilthey and Wilhelm Wundt also played influential roles for Boas, which thus imprinted a heritage of German idealism and postidealism on the whole first generation of American anthropologists.[5]

From Herder, Boas would import a cluster of ideas, such as the idea of the enormous variation of human mentality in time and space; the idea of interpreting other such mentalities by avoiding assimilating the alien position to one's own and an ensuing emphasis on empirical field work and participant observation; the idea that language determines and delimits the possibilities of thought (cf. Boas' famous disciple, Edward Sapir), and most of all Herder's *holism*—his idea that a nation is constituted by culture, a whole consisting of history, language, myth, arts, customs, all human accomplishments which should not be understood in a piecemeal way, but only from the background of that cultural whole. From this sprang the idea of understanding rather than explaining (which was also developed by Dilthey) as well as the idea of incommensurability, incomparability between the cultures of different nations. Michael Forster argues that Boas also inherited what he calls Herder's "pluralist cosmopolitanism," the ethical insistence on the right of single nations or single cultures to develop their individuality.[6] This appeared in Boas's appeal on the occasion of the involvement of the USA in World War I, when Boas demanded that one should "seek to understand and to respect the individuality of other nations."[7] This "pluralist cosmopolitanism," however, remained rife with tensions and did not prevent Boas from protesting against Nazi persecution of Jews in 1938. In the former case, Germany should have been understood and respected, but not so in the latter.

It is important to realize that the anthropological concept of culture shares a very decisive ancestor—Herder—with 19th century nationalisms and their descendants and, to a large extent, shares the nationalist conception of culture. It is well-known how Herder's cosmopolitanism easily lost out to his other principles about the organic wholeness of national cultures and the incommensurability between them, which came to form the basis of the emerging European nationalisms, both in their benign and their more malignant versions. Large parts of Herder's romantic cult around the uniqueness of the single nation were thus passed on by Boas to American anthropology which could now apply it in a broader sense than national states—namely the stateless peoples, who became the central research object of anthropology.[8]

A decisive development of this anthropological concept of culture takes place in the book *Patterns of Culture* (1934) by the American anthropologist and Boas disciple, Ruth Benedict. The book became an instant classic, translated into many languages and reprinted in many editions to this day. Its influence on the anthropological concept of culture is enormous and can be seen from checking its status in anthropological standard textbooks today. It is "one of the most widely read books in anthropology,"[9] and its special status explicitly refers to its concept of culture: "... the perspective which emerged as the most crucial for its [the concept of culture] position was that of Ruth Benedict."[10] Its position is emphasized by admirers and opponents alike. Among the adherents counts Benedict's friend Margaret Mead who writes, in her preface to a later version of the book: "That today the modern world is on such easy terms with the concept of culture, that the words 'in our culture' slip from the lips of educated men and women almost as effortlessly as do the phrases that refer to period and to place, is in very great part due to this book."[11] Among opponents counts the anthropological researcher of human universals Donald E. Brown[12], who characterizes Benedict's book as one of "the most important and popular of all texts in cultural relativism."

The book has served for many years as an introductory text in anthropology departments, especially in the US, but, well-written and easily read as it is, it also surpassed the walls of academia and, as Mead mentions, came to influence the idea of culture among "educated men and women" in the broader public. Especially among American liberals, "her cultural relativism came to define Boasian anthropology in the eyes of the American public."[13] The book was not only academic anthropology, but also had a political agenda: to spread the idea about the equal value of all cultures. There is no doubt about the fact that Benedict's concept of culture, in more and less diluted and vulgarized versions, plays an enormous role in the Western political and cultural public even today, even for people who have no first-hand knowledge of the book and perhaps even do not know it exists. The book has, in itself, created a *pattern of culture*. There is a very good reason, then, to investigate the concept of culture established by Benedict in this 20th century classic.

The book puts forward a concept of culture with a great emphasis on the autonomy of each culture. This, of course, goes against the loose theories in earlier anthropology of cultural evolution, in which different, currently existing groups of people could be identified with earlier and later levels of evolution. Benedict has an acute sensibility for the possible development of such doctrines into outright racism (the book was published in 1934, the year after the Nazi *Machtergreifung*) and in her first chapter she attacks "scientific" racism as well as contemporary American racism against black people. She admits that all cultures distinguish group members from "outsiders," but attacks Western racial prejudices which continue this distinction between "in-group" and "out-group" on an alleged biological basis: "not one item of his tribal social organization, of his language, of his local religion, is carried in his germ-cell" (12).

Just like her teacher, Boas, Benedict strongly argued against the idea that the behavior of ethnic groups was determined by their biological race, and in doing so, she formed an important figure in the discrediting of the idea of distinct, biological races in anthropology. The concept of race is a modern myth, which is contradicted by the simple fact that everywhere, human beings from one group who are born into another will, unproblematically, learn this new culture. It is from the background of this sound and relevant criticism of racism that Benedict constructs her theory of culture as an alternative explanation of human diversity. Ironically, she ends up with a notion of culture which is not much less totalizing, suppressive, and exclusionary than the concept of race, and which is even similar to the race concept at many points, maybe indeed because everything which the race concept has pretended to explain should now be explained by culture instead. In the structure of the book, she selects the study of three cultures as remote from modern Western culture as possible—the Pueblos of Mexico, the Dobu islanders south of New Guinea, and the Kwakiutls of British Columbia—to clearly illustrate her main point about cultural diversity.

We shall not go into her specific analyses here, but rather investigate the details of the concept of culture which the analyses are taken to illustrate. As preparation for her analyses, she puts forward two almost axiomatic definitions of her concept of culture: that cultures are different, and they are organic. Both are illustrated by a quote from a Californian Indian chief during a dialogue with Benedict: "'In the beginning,' he said, 'God gave to every people a cup, a cup of clay, and from this cup they drank their life'" (21). It was a claim of such extension and such power that Benedict chose it as her motto for the whole book. Culture is a vessel which contains the whole of life and which is given to every people from the beginning. The cup of Chief Ramon, however, is broken; the whole fabric of cultural relations which made it up, does not subsist after the colonizers' conquest of Native American lands.

As an illustration of this whole, Benedict selects language: the well-known linguistic fact that every language cuts up the phonetic continuum each in their own fashion is quickly generalized to all other social institutions. Every culture selects its own set of institutions (in a broad sense of the word), which appears arbitrary and irrelevant if seen from other cultures. With reference to Margaret Mead's well-known Samoan studies, puberty rites are taken as an example: they vary between cultures and may be completely absent. Similarly, warfare (maybe a little naive; war is hardly always a matter of free choice) is taken as a cultural option only selected by certain cultures. This gives rise to the hasty conclusion that:

> The truth of the matter is rather that the possible human institutions and motives are legion, on every plane of cultural simplicity or complexity, and that wisdom consists in a greatly increased tolerance toward their divergencies. No man can thoroughly participate in any culture unless he has been brought up and has

lived according to its forms, but he can grant to other cultures the same significance to their participants which he recognizes in his own (37).

The range of possible human institutions and motivations is infinite. The fact that this surprising claim is followed by a very sympathetic request for tolerance should not keep us from wondering about the radicality of the claim. Human beings, as a species, represent a relatively recent biological fact with small genetic diversity (as compared, e.g., to the genetic spread of other primates), and the preparation and digestion of food, language, myth, ritual, arts, warfare, family structures, systems of prohibitions and much more seem to be social institutions that we find in varied form in all human societies: see for example Brown's (1991) listing of human universals). Despite these facts, Benedict emphasizes the infinity of this variation time and time again: "The diversity of the possible combinations is endless" (44).

Here, Benedict takes an important and fatal step. She transforms a methodological rule in anthropology into an ontological postulate. She not only opens herself to whichever cultural differences may appear—she declares beforehand that the range of such differences is infinite. Benedict's teacher Franz Boas had attacked the all-encompassing and speculative theories of cultural evolution and instead called for precise empirical studies of actually existing cultures. He had recommended, as a methodological tool, field study as a participant observer in order for the anthropologist to observe the different cultural features in the context of use where they receive their meaning—and in this way to make it possible for the anthropologist to maintain a distance from his own cultural prejudices. He should, moreover, compare as vast a corpus of ethnographic data as possible—with full awareness of the differences between the positions of individual features in their specific cultural organizations.

Benedict herself repeats this rational methodology which revolutionized anthropology: "The fieldworker must be faithfully objective. He must chronicle all the relevant behavior, taking care not to select according to any challenging hypothesis the facts that will fill a thesis"(229). Already, the further step from culture relativist methodology and to culture relativist ontology and norm was prepared in Boas, and in Benedict the decisive radicalization of these principles of research become both central and popular. Now, it becomes an ontological axiom that cultures *are* radically different. It is no longer just a methodological axiom that one must investigate cultures in a neutral way so as not make oneself blind to those differences that might show up.

If cultures are thus radically different on the one hand, then they are, in return, strongly cohesive internally on the other. In Chief Ramon's metaphor: each culture constitutes one integral cup. This constitutes Benedict's second central axiom, that "the whole, as modern science is insisting in many fields, is not merely the sum of all its parts, but the result of a unique arrangement and interrelation of the parts that has brought about a new entity" (47). Cultures must also be understood as such "articulated wholes." Benedict refers to the contemporaneous gestalt theory, whose implications, for her, far surpass the psychological experiments and philosophical hypotheses of that theory. The cool and well-documented research of wholes in perception and thought of gestalt theory are directly coupled by Benedict with far more fey and romantic ideas of much more comprehensive wholes and their organic, autonomous and almost living character, with arguments taken from the philosophy of life and vitalism of the period (Dilthey and Oswald Spengler).

To Dilthey, philosophical systems are mere expressions of comprehensive and deeper "sentiments of life," (that is, cultures), and in Spengler, Benedict resumes the opposition between Apollonian and Faustian as prototypes of two different cultural systems. Spengler used these concepts to analyze two different aspects of Western culture, but to Benedict this opposition is difficult to investigate further because Western culture is still too large and complicated to be subjected to anthropological analysis. Here, Benedict finds that the study of primitive cultures is simpler and thus provides a more direct window on the central issue, which is less visible in the West, namely the cultural determination of the individual: "The whole problem of the formation of the individual's habit-patterns under the influence of traditional custom can best be understood at the present time through the study of simpler peoples" (55). Benedict's vitalist holism is very radical: "The whole determines its parts, not only their relation, but their very nature" (52), she claims. There is no discussion here about wholes of different strength, type or degree of organization, but a quick and resolute claim for a holism which is so radical that the whole has the power not only to organize the mutual relations of its parts, but even their very being.

Benedict's empirical studies have, of course, encountered cultures with very different degrees of organization, but they are only described as being integrated versus a "lacking" integration. This negative characteristic—lacking integration—interestingly covers cultures which are also deemed inferior in other respects, such as marginal cultures, cultures that are victims of conflict, cultures with a "facile" receptivity to other cultures, or cultures subjected to foreign influence (225-6). That which, for another observer, might appear as a freedom for the individuals in less integrated cultures are seen as deviations, even pathologies, by contrast to properly integrated cultures which are taken as the yardstick and goal for cultural development. Integration is something cultures strive to "achieve." On top of this comes, for Benedict, the possibility that cultures which appear to be badly integrated are merely an expression of bad fieldwork and badly integrated description on the part of the anthropologist. More professional descriptions of the same cultures are supposed to be able to document the presence of an integration which was not immediately obvious (228). The fact that the opposite possibility— that a relatively loosely integrated culture is rendered more integrated in the description of the anthropologist— is not even considered clearly proves that "the integration of cultures" is not the object of empirical investigation, but rather an undoubted presumption before investigation takes place.

All in all, a concept of culture is articulated with a decisive emphasis on:

1. mutual differences between cultures and the impossibility of understanding any aspect of one culture as seen from another.
2. internal integration of cultures and the impossibility of isolating and understanding single features from the organizing whole of culture.

The first of these ontological principles tends to make the anthropologist systematically blind for possible *similarities* between cultures. It is assumed in advance that all features in a given culture are absolutely different from all other cultures; even if the very same feature appears, it will assume a completely different meaning in the context of the different whole. It is not considered whether aspects of cultures on higher levels—parts of or whole cultural patterns—might be identified across cultures. It is not considered whether lower levels, such as basic human needs or behaviors, might be identified across cultures. The second principle threatens to blind the anthropologist to internal cultural differences which, given Benedict's principle, are hard to conceive of in any other way than decadence, as a sign that the integrity of that culture is lacking or decaying. By the same token, this principle makes the anthropologist antagonistic to cultural hybridization: a feature in one culture borrowed from another will be already preconceived as being there as the result of "facile openness." On such a basis cultures may never really meet. They are separated worlds of life which would rather decompose than communicate with other cultures. To take another metaphor, they are like continental plates: when culture moves, the individuals unwillingly follow, even when earthquakes result from the clash between plates. While the former idea claims the total variability of man, the latter claims that when the process of socialization has been completed, the infinitely variable individual stiffens completely in his culture and becomes totally incapable of grasping other cultures. Culture becomes an ineradicable imprint on a blank slate containing no other determinations. With the combination of these two principles, we have one of the clearest expressions of anthropological cultural relativism.

This doctrine is summed up neatly in Benedict's most pervasive metaphor: the single culture is like an individual with its own personality, "a personality writ large." It is striking that there is a sharp and unintended opposition in this metaphor: the culture as an individual. "Hard" cultural relativism will claim that the individual is thoroughly determined by his culture and now the radical closeness of the same culture is described by reference to the individual! In a certain sense, it is the group or society as "organic whole" which is the only relevant individual in Benedict's anthropology, which goes so far as to claim that psychological experiments show there are no "honest-dishonest persons, but honest-dishonest situations" (236), just as leaders, in our society as well, do not possess any special properties whatsoever as compared with other people, but are awarded the required competences by society. Thus, psychological properties on the individual level are mere surface effects, even illusions when compared to cultural-social determinations. On the other hand, it is also culture which assumes individual-like properties so as to have a psychological profile. A culture may be described in psychological terms, and it may pursue specific purposes to the extent that its members acquire the same set of psychological properties. This forms the basis for Benedict's appropriation of Nietzsche's concepts of Apollonian/Dionysian and their application to cultures. In reality, it is culture, not the individual, which has a psyche, according to Benedict.

This, surprisingly, makes possible certain universal claims across cultures: "great occasions" (initiations, marriages, burials, invocations of supernatural powers, etc.) are "situations which every society seizes upon to express its characteristic purposes" (243). Here, each and every culture expresses itself like an individual, wishing to express its goals in celebrations of big events in life (the individual culture of course not expressing the same things as other cultures in these rituals). Thus, it is not possible to compare family structure, economy, moral ideas, etc. across cultures; this would be the same as breaking up the individuality of each culture: "The significant sociological unit, from this point of view, therefore, is not the institution, but the cultural configuration" (244). It is the whole of the cultural structure, the pattern of culture, which has individual character, impossible to split up or analyze further. This is why anthropology aims at making us understand the culturally specific which is assumed, a priori and without argument, to be radically much more comprehensive than what might be common across cultures: "As we become increasingly culture-conscious, we shall be able to isolate the tiny core that is generic in a situation and the vast accretions that are local and cultural and man-made" (245). The common, universal core is tiny, and the further cultural elaboration enormous; we already know that this is what we will eventually end up knowing when the culture-conscious investigation has been completed.

The last chapter of the book is about culture and the individual, even though Benedict starts out by claiming that she does not recognize this opposition at all. She dismisses it as a 19th century idea which has given rise to "philosophies of freedom, political creeds of *laissez-faire*, revolutions that have unseated dynasties" (251), events she consequently does not endorse. It sounds suspiciously as though she has a longing to go back to an era before the bourgeois revolutions. The bottom line remains that the distinction between individual and society is a dualist ideology, against which she maintains that, "In reality, society and the individual are not antagonistic" (251).

She must admit, however, that all the cultures described in the book have means for marginalizing unwished persons (258), though they also have different ways of resocializing and making such marginal persons useful (267). Depending on culture, different types of persons are expelled, but she is surprisingly able to identify common reasons for expulsion across cultures (homosexuality, trance, epilepsy, for example)—and compare the culturally variable ways of treating such individuals on that basis. It seems as if the existence of cultural codes for which individuals are marginalized constitutes, in itself, an argument for the fact that it does not hurt any individual; it is whole groups which are stigmatized as witches or ostracized in other ways. This does not, however, prevent Benedict from finally outlining a criticism of the conformity-seeking American culture of the period: "Middletown" where it may be scandalous to have the wrong stockings or a wrong car and where "Eccentricity is more feared than parasitism" (273). This was before deviation became a middle class norm!

This throws light upon the political implications, in terms of cultural criticism, which Benedict draws from cultural relativism. It becomes clear that her relativism by far surpasses merely methodological issues. She takes relativism to possess an ontological status and, what is more, claims a new ethics on this ontological background. It is important to investigate this step in detail, for it contains a tension, even a contradiction, which is inherited by many later manifestations of multiculturalism.

On the one hand, it is claimed that all cultures are equal and it is therefore necessary to tolerate other life forms. Let us quote the conclusive credo of the book:

> "The recognition of cultural relativity carries with it its own values, which need not be those of the absolutist philosophies. It challenges customary opinions and causes those who have been bred to them acute discomfort. It rouses pessimism because it throws old formulas into confusion, not because it contains anything intrinsically difficult. As soon as the new opinion is embraced as customary belief, it will be another trusted bulwark of the good

life. We shall arrive then at a more realistic social faith, accepting the grounds of hope and as new bases for tolerance the coexisting and equally valid patterns of life which mankind has created for itself from the raw materials of existence" (274).

Here, we get the final expression of the doctrine of the equally valid patterns of life of all cultures, a doctrine which will protect other cultures from our prejudicial attacks and call for tolerance instead. If tolerance is supposed to be practiced also *by* other cultures, however, then cultural relativism here erects a common value system for all cultures—exactly what it just claimed is impossible. No restrictions are laid upon tolerance, the new value claimed by anthropological cultural relativism. It is expected to be embraced as a new creed, even a new "social faith," and it will become the protection of the good life. Not without a fight, however, because it incites resistance and pessimism in those who must give up their old beliefs, the belief that not everything cultural is equally valid, we must assume.

The strange tension, however, lies in the fact that this whole revolution must be assumed *itself* to take place within a culture, supposedly "Western culture." But how can a culture, holistic as it is, thus give up some of its "customary opinions" and substitute others for them? Would that not disintegrate it—cf. Benedict's lament over badly integrated cultures with "facile hospitality" (226) towards new influences from outside? It becomes clear that there are not only three cultures to analyze in *Patterns of Culture*, but four. The fourth one is Western culture and its American variant specifically, which does not have its own chapter in the book but to which Benedict returns pinprick-like, over and over again, during the course of the book.

Western culture is so complex and stratified that it does not yet yield to anthropological analysis, she wrote, but this does not restrain her from attacking it on a whole series of points throughout the book. We must criticize the points in which the features of our own culture are forced, local, and overgrown, she says; she thinks of things like warfare and capitalism (250) and Spengler's analysis of the "Faustian" character of modernity (52). The latter ought to be more deeply investigated by the ethnological description of recurring types in our own culture: "It is quite as convincing to characterize our cultural type as thoroughly extrovert, running about in endless mundane activity, inventing, governing, and, as Edward Carpenter says, 'endlessly catching its trains,' as it is to characterize it as Faustian, with a longing for the infinite" (54-55). But are these claims scientific results she has reached by the meticulous and detailed objectivity of the field worker? Is it at all possible for the anthropologist to reach such results, given the methodology defended? How may she, an individual within Western culture, break with its wholeness and attack parts of it? She is by her definition unable to transcend her culture. How can one place oneself outside and compare one's own culture to others and conclude that features she does not happen to like are "overgrown"—overgrown as compared to what?—and "local"—local as measured by which universals?

Here, all talk about the "equal value" of cultures abruptly disappears, and one is reminded of the old joke that an anthropologist is a person who displays full respect for all forms of life, except for his own. It is not that there are not many aspects of Western societies that ought to be criticized; the problem is that Benedict has to break with her own methodology and ontology—the difference, homogeneity, incomparability, and equal value of cultures—to make cultural relativism into a critical doctrine.

The strange thing is that the book does, in fact, display a sensibility for the difference between the three small societies explicitly analyzed in its middle part and "Western civilization." It is by no means given that cultures consisting of a few thousands persons on a limited geographical area constitute a type of social, scientific object which is directly comparable to the enormous current involving billions of people, several continents and considerable internal differences which we call "Western culture," A similar argument could be made regarding "Chinese culture." Here, "culture" seems to be an elastic concept which may be stretched to subsume enormous differences, from very small, limited groups to comprehensive social entities. Despite the fact that Benedict, unlike much vulgar anthropology, realizes this, she does not stay away from entering into an ongoing criticism of the West, which (contrary to the basis of the three analyses in field work and data collection) has the character of loosely supported idiosyncrasies, legitimized by cultural relativism as a critical doctrine. Democracy, rule of law, science, civil, political and human rights—principles which have arguably played a certain role during the recent centuries in the West—are not mentioned at all in her cursory description of the West, where negative characteristics such as capitalism, racism, war, conformism (and individualism!) play center stage.

A decisive and typical consequence of Benedict's cultural holism also becomes obvious: features of very different character and influence are involved side by side in the "pattern of culture." Racism and war form part of the characteristic culture of the West alongside canned food and the fact that children want the same clothing as their playmates. Everything, tiny or large, important or ephemeral, becomes a "social value." When the concept of culture becomes so all-encompassing as is the case here, any human choice on any level is supposed to be a cultural value and it becomes impossible (except when regarding western culture, apparently) to distinguish what is essential and what is not, what should be criticized and what should not—because these distinctions themselves are specific evaluations taken to depend on the relevant culture.

From Anthropology to Politics: Anthropologists against the UN

It is remarkable that political forms of government in the West are not at all mentioned in Benedict's analyses of Western culture. When racism is criticized, it takes place in a generalized tone, without specific emphasis on contemporary Nazi Germany. The strong tension between anthropological cultural relativism and democracy became explicit, however, thirteen years later when another Boas disciple, Melville Herskovits, took to action. The pretext was that the newly founded UN had begun its work upon the UN Declaration of Human Rights in 1947, to be published the following year. Herskovits, as an anthropologist, felt insulted by the universalism he saw developing in the UN. He authored a protest note as chairman of the American Association of Anthropologists, which he submitted on behalf of the Executive Board. It was also published under the name of this committee in *American Anthropologist*.[14] Here, Herskovits and the Board wrote (539):

> The problem faced by the Commission on Human Rights of the United Nations in preparing its Declaration on the Rights of Man

must be approached from two points of view. The first, in terms of which the Declaration is ordinarily conceived, concerns the respect for the personality of the individual as such, and his right to the fullest development as a member of his society. In a world order, however, respect for the cultures of differing human groups is equally important.

These are two facets of the same problem, since it is a truism that groups are composed of individuals, and human beings do not function outside the societies of which they form a part. The problem is thus to formulate a statement of human rights that will do more than just phrase respect for the individual as an individual. It must also take into full account the individual as a member of the social group of which he is a part, whose sanctioned modes of life shape his behavior, and with whose fate his own is thus inextricably bound.

We find the same basic figure of argumentation here as in Benedict: the individual is inextricably bound to his culture. This time, however, this idea is turned directly against the work of articulating universal human rights. If the individual is so inextricably bound to his society that his values cannot deviate from its, then no universal right can get its razor blade in and criticize one on behalf of the other. In particular, the individual cannot be protected against his society—for a conflict between the two is a priori excluded. As Benedict expressed it, "in reality, there is no opposition between the individual and society." In Herskovits, "the personality of the individual can develop only in terms of the culture of his society." The individual even *must* necessarily support the values of his culture. "…the individual cannot be but convinced that his own way of life is the most desirable one" (540).

This categorical assertion seems to hold only to a limited degree for anthropologists themselves. Herskovits, of course, intends to protect the small cultures under pressure from colonialism and imperialism, but the ideology he constructs with this praiseworthy ambition entails a relativism which gives carte blanche to everything which may go on in these cultures. This was perhaps the reason why other cultures than the West are seen as living peacefully with each other, as in a paradisiacal state before the Fall of Man, "In the main, people are willing to live and let live, exhibiting a tolerance for behavior of another group different than their own, especially where there is no conflict in the substance field. In the history of Western Europe and America, however, economic expansion, control of armaments, and an evangelical religious tradition have translated the recognition of cultural differences into a summons to action" (540).[15]

The only exception from natural tolerance and mutual cultural recognition seems to be the West, which has driven man out of this anthropological Eden. On that basis, the AAA put forward three demands for a declaration of human rights on a sound anthropological basis:

> 1. The individual realizes his personality through his culture, hence respect for individual differences entails a respect for cultural differences. (...)
> 2. Respect for differences between cultures is validated by the scientific fact that no technique of qualitatively evaluating cultures has been discovered. (...)
> 3. Standards and values are relative to the culture from which they derive so that any attempt to formulate postulates that grow out of the beliefs or moral codes of one culture must to that extent detract from the applicability of any Declaration of Human Rights to mankind as a whole (541-42).

The number of contradictions and problems in these proposals is almost infinite (cf. Schmidt 1955 which provides a strong and early philosophical criticism of the cultural relativist position). Is it not equally true that individuals often realize themselves against their cultures? If that is the case, then is it true that respect for individuals need not entail respect for cultures? Is there not a large array of fairly simple economical, political, health, education and other yardsticks that make possible the judgment of differences between societies? If standards and values really only hold for the culture they come from, how may cultural relativism be applied to other cultures? Is it really true that all standards and values stem from cultures (and not from a variety of sources including a priori states of affairs, biology, geography, economics, history, individual choice)? And is it, in fact, correct that the origin of values determines their validity?

Herskovits' protest terminates in the well-known claim (from the current attack on human rights from both the political right and the political left) that these rights are standards from one single culture which consequently will frustrate people living under other value systems, because they will be "excluded from the freedom of full participation in the only right and proper way of life that can be known to them, the institutions, sanctions and goals that make up the culture of their particular society" (543); the individual simply *cannot* know anything else than the institutions, sanctions, and goals of his own culture. Only rarely has cultural relativism so clearly expressed the doctrine of the individual as prisoner of his culture.

It is a strange airy world populated by these otherwise empirical anthropologists in the second year after the disclosure of Auschwitz, which might have opened the eyes of even the dullest to the fact that there might be a tension between an individual and his society. The number of refugees in the wake of the World War might also have made it plain that individuals are not always as "inextricably bound" to their culture as Herskovits assumes. It is remarkable, moreover, that these contemporaneous experiences with totalitarian societies have not made clear the flip side of the coin: that the idea of the individual submitting totally to his society is nothing but the fantasy of totalitarianism. Such a thing is possible only by means of the severe disciplining of individuals, which requires comprehensive apparatuses of subjection, such as one might believe the 1947 public realized had ruled in the fascist parts of Europe and were still ruling in its communist parts. There is only a slight reference to this perspective in the protest note of the American anthropologists against human rights. In the conclusive statement of the note, they write:

> Even where political systems exist that deny citizens the right of participation in their government, or seek to conquer weaker peoples, underlying cultural values may be called on to bring the peoples of such states to a realization of the consequences of the acts of their governments, and thus enforce a brake upon discrimination and conquest.
>
> World-wide standards of freedom and justice, based on the principle that man is free only when he lives as his society defines

freedom, that his rights are those he recognizes as a member of his society, must be basic (543).[16]

The first point treats the existence of political systems which do not allow citizens to participate in government, or which aim at swallowing up weaker people. Such cultures should obviously not be fought in any direct way; the only weapon against them is the appeal to (their own) "underlying cultural values" to awaken the people of such states to face the implications of the actions of their governments.

Even at the time, this was read as a powerless attempt to address the just-vanquished fascisms (Julian Steward 1948). For how should the Allies have applied this principle against Nazi Germany? Carpet bombing the Third Reich with leaflets of quotes from Kant and Goethe? The naivety of the quote is scary: the only weapon against a repressive culture is that very culture itself. And if culture is so holistic, homogeneous and tensionless, as organic culturalism presupposes, then such tensions cannot exist at all. The upshot must be that if a culture is barbaric, then all its individuals are the same, and then there cannot be any "underlying" values to which to appeal against dictatorship or warfare. The extremely weak way of addressing totalitarianism, tyranny, dictatorship, authoritarianism—the lack of "right to participation in government"—of course covers the fact that the majority of societies that anthropologists study do not have democracy in our sense of the word and easily might fall under the concept "undemocratic," if a more outspoken style was used.

But the second conclusive point in the manifesto of protesting anthropologists is also interesting; world-wide standards for freedom and justice are called for, dependent on the claim that man is free only when he lives in terms of how his society defines freedom. The concentration camp inmate must realize that when slaving to death under the motto "Arbeit macht Frei" (Work makes you free), then he lives according to the definition of freedom of his society, and then he actually *is* free. According to the anthropologists, there exists no other definition of freedom across cultures, and the initial universalism of the claim is contradicted already in the next line. Freedom was, according to another famous totalitarian doctrine of the period, the same thing as "insight in necessity" (Lenin), just as today we can often hear Islamists supporting a concept of freedom involving full free speech, provided, of course, you only say the right thing. There are, to put it briefly, many different cultural definitions of freedom, but it is a tough thing to require that individuals living in such cultures automatically assume or ought to assume the same strange concepts of freedom as propagated by their tyrants.

At the time, however other anthropologists discovered the problems inherent in the AAA's protest against human rights. Julian Steward, also a Boasian and the founder of ecological anthropology, replied in the journal of the Association the following year. He realized that the conclusion with the "underlying values" was a crooked and vain attempt to exempt Nazi Germany from an all-embracing tolerance, and he realized the dilemma more clearly than Benedict and Herskovits: "either we tolerate everything, and keep hands off, or we fight intolerance and conquest— political and economic as well as military—in all their forms" (Steward 1948, 351). He saw that it was the very transformation of the cultural relativist methodological principle into moral relativism which was the core of the problem, and he sharply asked whether anthropologists were then assumed to accept the caste system of India, contemporary American racism and other discriminatory systems. To him, hard culturalism must mean one of two things: either that intolerance must be tolerated in the name of tolerance—or it meant that the principle of tolerance must be intolerant towards societies which lacked Western principles of toleration. No third way was possible. To him the conclusion was that anthropologists must cease to pass value judgments and believe they could apply their science critically; they must remain descriptive scientists, and only as private citizens draw further, political conclusions.

In the same issue of the journal, another anthropologist, H.G.Barnett, expressed strong dissent against the leadership of the Association. He regretted that the very first important public stance taken by the AAA is directly embarrassing to its scientific reputation. There is no scientific definition of human rights—and generally anthropologists should not indulge in the jump from "is" to "ought:" "an intimate knowledge of a people throws no light upon their 'needs'"(353)—except on the basis of a yardstick which is added from outside science. He clearly saw the mixing up of facts and values in AAA's alternative human rights proposal and concluded that anthropologists must not fool themselves into believing that they are able to define what is good, true, and just on the basis of their scientific knowledge of man, such as the note of AAA concludes by claiming: "only when a statement of the right of men to live in terms of their own traditions is incorporated into the proposed Declaration, then, can the next step of defining the rights and duties of human groups as regards each other be set upon the firm foundation of the present-day scientific knowledge of Man." (543)

Culturalism: From Idea to Unconscious Presupposition

Many of the ideas we find in the harder versions of multiculturalism already lie preformed in mid-20th century anthropology, both in central and popular writings and in political activism. This cultural relativism, taking the leap from anthropological method to ontological claims about the organic essence of cultures, can be named "culturalism." By this notion we understand a theory of culture which assumes the central anthropological ideas: that culture precedes and determines the individuals belonging to it; that cultures have unlimited freedom to generate differences, uninhibited by any human nature; and that cultures form closed, organic units where all their different articulations, from gastronomy to theology, form an unbreakable whole which implies that these value systems are unique and in no way may be compared with or judged against other value systems. It is important to realize that this culturalism is very closely related to the nationalism which it counts three generations earlier in its ancestral tree in the history of ideas—Franz Boas basing his anthropology on Herder's romantic concept of the nation.

Boas himself did not, however, take the full step from cultural relativist method to culturalism; this step took place particularly in the generation of his disciples. Culturalism is, so to speak, nationalism transferred from state to society. The whole idea of combining an organic concept of culture with regimentation of individuals which so strongly incited 19th century nationalisms and made them fight for the formation of new states, the articulation of national cultures and expulsion of minorities was now, remarkably unchanged, applied to the largely stateless peoples that anthropologists studied. While 19th century nationalism had been allied with liberalism and had a status as an emancipation ideology turned against absolute monarchy, nobility and old, multinational empires, nationalism had, during the 20th century, matured into a primarily right-wing ideology, turned against the international character of liberalism as well as socialism.

It is a strange fact than in the mid-20th century, when nationalism is supplemented by culturalism built on the very same cluster of cultural concepts and the same tradition in the history of ideas, that this culturalism primarily (but not exclusively) finds its place on the political left, just as nationalism had done a century earlier. This might have happened, of course, because anthropology aimed to defend its "cultures" against the then still prevailing Western colonial empires with national bases.

Thus, from around the middle of the 20th century we have the strange constellation of a right-wing culturalism in the shape of nationalism and fascism, and a left-wing culturalism referring to stateless peoples, minorities and former colonies. The only difference is that the former talks about cultures, nations, and states, while the latter talks about cultures, peoples, and communities—but the underlying culturalist and anti-individualist cluster of concepts in the two is exactly the same, and their political idea of the comprehensive rights of the community vis-à-vis the individual is equally tough. This relatedness was hardly evident to everybody in 1948, even if it is striking how hard a time Herskovits had trying to articulate a cultural relativist position which must not, logically, lead to a tolerant acceptance of nationalist socialism—Nazism. But the reason why it was not obvious by then was of course the fact that most of the political left in the West was by then internationalist, be it in social democrat, New Deal, or communist variants. But with the seeds of culturalism sown, a culturalist germ was growing on the left which would become strong once the left eventually relativized or even totally gave up its commitment to internationalism and universalism. The result was multiculturalism.

Yet, the culturalism of Benedict and Herskovits lacks the prefix "multi"—and this of course was because they, just like nationalists, unproblematically assumed a bond between people and territory. Each anthropological culture generally occupied each their own territorial site, and when they did not, the reason was Western imperialism which broke up natural habitats and destroyed the clay cups of Chief Ramon. To become "multi," culturalism just needed a small amendment: that more than one of these broken cups should be present at one and the same place and compete for one and the same political power.

Even if cultural relativism thus had a strongly institutional position, as well as in the public perception of anthropology, a tension has remained within anthropology throughout this time. It has always contained many different currents, and the debate on cultural relativism resurfaced decade after decade, for example, in the pages of *American Anthropologist*.

It is curious to trace the anthropological discussion about culturalism during the second half of the 20th century. What had been avant-garde in the generation of Benedict and Herskovits had been the insight of a few pioneers struggling to found a novel and all-encompassing Science of Man, which had faced ethnocentrism in science and imperialism outside it. All this had soon given way to a quite different picture. During the 1960s, cultural relativism had become popular, supported by the fancy for exotism of the '68 generation and its cult of "primitive" and "authentic" forms of life.

At the same time, anthropological relativism had, to a large extent, proved academically victorious and even received support from other disciplines. In the theory of science, the prevailing interpretation of Thomas Kuhn's idea of science as based on different and mutually exclusive "paradigms" was that the paradigm was holistic and thoroughly determined the single scientific facts, just like a Benedictian culture determines its individuals. Gradually, as anthropology studied the dwindling number of remaining "primitive" societies, interest grew in studying the different classes, layers, and subcultures of Western culture, and the new discipline of Cultural Studies appeared, based for example at the Birmingham School of Cultural Studies in the UK. Subcultures, such as working class culture, youth culture, and immigrant cultures were studied. With the assumption of the idea of subcultures as "a whole way of life," large parts of Cultural Studies developed a holistic concept of cultures of a structure similar to Benedict's. With postmodern relativism and the growing social constructivism of the 1980s, it might almost seem as though anthropology was losing the race to its own relativist offspring in other disciplines. In anthropology, a more universalist pocket of resistance formed around the leading mid-century anthropologist, Claude Lévi-Strauss—had never been eliminated, and other currents, skeptical of the radical relativity of culture, also developed during the 80s, such as the growing interest in human biology and human universals on the one hand and research on the human mind in the cognitive sciences and neurosciences on the other hand.

This scenario forms the background for yet another round in the anthropological debate over relativism, initiated by a paper by the most influential anthropologist towards the end of the 20th century, Clifford Geertz. Geertz's idea of an "interpretative" anthropology takes field studies further, but now with the addition of a semiotic relativism. Descriptions are always already interpretations, dependent upon the language and the semiotic devices they employ; this forms a second-order relativism in the very description, which is laid on top of Benedictian relativism in the anthropological object. This gives a relativism whose radicality by far surpasses that of Boas, Benedict, and Herskovits: now science is but a specific cultural institution in a specific culture—Western culture—and it has no further claims to truth than magic, witchcraft, shamanism, and similar institutions in other cultures.

From the background of this linguistic relativism, it is logical that Geertz's attack on anti-relativism must assume the shape of a rhetorical feast. His relativist program paper "Anti-anti Relativism" (1984) is, as indicated by the title, no direct defense of relativism, but rather, based on the idea that an attack is the best defense; it forms a howling assault against what he sees as a growing anti-relativism. The paper and the debate around it is the history of the 1940s, now repeated as a farce. Geertz had assumed, he writes, that anthropological cultural relativism had prevailed once and for all, but now he sees the old arch enemies as rationalism (in the shape of cognitive science) and naturalism (in the shape of human biology) creeping back on stage. His attack is a joyful affair. The two enemies are dressed up as absolutist straw men with scare quotes and capitals. They believe in "The Human Mind" and "Human Nature" as unitary, dictatorial idols, and these ghosts are drowned in a tornado of glittering metaphors. At the same time, Geertz, without further details, claims that it is incorrect that he should be understood as meaning everything has equal value.

It is striking to record the difference as compared to the serious and hard-fought discussions among the anthropologists in the 1940s; a different academic culture had developed, and ridicule of the opponent (so much for tolerance!) had acquired a far more central position than the attempt to give a coherent description of one's own position. Geertz's position is described in the negative only. On the one hand, he spends most of the paper laughing at the new dangerous absolutes, "Human Mind" and "Human Nature"; on the other hand, he goes against the attacks on cultural relativism by defining himself in purely negative terms: "I, no nihilist, no subjectivist, and possessed, as you can see, of some strong views as to what is real and what is not, what is commendable and what is not, what is reasonable and what is not" (275).

In contrast to the old, doctrinaire (but also struggling and admirably honest) cultural relativism of Benedict and Herskovits, we now see a victorious cultural relativism which no longer has any need to make explicit and defend its position, but takes it to be sufficient to ridicule its opponents. The victories of anthropology are consequently also conceived of in the past tense: "Anthropology has played, in our day, a vanguard role. We have been the first to insist on a number of things: that the world does not divide into the pious and the superstitious; that there are sculptures in jungles and paintings in deserts; that political order is possible without centralized power and principled justice without codified rules; that the norms of reason were not fixed in Grecce, the evolution of morality not consummated in England" (275).

Real and dubious results are mixed up in this anthropological self-congratulation with ease, but the relativist credo remains unchanged: "most important, we were the first to insist that we see the lives of others through lenses of our own grinding and that they look back on ours through ones of their own" (275). The only proper argument present in the paper is worthy of being exposed: "The supposed conflict between Benedict's and Herskovits's call for tolerance and the untolerant passion with which they called for it turns out not to be the simple contradiction so many amateur logicians have held it to be, but the expression of a perception, caused by thinking a lot about Zunis and Dahomeys, that, the world being so full of a number of things, rushing to judgment is more than a mistake, it's a crime" (265). But Steward's and Barnett's argument against the two relativists were not that they displayed an intolerant passion; it was that their very doctrine was ripe with contradictions. The same thing goes for Geertz's claim. How can a "perception" result from thinking much about Zunis and Dahomeys? The results of the trains of thought of Benedict and Herskovits was a series of claims, propositions, judgments, rather than perceptions. But the reason why Geertz cannot say this is that to him the very "rushing to judgment" is already a crime; to claim something about the world is a criminal act, because the world is full of many things! It is remarkable that a scientist, even seen as leading in his field, may assert such a thing: that because there are many things in the world, it is a crime to make a judgment about it. So sloppy a condemnation of opponents is only possible in a person who feels very secure in his case, a victor proudly listing his strong allies in the war: "the appearance of deconstructionist literary criticism, the spread of nonfoundationalist moods in metaphysics and epistemology, and the rejection of whiggery and method-ism in the history of science" (257).

It is evident from the text that against such an alliance the study of human cognition and nature stands no chance. Even if these opponents are dressed up as dangerous fools, this has to be done in order to get the metaphorical carnival running; the text leaves no doubt that they do not constitute any real danger and are only pathological cases of "hyper-logicism" and "hyper-adaptationism," and Geertz's own position is so evident that there is no reason to present, explain, nor defend it.

Just as in the previous rounds, however, objections came against Geertz's anti-anti-relativism. Nissim-Sabat (1987) criticized details in both Herskovits' and Geertz's field studies which he finds are systematically blind to decisive facts, exactly because of their programmatic relativism. Herskovits describes at length the general polygamy of the Dahomeys without wondering for a second where this enormous surplus of women actually came from. It came from warfare, slave trade, and the killing of male slaves—things Herskovits is too well-mannered to investigate, Nissim-Sabat claims. In Geertz, he points to the fact that women do not appear at all in his famous Moroccan field study on Islam: here, Geertz blindly takes over the invisibility of women in Moroccan Islam to the extent that he does not register it and even reproduces it in his own presentation! Nissim-Sabat thus claims that cultural relativism is not only politically problematic but it may also lead to a systematic blindness in science; if a certain culture is constructed around overlooking or making invisible certain aspects of its own foundation, then it is easy for the cultural relativist field worker to be so much "participant observer" that he also keeps tacit about them, and maybe even does not even discover the embarrassing facts which the culture in question conceals.

The principal problem behind such errors is, according to Nissim-Sabat, the *cultural determinism* of relativism, which he compares to Geertz's criticism of sociobiology for implying biological determinism. But is cultural determinism any better than biological determinism? The assumption that culture has the ability to completely determine the individual appears again, forty years later, as the decisive problem in culturalism. It entails that any culture demands respect, only because it functions, no matter what price this functioning has for the individuals: "What most people learn from Benedict is that every culture deserves respect because it works" (938).

In a certain sense, the same arguments re-circulate in the 1980s as in the 1940s, but the whole scenery around the argument has changed. The picture of the few, truth-seeking anthropologists against a vast scientific and political power structure has given way to victorious anthropologists who may enlist a whole army of allies in scientific neighbor disciplines and who do not need to use arguments against rationalists and naturalists but may let fun and ridicule do the work. The price of this victory is coolly summarized in Washburn's looking back on the fight of the 1940s in 1987; it is the very idea of anthropology as a science—"The Science of Man," "The Scientific Theory of Culture"—which was so highly prized by the first generations of American anthropologists, but which is now eroded.

Geertz gradually came to think that anthropology itself was merely a form of "writing" which said more about the writer and his own culture than it said about the culture portrayed. As a logical consequence of his radicalization of relativism to epistemological relativism, one is not only unable to *judge* about matters in other cultures; one is now also unable to *describe* them at all, because one is inevitably caught up in the language of one's own culture. Relativism thus, in reality, devoured the very *scientific* ambitions of anthropology, while the *critical* ambitions remained, and even grew, in a certain sense. This is why the anthropologist may feel a certain nostalgia: "anthropologists may long for the good old days when one could easily identify with the good guys (natives), struggling for freedom against the bad guys (the West), preventing their emergence as independent and self-regulating states. It was the attitude that underlay the AAA Executive Board's Statement on Human Rights in 1947. But in the intervening 40 years, the simple picture of the post-war period has dissolved into the complex picture of 1987. It has become impossible to apply the Executive Board's policy recommendations of 1947 to the specific situations of today" (Washburn, 942).

To Washburn, the critical ambitions from the 1947 manifesto were now past, but to other anthropologists, criticism was rather what remained, now the scientific ambitions were withering away. The strange thing in this development is that, in the meantime, large parts of the middle class public, academia and the political left had taken over the same cultural relativist ideas of criticism. Boas and Benedict had taken the step from cultural relativism as research method and to a normative doctrine, but they had been unambiguous as to the possibility as well as the necessity of objective empirical field study. In the spread of cultural relativism as *versunkenes Kulturgut,* which had taken place in large parts of the Western middle class towards the end of the century, it was often only culturalism as a normative, critical doctrine that remained. Now that doctrine could almost be used as an argument for *not* being interested in other cultures: if we have decided beforehand that they have equal value and dignity, and if we are imprisoned in our own culture and language all the same, then there is no reason to take any interest in them, and there is no reason to believe in or investigate claims about barbaric customs and suppression in other cultures, for we have always already decided that they are respectable.[17]

No professional anthropologist would ever support such a claim, of course, but in a strange twist, it seems to have become the public result of the fact that only the worst part of the original cultural relativism survived in the popular version of the middle-class audience: the automatic tolerance towards anything alien, just because it is alien, and, correlatively, the automatic criticism of every part of one's own culture and the home of cultural relativism itself: America, and Western culture more broadly.

This boiled-down culturalism dominated the mindset in large parts of Western academia and the middle-class in the 1990's when growing immigration put a new type of culturalism on the agenda: multiculturalism.

129

The Argument of Culturalism Dissected

Before we proceed to multiculturalism, let us analyze the details of the culturalist argument.

As early as 1955, the philosopher P.F. Schmidt presented a clear and detailed charting of central steps and problems in the culturalist complex of arguments in his paper "Some Criticisms of Cultural Relativism." He distinguishes three different claims: a fact, a hypothesis and an ethical doctrine. The anthropological argument takes its point of departure in a *cultural relativist fact* which can be rephrased as follows:

(1) Different cultural systems of value and thought exist.

This premise is empirically indubitable and furnishes the reality base on which Benedict & Co. may claim that cultural relativism forms a scientific theory. But from this, the normative relativism in no way follows which Schmidt calls the *cultural relativist thesis*:

(2) There is no cross-cultural norm which may judge between the different standards of different cultures.

This is a meta-ethical hypothesis which is in no way entailed by (1). It might for instance be the case that cultures are different, but that there still exists a set of true values or true claims on which different cultures may be judged, maybe a set of truths we have not yet investigated thoroughly. In the same way as there exist many different claims and propositions, true and false, about any certain states-of-affairs which may only subsist in one way. That cannot be the case if (2) holds. But (2) is not incompatible with what could be called empirical universalism either: that the meticulous investigation of the cultures of the world might, someday, result in the fact that all of them share certain values or thoughts, even if (2) claims that no meta-theory may exist which may confirm that these common values or thoughts are in some sense correct. But no matter whether the meta-ethical claim of (2) is in fact correct or not, it is surprising that cultural relativism very often hastens on to the normative claim that "tolerance is good," the *cultural relative norm*:

(3) Therefore all cultures have a right to tolerance.

As Schmidt asserts, this claim in no way follows from (1) and (2). In a certain sense, (3) is even in flagrant contradiction to (2). Whilst (2) claims that there can be no normative cross-cultural demands which are valid, (3) quickly erects exactly such a demand: tolerance. Quite to the contrary, a more probable result of claim (2) would be the never ending battle between cultures (strife or outright warfare between ethnocentric values), exactly because no cross-cultural doctrine is possible which might settle the dispute and end the strife. As Renteln says: "if relativism is associated with any value, it is ethnocentrism and not tolerance" (1988, 63).

We can add that it may be for that reason that (3) is seen as necessary, that is, exactly because (3) does *not* follow from (2). (3) is taken as a necessary remedy to stop the strife which (2) makes inevitable. But for many cultural relativists, (3) primarily seems to be motivated by the more or less brutal actions by the West against various colonized populations, which early anthropology laudably opposed. Maybe the urgent character of this appeal has blurred the principal problem for the relativists—cf. Herskovits above, who seems to mean that cultures outside the detrimental sphere of influence of the West have by and large lived tolerantly in peace with each other. If you take this rosy idea as a point of departure, you miss the point that (3) maintained with equal force for all cultures potentially leads to tolerance towards intolerances of all sorts.

There are, however, more aspects of the cultural relativist doctrine than those three basic ideas listed by Schmidt.[18] As a consequence of (1), we can place the methodological idea that

> (4) If you investigate an alien culture, it must take place in a neutral way, so that the anthropologist strives to place his own cultural assumptions in brackets.

As we have seen, (4) may motivate ethnographical (field work as participant observer) and ethnological (comparative cross-cultural studies) rules of conduct which have shown scientific validity. (4), however, entails a restriction on (2): the anthropologist is assumed to be able to be or bring himself a suitable distance from his own culture so that he does not simply reproduce cultural prejudices in his research. It is thus presupposed to be possible that the anthropologist may, at one and the same time, participate in the culture studied and maintain an objective distance to what he sees and participates in. But already before the next step to maintain the difference between cultures, there are important problems in the principle (4). How do you warrant that the anthropologist does not blindly reproduce the culture's own biased understandings of itself and does not systematically overlook important issues which the culture studied is, in itself, organized in a way not to discover?

Another important addition to (1) says not only that different systems of value and thought exist, but:

(5) Systems of value of thought are *infinitely* variable.

It is not entailed by the naked fact of (1) and is, as a matter of fact, a daring generalization. How could we know that? It is presented as an explicit claim in Benedict, but also implies certain dangers in the work of the anthropologist: he may easily overlook resemblances between cultures, if from the very beginning he only intends to find differences. The specificity of cultures may be exaggerated in description, and cross-cultural loans, communication, hybridization and influence between cultures may become invisible, just like cultural, biological, or other universals may be. But (5) is also problematic for another reason: is it really correct that cultural variability is infinite? Could any possible bundle of cultural features, practices, ideas, and values be put together and be made to function as a culture? Could there exist a culture which celebrated murder as the highest value, or a culture which saw any kind of appetite as a vice? Could a culture which claimed that all things fall upwards exist? As Barry Smith says: could a culture where the acceptance of any agreement required that the two parties subjected themselves to painful surgery or proved a hitherto unproved mathematical conjecture exist? There are, in fact, two distinct problems here: could a culture with consequently counterproductive value systems exist? Could a culture with systematically erroneous systems of facts exist?

As a further important point about (1) is that we can thus see it has two variants:

(6) There are different cultural value systems.

(7) There are different cultural thought systems.

Naturally, they are just as unproblematically true as (1), but they do not have the same radicality if they are taken as a basis for relativism. If we take cultural difference as an indication that there is no system which is more correct than another (2), then (6) gives rise to moral relativism, while (7), even more radically, gives rise to epistemological relativism (as we encountered in Geertz). Epistemological relativism, resulting from (2) plus (7), had already developed in early American anthropology in the shape of the Sapir-Whorf hypothesis, presented by the two anthropological linguists, the Boas disciple Edward Sapir and his disciple Benjamin Lee Whorf, whose main idea can be expressed as follows:

(8) Linguistic distinctions determine the distinctions of thought.

The categories employed by a given language are assumed to shape the thought of the individual speaking the language, so that he cannot, in fact, think counter to his language. This idea, of course, can be found in more and less radical variants. If (8) just means that the distinctions of language (along with other determinations) influence thought, then the claim seems unproblematic, but if it means that the distinctions of language present precise and unchangeable limits for what can be thought by an individual speaking that language, then it is far more problematic. (8) appears in further sub-variants, such as:

(9) The lexical distinctions of language determine thought.

(10) The grammar of language determines thought.

The former claim refers to the observations such as different languages have different color taxonomies with greater or lesser degrees of granularity and different borderlines between color concepts, while the latter refers to the fact that different languages have different grammatical structurings of the same domain, e.g. as to the tempus forms of verbs. Here, a variant of (2) may play a role to the extent that it has been imagined that language is the *only* thing determining thought, so that color and time, respectively, should in themselves be undifferentiated continua which are arbitrarily cut up by means of language (a basic idea in American as well as European structuralism). Berlin and Kay (1969) have disproved the radical version of (9) with an empirical investigation of color terms in many languages.[19] (10) taken along with (2) is more radical than (9) coupled with (2), because (10) is then taken to imply that thought categories which are not explicitly present in grammar cannot be used by a speaker of that language.

Such an idea gave rise to some of Whorf's more airy ideas such as the claim that the Navajos did not have any grammatical future category and hence had a completely different time conception from us, ideas which have been, to a large extent, disproved, not least because languages have a manifold of alternative ways of expressing things which they do not have grammatical categories for. English does not have a grammatical futurum either but gets along with an auxiliary construction with "will" and "shall" (though hardly anyone will claim that English speakers live in the present now only and have no ideas about the future). The Sapir-Whorf hypothesis has, however, had a huge effect, and it can still be encountered today, often accompanied by the "linguistic turn" in philosophy. The idea has thus given rise to popular but incorrect cultural relativist imaginings, such as that about the manifold Eskimo concepts of snow and the like—a variant of (9). If "language" in the generalization often promoted by "the linguistic turn" thus may mean "cultural systems of value and thought in general", then the Sapir-Whorf hypothesis becomes easy to reconcile with (2) with the idea that culture, as a whole, is learned like a language and is as systematic and coherent as a language. (8) through (10) are often conceived, either separately or together, as equivalent to the idea that a language comes with a world view. This idea is highly problematic, if only for the simple reason that it is well known that several and even antagonistic world views may be articulated and struggle within one and the same language (and, a fortiori, culture). This idea leads to the widespread assumption that cultures as such imply a world view or an ideology which is shared by all its members.

This leads us to a further assumption in classic cultural relativism which was explicit in Benedict and adds to (1):

(11) Cultures are holistic, organic entities, in which the meaning of each single feature can only be understood from the whole.

This follows in no way from (1); there might easily exist different cultural systems of value and thought without forming closed, organic wholes of type (11). The idea is presumably influenced by the fact that most of the cultures studied by early anthropology were geographically well-defined on small and separate territories, just as the cultures studied were most often rather small so that they were rarely segregated into highly visible, different, and competing subgroups. But (11) constitutes in fact, a highly problematic addition to (1), because (11) systematically overlooks a long series of important features in cultures. They are dynamic; they interact with other cultures; they form hybrid cultures; they often display internal oppositions between different subgroups, and many of the ideas of a culture may be weapons of one subgroup's fight against another. They are often fuzzy and contradictory and often have the character of a more or less loose sum of cultural parts than the powerful organic metaphor admits. (11) is thus a very important addition to (1) in order to get at the categorical articulation of meta-ethical relativism (2).

If radical holism does not hold, it might be fairly difficult to compare cultures and judge them to be different, because they no longer form separate wholes, especially not in mixed societies. As a hypothesis, (11) entails the danger that the anthropologist comes to conceive of a culture as much more static than it is, to eternalize features which are only temporary, to exaggerate the unity of culture and overlook plurality, tensions, contradictions, and social oppositions internally in culture.[20] Politically, it immediately entails the danger that anthropology allies itself with the most traditionalist, most reactionary, even authoritarian forces which have an interest in keeping tradition "pure" and unchallenged, in enforcing the doctrines of culture and persuade or force ill-adjusted, deviant, or rebel members of the culture to submit. This is one of the most decisive premises of "hard" cultural relativism which is presented very explicitly in Benedict but which often lives a more secluded life as an undoubted but merely implicit premise. But how can cultures be assumed to be organic wholes? Only if they possess the power to imprint the totality of cultural systems in all individuals in a successful socialization process, cf. Herskovits above on "enculturation:"

> (12) Cultures determine their members, and the cultural systems are learned through socialization, often to a large extent without conscious access of the individuals.

This claim is very often supplemented by the following:

> (13) When an individual is culturally imprinted, he possesses as a capacity the decisive features of his culture, and they make him unable to see the world from the point of view of another culture and incapable (or only with great difficulty and bit by bit) to learn the value and thought systems of other cultures.

This determination hypothesis is often overlooked, but it constitutes a very important ingredient in the overall cultural relativist package, even, as Renteln puts it, the very core of cultural relativism.[21] This hypothesis also has its blind spots. The anthropologist may have a hard time discovering individuals who innovate or develop their culture, individuals being inimical towards (aspects of) their culture, individuals who want to flee to be integrated into another culture. But the potentially political implications of (13) may be highly problematic. Just as racism turned biology into a destiny, thus (12) and (13) make of culture a destiny. It is these assumptions which make the individual into an apathetic, spineless product of his culture from which he may never escape. Seen from this point of view, dissidents, deviants, apostates, converts, nonbelievers, culture-mixers of all sorts become problems because they do not satisfy the requirements of culture. In (12) and (13), the individual becomes, in fact, imprisoned in a specific world view and is placed beyond the reach of argument. The anthropologist may not only easily overlook figures like these, if he takes his point of departure in (13), he may also easily position himself on the same side as the most conservative forces in a culture, those who want to force, punish, even expel or exterminate such figures who do not in a suitable way conform to cultural determination and "enculturation." In turn, (13) presupposes a very decisive and problematic assumption which is far from always made explicit, namely:

> (14) Systems of value and thought originate exclusively in culture.

This often lies as a premise in the interpretation of (1), cf. Herskovits' note against human rights: "Standards and values are relative to the culture they come from" (1947, 542). But there might easily be a manifold of systems of value and thought, without culture being their sole source, it even seems fairly obvious that such systems actually *do* have a manifold of sources. The values and stocks of observations, knowledge, and hypotheses of the world held by individuals have many more sources than the culture of those individuals; they may stem from innate tendencies, from individual observations, experiences, and inferences, from cross-cultural economic, social, or political regularities, from a priori structures, from ideas borrowed from other cultures or other individuals.[22] (14) is the idea which makes the concept of culture superior to all other levels of description such as, for example, biological, sociological, economical, technological, and which has allowed, to a large extent, the culturalist notion of culture to expand at the expense of those other descriptions in media and academia.

Finally, there is the whole complex around relativism as a critical doctrine, such as maintained by (3). In reality, you could claim (1) and (2), along with the whole cluster of ideas from (4) to (14), without supporting tolerance at all. This would give a picture of ethnocentric, incommensurable cultures, unable to communicate and probably mostly oriented towards mutual strife and warfare.[23] Thus, (3) is not added as a logical consequence of (2) but, quite on the contrary, as a proposal for a means to avoid the consequences of (2). As already mentioned, this specifically anthropological concept of tolerance refers to cultures, not to persons. It is the culture as a whole which should be tolerated, not the individual whims of its members, particularly not if they do not fit into the cultural pattern tolerated. But what is more, it is far from always clear who is supposed to be the *subject* for (3). Does it include (a) the anthropologist, or does it also include (b) the Western society which has sent him out? Most people will probably think (b), but does it also include (c) the different cultures studied by the anthropologist? Are they also supposed to learn from the anthropologist to behave in a more tolerant way towards each other? If that is the case, then (3) constitutes an explicit anthropological order of mission aimed at other cultures, and may easily conflict with cultural relativism as a methodological principle (4).

It is important to note that (3), as a rule, says nothing about individuals; it does not constitute a demand for cultures to be tolerant towards their members. It is thus a conception of tolerance which is very far from the notion of tolerance stemming from the Enlightenment and codified in human rights, where a decisive element is to constrain the powers of the state from suppressing its own citizens, and thus force the state to a basic tolerance of different types of behavior from its citizens. Such a thing is by no means implied by (3), which rather points in the direction of something like the Ottoman "millet" system, with its permission of certain organized religious groups, but with no liberty for individuals. Very often, a self-critical elaboration of (3) can be found, claiming--and supported by the cultural relativist fact (1)—that one ought to realize that one's own values are culturally specific and hence give up (naive) ideas of universality which one might have entertained because of knowing only one culture:

> (15) You should see your own norms and ideas as specific for your culture.

Again, this self-critical maneuver is most often recommended by the anthropologist to the (Western) reader, who is supposed to undertake the self-critical task on behalf of the West (cf. the Mead quote above, praising educated men and women for their habit of saying "In our culture..."), but is (15) also valid for the cultures studied by the anthropologist? Should they also learn to see their own ideas as contingent, culture-dependent and one-possibility-among-many? In that case it is hard to deny that such a lecture could add to the dissolution of the culture in question which may lose its self-evident character when individuals realize the possibility of substituting other patterns of culture for their own. If the other cultures are exempt from this self-critical task is it not some sort of racism in which they are deemed less capable than Western self-criticizers? If all cultures are presumed to adhere to (15), and "we" are supposed to teach "them," then it easily comes to contradict (3). In any case, (15) often contributes to a radicalization of (3), with which it is often confused:

> (16) Each culture has its own dignity which requires respect.

It is, in fact, a far stronger demand than (3), which is compatible with a laissez-faire stance that one should not harm other cultures and just let them live, or protect them without critically judging their behavior. (16) erects a requirement for recognition of cultures because they are assumed to possess a "dignity" (Benedict), without it being explicit what exactly this "respect" should consist in or who is supposed to practice it—all members of one culture towards all members of the other, or political, religious, or scientific representatives sent out to express respect? A related idea is developed further in the discussion on multiculturalism by Charles Taylor and his idea of "recognition" of cultures (we shall return to this below). "Respect" is, in any case, a far more ambiguous concept than tolerance, and it may be difficult to establish what a claim like (16) exactly means or what it should entail in practice. With (3), it may already be problematic to tolerate a whole culture where very bloody and inhuman practices regularly occur, but it seems much more difficult explicitly to be required to "respect" such things. Does respect also entail that you should, as an outsider, obey certain prescriptions which the other culture considers basic? Such a question becomes especially acute in cases where cultures are not geographically distinct but to some extent live together. In such cases, "respect" might constitute a renunciation of parts of one's own culture. Will it then constitute an insult to *its* "dignity"? We shall return to the issues of "respect" between cultures.

Cultural relativism, as we find it in its classic formulation in American anthropology from the 1940s onwards, is a far from simple doctrine. It consists of a whole cluster of loosely connected facts, axioms, prescriptions, etc., ranging from the completely unproblematic, such as (1), to strongly problematic and even hardly understandable ideas, such as (16).

It is instructive that among the different variants of actual political culturalism and multiculturalism we very often find large clusters of assumptions directly inherited from classical cultural relativism.

Left- and Right-Wing Culturalism: UNESCO and Lévi-Strauss

One of the ways in which anthropological culturalism gained influence in international politics and participated in the formation of multiculturalism was through UN organizations such as UNESCO. After World War II, the new international organizations established within the framework of the UN attempted to actively combat the pseudo-scientific concept of race which had been so disastrous in European fascism. Thus, UNESCO widely propagated the idea that "culture" or "ethnic group" should replace "race" as a concept for different groups of human beings.

A classic and famous example of UNESCO's strategy is provided by the collection of essays with the title *La question raciale devant la science moderne* ("The race issue faced with modern science"), which was published by the organization in 1952. The book contained, among others, an influential paper by the father of structural anthropology, Claude Lévi-Strauss: "Race et histoire" (Race and History). Here we find a showdown with pre-Boasian anthropology which is related to the culturalism of American anthropology in a number of ways: "... the original sin of anthropology consists in the confusion of a purely biological concept of race (presupposing that this concept can meet objectivity requirements even within its own limited domain which is doubted by modern genetics) and the sociological and psychological products of human cultures" (378).[24] The anthropological original sin mixed the contested objectivity of race biology with sociology and psychology, such as had taken place in different social evolution doctrines from Pascal to Spencer and Tylor. This healthy point of departure becomes, also in this case, the basis for a culturalism which has strong resemblance to the Boasians. Like them, it emphasizes:

1. Diversity (379-80)
2. The equal value of cultures: "The barbarian, it is first and foremost the human being who believes in barbary." (384)—There are no barbarians; the only barbarians are those who think others are barbarians.
3. The character of human rights as abstractions disregarding the concrete binding to culture, time, and space; they have "... the strength and weakness in outlining and ideal which all too often forgets the fact that the human being does not realize his being in an abstract humanity, but in traditional cultures where even the most revolutionary changes let whole structures re-

main, and which must itself be explained as a function of a situation, strictly defined in time and space" (385).

Still, the differences from the Boasians must also be maintained: here, emphasis is placed, unlike with the Boasians, on the fact that diversity holds not only between cultures but also within cultures, between classes, professions, castes, etc. (381). Similarly, cultures are not seen as separate, as is the case with the Boasians; rather the cultural differences are articulated against each other, exactly because no culture lives alone (382), and it is not only Western observers who may have the inclination to call other groups "barbarians". Such groups constantly do the same thing aimed at other such groups (383) because all cultures are necessarily ethnocentric.

Only a few years after the Declaration of Human Rights of 1948, a parallel, influential action was undertaken under the auspices of the UN, now based on culturalism, and thus skeptical of the universalism of those very same rights. Lévi-Strauss does not reject the notion of progress but maintains that it must be seen in a less linear and continuous way than it is by the evolutionists—and with a sensitivity for how progress accumulates and gathers contributions from a variety of different cultures (here, the American cultures' domestication of potatoes, rubber trees, tobacco, and cocoa are mentioned), just as the same progression may occur several times and in several places (the Mayans who invented the zero independently of the Indians and made a calendar which was more precise than those of the high cultures of the Old World). Some cultures are indeed more cumulative than others, but that is not due to any internal cultural capacity; rather, it is an effect of their degree of contact with other cultures: "The possibility which a culture has to gather this complex amount of inventions of all sorts which we call a civilization is a function of the number and the diversity of the cultures it collaborates with about the elaboration—often unknowingly—of a common strategy." (414)

The fact that certain cultures display greater progress and accumulation than others is thus an effect of a greater degree of connectedness and exchange with others of those cultures: "It results from their *behavior* rather than their *essence*. It expresses a specific way of existing in cultures which is merely the *way they coexist*" (415). This interesting hypothesis of philosophy of history—that cultures which, perhaps unwillingly, stick together in networks, have a greater potential for cumulative development than those which remain more loosely connected—now forms the basis for a normative claim which fits the context of the paper in a campaign of an international organization nicely: namely that cultural cooperation forms the way forward. A delicate tension remains, however, for cultures do not only consist of inventions without contexts; when powder, paper, and pasta are learned from the Chinese, it is decisive how these artifacts are used in the new culture adopting them (401). This is why the very style of life of a culture is irreplaceable: "The originality and irreparability of these forms of life, or as the Anglo-Saxons say, these *patterns*, cannot be denied, but they refer all to exclusive choices, and it is difficult to see how a civilization could hope to profit from another's form of life, not without giving up being itself" (416).

Even if the single culture's separateness and closeness is far from as radical as in the Boasians, the Benedictian "patterns" remain irreducible, which gives us the double formula for Lévi-Strauss's political recommendation on behalf of the UNESCO: "World civilization can be nothing but a coalition, on a global scale, of cultures each of which maintain their originality" (417). World society must be a cooperation between cultures (defined by borrowing features from each others, facilitating a cumulative progress), but each of them should, at the same time, preserve their originality. Here, we see the analogy to Benjamin Dawson's critical portrait of Malaysia where Malayan, Chinese, and Indian culture constitute a mosaic, but must under no circumstance mix with each other.

This inbuilt tension between coalition and particularism might easily have been glossed over by the rhetoric of the ceremonial speech and the expected applause, but Lévi-Strauss is honest enough to subject this tension to further analysis. The upshot is that if diversity is the necessary initial condition for the cooperating coalition, then an ever-decreasing output of cooperation must be expected, because it will, at the same time, gradually homogenize the participating cultures (418). This somber heat death of cultures where the marginal utility of cultural exchange converges to zero, in the long run, gives only two possibilities for the further injection of cultural difference: One, cynical, possibility is the construction of internal differences within each culture, just like the agricultural revolution gave rise to a fast and radical new social differentiation in the old high cultures with cities, states, classes, castes. The second possibility is provided by the steady addition of new cultures to the coalition, just as imperialism and colonialism have done—a strategy with a natural upper bound on a sphere-shaped planet. In both cases these are strategies which may do nothing but draw out the process.

A third solution might be the appearance of conflicting powers on the earth which may reinforce the necessary imbalance on which the biological and cultural survival of man depends—as Lévi-Strauss momentously declares (420). On the one hand, man must hence turn against blind particularism—(the necessary ethnocentrism of individual cultures), but on the other hand, he must also avoid that eventuality in which one form of life engulfs the whole planet in one ossified humanity. Therefore, the diversity of cultures must be preserved—not necessarily the specific content of each and every culture, but rather the fact of diversity as such. Hence, tolerance is not only a contemplative attitude which oversees what has already been created or that which is, he claims in a final fanfare; it consists in predicting, understanding, and nursing that which will become. The text thus ends with normative claims of very broad extension, which entail, in reality, an extremely conservative criticism of what was later called liberal multiculturalism—a conservative criticism of the equalizing tendencies inherent in globalization. But for whom is the flowing together of cultures ugly to behold? Is it for the participants within the particular cultures? Is there anyone who dislikes getting more cultural possibilities and rights? Or is it for the anthropological observer on UNESCO level? Or is it the idea that cultural difference and tension are necessary in order for history to move? In this case it is a very ambitious hypothesis; many other ideas as to the causes and structures of historical evolution exist. We shall return to this.

The tolerance that is called for here is thus very different from that of the Boasians, where it referred to the attitude of an already existing culture towards another. Here, by way of contrast, tolerance refers to new, growing, not yet established differences, and tolerance is even urged to assist in them gaining a foothold. But in common with the Boasians remains the idea that tolerance pertains to groups, not to the individual, as well as the fact that diversity itself remains the highest value; no criteria are given which might distinguish between good and bad internally in diversity. Thus, this unconditional celebration of diversity is what is propagated by UNESCO in the early 1950s, without commenting upon the radical tension between these ideas and those of the contemporaneous human rights declaration of the UN to any great extent.

A more piquant result appeared twenty years later when the organization asked of Lévi-Strauss to repeat the success. Now he should inaugurate UNESCO's international anti-racism year of 1971, this time resulting in a much more ill-famed paper: "Race et culture" (Race and Culture). Very often, these two texts are opposed so that the early, humanist Lévi-Strauss, oriented towards international collaboration, becomes transformed into his demonical opposite, where human differences were darkly absolutized, almost into a new racism. This is not the case. There is far more continuity between the two famous UNESCO texts; Lévi-Strauss had not wanted merely to repeat old points, but developed further some of the problematic points which we have already indicated in the old text.

Initially, it shocked the international audience that Lévi-Strauss, in a certain sense, rehabilitated the concept of race, yet in a way that it was now subsumed under the concept of culture. He proposed that it is human cultures and their diversification which decide the roads which human biological evolution may take. Ethnology had made the case too easy when it answered the question of the relation between cultural differences and biology by repeating Laplace's famous formula about God: "We have no need for such a hypothesis" (433), Lévi-Strauss says. Rather, the formation of race is one of the very functions of culture, because "cultural barriers have the same character as biological barriers: they anticipate them in a way in reality, to the extent that all cultures imprint their marks on the body: by the style of dress, by hairstyles and jewelry, by bodily scarification and gestic behavior the cultures mimic differences which are comparable to those which can be found between races; by preferring certain physical types to others, cultures stabilize these types and expand them in the long run."

The hypothesis is that acquired (cultural) behavior which influences partner selection has a feedback function so that this cultural behavior directs biological evolution. This hypothesis is now known under the label of "Baldwinian evolution"[25] after the American psychologist who originally proposed it, and it now forms a common and unproblematic part of the investigation of the origins of the human race. It has, for instance, been proposed that human language and the human brain are the results of a mutual process of evolution where the cultural achievements of language feed back upon biology. The hypothesis is articulated clearly in Lévi-Strauss: "All cultures demand not exactly the same capacities in their members, and as it is probable that a certain amount of these capacities have a genetic basis, then the individuals who possess them to the highest degree will be favorized" (453).

In 1971, however, it shocked the audience to hear the man behind what is almost considered the birth certificate of UNESCO take up the disputed relation between biology and culture which was believed to have been expelled once and for all in 1952, even if it was now a synthesis of biology and culture with collaboration between anthropologists and biologist that he propagated, and the direction of determination was now completely different, (from culture to biology rather than the other way around). Such hypotheses may hardly shock anyone today, but what was less in focus at the time was the fact that Lévi-Strauss's culturalism had, in the intervening twenty years, undergone a dark radicalization. He now claimed that the very idea of collaboration, coalition, and fight against racial prejudice which he celebrated twenty years earlier, should be seen in intimate connection to what had not yet been given the name globalization and which threatened the global ecosystem of biological species as well as cultures: "But it is impossible to hide, that the fight against discrimination, despite its pressing practical necessity and the grand moral objectives it gives itself, participates in the same movement which takes humanity towards one world civilization and which is destructive for the old particularisms which have the honor of having created the aesthetical and spiritual values which give life its value, because we feel less and less confident to be capable of producing any which are equally evident" (461).

The whole fight against discrimination (and hence the whole of UNESCO's campaign, which was inaugurated by the lecture) only adds to the problem, namely the demise of particular cultures. This time, Lévi-Strauss is radical in his partisanship, and this constitutes the precarious development since 1951. Now he goes against the coalition of cultures and takes the side of their particularities, because it is now seen as impossible to support the former without eroding the latter: "For you cannot, at one and the same time, flow out in enjoyment of the other, identify with him, and remain different." When the latter remains the most important (the unconditional cult of diversity), the fight against prejudice must yield. Now the cultural meltdown and loss of difference must be avoided by means of a "change in the course of history", he vaguely and ominously adds at the end of the talk. What could that change be?

It is difficult to see that it could mean anything other than a return to the territorial segregation of cultures. Lévi-Strauss claims, a little before the conclusion, that all the large creative epochs in the history of man took place when the means of communication were sufficient to let remote parties stimulate one another, but without the contact becoming so frequent or intense that the cultures involved disintegrated (460). Similarly, he ponders what the ethnologist may teach others about the conditions for tolerance. Among so-called primivites, two such conditions prevail, Lévi-Strauss says: the first is relative equality and the second is sufficient physical distance.

That conclusion is not made evident in the final paragraph of the talk, where only unspecified "change" is called for—it might have been considered too explosive to claim such a thing in the opening ceremony of the anti-racist year 1971. But to the attentive reader, the conclusion is obvious: the change which is advocated is one which protects cultures against cultural exchange and lets them subsist unchanged. This idea is shared with contemporaneous Canadian multiculturalism, but claimed that this is only possible if the cultures are kept geographically distinct, each in their territory and with large communication distance. Lévi-Strauss speaks here as an anthropological expert and may thus appear as a central support for the most arch-conservative variant of multiculturalism, namely the so-called "ethnopluralism" of the extreme European right wing. This current claims exactly that cultures should be preserved unchanged in each their territory (which is why immigrants should be shipped home or, at the very least, assimilated), a political conclusion which is opposite to those left-wing multiculturalists who also claim that cultures can and must survive unchanged, but in one and the same territory.

Lévi-Strauss's two famous papers present to us two variants of culturalism: the former with an emphasis on the collaboration between distinct cultures, the latter with the weight on the distinctness, taken as the precondition for a (limited) collaboration. It was of course the former which became and remained the official ideology of the UNESCO, and has—as Alain Finkielkraut critically analyzes it in his *La defaite de la pensée* (The Defeat of Thought, 1987)—contributed to shape international politics in the half century since its foundation. But the honor goes to Lévi-Strauss for demonstrating, with his second, controversial speech from 1971, how radically conservative, anti-Enlightenment implications may be drawn from culturalism, behind the curtains of ceremonial celebrations and speeches. To Finkielkraut, UNESCO's ideology, as presented in Lévi-Strauss's two speeches, constitutes a fateful international counter-Enlightenment movement. Let us briefly recapitulate his argumentation.

Finkielkraut and UNESCO Culturalism

Finkielkraut's basic criticism points to the fact that UNESCO's idea about preservation of cultures (as it is put forward, inter alia, in the two papers of Lévi-Strauss) goes directly against enlightenment and democracy. Finkielkraut recognizes that this return to a romantic conception of culture signaled by UNESCO does not have its roots in a sudden eruption of tribal pride, but is rather the result of an attempt at atonement after World War II and the dismantling of the Western colonial empires (61). Where Herder spoke on his own behalf, the philosophy of decolonization speaks on behalf of "the other," and therefore consequently against the West. This is why the new romanticism of culture not only goes against distasteful Western currents such as fascism and imperialism, but goes against "Western culture" as such.

The UNESCO ideology has the best of motives: it is friendly to strangers, it takes the side of the damned and those with no possessions, and it declares the death of man in the name of the different men, as Finkielkraut says with an indirect reference to Foucault's famous claim about the death of man. All this, however, drives UNESCO towards the consequence of declaring the impossibility of universal values (62). To Finkielkraut, it forms a part of the whole catastrophe of decolonization that the young nations in the Third World inherit the romantic, anthropological concept of culture in their self-understanding. "Millions of people who had been torn away from their gods, their soil, their habits, life, dance, and wisdom" were given their culture back (Finkielkraut is quoting Aimé Césaire, 63). But that culture which might serve as a pocket of resistance against Western colonizers has immediately transformed into a new tool of oppression as soon as the Western oppressors left, because (as Finkielkraut expresses it) it constructs a collective identity where you lose the right to express yourself in any other way than first person plural.[26] A "thick" conception of culture, originating in Germany, heavy with sentimentalism, authenticity and collective suppression of individual deviation, was preferred to a "thin" conception of nation defined by citizenship, rule of law, democracy and rights.[27]

Very often, these new nations supplemented their radical culturalism with a Marxist claim for revolution, so that, as Finkielkraut says, they could play the two different cards of ethnologism and class struggle at one and the same time. Without knowing it, they reconcile Marx with the deep conservatism and particularism of a Joseph de Maistre. In these national socialisms of the Third World, the tendency is—and it has continued during the twenty years since Finkielkraut's book—that the socialism part of the ideology has withered away and nationalism has taken its place. A similar development can be recorded in those Muslim countries where various forms of Islamism are on the rise; they have, to a large extent, replaced and even actively fought against earlier left-wing positions such as communism or Arab socialism, and the Islamists have, despite the traditional universalism of Islam, learned the culturalist lesson and have acquired the particularist jargon of culturalism (see the column on "Islamic rights" below).

Seen from the West, the spokesmen of culturalism make the Other into one homogenous block, as Finkielkraut says, and to this whole, the really existing others are sacrificed in their individual reality (71). Frantz Fanon's *Damnés de la terre* incarnates this tendency when it condemns the "deeply cosmopolitan shaping" of the bourgeois classes of Third World countries as one of the decisive reasons for their weakening. Just like 19th century nationalists and the Boasian anthropologists, the Third World culturalists of today will lock the individual up in their cultural categories. Culture becomes destiny.

UNESCO supports this particularism, but unlike Lévi-Strauss, who outspokenly claimed that ethnocentrism and particularism were the necessary price to pay for diversity and territorial distance the necessary price for its conservation, the rhetoric of UNESCO is, to Finkielkraut, a saccharine cult of "difference" and "universal understanding," which does not mean anything else but lack of individual freedom. The word "culture" serves as a "humanist flag for the splitting up of humanity into collective, insurmountable, and unchangeable wholes." (80)

A more recent analysis of this UNESCO discourse comes from the Norwegian social anthropologist Thomas Hylland Eriksen. He has remarkably attempted to go against "hard" culturalism as an ideology which claims that cultures exist separately, like islands in an archipelago. He sets himself the task of analyzing the UNESCO report *Our Creative Diversity: Report of the World commission on Culture and Development* from 1995. Here, he finds the following interesting tension:

> The political conclusions to be drawn from the description of the world inherent in the report are not necessarily the liberal, tolerant and universalistic ones suggested by the authors (and here, at least, one must approve of Finkielkraut's unreformed Enlightenment universalism-cum-provincialism): both separatists, difference multiculturalists championing exclusive criteria of judgement for "my culture," nationalists seeking stricter border controls and restrictions on the flows of meaning across boundaries, inquisitors chasing the Salman Rushdies of the world into hiding and myriad nationalisms writ small could find a sound basis for their isolationism and political particularism in the report, notwithstanding its periodical assertions to the contrary (Eriksen 2001).

The universalist proclamations at the surface level of the UNESCO report give way, as soon as you delve deeper into its recommendations, to "hard" culturalism, a property this discourse shares with the different attempts to articulate Islamic rights (see the intervention below). Correspondingly, you find again the Boasians's and Lévi-Strauss's recurrent focus on "diversity" as a central good in itself: [28]

> Since the report does not distinguish between culture and ethnicity, it may perhaps be inferred that the "deep" culture of tradition

> is associated with ethnic identity, while the "superficial" culture of modernity is not. As long as such a view is not supported by evidence, it must be questioned. The many passages on "minority cultures", further, reveal a conservationist view of cultural diversity; in several places, "diversity" is seen as "a value in itself." To whom? To the conservationists? The pluralism endorsed in the report, further, does not seem to include post-plural hybrid forms, the millions of mixed neither-nor or both-and individuals inhabiting both global megacities and rural outposts in many countries. In other words, the right to an identity does not seem to entail the right *not* to have a specific (usually ethnic) identity.

Eriksen here puts the spotlight on a cluster of related problems in the UNESCO ideology: cultures are conceived of as (1) holistic, (2) in themselves worthy of conservation, (3) supporting identity—all of them classic claims from the Boas-Benedict tradition. Eriksen, the social anthropologist, studies modern city culture, today comprising more than half of the population of the planet, and he may refer, (given his foundation in this research), to the fact that such culturalist ideas are completely incompatible with such current anthropological objects. The "post-plural hybrid forms" which shape the horizon for most modern human beings in the megapolises of the globe are neither holistic, necessarily worthy of conservation, nor carriers of identity in the deep sense imagined by culturalism, and they develop, hybridize, and change all of the time.

As Eriksen says, the report refers both to individual human rights and to collective cultural rights without reflecting on the fact that you cannot have an unlimited amount of both at the same time. The report is thus typical of a certain discourse of exaggeration in international fora which embraces an array of fine principles by listing them one by one, without in any way reflecting upon the implications of celebrating mutually contradictory principles.[29] It is, in fact, an idea of politics as a sum of values, not as a demanding task of reflection where you are forced to prioritize and compromise between irreconcilable demands:

> Finkielkraut (1987) is, therefore, only partly right when he writes that the UNESCO quickly moved from a universalistic Enlightenment way of reasoning to a relativistic Romantic attitude: The

recent report tries to encompass both, but it glosses over the contradictions rather than attempting to resolve them (Eriksen 2001).

Even if Finkielkraut's analysis was one of the first to focus upon a sore spot (UNESCO's culturalism), Hylland Eriksen's characterization of the UNESCO discourse is more precise. What Finkielkraut saw is indeed an ongoing tendency in UNESCO, but it is constantly amalgamated with a universalism of rights with which it directly clashes, when examined closely. The problem is not, then, that UNESCO has taken over culturalism lock, stock, and barrel; the problem is rather that UNESCO is speaking with forked tongue, because it does not realize that you cannot be a universalist and a culturalist at the same time.

On April 13 2006, at its 174th meeting in Paris, UNESCO adopted the proposal submitted by OIC, the Organization of the Islamic Conference, resolution 174 EX/46 entitled *Respect for freedom of speech and respect for sacred beliefs and values and religious and cultural symbols*, which "urges mutual respect for cultural diversity, religious beliefs and religious symbols." It assigns to the General Secretary the task of working, in different ways, to strengthen the striving for achieving this goal, and to compose a report on the international tools at hand for this work, to be put forward at the 176th meeting.

This resolution, directly coupling "respect for free speech" with "respect for sacred forms of belief and values and religious and cultural symbols," provides a nice example of how the kind of double talk analyzed by Eriksen has become standard discourse, not only in UNESCO, but also in other UN organizations such as the Human Rights Council and even the General Assembly. Eriksen is obviously right to assert, against Finkielkraut, that the UNESCO and the UN system as a whole is not completely based on culturalism. Rather, universalist and culturalist jargon is constantly mixed but in a way where the culturalist demands are, by their very essence, more specific than universalist principles, and hence appear as particular, concrete recommendations which in reality invalidate universalism. Of course, freedom of speech cannot be maintained if "respect for religious symbols" is adopted at the same time, and the latter then becomes the ruling criterion. UNESCO's resolution does not claim anything concretely about how this "mutual respect" should be realized politically. As we shall see in more detail below, the UN Human Rights Commission has gone a long way further in the culturalist direction, even as far as to require that member states implement legislation which shall criminalize "defamation of religion," while also insisting that freedom of speech be preserved.

The UN and UNESCO have thus contributed and still contribute to the international expansion of culturalism and to the political realization of what was originally an anthropological hypothesis. In that sense, the UN system has become co-responsible for the spread of that general culturalist ethos in international politics which the development of multiculturalism has as its background.

From Culturalism to Multiculturalism

In contrast to culturalism, which constitutes a wide current of thought prior to any attempt at its political actualization, multiculturalism has been, from the very beginning, a political endeavor. The adjective "multicultural" stems from the 1940s, but as the name of a political "ism," its beginnings can be traced fairly precisely, namely to Canada in 1971, and its further development can be traced especially to the four immigrant states and former British colonies of Canada, USA, Australia, and Malaysia.[30] The concept here refers to policies which strive for the integration of immigrants with broad regard for the conservation of their original culture—this taken as the opposite of assimilation and the old American idea of the "melting pot."[31] Very often, alternative metaphors, such as that of a "mosaic" or "salad bowl" are put forward as images of multiculturalism.

In a more theoretical vein, "multiculturalism" is used with a broad cluster of very different meanings, ranging from serious attempts at integrating it into the framework of a liberal theory of politics (as Will Kymlicka, see below), to theories combining the concept with respect for "the Other," a celebration of difference as such and marginalization in and of itself, and an anti-essentialism which claims, as something very essential, that essences do not exist (see the columns about these issues below). Finally, this forms a continuum of different meanings of the word which, at one end, refers to the conservation or segregation of a plurality of cultures (especially minority cultures) and at the other end refers to hybrid societies where cultural identities flow together, mix and give rise to new syntheses, as with the "melting-pot" metaphor.

It is evident that these uses of the concept exhibit a tension, even a direct opposition. Hybridization refers to a dilution and change of culture in contrast to the struggle for conservation of cultures. Many "multiculturalists" expressly celebrate the hybrid culture mix—it seems to be such a thing Will Kymlicka talks about when envisioning multiculturalism as "vibrant"—but in the states which have actually pursued multiculturalist policies it is in no way hybridization which has been the goal. Rather, the existing political multiculturalism in its different forms, for example, Canadian or Malaysian, consists of different policies which aim to preserve existing cultures and guard them against change and hybridization, rather than celebrating the latter.

The prehistory in the Canadian case is the tension between the Canadian government and the French minority of Québec. The concept "multicultural" seems to have been used for the first time in a senate speech by the conservative Ukranian-Canadian senator Paul Yuzuk in 1964, and, around 1970, the Trudeau administration planned a new policy with more political rights for francophones. The "Royal Commission on Bilinguism and Biculturalism" held hearings which resulted, in 1969, in the adoption of the *Bicultural and Bilingual Act*. The commission had, however, received claims from immigrant groups with other backgrounds than French, as well as indigenous groups such as Indians and Inuits, who demanded similar political recognition. The Commission hence proposed a policy, which (by contrast with the famous American "melting-pot") should constitute a "cultural mosaic" where no ethnic identity should exclusively constitute the Canadian identity, which should rather be composed out of the collected mosaic of such identities. The proposal of the Commission was adopted by Pierre Trudeau in 1971 as official ideology and characterized as "multiculturalism" (as opposed to "biculturalism") which should conserve a plurality of ethnic identities within a bilingual framework. By this policy, the indigenous peoples of Canada also received cultural rights.

Multiculturalism has, since then, developed into the official political ideology in Canada and has given rise to several pieces of legislation. In 1982 Canadian multiculturalism was introduced into the Constitution in the shape of Section 27 of the Canadian Charter of Rights and Freedoms and, in 1988, Bill C-93, the "Canadian Multiculturalism Act" was adopted. It states:

> "3. (1) It is hereby declared to be the policy of the Government of Canada to
> (*a*) recognize and promote the understanding that multiculturalism reflects the cultural and racial diversity of Canadian society and acknowledges the freedom of all members of Canadian society to preserve, enhance and share their cultural heritage;
> (*b*) recognize and promote the understanding that multiculturalism is a fundamental characteristic of the Canadian heritage and identity and that it provides an invaluable resource in the shaping of Canada's future;
> (*c*) promote the full and equitable participation of individuals and communities of all origins in the continuing evolution and shaping of all aspects of Canadian society and assist them in the elimination of any barrier to that participation;
> (*d*) recognize the existence of communities whose members share a common origin and their historic contribution to Canadian society, and enhance their development;
> (*e*) ensure that all individuals receive equal treatment and equal protection under the law, while respecting and valuing their diversity;
> (*f*) encourage and assist the social, cultural, economic and political institutions of Canada to be both respectful and inclusive of Canada's multicultural character;
> (*g*) promote the understanding and creativity that arise from the interaction between individuals and communities of different origins;
> (*h*) foster the recognition and appreciation of the diverse cultures of Canadian society and promote the reflection and the evolving expressions of those cultures;
> (*i*) preserve and enhance the use of languages other than English and French, while strengthening the status and use of the official languages of Canada; and

(*j*) advance multiculturalism throughout Canada in harmony with the national commitment to the official languages of Canada."

As is evident, many of the tensions inherent in the "hard" concept of culture remain in the political concept of multiculturalism in its Canadian variant. In the broad declarations of intent found in the "Multiculturalism Act" lies a series of rather different assumptions and ideas. Without any apparent problems, "different cultures" are referred to as something individuals can belong to (it is not evident whether the same individual can be a member of several such cultures, but it does not seem to be the case). The concept of culture seems to be synonymous with "communities of different origins" and is thus defined by origin and not as anything which may be the object of individual choice.[32]

At the same time, culture appears as something which must be recognized and appreciated without it being clear who should be the subject for these actions; (the government should "cultivate" recognition and appreciation, but it is presumably something other cultures and individuals should enact). Furthermore, it must be noted how multiculturalism extends both to "preserve" the single culture—and to "enhance its development" as well. These aims are far from equivalent and may in reality enter into considerable dispute. It is surprising that the concept of identity in this legal text does not (as happens so often) refer to the single culture, but rather to the Canadian "heritage and identity" as such, of which multiculturalism as a principle is claimed to be a central feature.

This legislation thus shares a basic assumption with many other multiculturalisms:

(1) Several distinct and different cultures can co-exist unchanged in a modern society.

Here, "modern society" refers to democracies with rule of law, characterized by equal rights for all citizens, basic human rights, etc. As compared to the culturalist concept of culture, a decisive change has taken place here. Even if the concept of culture seems to be just as organic and determining for individuals as in culturalism, an important change has been made, albeit implicitly: it is no longer presupposed that the single culture has its place in its own territory which it considers its own. In some sense, the single cultures exist in one and the same territory and within one and the same more comprehensive political entity, without one modifying the other or entering into a state of strife. The decisive problem—which is not at all thematized in the Canadian law and which is very often also covered by silence in the ordinary use of the word "multiculturalism"— is whether cultural behaviors and practices which to some extent clash with the basic principles of democracy and rule of law may survive unchanged, and how much of them can be "preserved" and "enhanced?" If it is claimed that they can be preserved and enhanced, how should this be realized? It is naturally presupposed in the normative addition to (1), which is often taken as the very core of multiculturalism, that:

> (2) Several distinct and different cultures ought to co-exist unchanged in a modern society.

The Canadian law explicitly claims this in its call for preservation of cultures. But it remains unclear what the state, while "enhancing their development," should do regarding the clashes between one culture and another, as well as regarding the clashes between cultural values and democratic principles which are maintained by the larger political entity, within which the different cultures are assumed to exist. Should the state, for example, permit or even support schools whose aim it is to pass on a particular culture to the next generation, as is usual in Anglo-Saxon multiculturalism? Should it support special media for cultural groups, such as it is the case in Holland with state support for Islamic radio? Should the state accept or even support the construction of parallel systems of courts, as in Malaysia and to some extent in Great Britain? Canada has, over the years, reached a formula claiming that multiculturalism should be supported without offending normal individual rights such as those expressed in the Canadian constitution's Charter of Rights and Freedom from 1982,[33] but it remains a constant source of ambiguity and problems as to what extent individual cultures should be supported and thus enjoy group rights without this offending basic individual rights.

Group rights may, of course, offend non-members of a given group who are not beneficiaries of the special rights awarded, just as they might offend individuals belonging to the group who do not wish the group to receive the right in question because it may delimit their individual rights, formally or informally. For example, in 2003, the Muslim lawyer Syed Mumtaz Ali published that he intended to establish a sharia court in Ontario under the Arbitration Act of 1991, a law which permits persons to settle civil law disputes by means of mediators and subsequently have an ordinary court confirming the result of arbitration to make it legally binding. A large debate took place. Opponents of Ali's proposal were led by the Iranian refugee Homa Arjomand, who specifically attacked the proposal for its gender discrimination (because of the well-known gender biases in sharia family law)—and the Prime Minister of Ontario, Dalton McGuinty, decided in September 2003, after an investigation by former General Attorney Marion Boyd, to state "No sharia courts in Ontario!" He simultaneously proposed an amendment to the Arbitration Act which emphasizes the continued possibility of private arbitration along with the requirement that such arbitration must conform to the Canadian Charter of Rights and Freedoms.

In any case, (2) entails that

> (3) Culturally based group rights can, in some cases, outdo individual rights

and

> (3') Such group rights ought to be developed as an implication of (2).

An important question is what this specifically implies for the general foundation for democracy and rule of law. Does (3) require the relativization of certain aspects of this foundation? Or, by contrast, should multiculturalism develop under the constraints of general liberal rights? (3) may stretch from relatively innocent cases (e.g. that Danish "communities of belief" are exempted from taxation, unlike other associations), to very extreme cases (e.g. that group rights are taken to include the right to discriminate against members of the group, special legislation with special courts, special police forces, etc.), and (3) does not, in itself, give any criteria for which group rights might rule over which individual rights, etc.

There is a further complication here. "Group rights" may mean rights admitted to a group as such (the right to self-government, collective land property rights, right to its own court system etc.), but it may also refer to individual rights, which are given to members of a specific group only (Affirmative Action; or, the exemption of British Sikhs from the legislation prescribing helmets for motorbike riders). The latter type of group rights is especially pertinent in the case of immigrant groups, and it does not involve the direct clash between group rights and individual rights. Still, it involves clashes in differences between individual rights as when the individual rights of persons not belonging to a group may be diminished by the individual rights given to group members, as is the case with the rights of those who do not get access to higher education because their place has been given to a less qualified applicant from a "cultural" group under Affirmative Action legislation. Group rights of this kind are in opposition not to individual rights as such, but to the individual rights of non-members of a group. We take (3) and (3') to include both of these types of opposition. In any case, (3) may be interpreted in two widely differing ways, and an important part of the discussion of multiculturalism relates to the discussion of these:

> (4) Culturally based group rights ought to be established, but in a way so that they conform to general liberal principles.
> (4') Culturally based group rights ought to be established, but in a way so that they may transcend and modify certain general liberal principles.

In Will Kymlicka's comprehensive discussion of multiculturalism, for instance, this discussion plays center stage. (4) and (4') refer to the potential changes which multiculturalist society must make in order to accommodate to the multicultural fact. But should the individual cultures also undergo changes? Here lies a parallel dilemma:

> (5) Multiculturalism allows the individual cultures to survive completely unchanged.
> (5') Multiculturalism allows the individual cultures to survive largely unchanged, but they should conform to larger society in certain ways.

(5'), of course, goes against (2) or, at least, relativizes it. (5') exists in two importantly different variants:

> (5'a) The individual cultures should conform to basic liberal and democratic principles.
> (5'b) The individual cultures should conform to aspects of the majority culture in the larger society.

The "Multiculturalism Act" must be read to claim that the single member of a culture must develop a sort of political double identity, so that the traditional cultural identity is preserved (and developed?) at the same time as a more general Canadian identity evolves on a higher level, of which multiculturalism as a principle forms a central part. Hence, a double identity emerges of which the "cultural" aspect constitutes only one part, while the more general, "Canadian," "multiculturalist" aspect constitutes the other part. It is not made clear whether this requirement is conceived of as variant (a) or (b). In any case, it is very often assumed that the whole of the complex (1) through (5) may only develop if certain policies are adopted, so that multiculturalism in this sense is largely an issue of legislation (cf. the intervention on Multiculturalist Ethos).[34] Even if (1) mentions the possibility of multiculturalism, this basic notion does not in itself indicate which policies may realize that possibility. Thus the different combinations of possibilities (2) through (5) are also possible bases for other policies. These different policies constitute multiculturalism as a political program:

> (6) A set of policies can and should be developed to make possible the actualization of (1).

But what *is* this set of policies? They involve, of course, some degree of group rights (3), but what should be the criteria for development of and implementation of them, and what relation do they have to basic structures of modern society (4)–(5)? The lack of clarity as to the character of (6) also arises from the fact that it is far from clear *why* (2) is deemed desirable. Is that because, as some claim:

> (7) Cultural diversity is a good in itself

or because:

> (8) Cultures (or their individuals) cannot participate in society on an equal basis without group rights

or because:

> (9) Cultures (or their individuals) cannot participate in society on an equal basis without receiving special recognition

or is it because:

> (10) Cultures (or their individuals) cannot participate in society on an equal basis without enjoying respect?

These widely differing reasons—and more—can be heard as justifications for the principal multiculturalism of (2). Multiculturalism, such as it appears in one of its main legal documents, the Canadian Multiculturalism Act, is thus a rather ambiguous program, and it may assume many different shapes depending on which combination of propositions is selected from the basic possibilities outlined here. Let us return to these combinations after having investigated some of the more principal deliberations.

From Communitarianism to Campus Radicalism

The principal discussion of multiculturalism has a series of affinities with the so-called communitarianists in political philosophy (Charles Taylor, Michael Sandel, Michael Walzer, etc.) and their attack, in the 1980s and 1990s, on the "atomized" conception of the individual in general liberalism, as well as in the influential liberalism of John Rawls particularly. To the communitarianists, the community as a basic social unity in which individuals participate should play a central political role. Thus, communitarianists tend to emphasize those cultural "values" which bind individuals together in pre-political entities (families, civil societies, associations, and cultures), which agree upon a "common good" as the presupposition of their lives and their political decisions. To that extent, they express an emphasis on culture that does not necessarily lead into culturalism, but may easily do so in strong cases.[35] The approach of communitarianists has been monoculturalist in tendency, however, in so far as their philosophical ideas have been largely based on the pre-political conditions for ordinary—that is, state—politics. Thus, they have had a tendency to identify the politically relevant community as that which supports a given state. Not that they are, for that reason, nationalists or exclude multiculturalism; many of their ideas have indeed been able to influence and be further developed by multiculturalists, such as Charles Taylor.

Parallel to the existing multiculturalisms in, for example, Malaysia or Canada, a comprehensive, philosophical discussion of multiculturalism has developed. One such current springs from political philosophy and the discussion about basic liberal principles which stem from Rawls's influential work; another springs from that mixture of continental philosophy, deconstructivism, cultural studies, and campus radicalism that characterized Western literature departments in the late twentieth century, around figures such as Jacques Derrida, Edward Said, Gayatri Spivak, Homi Bhabha, and Iris Young.

While the former philosophical current is closely related to an interpretation of the specific adoptions of multiculturalist policies and often acts as a spokesman for them, the latter is much more general and, in its self-conception, much more radical. It correctly observes that both political multiculturalism and its philosophical interpreters adopt the idea of stable, well-defined cultures, an idea which may then be attacked for "essentialism." On the theoretical-philosophical level, "multiculturalism" is thus a highly ambiguous issue which ranges from specific and detailed discussions regarding the protection or privileges of minorities to the general possibility of encountering "the Other" in a direct, non-reductive way and the call for political "processes of culturalization" instead of stiff and essentialist cultures.

Thus, this "multiculturalism" of campus radicalism develops at a distance from the concrete multiculturalist policies and is often highly critical of them. It may argue that the very act of defending a minority is already an act of essentializing it and making it invisible, thereby overlooking the responsible mechanisms of exclusion which have shaped marginalization in the first place through an ongoing process of so-called "Othering." Campus radicalism has a keen sense for some of the central problems in actually existing multiculturalism: its tendency to reify, eternalize and sharply delimit cultures as well as its tendency to lay too heavy an emphasis on cultural determination. Thus, campus radicalism points to the fact that the emphasis on culture may easily overlook gender, class, race, and other categories, which may also contribute to marginalization. Even if campus radicalism realizes some of the central problems in the culturalist concept of culture in multiculturalism, it is easily caught up in paradoxes. For instance, any attempt to give voice to a minority is an almost impossible project in this optics, because, it is claimed, this requires that the "culture" at issue must first reconfigure itself in the image of the dominant culture and its concepts and then subject itself to speaking its language; if it spoke its own, marginal, ungraspable language it would, *eo ipso*, remain un-hearable or incomprehensible.

Because of such paradoxes, the answer to Spivak's question "Can the Subaltern Speak?" (1988) is thus almost necessarily negative. Against any entity or unit, an infinity of internal, boiling differences is imagined, as in Bhabha's notion of "dissemiNation."[36] Yet, academic radicalism imagines that its references to subjectless, streaming processes (often described with present participles)[37] provide a much bolder and more radical political program than the small dusty steps of multicultural legislation. Often its focus on discourse rather than the things themselves leads to the idea that the very *mise-en-discours*, the discursivation, of cultural problems is what creates them. Hence it may be seen as a sufficient political action to campaign for speaking about the problems in other terms. In this, it is related to "political correctness" and the idea that if the word creates what it mentions, then a less offensive way of speaking will in itself solve the problems. Radical multiculturalism may thus claim a linguistic purism where manners in talking about cultures is seen as seminal—if you believe that discursivation is what creates problems in the first place, it becomes of very great significance how you put your words. If, however, you do not subscribe to this radical nominalism, the idea instead appears as a somewhat exaggerated doctrine of stiff politeness, which may often contribute to hiding real problems rather than solving them. To insist that you must not say "black" but must always say "African-American" or that you must stop using expressions like "girls" and prefer "young women" has, from this point of view, hardly the wide-ranging political implications, which campus radicalist spokesmen for political courteousness assume.[38]

Radical multiculturalism is often decidedly illiberal and may assume democracy and human rights as such are but the restricted expression of one "culture" which, in an act of hegemony, suppresses other cultures by feigning to be universal. When Iris Young refers to the social groups which are suppressed and, for that reason, should claim "differentiated citizenship" with special group rights, she may list "women, blacks, Native Americans, Chicanos, Puerto Ricans, and other Spanish-speaking Americans, Asian Americans, gay men, lesbians, working-class people, poor people, old people, and mentally and physically disabled people." In response, Joppke dryly remarks that differentiated citizenship would be rather difficult to realize for around 75% of the US population.[39] Correspondingly, the radical idea that all universalism is but a hegemonic particularism in disguise seems to be in direct opposition to the idea that differentiation should make possible participation and inclusion—why should you participate and be included in institutions which are based on a suppressive universalism?

Even if campus radicalism is thus very far from providing any very concrete policies, it must be assigned an important role in the ongoing discussions of multiculturalism: it sticks to a floating, utopian, and vague version of multiculturalism and dreamily hints at solving the problems of cultural clashes by changing the very discourse in which problems are addressed (and allegedly created) in dualist dichotomies. This radicalism thus points to an ideal of ongoing cultural hybridization where cultures are not fixed essences but rather continuously mix and engender new articulations, but at the same time without any leveling or homogenization taking place. By contrast, it celebrates a state of constant openness to difference, to the event, to future, without making clear what this might entail for the concrete immigrant, teacher or politician. But the multiculturalism of campus radicalism contributes to the strange phenomenon that many multiculturalists seem to dream about realized: multiculturalism as a state of mutual influence and hybridization among cultures, at the same time as the concrete policies they support most often regard preservation and conservation legislation of minority cultures *against* hybridization and influences.

Many voices who adopt multiculturalist arguments in the ongoing debate likewise seem to remain unconscious of such inner tensions in the concept of multiculturalism. They often claim that "all cultures should respect one another" and "any culture has a right to respect" without reflecting upon their implications in relation to general democratic, liberal and rule-of-law principles.

Multiculturalism and Recognition: Charles Taylor

A considerably higher level of reflection than campus radicalism, with its extravagant and paradoxical celebration of "the Other" and the automatic acceptance of anything in "other cultures" *en bloc,* may be found in the work of Canadian philosophers such as Charles Taylor and Will Kymlicka, thinking in parallel to the actually existing and evolving Canadian multiculturalism. Taylor is, at the same time, the communitarianist who most directly involved himself in multiculturalist issues.

As a Hegelian, Taylor is naturally interested in how moral and political principles may be realized in the real world in practiced habits and customs. His answer to this question is likewise Hegelian and is based on "recognition," the concept used by Hegel in his famous so-called dialectics of master-and-slave in the *Phenomenology of Spirit* as that fight in which oppressors and oppressed have have been involved through history. In the "anthropological" interpretation of Hegel, which in the 20th century is represented by Alexandre Kojève and Francis Fukuyama, this recognition becomes the very motor of world history. In a struggle to the limit of death, he who gives up fighting in fear of death becomes a slave and recognizes the more brave as his master. The slave instead realizes himself through work and gains strength to repeatedly attack the master in the series of revolutions in world history, where the slave may assume power as the new master, marginalizing in turn a new group of slaves. This ongoing dialectic only reaches its end in liberal society where everybody recognizes everybody. But the problem then remains of where individuals thirsty for extra recognition should now go to get it (the right wing) or how individuals and groups can pursue more equality (economical, social, political, etc.) than the mere equality inherent in liberal rights (the left wing). Taylor (1994) puts the multiculturalist issue into this context in his famous paper "The Politics of Recognition." As philosophical predecessors, Taylor refers to Rousseau and his ideas of personal pride and authenticity, which are developed further by Herder, for whom this pride stems from being recognized for exactly who I am, different from others, both as an individual and as a member of that *Volk* which constitutes a sort of authentic and proud person on a higher level:

> With the politics of equal dignity, what is established is meant to be universally the same, an identical basket of rights and immunities; with the politics of difference, what we are asked to recognize is the unique identity of this individual or group, their distinctness from everyone else. The idea is that it is precisely this distinctness that has been ignored, glossed over, assimilated to a dominant or majority identity. And this assimilation is the cardinal sin against the ideal of authenticity (38).
>
> But at least in the intercultural context, a stronger demand has recently arisen: that one accords equal respect to actually evolved cultures (42).

As against the individual rights of liberalism, tied to the idea that all individuals as moral subjects have an equal dignity, the Herderian tradition thus forms the basis of a "politics of difference" where we are assumed to recognize the special originality of the individual and his group, and their difference from everybody else. Taylor claims that to ignore this constitutes the original sin against the ideal of authenticity.[5] Already, a central problem in politics of recognition and identity after this model becomes apparent: it is wholly unclear *who* should perform this recognition and how it should take place. This problem is quite different from that of individual rights, where the democratic state with rule of law is the subject and forms the guarantee that its citizens enjoy those rights in equal measure, incarnated in political, juridicial, educational and other institutions, and where other individuals, qua citizens of the same state, are obliged to recognize each others' constitutional rights.

> The charge leveled by the most radical forms of the politics of difference is that "blind" liberalisms are themselves the reflection

of particular cultures. And the worrying thought is that this bias might not just be a contingent weakness of all hitherto proposed theories, that the very idea of such a liberalism may be a kind of pragmatic contradiction, a particularism masquerading as the universal (44).

The problem for Taylor is that liberal democracy, claiming to be "colorblind" to the specific properties of the citizens, is not really colorblind but just promotes its own cultural forms as if they were universal, partly because of their imperial past, and partly because of their marginalization of ethnic minorities and immigrant groups in the present day:

> Western liberal societies are thought to be supremely guilty in this regard, partly because of their colonial past, and partly because of their marginalization of segments of their populations that stem from other cultures. It is in this context that the reply "this is how we do things here" can seem crude and insensitive. Even if, in the nature of things, compromise is close to impossible here—one either forbids murder or allows it—the attitude presumed by the reply is seen as one of contempt. Often, in fact, this presumption is correct. Thus we arrive again at the issue of recognition (63),

Allowing murder is thus seen as a cultural practice, while the real problem is taken to be insensitivity *vis-à-vis* other cultures. The upshot seems to be that murder is less evil than cultural insensitivity. The example of murder stems from the discussion of the Rushdie case; the implication is thus that some cultures permit murder, others do not. As the British philosopher Brian Barry says (2001, 280), it is wrong when Taylor claims no compromise is possible. The British government might, for example, fly Rushdie to a pre-designated location where a professional amputator from Tehran is flown in to cut off one of his limbs. The reason why Taylor does not contemplate such a compromise is not that it is not possible, but that it is disgusting; execution or dismemberment for writing a novel is not a cultural practice on which liberal societies are willing to make a compromise because they regard free speech as a basic principle not open to negotiation. Taylor's argument, however, is that the problem has a character which disallows compromise—you have one legislation or you have another. This is why he claims the problem cannot be solved on a juridicial level, as is claimed by other multiculturalists, but only on the level of "recognition:"

> But the further demand we are looking at here is that we all recognize the equal value of different cultures; that we not only let them survive, but acknowledge their worth. What sense can be made of this demand? (64).

The question is, quite rightly, what can recognition of the equal value of different cultures mean in practice?[41] As Barry points out (2001, 270), it is an elementary problem for the idea of recognition of the equal value of all cultures that cultures possess "propositional content," that is, they involve claims about the world which are often contradictory. You cannot both claim that God wrote the Bible and that He did not. Taylor tries to avoid this by seeing cultures as something which address self-images. Here, he draws upon the central *tiers-mondiste,* Frantz Fanon. He takes care, though, not to subscribe to his recommendation of violent revenge against the West as the adequate political means (which would not have been an un-Hegelian idea), but instead refers to the struggle for recognition as a change in self-image:

> Fanon recommended violence as the way to this freedom, matching the original violence of the alien imposition. Not all those who have drawn from Fanon have followed him in this, but the notion that there is a struggle for a changed self-image, which takes place both within the subjugated and against the dominator, has been very widely applied. The idea has become crucial to certain strands of feminism, and is also a very important element in the contemporary debate about multiculturalism (65).

The idea is that the self-image of marginalized groups—Rousseau's and Herder's source for authenticity and pride—has been corrupted by by oppression and hence must be changed in order to be properly recognized. This makes Taylor claim the following ambitious and wide-ranging idea:

> As a presumption, the claim is that all human cultures that have animated whole societies over some considerable stretch of time have something important to say to all human beings (66).

All human cultures which have characterized whole societies during a certain period are deemed a priori valuable because they have an important message to humanity. No examples are given, but here Taylor narrows, without saying so, the concept of "culture" considerably, presumably to exclude different sub-cultural claims for recognition. But in doing so, he simultaneously sets the lower limit for demand at a very high point, because it is not evident that national minorities and immigrant groups in themselves constitute such "whole societies over some considerable stretch of time." Kymlicka attempts something similar with this notion of "societal cultures" and runs into similar problems below.

> Just as all must have equal civil rights, and equal voting rights, regardless of race or culture, so all should enjoy the presumption that their traditional culture has value. This extension, however logically it may seem to flow from the accepted norms of equal dignity, fits uneasily within them, as described in Section II, because it challenges the "difference-blindness" that was central to them. Yet it does indeed seem to flow from them, albeit uneasily (68).

The demand for recognition stands in an uneasy relation to basic democratic notions concerning the equal dignity of individuals. On the one hand, it is claimed that this demand follows from them; on the other hand, it is claimed that it fits them badly. A similar tension is obvious below in Kymlicka, and this remains a central problem for all sorts of liberal multiculturalism. On the one hand it is claimed that multiculturalism follows logically and directly from equality-seeking liberal traditions of rights; on the other hand, it is admitted that it is in opposition to those traditions. Both cannot, of course, be true. More consequent liberals among the Hegelians, such as Fukuyama, have seen this clearly: the demands for further personal or group recognition are necessarily a sort of excess politics as compared to basic liberal equality, and, what is more, it is ripe with internal contradictions in so far as you cannot demand more equality and more recognition at one and the same time. These two demands, even if often rhetorically composed into beautiful phrases such as "equal recognition" or "equal dignity" of different groups, remain tension-filled.

A further problem is, of course, that agreement upon recognition of different cultures requires an agreement upon the criteria for such recognition. But if cultures are indeed radically different, they cannot be expected to agree on such criteria. Something similar holds for other ideas of justice across cultures: if justice is a "just distribution" of something, then different cultures must agree about this, on a meta-level, just as well as they must agree about *what* should be justly distributed (happiness, resources, possibilities, rights, recognition, dignity, etc.).[42] And if agreement about this is reached, then a position *outside* the individual cultures has already been established to take care of that recognition.

This is why Taylor very well realizes the problems of a politics of recognition:

> Then, however, the act of declaring another culture's creations to be of worth and the act of declaring oneself on their side, even if their creations aren't all that impressive, become indistinguishable (69).

> Moreover, the giving of such a judgment on demand is an act of breathtaking condescension. No one can really mean it as a genuine act of respect. It is more in the nature of a pretend act of respect given on the insistence of its supposed beneficiary. Objectively, such an act involves contempt for the latter's intelligence (70).

If the culture that is supposed to be recognized has never actually produced anything especially interesting or valuable, then the act of recognition easily becomes a pretense. Taylor vacillates back and forth, for even if he clearly realizes this danger of pretended praise, he keeps on insisting that all cultures *must* have produced something praiseworthy. The claim that it must a priori be the case is yet weakened to the softer idea that you cannot a priori assume the opposite. You cannot, of course, claim that a culture is worthless without first having investigated it meticulously:

> But merely on the human level, one could argue that it is reasonable to suppose that cultures that have provided the horizon of meaning for large numbers of human beings, of diverse characters and temperaments, over a long period of time—that have, in other words, articulated their sense of the good, the holy, the admirable—are almost certain to have something that deserves our admiration and respect, even if it is accompanied by much that we have to abhor and reject. Perhaps one could put it another way: it would take a supreme arrogance to discount this possibility a priori. (72-73)

The core problem of Taylor's controversial and, in many ways, unclear paper thus remains what the "recognition" of the title actually *is*. Is it something which is a priori owed to all cultures, or is it something which must be given only to cultures which have, in fact, yielded something praiseworthy? Neither of the two alternatives is attractive, hence Taylor's vacillation between them. If the former is the case, then it is no real act of recognition you make, for if everybody is recognized it is a recognition which needs not be interested in the properties of the particular culture under scrutiny, and then you are, in a way, back to the ordinary liberal, equal, and "colorblind" recognition which was supposed to be transgressed.[43] But if the latter is the case and recognition should be given on the basis of real results and products in a culture which have an interest not only for that culture itself and its members but "to all human beings," then this recognition can only be given after a meticulous investigation and evaluation of the culture in question and its many aspects, and then you cannot predict that such recognition will flow in equal measure to all cultures. Rather, there could in reality be cultures which receive considerably less recognition than others.

Taylor wants both: full and equal recognition of all cultures. His vacillation and hesitation, however, demonstrates the impossibility of such a politics of recognition.[44] This problem characterizes all sorts of talk about "recognition of," "respect for," "acceptance of," "living interest for" cultures as political demands, while it does not affect the more modest demand for tolerance because it does not presuppose a positive evaluation of the thing tolerated.

Liberal Multiculturalism as Political Philosophy: Will Kymlicka

Taylor is willing to go very far in the direction of renouncing general liberal principles and may thus count as a "hard" multiculturalist (even if one with scruples). The leading theoretician of multiculturalism in political philosophy, the Canadian Will Kymlicka, has attempted to involve the central liberal ideas of individual rights and tolerance to a greater degree. With *Multicultural Citizenship* (1985), he produced a new classic in the field, which he has recently continued in *Multicultural Odysseys* (2007). Kymlicka is especially interesting, because he directly addresses the problem discussed above concerning the tension between multicultural norms and general principles of liberal democracy, as is indicated by the subtitle of his *chef d'oeuvre*: a liberal theory for multiculturalism. His explicit idea is that it is possible to articulate a multiculturalism which constitutes a further development of basic liberal ideas of democracy, human rights etc. It might be expressed more problematically in a way that he would not himself be satisfied with: Kymlicka seeks a middle road between culturalism and liberalism.

His project rests on an attempt to reconcile some of the ontological presuppositions of culturalism with a basically liberal political philosophy by trying to develop the former out of the latter. His concept of culture is obviously culturalist: he delimits it from the broad use of the notion of culture comprising "gay culture" or "Western culture," (18) by focusing upon what he calls "societal culture... that is, a culture which provides its members with meaningful ways of life across the full range of human activities, including social, educational, religious, recreational, and economic life, encompassing both public and private spheres" (76).[45]

This forms a relatively unmodified version of the all-embracing culture concept of culturalism—even if we remark the conspicuous absence of adjectives like "juridical" and "political" in his list of the full range of human activities. He emphasizes that such a full culture necessarily exists in institutional incarnations. If a culture should be able to survive and develop in the modern world, it must necessarily be such a "societal culture," he claims (80). The intimate connection of such a culture with the concept of liberty forms the basis of the central argument axis in the book: "... freedom involves making choices amongst various options, and our societal culture not only provides these options, but also makes them meaningful to us. (...) And to have a belief about the value of a practice is, in the first instance, a matter of understanding the meanings attached to it by our culture" (83). As is evident, this is a variant of basic culturalist ideas, more precisely, that claim which in the preceding chapter we recorded as (14): thought and value systems originate exhaustively from culture. As the protest note from AAA had it, man is inextricably bound to his culture. Kymlicka even goes so far as to quote Margalit and Raz with acclamation for their claim that, "familiarity with a culture determines the boundaries of the imaginable" (89). This Wittgenstein-like idea that the limits of culture form the limit of fantasy constitutes a really hard and conservative version of culturalism.

To the same complex of ideas also belongs the radical idea that the self-esteem of persons is determined by the dignity ascribed to their culture (89).[46] Kymlicka's trick is now to connect this hard culturalism (appearing in much multiculturalism) with a basic liberalism, with its emphasis on individual autonomy and liberty. His key idea here is that it is culture which provides the individual with the series of options which makes him or her free[47]—a liberalized version of AAA's old claim that the "the individual realizes his personality through his culture, hence respect for individual differences entails a respect for cultural differences" (541). In a certain sense, then, the individual has no other liberty than that which his culture provides, just like AAA's idea that the freedom of the individual depends on which concept of freedom is maintained by his culture.[48] There is, however, the difference that culture, according to the AAA, governs the choice of the individual; in Kymlicka the individual does have a choice but only between the options provided by culture. And yet, the liberal Kymlicka does not want to subscribe to the communitarianist (like Michael Sandel) idea that a community defines a common good, which it is beyond the power of individuals to problematize. He realizes that persons in one and the same culture may have widely differing ideas about the good life. Kymlicka does not want to give up the core idea of liberalism that man is free to problematize and revise his own ideas.

The idea that any notion of the good life is fallible and thus open to revision is a cornerstone in the liberal tradition from Stuart Mill to John Rawls and Ronald Dworkin, and Kymlicka will not give in on this point. The individual has the possibility of "stepping back" from his actual actions and purposes, and critically evaluating them (81). But if the individual may do this, (contrary to the claim of the communitarianists) then why is culture taken to be the only provider of human choice possibilities? Kymlicka does not solve this opposition, which is wrapped up in a weak compromise which persists in his more concrete proposals. Do immigrants, for instance, need a whole "societal culture" of their own? We were just taught that a wholly developed "societal culture" with a full range of institutions was required in order to run a culture (80), but at the same time Kymlicka admits that immigrant groups do *not* have such a full culture and most often must make do with a "symbolical ethnicity" (98). At the same time, he seriously considers the utopian possibility of empowering immigrants from poor countries and compensating for our lack of ability to erase the inequalities of the world by recreating a full "societal culture" for them in their country of immigration (99). Both are not possible, of course, and the latter possibility would in reality consist of the support for fully separate parallel societies with their own institutions including language, legislation, police forces, territory etc.—a consequence which Kymlicka does not explicitly draw and never discusses, but which becomes openly relevant in a case like Malaysia.

Elsewhere, he makes the cooler observation that, in many modern liberalized societies, both minorities and majorities give up moral values, common ideas of the good as well as cultural traditions, and *yet* remain strongly connected to their "language and culture" (whatever "culture" now means in this context, where it can no longer refer to a fully developed "societal culture" with all its institutions, but rather must be restricted to something like a folkloristic repetition of traditional gastronomy, dress, and folk dance, etc.). Another problem indicated by Walker (1997, 230) is that Kymlicka describes cultures in terms of past-oriented preservation and thus overlooks the future orientation of cultures or nations, which may even contain very problematic overtones ("Le Québec aux Québecois!"). Cultures are merely harmless conservators of traditions, not political agents with clashing claims pertaining to future policies. Kymlicka never really succeeds in creating a stable synthesis of his all-embracing culturalist culture concept and his liberal contention about individual autonomy and liberty. This does not, however, prevent him from presenting some interesting ideas as to the constraints on multiculturalist group rights, exactly motivated by a liberal restraint on the total concept of culture.

A central distinction of the book is between two types of minorities—the "national minorities," which have been present since the foundation of the state and typically inhabit a well-defined part of the territory; and immigrant groups of more and less permanent kind. Kymlicka argues that the two types are fundamentally alike, even if the notion of multiculturalism is most often used in discussion of the latter.[49] The former have a greater right to special treatment than the latter, which has typically arrived lately and willingly, and thus must be expected to assimilate to a greater degree than the former. He emphasizes that acceptable types of special treatment and group rights must conform to liberal principles; he even sees them as growing directly out of liberal principles and of that "culture of rights" (Kymlicka 2007) which has spread internationally from the UN's human rights declaration after World War II. His version of liberalism, however, is taken so broadly as to include several features which would normally rather be classified as communitarian. Thus, his liberalism opposes traditional liberalism with its focus upon individual rights and few or no group rights, claiming that group rights may be necessary to achieve classical liberal goals. By doing so, he exposes himself to the criticism that his liberalism is not really liberal any more. In any case, he now makes a distinction between three types of such liberally legitimate group rights:

1. Self-government rights
2. Polyethnic rights (such as exemptions for British Sikhs from motorcycle helmet regulations, because their religion claims to oblige them to wear turbans)
3. Special rights of group representation (such as Affirmative Action) (27-31)

Points (1) and (3) are especially relevant for national minorities; (3) and especially (2) for immigrants (societies with immigrant groups are termed "polyethnic states" by Kymlicka). The latter can include political campaigns against racism and discrimination, special rules for education, "affirmative action," exemption from laws which offend religious practices, and state support for cultural and religious practices.⁵⁰ All three types of rights, however, contain possibilities of clashes with general democratic and rule-of-law principles, such as equality before the law. Kymlicka tries to contain this problem by a distinction between two basic types of motivations or needs in a minority: external protection and internal restriction. The outer protection refers to the exemption of the minority from legislation and practices of the majority society which are unequal for their members; for Kymlicka, this is the main motivation and legitimation for any group right. Internal restrictions which are desired by the minority to hold for their own members do not have the same legitimacy (of course, they directly clash with individual liberty) and they ought to be used only to a limited extent or not at all. (3) is also relevant for immigrant groups, Kymlicka claims, because legislative bodies are overwhelmingly composed of "middle-class, able-bodied, white men" (32), which is why it is a legitimate political aim to reduce those "barriers" that prevent women, ethnic minorities, poor, disabled persons etc. from representation. Kymlicka remains silent about which "barriers" he refers to (generally, there are no juridical or political barriers against the election of such persons in modern democracies), and the only means he proposes to make up for this problem is that of "proportional representation" (32). He does not develop this train of thought further. Should we really believe he will reserve quotas of parliament seats for groups characterized by income, race, gender and ability, in analogy to national minority representations?

As to the decisive point, the liberal basis for group rights, Kymlicka lists four arguments: (1) the equality argument claiming that certain group rights augment equality so that "true equality" should be reached by treating different groups differently, and that the lack of such rights may leave a social group "culturally disadvantaged" and incapable of fully participating in society; (2) historical special rights (relevant especially for national minorities, not for "polyethnic" groups); (3) cultural diversity as a good in itself (Kymlicka is rather skeptical of this argument); and (4) the unity of society supported by integration; Kymlicka imagines that cultural identity is supplemented, on the social level, by a "civic identity" common to all cultural groups (as it was also assumed in the Canadian charter). He develops points (1-3) on pp 107-23, and (4) on pp. 173ff.

The equality argument builds on the observation that majority society is not "colorblind" in all respects, but involves a series of cultural choices (language, education curricula, and the ever recurrent example of official holidays) which give minority groups disadvantages. They should be compensated accordingly with special group rights for language teaching and other education (114; he never proposes a solution as to holidays, even if it is probably the most frequently quoted example in the book to prove the dominance of majority culture).[51] Another of his recurrent examples, the permission for Sikhs or orthodox Jews to wear their special religious head-dresses in the police and military as a modification of uniform requirements, is supported by an analogous argument: if such a concession was not made they would have unequal opportunities for a career in those bodies. As is evident, the concrete examples discussed are remarkably modest as compared with Kymlicka's culturalism on the theoretical level. These examples, however, force Kymlicka to say that the liberal doctrine of "benign neglect" of cultural differences is nothing but a myth. Given his own self-declared liberalism and the thin list of examples, could it not just as well be argued that the principle of "benign neglect" is fine as a regulative idea, which, as all such ideas, must entertain certain compromises when it is realized piecemeal in the world? The widespread argument about "diversity" as a good in itself is not rejected, but Kymlicka hesitates to ascribe any central role to it, because it does not (as opposed to the criteria of equality and history) constitute any obligation for the majority culture, but seeks to "fool" the majority by dressing up multiculturalism as if it were in its own interest. This interest is real indeed, but fairly modest, even if it can be seen as a state interest parallel to support for the arts, public service TV and the like (123).

However, the final argument discussed in the concluding chapter of the book, is that of social cohesion. Kymlicka claims that cohesion is strengthened by group rights and what he calls "differentiated citizenship" (174). This proposal immediately clashes with the general democratic principle that it is the *same* citizenship, which provides a strong integrative power between different groups in society, making it evident that they constitute parts of one and the same social unity with the same political and juridical rights and duties. Is segregation really the key to better social cohesion? Paradoxical as the claim may sound, it is not corroborated by reference to specific cases supporting the argument. The argument is rather motivated by references to emotions and intentions, and it is somewhat difficult to judge who is supposed to be the bearers of those feelings: "Groups that feel excluded want to be included in the larger society, and the recognition and accommodation of their 'difference' is intended to facilitate this" (176). Here lie several problems. First, the fact that somebody "feels" excluded is not in itself any proof of the fact that in any politically interesting sense they *are* so excluded (and why should this feeling not have its proper release in the voting for certain candidates in the ordinary parliamentary election process?). Second, should state or society "recognize" certain groups at all, if they so wish? Many different groups organize themselves in associations and lobbies which exert political pressure—is this possibility sufficient for "recognition"?—and if not, why not? Third, the most important point: Is it really in all cases correct, as Kymlicka assumes repeatedly, that the demand for group rights is really motivated by the wish for integration into the "mainstream" of society? Could this demand not quite have the opposite motivation; namely the wish to distinguish oneself from that mainstream and form separated parallel societies? Kymlicka does not even address this issue, but when it comes to the discussion of national minorities (as opposed to polyethnic groups) he is aware of the slippery-slope argument: "there seems to be no natural stopping point to the demands for increasing self-government" (182). In contrast with his treatment of the immigration issue, Kymlicka thus surprisingly remains radically pessimistic with regard to the long-term problem of national minorities to which he does not see any general solution. Switzerland and his home of Canada may serve as ideals, but there is a scale of problematic cases stretching from Belgium to the ex-Soviet states and to worst case scenarios such as ex-Yugoslavia and Rwanda, which may be cited as counterexamples.

This is not our main issue here, but the strange thing is why Kymlicka does not consider a similar slippery-slope argument with regard to polyethnic rights. If more wants more, when it is about self-government, why is it not the same for polyethnic rights? Is there a "natural stopping point" for ethnic special rights? And if so, where? If you have gained language rights, affirmative action and a long series of other special rights and exceptions, then why not wish for special legislation and courts just as the imams of Canada, England, Denmark and many other places desire, and which is already reality in Malaysia? Why not crave special police forces, as Swedish Muslims have proposed? Not that such a slippery-slope argument necessarily holds, but it is striking that it is not even considered. Here, one can think of Benjamin Dawson in Malaysia, who accounted for how it began with local religious laws for Muslims only to accelerate during the 1980s to the codification of proper sharia laws on a state level which even, in certain cases, overrule general law, and which is now proposed to have binding validity even for non-Muslims when they come into contact with Muslims. Here, such a slippery-slope argument seems to be valid.

This leads to the very central problematic knot of the whole edifice, where the tensions between Kymlicka's compromise between culturalism and liberalism really face the test: the limits of tolerance and the issue of anti-liberal cultures.[52] Here, his interesting hypothesis is that of two limits which must constrain group rights: one is that group rights serving "internal restrictions" in the group (rights ascribing power to the group to restrict the basic democratic rights of the individual group member) should not be allowed. Group rights should only serve to protect the group against wider society's decisions and powers. To this he adds another restriction: only so far as these rights do not make it possible for a group to suppress or exploit another: "...*freedom within* the minority group, and *equality between* the minority and majority groups." This then is Kymlicka's basic motto (152).

His argument is interesting. "Internal restrictions" should not be allowed because they contradict the liberal reasons for protecting groups: the fact that it is the membership in those groups which provides the informed choice options for how to conduct life (153). But the group does not stop doing this, only because it excludes certain choices. Rather, it must be said that *any* culture excludes some options for the individual, otherwise it would be no culture at all. Some of the attraction of cultures probably lies exactly in this; they *relieve* the individual from a measure of difficult and painful choices and liberate time and power for things other than choosing. Options excluded from a culture are, *eo ipso*, not options in that culture, so they must necessarily be supernumeral as compared with the choices specific to this "societal culture." It is for that reason that what is interesting is not only the exclusion of certain options for the cultural individual, but rather the active pressure against options *outside* of that culture (such as apostasy).

Kymlicka's idea that it is the culture as such which provides the options for the individual here appears as an impossible contradiction. Either the culture is characterized by opening a specific cluster of possible choices and no more, or else *all* choices (including those outside that culture) must be open to the individual, but then the culture would no longer be the culture it was.[53] Kymlicka's example is the Pueblos in the US who practice a sort of theocracy where only the tribe members taking part in the traditional cult enjoy full rights (not covering, for instance, protestant Pueblos). This is condemned by Kymlicka, and rightfully so. But is a protestant Pueblo a "real" Pueblo, given the culturalist notion of culture? Is this discrimination not a measure taken in order to protect culture? If that is the case, the sharp distinction between Kymlicka's two categories—outer protection and inner restriction—is not so easily drawn in practice. Consider, for example, the Malaysian imams' argument for the proscription of apostasy: it is there to protect Islam, but the right to leave a minority group is naturally a grave threat to its collective right to uphold its own cultural traditions; to that extent, there is a tension between liberal individual principles on the one hand and inner restriction *as well as* outer protection on the other.

Other liberals may take a more laissez-faire-like approach to antiliberal groups, such as the anarcho-liberalist Chandran Kukathas whom Kymlicka argues against. According to Kukathas, the larger society should not interfere in offenses against individual rights within cultural groups (one might then ask if you could not just invent a group to be a member of, if you want your crime against somebody to go unpunished). Consequently, the state must allow female circumcision or permit Jehovah's Witnesses to deny important medicine to their children. To Kukathas, the defense for such illiberal practices of cultural groups does not depend on respect for cultures or anything like that, but on the freedom of association which obliges the state not to interfere in associations but to tolerate what goes on. Brian Barry correctly objects that this tolerance should then also be extended to cover similar crimes, from female circumcision to killing, in non-religious groups (2001, 319).

The problem with anti-liberal groups forces Kymlicka to discuss an important problem: what is more basic to the liberal, tolerance or autonomy? Both have long ancestral lines in the liberal history of ideas. Kymlicka takes the Ottoman "millet" system (which has been seen by many naive observers as an anticipation of, or even an ideal of, religious tolerance) as his example. The governing Muslim majority allowed other organized book religions to survive—Judaism as well as Greek Orthodox and Armenian Orthodox Christianity. They were permitted to continue their religious cults and the internal political structures of the groups of believers, but no new churches or synagogues could be built, no mission undertaken, and conversion (to, not from these religions) was prohibited. The believers had to pay an extra poll tax, which Muslims did not.

Here, according to Kymlicka, we see full tolerance, but no personal autonomy. The individual does not have the liberty to choose his religion, but the single religious organization has freedom within its own ranks. The kind of "freedom" found in such systems seems to attract many anti-liberal minorities, and, as Kymlicka realizes, it is often such a system that is desired when "tolerance" is demanded from such groups (158). But it is important to realize that this has nothing to do with tolerance in the liberal democratic use of the word, where the emphasis is on the autonomy and freedom of the individual. (This issue explored further below in the column on respect and tolerance.) In that sense, Kymlicka chooses autonomy, and tolerance must be of that special kind which follows from autonomy.[54] On this point, his liberalism defeats his culturalism, which is also why he devotes some thought to how anti-liberal groups may be integrated. To what extent may society demand of such groups that they assume liberal principles? Kymlicka does not think liberalism can force such groups (this would amount to "secteric liberalism"), but it may seek to promote "... liberal principles, through reason or example, and liberals outside should lend their support to any efforts the group makes to liberalize their culture" (168).

Even if he clearly finds the exception clauses of the Pueblos and different American sects (Amish, Menonnites, Hutterites etc) despicable, his (reduced) culturalism becomes the shield that protects them against state enforcement of consistent democratic principles within them. In practice, he ends up close to Kukathas: the state should not interfere in anti-liberal groups' suppression of their own members, but merely avoid directly supporting such "restrictions." Liberally oriented groups should do nothing more intrusive than support such currents of liberalization which may occur.

Kymlicka is quite aware of many offenses against democratic principles (such as slavery, genocide, mass torture and expulsion which necessitates interference with anti-liberal groups), but he backs off from giving any criteria for when such an interference is valid, neither in the international case in respect of other states, nor in the national case in respect of minorities. The former—the interference in sovereign states—is not an easy question. The latter seems more difficult; in reality it depends upon how much emphasis is put on culturalism and liberalism respectively. Barry also finds that, in this conclusion, Kymlicka proves considerably more culturalist than liberal: "It is an illiberal theory with a bit of liberal hand-wringing thrown in as an optional extra" (Barry 2001, 140).

Kymlicka's argumentation is not rich in examples, but the introduction of some concrete cases might shed some light upon the problems in his mild version of hard multiculturalism.[55] Take the Danish Muhammad Crisis or Cartoon Crisis (discussed extensively in the next chapter), where a widespread argument from Danish Muslim organizations and their intellectual, Danish defenders was that Danish Muslims constitute a persecuted minority which has, for that reason, a right not to be insulted by caricatures of the prophet. Danish (and generally, Western) law does not recognize a general right not to be offended, and attempts at having the drawings convicted for blasphemy have not been effective, but what status would this proposal have in Kymlicka's system? It is not, of course, based on legislation. Only few Danish protagonists have imagined a change in the free speech clause of the Danish constitution. But other examples from Kymlicka (such as state campaigns against racism) are also extra-legal remedies. Would a right not to be offended be an outer protection of a minority (so that Danish Muslims avoid the offence of seeing or knowing that other people see the drawings in *Jyllands-Posten*), or would such a right be an internal restriction (so that Danish Muslims are not informed about criticism of Islamist use of terror, and are forced not to ridicule the prophet themselves)?

The idea of a right against offence is not easy to place exhaustively in one of Kymlicka's two categories. Something similar holds for the comprehensive Muslim special legislation in Malaysia (which is claimed to be "intended" as a protection of Islam). The ban on apostasy is, of course, a severe curtailment of individual rights (reminiscent of the millet system) and would thus be criticizable according to Kymlicka's criterion (1),[56] but the most widespread argument for this proscription is the protection of Islam, that is, the protection of a group against the surrounding society. If conversion or apostasy were allowed, Islam might envisage a gradual seeping of believers to other faiths, to agnosticism or atheism, which is prevented by the prohibition. So this rule is also difficult to place unambiguously in one of Kymlicka's categories.

Of course, an extra criterion might be introduced, saying that if some rule falls under both categories it will be, in all cases, liberally indigestible (it is conceivable that Kymlicka means such a thing), but the question then is, will there only remain a relatively small subset of pure protection initiatives which do not also have effects of internal restriction? A problem here is also that "internal restrictions" is not a precise term. It can be taken in a narrow sense where the ethnic group demands formal, recognized exemptions from some general law in order to restrict its members and suppress other groups. Examples here could be the Malaysian apostasy ban, Malaysian divorce and marital law, discriminating against women and non-Muslims, and the Malaysian legislation on lower prices on real estate for Muslims. But "internal restrictions" may also be taken in a broader sense, where the suppression of its own members and other groups take place in a less legalistic sense—that is, if women are expected to be satisfied with half an inheritance even if it is not codified in law, or if children are raised to despise democracy and enlightenment. One of Kymlicka's central arguments for having group rights at all is exactly that there may be inequalities which have a non-legal character and are not prevented by the existing equality legislation; it becomes obvious to interpret the "internal restrictions" in the same, non-legalist way. But this entails, ironically, a large measure of hesitation with regard to group rights, because they may easily be put to use in "internal restriction," even if their purely legal consequences only seem to pertain to "outer protection."

Does Liberalism Need Multiculturalism?

Kymlicka's recent book, *Multicultural Odysseys* (2007), looks back on the international destiny of the multiculturalism concept during recent decades, and therefore offers a welcome concretization of the often very general principal claims of *Multicultural Citizenship*. The tone is initially triumphalist, because older ideas such as homogenization and assimilation seem to give way internationally to the cultural and religious accommodation of immigrants, also insofar as international organizations have adopted variants of multiculturalism, while encouraging or even pressuring states to adopt multiculturalist policies, just as they sanction states for assimilation initiatives (3). The multicultural discourse spreads, and attempts are made to codify it in international legislation. In a paradoxical formula, Kymlicka sees this development as a natural further development of existing human rights and at the same time as something, which goes on within the confines of those rights (7). At the same time, he realizes that this development gives rise to certain tensions and problems. Should multiculturalism constitute one set of policies for all groups, or should it refer to different policies for different groups, national minorities, indigenous groups or immigrant groups? Should it be "generic," valid for all cases, or should it be "targeted" in each specific case? Can multiculturalism be introduced before a democratic state is established? This question is connected to the balance between justice and security: "Is the goal to open up space for a vibrant democratic multiethnic politics, or is the goal to suppress and contain destabilizing ethnic mobilization?" (p. 8-9). Already in *Multicultural Citizenship*, "vibrant" was a recurring plus-word which stood out surprisingly against Kymlicka's otherwise cool, scholarly prose. In many cases, these goals may coincide and give rise to related or identical policies. Worse is the possibility that they may, in other cases, conflict; as always when security clashes with other policy goals, there is a tendency for safety and security to come out victorious. Kymlicka also observes that even if many international organizations have adopted different variants of multiculturalist terminology, they may mean rather different things by it (22).

The basic development towards a more "different-friendly" approach in international organizations has, according to Kymlicka, its basis in the reinterpretation of the UN *International Covenant on Civil and Political Rights* from 1966 (art. 27):

> In those states in which ethnic, religious or linguistic minorities exist, persons belonging to such minorities shall not be denied the right, in community with the other members of their group, to enjoy their own culture, to profess and practice their own religion, or to use their own language (Kymlicka, 34).

After originally having been interpreted as referring to the securing of the same ordinary rights for minorities as for other citizens, the phrasing was reinterpreted during the 1980s to pertain to special minority rights. Kymlicka deals with these changes at length in international organizations which he—differently from Finkielkraut (1988)—conceives of as a unanimously democratic progress. The very text remains, however, absolutely ambiguous: what does it mean precisely to have the right to practice your religion and culture in community with other group members? What does it comprise? Collective prayers or prohibitions against blood transfusion? Ritual meals or female circumcision? Apostasy ban or capital punishment? How are borderline cases regulated? How about clashes with other groups and other rights? The fact that Kymlicka realizes this problem appears only indirectly from his problems in relating the development of the race issue in the US from forced segregation to civil rights and to new segregation in terms of identity politics:

> In most countries, however, the situation of minorities needing protection differs from that of African-Americans, and so too do the sorts of civil and political rights they require. African-Americans were involuntarily segregated, solely on the basis of their race, excluded from common institutions and opportunities to which they often wanted access. Many minorities, however, are in the opposite position: they have been involuntarily assimilated, stripped of their own language, culture, and self-governing institutions (91).

The double use of "involuntarily" is revealing. If segregation is involuntarily, it should be criticized; if assimilation is involuntarily, that should be criticized. This implies that the free will of the group—whatever that is and however it may be measured—is the decisive criterion, not segregation or assimilation in themselves. The possible tension between cultural group rights and human rights which was addressed in *Multicultural Citizenship* is now bluntly refused as follows:

> The leaders of minorities can appeal to the ideals of liberal multiculturalism to challenge their historic exclusion and subordination, but those very ideals also impose the duty on them to be just, tolerant, and inclusive (93).

This indeed sounds beautiful and refers to the previously mentioned ideal of a cultural/multicultural double consciousness, but attention should be paid to the reference to "leaders of minorities". Here lies part of the problem, for how do you qualify to become such a leader? The figures that act as such, and are often also treated by the surrounding world as such, rarely have any explicit mandate, and in many cases they may be suspected of not being representative.[57] In the following section, Kymlicka admits that the ideal of such a double identity often does not hold in practice, where he considers the possibility that the use of rights lingo may be merely strategic and refer to the wish of a minority to fight the dominant majority at the same time as it wants to extend its own dominance over internal minorities—the tension between external protection and internal restriction again. But here, this tension is rejected with a legalist argument:

> Put simply, there is no legal space for minorities to set aside human rights norms in the name of multiculturalism, and, in the case of most minorities, there is no wish to do so (ibid.).

This argument is double and paradoxical; no legal space exists for rejecting human rights—and moreover, most minorities do not do it! But if just a few minorities do it in reality, then there *is* eo ipso a space, be it legal or not. It is a strangely sloppy approach to human rights violations on Kymlicka's part. Could it cover the fact that a more considered reflection on the issue would require restrictions against ethnic groups and "cultures" which systematically violate human rights? This "legal space" is constituted by the fact that only court practice (or further legislation) can decide the undecided tension between the original, individual human rights and the multicultural group rights between which Kymlicka wants to compromise.

However, this makes Kymlicka realize a problem he has not addressed before and forces him to argue directly against a type of problematical multiculturalism which emphasizes cultural identity and authenticity, that which Amartya Sen strikingly calls "communitarian" and "conservative." Here, Kymlicka sharpens the "liberal multiculturalism" position from 1995 which deftly avoided putting a name to the implicit opponent of "illiberal multiculturalism". This anti-liberal multiculturalism is now placed directly in opposition to his own allegedly liberal multiculturalism: "The liberal view of multiculturalism is inevitably, intentionally, and unapologetically transformational of people's cultural traditions" (99). Multiculturalism is no longer only a defensive ring allowing for the preservation of cultures; instead, it is "transformational," it forces cultures to enter into new mutual relationships, learn new concepts, and it changes deeply the identity and behavior of people, a decidedly liberal sharpening of the 1995 position.

Here, Kymlicka realizes a series of the problems which "conservative" multiculturalism inherits from culturalism, and which he had earlier passed over in silence: (1) the "conservative" multiculturalism is anthropologically naive, because "cultural authenticity" is very often a late and highly constructed artifact in cultural groups, a result of traditionalist identity construction (of dogma, dress, rituals, etc.), in some cases even a direct "invention of tradition" which may serve to separate the group and give it a new identity; (2) the "organic" character of cultural groups often glosses over deep inner tensions and struggles within the group; (3) a decidedly anti-universalist culturalism, like that expressed in the AAA 1947 protest note to which Kymlicka now refers; and (4) cultural identity may be used as a discussion stopper rather than as a part of a dialogue—any problematization of identity may be interpreted as disrespect for the person and his cultural identity.[58]

Kymlicka here admits, to a much greater extent than in 1995, the dangers in such a conservative "authenticity" multiculturalism. Still, he maintains this criticism is irrelevant for his own position, which he identifies with Canadian multiculturalism. His argument (103-5) that this position is immune to this criticism is, however, strange and indirect. He resorts to a meta-level and asks: how should a conservative policy be possible in a West obsessed by human rights? Kymlicka takes the empirical existence in Canada of an individualist and egalitarian left, supporting women, gay, and minority rights, as the decisive proof that these points of view are in fact consistent with his Canadian multiculturalism, but it is really no argument for the consistency of ideas that there exist empirical persons who actually believe in all of them at the same time. People may be inconsistent, perhaps even more often than not. You could argue for the democratic character of Nazism along the same lines: how should Nazism have appeared in a Western Europe occupied with liberal and democratic ideals, if it was not itself democratic? Kymlicka overlooks the banal fact that ideas may just as well develop as a reaction against other ideas, as they may represent an inspiration from them.

What Kymlicka ought to have done here, of course, is to clarify what is the deep difference between the conservative, anthropological, naive multiculturalism which he attacks and his own, far more sophisticated liberal version. Instead, he quickly turns to explanations of the spread of multiculturalism in terms of power politics. Just as the original UN 1948 human rights declaration can be interpreted as having a partial motivation in the Allies' attempt to win over the people of the world against Nazis and fascists, the spread of multiculturalism can be seen as an attempt at the "desecuritization" of minorities, so that they cease to appear as security risks (this argument pertains to national minorities who might get the idea of joining another state, like the Sudeten Germans or the Bosnian Serbs). Such dangers have disappeared from the West with the establishment of NATO, and more remote threats such as Islamic jihadism or China have, according to Kymlicka, no support among national minorities.

Another issue, of course, is immigration groups, and it is the multiculturalism relevant for them which Kymlicka now sees threatened by a wide "resecuritization" of the relation between states and Muslim immigrant groups, especially in Europe. Kymlicka gives "free-floating anxiety about 'the other,'" as well as racism and xenophobia dressed up as criticism of multiculturalism, the bulk of the responsibility for this reemergence of security connected to immigration. He remains serious enough, though, to mention that it might also have something to do with a change in the immigrant groups themselves—some groups now "are perceived as high risk" (127), as he enigmatically writes. High risk for what? Is this risk merely "perceived" or is it real? It cannot refer to much other than 9/11 and the growth in Islamism and Islamist terror since 1995, but none of these issues are explicitly mentioned. This silence seems, in itself, to constitute an example of how the multiculturalist "ethos" in the Canadian version makes open discussion of certain problems impossible.

In the following chapter, he turns towards an evaluation of multiculturalism in practice. Here, he admits a possibility which was not discussed in 1995:

> We can expect the different factions within immigrant groups will compete to control the institutions and programs established under multiculturalism policies. And this raises the potential that the infrastructure of liberal multiculturalism will be captured and abused for illiberal or undemocratic processes (160).

Though Kymlicka suddenly admits the existence of that "legal space" he denied above, it is now claimed insignificant because, since the 17th century, Western democracies have known the paradox of the anti-liberal abuse of democratic possibilities; such abuse of liberal multiculturalism can be—and is—fought with the same means:

1. Citizen education and political socialization which create a culture based on human and civil rights
2. Mechanisms which identify and publishes actual and potential abuse
3. Legal and constitutional guarantees which give the state the power to hinder or act against such abuse (161)

Kymlicka seems to find that such mechanisms actually function satisfactorily, and he refers to the above-mentioned case concerning the rejection of sharia courts in Ontario. The introduction of sharia in Britain is a later development, but it is not easy to see how Kymlicka's argument would address that. Examples from the actual discussions of different strategies regarding Muslim immigrants in France, Germany, and England and other European countries are absent.[59]

One of the reasons for this omission might be Kymlicka's considerable naivety as to the democratic character of Muslim areas in Asia, Africa, and the Middle East; we need here only refer to the Malaysian example. The actual, homogenized policies in postcolonial states, he says, "are clearly inconsistent with the historical traditions of the peoples and cultures of Asia, Africa, or the Middle East. Most of the political systems that predated European colonization had complex systems of inter-ethnic tolerance and co-existence" (253). He writes, surprisingly naively, as if he had never heard about caste systems, wars of conquest, subjection of nonbelievers, forced conversions, slave trade and a manifold of other suppressive political practices in those areas very far from "interethnic tolerance," as if he had not himself in 1995 described the Ottoman "millet" system as the direct opposite of liberal tolerance, and as if central countries of the area such as Iran, Afghanistan, Turkey, and Saudi Arabia had not escaped colonization.[60]

Naturally, the conclusion of the book considers the prospects for the further propagation of the multiculturalist idea. Either you can go back to before 1990, when minority issues had a low priority in the international community, or you can go further to articulate proper international principles and rules for a liberal multiculturalism. The state in-between is deemed unstable; you must either go backwards or forwards. It is no surprise that Kymlicka, the prophet of the concept, prefers the latter. The great problem, he says, remains the lack of criteria for "targeted" policies aimed at specific groups, which constitutes the core of multiculturalism—the criteria for when and to what extent which policies needs to be added on top of the universal principles of multiculturalism (which are hard to distinguish from ordinary, basic liberal rights).

These "targeted" rights are oriented towards identifying and rejecting standard threats against unjust treatment of groups, he says, but he has no precise proposals of how these rights should be shaped after the character of the problem, apart from the idea that they should be combined with short- and long-sighted policies as needed! It can be added that it is also unclear how specific the "targeting" should be. That Sikhs are exempted from the head dress regulations of the British police force is a highly specific version of a "targeted" special treatment—and it does not entail any right for other believers, or that quite different groups may wear kepis, tiaras, or hooligan outfit when in the police force. What is the argument for the "targeting" of Sikhs but not for other believers or groups? Another case is a "targeted" multiculturalism as that discussed in our next chapter: special legislation aimed at protecting religions against offense; this is an example of a very general but still "targeted" special group treatment. What these two examples have in common, however, is that they demonstrate that it is indeed very difficult to see what the *general* argument for this type of special rights should be. If the Sikh turban should be permitted, then why not other religious or non-religious headdresses, hats, and flat-caps? If religions and religious persons should be protected against insult, then why should non-believers not be protected against the constant insults from believers and their threats that the incredulous will burn in hell? If "self-image" forms the core of culture, why should not all kinds of social groups be protected against bad presentations of their self-images? In the absence of criteria for applying "targeted" multiculturalism to a specific demand on behalf of a cultural group, how can it be avoided that it is merely the group which lobbies the best or shouts most loudly which achieves to be "targeted?" Or, even worse, how can it be avoided that it is the group that best manages to employ threats or acts of violence which is awarded with special rights? Kymlicka is very far from solving such problems with "targeted" multiculturalism. The lack of criteria for what counts as a proper target is almost complete.

A fallback position, of course, is to focus upon the development of minimum criteria for the "generic" (non-targeted) multicultural rights which may be applied in all cases: full freedom of assembly and freedom of speech plus a minimum of "efficient participation" in the political process of the state (310), a backlash to an ordinary, safe version 1.0 liberalism without much "hard" multiculturalism. Kymlicka is not amused. The "targeted" part of multiculturalism, of course, forms its very core, and it appears rather disappointing that he, the foremost spokesman for liberal multiculturalism, is not able to suggest the least criteria for its use. And this at the same time that he thinks the adoption of such criteria in international law is the most pressing issue for multiculturalism! If Kymlicka cannot articulate proposals for such criteria, then who can?

The central problem in his position is, as already noted, that the "generic" minimal multiculturalism, with the same criteria for all groups is very hard to distinguish from ordinary liberal basic principles.[61] The more ambitious "targeted" multiculturalism, aimed at the specific needs of single cultural groups, is both difficult to articulate clearly, left to a principleless pragmatism (or, in any case, a pragmatism whose principles are never made clear), and, on the top of that, very difficult to conceive as a further development of liberal first principles, despite Kymlicka's constant claims to the contrary. He has now grown acutely aware of the dangers in going too far in the direction of "conservative" multiculturalism ripe with romanticism, authenticity, inertia of tradition and internal group repression, but it remains difficult to see any clear conceptual boundary between this and the allegedly completely different liberal multiculturalism.

Clearly, it is Kymlicka's intention that it should appear as the latter, as liberal, but his arguments (including in his recent book) constantly vacillate between liberalism and culturalism, at times contradictory and thus little convincing. The lack of a rich list of examples of well-argued, legitimate, "targeted" group rights adds to the doubt about whether the sympathetic project of a "liberal multiculturalism" is at all feasible or whether it is one, big, hopeful *contradictio in adiecto* instead. Liberal multiculturalism is increasingly difficult to distinguish from full, normal, liberal, rule-of-law democracy with civil and human rights. Maybe they are simply identical?

In constrast, examples abound in Charles Taylor's May 2008 report for the Québec government, (co-authored with Gerard Bouchard—Bouchard and Taylor 2008). The report is interesting because it displays a different approach from Kymlicka's, less centered on the concept of rights. If Kymlicka is the ever-ruminating Kant of multiculturalism, Taylor is multiculturalism's full-blown Hegel, and, as a Hegelian, Taylor is obviously far more interested in *Sittlichkeit*, morality, and concrete behavior, rather than legislation, which is why he, unlike Kymlicka, does not talk about citizenship and rights. Instead, he talks about the need for developing a compromise culture; cultural accommodation ought to take place by means of local compromises case-by-case. A restaurant owner allows Muslims to pray in a room which is out of use; a driving teacher takes care that the female Muslim pupil gets a woman examiner at the driving exam; airplane companies offer kosher meals in flight. Taylor is right that such local compromises are both plastic and practical, but that does not solve the general problem of what should be done in cases where none of the parties will give in and no local solution is at hand.

Taylor supports the call for a common culture of compromise where all parties are prone to give in with a list of eleven proposals for a Québécois "interculturalism" (40-41). It is interesting that the m-word has here been given up (it is only used about Canadian multiculturalism), just like the dichotomy of "assimilation" and "integration" has given way to the new concept of "accommodation," which is primarily taken to be something which a majority culture should offer cultural minorities. It is a little as if Taylor assumes that the very act of renaming the problems and the avoidance of the problem word "multiculturalism" will itself minimize trouble. The eleven proposals are thought of as a possible political program at government level in Québec. At the same time, the proposals do not have the juridical character of legislation, but form a sort of hymnic expression of good will; here, the "spirit of reciprocity," "interaction," the "defusion of fear or rejection of the Other" are celebrated. One should display one's own differences and learn about the differences of the Other, one should have the right to belong to one's ethnic group, everyone should be given the means to preserve their mother tongue at the same time as the learning of French is encouraged; diversity is praised, again and again, as a resource, etc. There remains only one more specific guideline: that both parties should display a willingness to compromise, and that this compromise must not result in "undue hardship" for any of the parties.

All in all, the recommendations of Bouchard and Taylor aim at what they call an "open secularism," as opposed, allegedly, to French secularism. They identify the latter (not quite correctly) with a direct fight against religions on the part of the state, while their more open version would not object to, for example, veils in schools (even if they would not accept such religious symbols in presidents, judges, general attorneys and police personnel), just like the state should be obliged to offer "accommodation" to religious demands wherever possible. Consequently, they turn against the Québécois' more French-like proposal of refusing "accommodation" of religions in any way. Compared to Taylor's earlier, far more radical but also more vague ideas of a "politics of recognition," it is a much more subdued and modest "interculturalism" that is now promoted, perhaps because it too has been tempered by the challenge of concrete examples. The upshot is that what was the "recognition of all cultures" has now become a difference of grade within secularism: should the state be neutral to religion in the sense that it should compromise to the same low degree with any religion, or should it be neutral in the sense that it may compromise with religious demands to the same extent as to non-religious demands (green meals for vegetarians, acceptance of veils for cancer patients, etc.)? In Taylor, the hard multiculturalism has softened with time and the wealth of examples. The extent of lyrics about the blessings of diversity, however, seems to grow proportionally with the words being replaced to refer to still smaller differences.

Kymlicka in the Liberal Field of Gravity

However, the discussion about the tensions between Canadian multiculturalism and general, liberal principles of freedom has also broken out in Canada. This has given Kymlicka the chance to clarify his position. The debate was triggered by a paper by Janice Gross Stein that takes its point of departure in feminist deliberations, parallel to those which were presented in Susan Muller Okin's *Is Multiculturalism Bad for Women?* (1999). Does multiculturalism imply the protection of extreme oppression of women internally in immigrant cultures? Stein's argument is parallel: she claims that Canadian multiculturalism does not, to a sufficient degree, require ordinary demands of gender equality in the cultures it seeks to protect and further, as a central example, she refers to gender biases in the Jewish congregation to which she herself belongs (ten men must be present before a service may take place, for example). Stein's influential paper has been reprinted in the anthology *Uneasy Partners* (2007), which contains several interesting responses. One strategy, advocated by John Ibbitson, is directly signaled by his title "Let Sleeping Dogs Lie," although who the sleeping dogs are does not become absolutely clear. Is it the internal oppression in immigrant groups, which might grow, if more light is shed upon it? Or is it the critics of multiculturalism who must not be awakened? The conclusion of the paper seems to assume the latter: "That's why we should let the dogs sleep. Waking them up will only create a lot of barking and ill will. And before we are anything else, let us be people of good will" (Stein et al. 2007, 69).[62] Ibbitson's conclusion is revealing: the decisive thing is to confess to a group of people "with good will," and if you desire this adornment to your self-image, you must simply keep silent about the tensions between religion and democracy. Otherwise, you may awake the wrong persons—those with ill will. But here (as elsewhere in these debates), you must reject the argument that by assuming certain points of view, you might end up agreeing with the wrong persons. As so often before, the wise words attributed to Arthur Koestler must be repeated: "I cannot assume responsibility for who agrees with me." The fact that persons you do not like and with whom you disagree on other matters, agree with you on certain points is no reason for giving up that point of view. You must present the arguments and points of view that you have; you cannot tactically predict what effects your points of view would have in the public debate. If you should play the tactical game that Ibbitson proposes, then you would constantly have to serve as your own spin doctor–the whole of public debate would be infected by the politician's disease, and you would no longer be able to tell who really means what. Ibbitson is interesting, because he forms a rare example of one who directly expresses what many seem to mean and think tacitly: that you should keep silent about repression internally in immigrant groups, otherwise, it might cause damage to the "good cause" and would thus not be "politically correct."

Kymlicka, of course, is a debate participant of a somewhat different stripe from Ibbitson, and he attempts to address the real problem brought forward by Stein, rather than just call for a collective, respectful silence on the issue. As early as 1995, we saw him touching upon the problem, but his current position makes some overlooked distinctions clear. He now distinguishes between two different problems in Stein: "What exactly is the connection between concerns about potential conflicts between religious freedom and equality rights, on the one hand, and concerns about immigrant integration, on the other?" (137). Stein claims that the connection between these two pertains to Canadian multiculturalism in theory and practice. But what is this multiculturalism? Kymlicka now distinguishes three aspects: multiculturalism as fact, as policy, and as ethos. The former two remind us about culturalism as fact and as norm (which we listed as numbers (1) and (3) in our analysis of culturalism), the fact that different cultural groups exist in Canada, and the fact that there is a policy based on certain multiculturalist norms regarding these groups. The third is an "ethos" of multiculturalism which is assumed to have developed in Canadian civil society during multiculturalism's long march through the institutions, an ethos which forms the way Canadians think and act regarding such issues and which has a far broader scope than the specific policies, not unlike Taylor's Hegelian morality of multiculturalism.

This ethos has two sides: the front side, as it were, is the will to be inclusive of ethnic groups and the identification with their perspectives and interests, but the back side is that this may "degenerate into tokenism or a stifling sort of political correctness" (139). The latter refers to the possibility that one is so desperate to avoid the defamation of minorities that one completely avoids touching upon difficult issues and closes one's eyes to the real problems of immigrant groups and their relation to the larger society (140). The conflict between religion and democracy is, according to Kymlicka, relatively independent of the two first aspects of multiculturalism because it was already present in the conflict between Christian sects and human rights long before the construction of Canadian multiculturalist policies, and because the contemporary sharpening of the conflict is due to the growth of religious orthodoxy in the world in general, this being, perhaps, partly a reaction against the liberal "aggressive promotion of a culture of rights" (141), which we saw him celebrate earlier.

To this, two things may be said. The fact that the problem has existed since the days of the early Enlightenment does not imply that it is irrelevant to multiculturalism, but only shows that it is a problem which is so basic that multiculturalism can not merely declare itself immune to it. If the real problem is indeed, as Kymlicka says, the century-old *libertas ecclesiae,* freedom of the church (147), this does not exempt multiculturalism from taking a stance regarding it. And if the growing wave of religious re-orthodoxification in Islam as well as Christianity has its background in the liberal "culture of rights" (of which Kymlicka himself claims that multiculturalism forms a prominent part), then multiculturalism as an actor indeed forms part of the problem. Kymlicka, however, wants to evade that issue and claims that Stein's real problem is only the multiculturalist "ethos" which may suppress the necessary discussions of the tension between religion and democracy.

Kymlicka's own solution to this problem also seems tactical. He admits, as a liberal, that there are strong arguments for the ongoing propagation of ordinary, general rights of equality (in gender and race, for example), but then he goes on to add, in a surprising call: "And yet we have to stop somewhere. Pushing equality norms all the way down would effectively abolish any meaningful right of religious freedom, or indeed freedom of association more generally" (143). The multicultural compromise here implies to him that, thanks to *libertas ecclesiae*, religions should be exempted from the demand to comply with certain human rights! In Canadian courts, family and religious association have been exempted and, according to Kymlicka, have the right to be so exempted—from liberal equality![63] It is quite difficult to see why religious organizations have any demand for special status as compared to other organizations in this regard, and Kymlicka does not seem to intend a deeper discussion of this.[64] It may be added that contemporary voices such as Jonathan Israel point to the fact that *libertas ecclesiae* may mean two quite different things. It may mean freedom of belief for the individual, or it may mean the right to special status for religious organizations, including, in extreme cases, their right to suppress their members. The former is liberal, the latter is not. Kymlicka does not realize this. Multiculturalism as legislation and policy remain outgrowths from basic liberal principles to him, even when they go directly against such principles.

The problem seems to lie in the fact that the widespread multiculturalist "ethos" is not any continuation of liberal basic principles, and may very easily turn directly against them. This ethos may quickly assume the character of a "conservative" multiculturalism, from which Kymlicka otherwise distances himself. Much points to the fact that he is right in his argument around this "ethos," which prevents well-meaning people like Ibbitson from seeing and discussing these problems openly for fear of leaving the good company of those with "good will". Kymlicka's conclusion goes as follows:

> According to John Ibbitson, 'it is wrong to say that political correctness, or a desire not to offend, is keeping us from facing a growing threat. There is no threat, pure and simple.' I broadly agree, but would put the point slightly differently. There may be no threat, but the adoption of multiculturalism does involve a gamble (151).

Kymlicka's position is at some distance to Ibbitson's, however, for this "gamble" is the following: Something exists which is called the "liberal expectancy,"[65] namely the expectation that liberal democracy exerts a sort of gravitational pull which gradually influences the practice and behavior of ethnic and religious groups. Catholics and Jews arrived in the US as conservative, authoritarian patriarchs and developed, during the course of some generations, into convinced full-blood democrats. The gamble is whether this analogy holds for more recent immigrants as well. In Canada, many have confidence in it, but in much of Europe, Kymlicka says, this belief is lacking.[66] The argument is surprising because it pulls the carpet from under the whole of Kymlicka's long-lasting project, since, if the liberal gravity really does pull, then the whole development of multiculturalist policies were but provisional and tactical, and every immigrant is destined to end up, sooner or later, in the liberal *melting-pot*—the only question remaining is how long it takes. Thus the ideas of "mosaic" or "salad bowl" instead of that melting-pot are merely temporary; the salad will be digested sooner or later. But if that is the case, then the whole program of declarations of "preserving and developing" immigrant cultures is just talk, which serves to cover the slow and steady pull of liberal gravity. Even Kymlicka's and Canada's nice-sounding ideas of not only preserving but also transforming immigrant cultures become a mere surface on the long-drawn journey towards the liberal democrat goal. When we, multiculturalistically, are assumed to accept gender separation in gym classes or in opening hours of swimming pools, it is only because such initiatives keep the immigrants within the institutions, so that liberal gravity may exert its pull on them, until such measures may again be discarded: "We can safely rely on the gravitational pull of liberal democratic institutions to diffuse a culture of rights over time, but only if people are in fact participating in those institutions" (153). But if multiculturalism is merely tactical and provisional, then is it really such an excellent idea to erect its norms into binding legislation in international institutions, such as Kymlicka is striving for? His actual position seems to have been reduced to arguing that the liberal gravity is better than the "aggressive intervention into every nook and cranny of civil society," as he says conclusively (154), but multiculturalism *began* precisely as such legislative interventions into civil society! It seems as if the pull of liberal gravity steadily exerts its force on Kymlicka's theory as well; it becomes less and less culturalist and more and more oriented towards normal, "colorblind" democracy and human rights.

The Chips from the Cup

Modern society irreversibly rejects the dream of culturalism to repair the broken cup. The functional differentiation of modernity gives the single individual a whole bundle of widely differing identities, depending on the contexts in which he participates. Taylor's and Kymlicka's theories try to save an idea that liberal society can be brought to consist of a mosaic whose single pieces are not the chips from the different broken cups, but are rather small, repaired versions of whole, different cultural cups: a society of state-supported ghettos. Multiculturalism is no doubt right in claiming that the melting-pot metaphor is not an adequate picture of the mixture of cultures in modern society. The mosaic rather consists of single chips from the broken cups, and even if people have their liberty to try to reconstruct larger parts of the single cups, it may only be attempted within the constraints of democracy, rule-of-law and human rights. And there are indeed chips, pieces of cultural traditions, which do not conform to these principles. The mosaic picture is further unsatisfactory, though, because it overlooks how new hybrids between different chips constantly develop in a trial-and-error process, and it does not see either that many chips will disappear completely because they correspond to cultural practices which no one continues to perform.[67] Furthermore, modern societies do not only consist of chips from broken cups from days of old, but they have their own institutions, habits, and dynamics which constantly generate a wealth of new different cultural traits, which are not necessarily any less worthy of survival than the ever so "authentic" traditions of the past.

Protection against Defamation:
A Multicultural Group Right?

Muhammad and Fogh Caricatures: A Comparative Analysis

An example of an argument for an informal variant of the demand for group protection can be found at the heart of the "Cartoon Crisis," or the "Muhammad Crisis." The outrage among Danish and international Muslims over twelve cartoons in the Danish daily newspaper *Jyllands-Posten* peaked with the destruction of Danish embassies in the Middle East in early February 2006 and forced politicians, media persons and intellectuals all over the world to consider the right to publish such drawings. Here, many observers argued—and still do—that out of consideration to Muslim immigrants in Denmark, or to the international *umma* in general, such cartoons should not be published; such drawings would insult the cultural group and defame its religion. Most observers who mobilize this argument usually begin by stating their unconditional support for freedom of expression and the inviolable right of *Jyllands-Posten* to publish such drawings, then hastily proceed to a "but," which takes over most of the ensuing argumentation, explaining why such offenses of religious or cultural groups should be avoided. For that reason, this argument won the nickname "Free Speech BUT." It most often relies on the claim that there is no formal threat to Danish or international freedom of expression in legal terms, which is why concentration focuses upon attacking the publication of the offensive drawings, allegedly without involving freedom of speech. Let us take a closer look at this case in order to establish the reality in the alleged offense of a cultural group, and whether it may give rise to a more or less formal group right to avoid defamation of religious feelings. But, as a very basic presupposition to this investigation, let us first do something surprisingly few observers have cared to do: take a closer look at those drawings.

In the international crisis triggered by those twelve cartoons, many observers have held different opinions about the status, permissibility, motivation, etc. of the drawings. Very few have cared, however, to investigate the type of cartoons, as a newspaper and drawing genre, before the vast and strange political game in which they were caught. The 12 cartoons were very different from each other. Some were caricatures of Muhammad, while some were portraits without satirical intent. Others put Muhammad into satirical contexts with other aims, e.g. attacks on the Danish right wing party leader Pia Kjærsgaard or even the *Jyllands-Posten* itself. There were only three proper caricatures among the twelve cartoons. One showed Muhammad in paradise receiving a long line of deceased suicide bombers; he greets them by pointing to the fact that there is now a lack of virgins in Paradise. Another displays Muhammad, sword in hand, flanked by two women in black burkas. The two rectangular holes for the eyes in the burkas are mirrored by a corresponding black rectangle covering Muhammad's eyes, consistent with the convention of concealing the identity of people on photographs. Here, we shall focus upon the most debated and most controversial of the twelve cartoons, namely the one portraying Muhammad with a bomb in the turban. That is the drawing made by the draughtsman Kurt Westergaard who has subsequently been the object of several Islamist plots—most recently on January 1st 2010, when a Somali broke into his home and tried to assassinate him with an axe.

The cartoon consists of two parts. One is the portrait of a bearded, male person, unidentifiable at a first glance. This is the iconic part of the drawing. The accompanying text (the headline of the newspaper page containing all of the drawings: "Muhammeds ansigter"—the Faces of Muhammad) indicates that this person is identical to the founder of the Muslim religion, Muhammad, often called "The Prophet" by believers.

This text forms the indexical part of the drawing, which fixes its reference and allows the observer to identify which person the iconic part of the drawing portrays and expresses something about. Without the indexical part, it would not be possible to know who the cartoon portrays, as there is no secure historical knowledge as to the appearance of the historical Muhammad; the iconic drawing taken alone might as well portray many other bearded, turban-wearing men, for instance its draughtsman Kurt Westergaard himself, if he was equipped with such a headdress. The coupling of icon and index, predicate and subject, in this specific way is the prerequisite for the drawing to function as a proposition claiming: "This is Muhammad." The indexical part thus forms a decisive pretext for the ensuing scandal, to the extent that it is the very claim that this cartoon portrays the prophet which makes controversial the otherwise harmless drawing.

We now focus upon the iconic part of the drawing, the manifest cartoon at the top of the newspaper page, which consists of three components. One is the sketchy drawing of a bearded male face with a slightly skewed, imponderable expression. The second is his black turban, in which lies a black, spherical bomb with a short, burning fuse. The third is a sign on the front side of that bomb which most western readers are probably unable to decode further than the fact that it refers to something Arabic or Muslim. The face is rendered comparably naturalistically, with deep-set black eyes, thick black eyebrows, an invisible mouth and a perhaps absentminded, even meditative, expression. The black turban is, in Islamic iconography, a sign of the prophet or one of his direct descendants who are the only persons allowed to wear such a headdress. The bomb, however, is far less naturalistically depicted and is stylized into a black, shining sphere in a Donald Duck-like cartoon tradition which is probably most observers' source for such an idea of a bomb which is very different from most existing explosives today. The use of such a stylized bomb is widespread in newspaper satire where it is, most often, a metonymy for weapons as such or for threatening and violent behavior in general, metonymy being the figure of style which represents a whole by displaying one of its parts or aspects.[68]

The iconic part of the drawing thus consists of three incommensurable elements put together. This zeugmatic strategy, the composition of incoherent parts, is very widespread in the satire tradition, and it is this device which makes the observer conscious of the fact that the drawing not only represents a concrete person, identified as the historical Muhammad, but that the drawing should somehow be read as a proposition claiming something about this person and is therefore in need of a further reading; this is no ordinary portrait of a historical person. The added attributes—the bomb and the text—should in some sense be read as predicates in a more or less general proposition pertaining to Muhammad.

Here many (enraged) interpreters find that the proposition of the drawing is something like "Muslims are terrorists," and even that the drawing provides a stereotypical and pejorative representation of Muslims as such. However, this is a much too quick interpretation. It presupposes many more steps than the mere identification of the parts of the drawing, namely a specific syntactical coupling of those parts—and all these steps are far from legitimized by the cartoon satire tradition. Let us take the first step first: from identifying the person in the picture as the historical person Muhammad to seeing this figure as representing Islam, or even Muslims as such. The first step is a metonymy of a widespread type: to take the originator of a doctrine as a sign for that doctrine. It is the same if we find in a drawing of Marx as a sign for Marxism (even if he said, famously, "I am not a Marxist"), or the drawing of George Washington as a sign for American independence. The drawing only indirectly, via this specific metonymy, refers to Islam as the doctrine, which Muhammad founded. But does this legitimize the further step, which goes on to claim that the drawing is also about Muslims as such, as many interpreters have claimed when interpreting the cartoon as a derogatory stereotype of all Muslims?

This is not nearly as automatically the case. The two-step metonymy, which goes from the creator of a doctrine to that doctrine and further on to the adherents of the doctrine, is a far more fragile and less stable figure than the one step from originator to doctrine. If you were a fan of the philosopher Karl Marx, for instance, and you saw a portrait of him which was ridiculing him in some way, would you then have the right to claim that that drawing also ridiculed all Marxists? Of course not. Marxists come in many different versions, and it might be that the parts of the doctrine which the cartoon targets are not those parts which you celebrate. This double step from originator to doctrine to adherents tacitly presupposes that the drawing is equipped with what logicians call *Universal Quantification*: "For All Muslims, it is the case that..." But this is in no way claimed in the cartoon which may just as well be read with *Existential Quantification*: "For Some Muslims, it is the case that..." It is, in fact, impossible to establish whether the drawing is about all or some Muslims, even if you take as granted the problematic two-step metonymy.

But *what* does the cartoon claim about these Muslims, be it some or all? The drawing associates some or all Muslims with a bomb about to explode. If we did not presuppose the one- or two-step metonymy, the cartoon would be strange: why does Muhammad look so calm, even if he has a bomb about to detonate in his turban? Is he a suicide bomber? One hardly associates a suicide bomber with calm, and the received picture of a suicide bomber is rather one with a bomb belt around his waist. If we take for granted that Muhammad is the subject of the cartoon (supported by the newspaper headline), then the bomb is added as a predicate to that subject, but in such a composite drawing there is no unanimous interpretation of the predicate. The grammar connecting subject and predicate in drawings is less strict than the more unambiguous grammar of linguistics. The drawing means, on a first gaze, that there is something "bomb-like" about Muhammad. As Mehdi Mozaffari from the Aarhus University has indicated,[69] if the drawing is taken as a portrayal of Muhammad it does nothing but update an old Islamic tradition of depicting (in picture and writing) Muhammad as a warlord. This is often indicated by him being equipped with his famous sword, a sword which is for example depicted on the Saudi Arabian flag. On that interpretation, the bomb is but a contemporary version of the Islamic tradition of a description of the prophet, associated to the idea in parts of Islam involving the spread of the faith by the sword.[70]

If we insert this into the two-step metonymy, this entails (1) that there is something bomb-like or belligerent in Muhammad's doctrine, and (2) maybe about all or some Muslims. Here, the interpretation with "all" is highly controversial and cannot stand alone, while the interpretation with "some" is less controversial to the extent that it can hardly be denied that there do exist strong networks of Islamists who accompany bombing actions with references to Islam and Muhammad, and that some adherents of Islamist revival movements such as Salafism, Wahhabism, or Deobandi, support such actions. In this reading, it may be difficult to see why the drawing does not simply refer to those variants of Islam which interpret the claims about Islam as the religion of the sword fairly literally, and, for that reason, make use of explosives and other kinds of violence in their political struggle.[71]

But taken strictly, the cartoon says nothing about whether Muhammad (and by implication, these Muslims) have an active relationship to the bomb or whether they may instead be victims if the bomb had been placed on top of their head against their will. The spherical bomb in the turban in fact twists the Danish idiomatic expression "at få en appelsin i turbanen"—to receive an orange in one's turban, as an expression of the luck of Aladdin.[72] Another of the twelve cartoons plays on the same idiom, in which the author Kaare Bluitgen, dressed in a turban, receives an orange marked "PR stunt" falling into his turban. In this interpretation, Muhammad would, unlike Aladdin, suffer from ill luck when he, instead of the expected orange, receives a bomb of the same shape. When this ambiguity (is Muhammad the subject or the object for the bomb?) is easily changed into unequivocality in many interpretations, it is of course due to context. Namely the fact the there has been, during the recent decades, a number of bloody bomb attacks in the US, Europe, Israel—and not least in the Muslim world—where different Islamist groups have assumed responsibility and invoked different radical interpretations of Islam.

This knowledge in the general public forms the context which allows this aspect of the cartoon to become unambiguous without further analysis, such as when we immediately assume that the cartoon portrays Muhammad threatening with a bomb, or, via the double metonymy, an Islamist threatening with a bomb (even if Muhammad's facial expression in the cartoon seems relatively peaceful and not threatening). But here lies an interesting tension: this fact makes possible the interpretation that it is not the prophet with his not very warlike apparition in the drawing who is the subject for the bomb threat, but that it is other powers, not present in the cartoon, who have taken him and his doctrine as the pretext for bombing by placing the bomb in his turban. This (rather obvious) interpretation, which distinguishes an innocent Muhammad from other (Islamist?) forces, using him for bombastic purposes, has attracted very few interpreters.[73] This is probably because much of the discussion has not been interested in the meaning of the drawing, but rather in whether the very act of depicting the founder of the religion, Muhammad, is covered by the free speech paragraph 77 of the Danish constitution or whether it has violated other formal or informal rules.[74]

A further question is whether the bomb depicted is literal or—as in many newspaper cartoons—metaphorical. Is the bomb a metaphor for the bombast which some critics have found in the Islamic religion, or even more in the Islamist doctrine of political Islam with totalitarian ambitions (dating from Mawdudi, Qutb, and al-Banna in the 20th century)? This possibility has too not been investigated by many. Or is the bomb, in its cartoon naivety, another metonymy, namely for warfare or terror as such? Most will probably choose the latter reading.

Finally, there is the third element: the calligraphic sign on the bomb.[75] It is a so-called *shahāda* in compressed form, that is, the Muslim declaration of faith: "There is no god except God [&] Muhammad is God's messenger." It is calligraphically omnipresent in the Muslim world (as vignettes in books and pamphlets, on banners and flags, etc.) and variants of it form some of the earliest documented written evidence of Islam, such as from the Dome of the Rock in Jerusalem from the year 691 (Muhammad died in 632). It is thus a fundamental sign in Islam. It is constructed as follows:

allâh
   illa
allah   *ilah*
  al-rasûl   *lâ*
    muhammad

The upper oblique line should be read first, from lower right to upper left, with the following translation, given that the verb "to be," as normally in Arabic, is implicit only:

God
   except
God   god
  messenger [there is] no
    Muhammad

This sign provides the only component in the iconic part of the drawing which connects it to Islam. It is a piece of writing which, with its unanimous reference to the basic credo of Islam, emphasizes the first metonymy: from the originator of the doctrine to the doctrine, from Muhammad to Islam. A basic component of that doctrine is simply presented in the transition zone from turban to bomb. The sign, however, is strangely flat, probably copy-pasted onto the drawing from some source. It is not perspectively rendered, as it would be if it followed the spherical shape of the bomb. In any case, it is a possible, even obvious interpretation to connect the programmatic monotheism of the sign with the bomb—the tension-filled relation of monotheism to other, not consistently monotheist or even polytheist religions which are often criticized or in some cases even attacked or exterminated—which the bomb then might be taken to symbolize. Here, the difficult conditions and lack of rights of "unbelievers" in many Muslim countries (with regard to Christians, Jews, and atheists—see reports on the single Muslim countries on the homepage of *Human Rights Watch*) may be an appropriate context. Even such a tough interpretation of the drawing in terms of aggression—that Islam as a doctrine has a tendency to suppress other faiths—does not legitimize metonymy number two, claiming that some or all Muslims should be bombers or something akin to bombers.

But this takes us to the consideration of the genre of the cartoon—newspaper satire or caricature. In this genre, such couplings between recognizable public persons and different metonymical or metaphorical predicates constitute a widespread and easily understandable syntax. Let us take a parallel cartoon for comparison—the cartoonist Roald Als from the center-left Danish daily *Politiken* and his long tradition of depicting another of the main characters of the Cartoon Crisis, Danish PM Anders Fogh Rasmussen (now secretary general of NATO), as a stone age man.

On this occasion, Fogh has his chin protruding rather far in a monkey-like position, and the dark lower part of his face with the shadow of a beard is depicted as even darker. He is dressed up in fur and is provided with a club as a weapon, while he indulges in desperate and often naive behavior. This particular drawing comments upon events during the Cartoon Crisis. Here, the upright, white, normal looking, calm editor-in-chief of *Politiken*, Tøger Seidenfaden, is standing with an overbearing glance as a contrast to the raging Fogh who, swinging his club and

cramped in a monkeylike posture jumps up and down on a copy of *Politiken*. There is a clear racial difference between the two men as rendered in *Politiken*'s drawing. Fogh exclaims "Of course you have your freedom of expression, but...." The "Free Speech BUT" argument, of which Seidenfaden had been one of the main proponents, is here transferred to his opponent who acts contrary to free speech with this destruction of a newspaper, the occasion being that the Danish PM had said that the Cartoon Crisis had separated the sheep from the goats in the Danish media.

The depiction of Fogh as a caveman rests on analogous devices to those of the Muhammad drawing with the bomb. This depiction of the person is a metonymy for the policies of Fogh, and just as in the Muhammad case, there is also the more remote possibility of a two-step metonymy so that the drawing is, at the same time, a portrait of all or some supporters of Fogh's party (the Danish liberal party *Venstre*), or even a portrait of all or some Danes. The predicates added to the person—ape face, fur, and club—also characterize some properties of the doctrine, even if in a somewhat more obviously metaphorical way than in the Muhammad cartoon. Fogh's person and doctrine are stone age-like, and a caveman cannot make anything but primitive politics. The Stone-Age dress is thus an easily decodable metaphor, resting upon the colloquial expression that something that you find primitive is from the Stone Age. This is emphasized by the ape-like character of Fogh's face that adds the significations of brutish and stupid. The less direct relations between prophet, bomb, and sign in the Muhammad cartoon is somewhat more unambiguous here. The difficult issue in the Muhammad case—whether the peaceful prophet might be innocent as to the presence of the bomb in the turban—is not a problem in the Fogh case, where Fogh is displayed as insecure, as if he is trying to solve a problem which he, given his caveman abilities, cannot. Maybe one could imagine that Fogh has ended up in caveman suit against his own will, just as Muhammad may have received the bomb without wanting it, but there is nothing in the cartoon that indicates that this is a modern, able Fogh who has just been forced into the costume, as it might possibly be the peaceful prophet who has been forced to wear the bomb. It is rather an ape-man who has been placed in the PM's office.

With regard to the decisive issue of quantification, the two drawings are completely parallel. In neither of the two cartoons is it explicit *how much* of the subject of the drawing is covered by the predicate. Is it *all* of Fogh's politics which are primitive, or only some? Is it *all* of Muhammad's religion which is primitive, or only some of it? The cartoons do not determine that. Or, if we proceed in the two-step metonymy: is it *all* adherents of the Liberal Party who are cavemen, or is it only *some* of them? Is it *all* Danes who are Stone Age men, or is it only *some* Danes? Skeptics in the Liberal Party against the party leadership (such skeptics can be found in all social organizations) hardly need to feel targeted by the cartoon and probably don't—just as Danes who have not voted for Fogh need not feel targeted by the metonymy. In exactly the same way, peaceful Muslims need not feel targeted by the metonymy of the Muhammad caricature.

This ambiguity between universal and existential quantification is actually one of the central artistic devices of satirical drawings. It encourages the observer to speculate: *How much* of the PMs politics are, in fact, stone age-like and primitive—the cartoon does not make it explicit. Correspondingly in the Muhammad case: *To what degree* is Muhammad's doctrine, Islam, in fact associated with bombs? The cartoon does not make it explicit. If we regard the two-step metonymy: *How many* Danish liberals are, in fact, primitive? *How many* Muslims are bombers or support bombers?

Read within the confines of this widespread, enlightened satire tradition it is thus not at all evident that the Muhammad drawing allows the observer to conclude that it claims that all Muslims are bombers. The cartoon does not say that anymore than the caveman Fogh says that all Danish liberals are primitive. It is because of this plasticity of interpretation that satirical drawings may not be contradicted or attacked in the same way as literal, linguistic utterances, such as "All Liberals are primitive," "All Danes are primitive" or "All Muslims are bombers," which are categorical and have a far smaller range of interpretation than the corresponding cartoons. It is for this reason, among others, that such propositions are not funny, while cartoons may well be.

As to the allegedly controversial combination between person and bomb in the Muhammad case, the Fogh drawing also equips the PM with a weapon: the club. But weaponry is no rare predicate for persons appearing in general international satire, particularly not bombs, which are widespread in newspaper satire. To characterize the aggressive or warlike intentions of people or doctrines by equipping them with a stylized bomb is, in fact, a stable, recurring device in newspaper cartoons.

To sum up, we may conclude that the allegedly most offensive of the Danish cartoons makes use of exactly the same semiotic devices as does the *Politiken* cartoon of Danish PM Anders Fogh Rasmussen, and, with regard to the bomb, employs a device which is standard among newspaper cartoonists. The depiction of the prophet, however, is somewhat more ambiguous than that of the PM, the former being also interpretable as peaceful, while the latter can hardly be seen as non-primitive. This, of course, is also due to the fact that Roald Als's drawing of Fogh forms one among a long series of Fogh cartoons over many years, so that the

The bomb as a metonymy for violent behavior is widespread in international newspaper satire, before and after the Muhammad cartoon crisis of 2006. In particular, the substitution of a bomb or other weaponry for a violent person's head is a customary device in international image rhetorics. In the cartoons reproduced here we find (1) US President George W. Bush with a bomb head and cowboy hat (Patrick Dea, 2003); (2) Iran's Ayatollah Khamenei with an atomic explosion off the top of his head (Jake Fuller, 2005); (3) North Korean leader Kim Jong-Il as a nuclear bomb (Dale Cummings, 2009); (4) an anonymous female suicide bomber with a bomb head (Kjell Nilsson-Mäki, 2005); (5) an Arabian response to Kurt Westergaard's Muhammad cartoon in which Muhammad is replaced by a Jewish stereotype with a bomb hat and the caption "Zionist" (Khaleel, 2006); and finally (6) the Dutch cartoonist Gregorius Nekschot's indirect portrait of Muhammad, also a reaction to the Muhammad cartoons (Nekschot, 2006). Two of the drawings, (1) and (6), play on Magritte's famous surrealist painting of a pipe with the caption "Ceci n'est pas une pipe."

It may be remarked that the Dear Leader Kim Jong-Il is hailed as a religious figure (in the so-called Juche doctrine), and North Korean extremists might thus claim the right to embassy burnings and related pressure, were they to follow the Islamist reaction patterns to the Muhammad cartoons. As to the Palestinian cartoon of the Jew with the bomb hat, it provides a direct answer to Westergaard's drawing and was produced in the midst of the Cartoon Crisis in February 2006. It uses the same predicate (the bomb) but with a decisive difference. The subject of the predicate here is a Jewish stereotype referring to Israeli Jews as such, not the originator of a doctrine as in the Westergaard cartoon (in that case, it would of course have been Moses).

Take the portrait of a suicide bomber whose head has been replaced with the cartoon bomb; it is evident that this drawing does not claim that all persons wearing veils are suicide bombers. Or take the example of a fundamentalist Christian, American, warmongering president. He is depicted with a bomb as his head, with a short, lighted fuse, just as is that in the Muhammad drawing, which goes to suggest that Bush's "War on Terror" has, in itself, a terrorist character. But parallel to the Muhammad and Fogh drawings, it is not the case that the assertion about Bush and his doctrine may, without further notice, be extended to cover all Americans, all Christians, or all Westerners, or anyone else President Bush may be imagined to be a representative for.

The cartoons are reproduced thanks to permission from the copyright owners.

interpretation of the caveman costume has gradually been automatized and does not require deeper reflection in the experienced observer.

It might be further discussed which of the two predicates used is more insulting. To a politician who has expended a great deal of effort in appearing modern, it is of course insulting when he himself, his politics (first metonymy), and maybe (some of) his adherents (second metonymy) are claimed to be primitive and prehistoric. And to a prophet who despite massacres is claimed to be the father of a religion of peace, it is of course insulting when he himself, his religion (first metonymy), and maybe (some of) his adherents (second metonymy) are associated with a bomb. Both predicates are thus antagonistic in relation to the doctrine they refer to—hence the critical character of both drawings—and both predicates have to do with weapons and violence (club, bomb), which indicates that the two figures are both more aggressive and warlike and less sophisticated than they immediately appear.

The two-step metonymy which, in both cartoons separates the immediate object of the drawing, the identifiable individual, from the set of persons it indirectly and maybe only partially refers to, is thus quite different in both these drawings from stereotype drawings of the anti-Semitic tradition, which the Westergaard drawing has been unfairly compared to (e.g. those of *Der Stürmer* in 1930s Germany or those of many present-day Arab newspapers).[76]

Those cartoons also depict persons, but in contrast to the Muhammad and, to some degree the Fogh cartoon as well (the monkey face), they form stereotypes equipped with racial features (crooked Jew nose, obesity, greedy facial expression, traditional Jewish dress). Unlike both the Muhammad and Fogh drawings, they are very often equipped with *generalizing* indices ("Der ewige Jude," the eternal Jew and the Star of David) that indicate that they directly refer to all members of the population which is stereotyped. Here, a whole group is characterized as different from and inferior to all other people. Here, that universal quantifier is present ("All Jews...") which was lacking both in the Muhammad and the Fogh cartoon. Such anti-Semitic cartoons do not retain the plasticity of interpretation and the relativity of reference which caused those drawings not to refer to all Muslims or all Danish Liberals.

Drawing from *Der Stürmer* special issue on ritual murders, May 1934.

Drawing from *Al-Watan* (Qatar), July 20 2006.

A classic strategy in Nazi anti-Semitic cartoons, which is repeated in the Arab anti-Semitism of the present day, is to stereotype Jews as such with black hats, sidelocks of hair, crooked noses, thick lips, often sweaty and greedy-looking. This stereotype then performs acts such as striving for world power, controlling the USA, suppressing ordinary people, and organizing massacres, often with the introduction of classic anti-Semitic myths: the drinking of blood from massacred babies, etc.. Very often, these stereotypes associate Jews with animals such as snakes, rats, and swine. Depiction strategies differ radically from those used in the analyzed cartoons of Muhammad and Fogh; they stereotype a whole population. The difference is aptly expressed in Rushdie's distinction: democracy defends people, not their ideas. The cartoons of Fogh and Muhammad attack ideas, while the Stürmer strategy attacks groups of people.

The two cartoons displayed here both exploit the anti-Semitic myth of the Jews slaughtering innocent children in order to drink their blood. The Stürmer cartoon has the subtext rhyme "Durch die Jahrtausende vergoß der Jud, geheimem Ritus folgend, Menschenblut. Der Teufel sitzt uns heute noch im Nacken, so liegt an Euch die Teufelsbrut zu packen"—During thousands of years, the Jew has followed a secret rite to spill human blood. That devil still bites our necks, now it is up to you to get rid of that devil's brood.

The drawing from Al-Watan (Qatar) also refers to the myth of Jews massacring innocent children. The large drop of blood identifies those children with the population of Lebanon; the text on the drop reads "the Lebanese people."

As the two drawings of Muhammad and Fogh are so parallel, the decisive difference between the reception of them must be sought elsewhere: in the context. There is a certain, if weak, Muslim tradition for avoiding the depiction of the historical person Muhammad—the issue of the Islamic image ban.[77] It cannot, of course, be claimed in a society with freedom of religion, like Denmark, that one religion has the right to impose its taboos, proscriptions, and rituals on non-believers or believers of different faiths. The ban on Muhammad depictions covers parts of Islam, but is in no way valid for the rest of society which has a legitimate interest in Muhammad as an important and influential historical figure whose doctrine, influences, and effects are the object of ordinary investigation, research, and debate, just as is the case with all other historical persons—other male mammals, as Christopher Hitchens has it. To claim that the Islamic iconoclasm should cover also *Jyllands-Posten*, as has been claimed, appears rather strange.

In addition, there is the interesting question of the prohibition of depiction. The theological background for maintaining this prohibition in the *Hadith* tradition is to avoid the appearance of a fallacious cult around the prophet Muhammad as if he were a god, since the only god is supposed to be Allah. Pictures of him should not be produced because of the risk of idolatry. This is an idea which is often contrasted with Christianity, whose depiction and cult around the pre-Muhammadan but Islamic prophet Jesus (Isa) appears, as seen from an Islamic point of view, as exactly such a case of erroneous idolatry and, in fact, polytheism. This Islamic depiction ban thus also covers Abraham, Jesus, and other figures common to Christianity and Islam, and there are many classical cases of Islamic destruction of churches and Christian depictions of Jesus for that reason, but, as the criticism against *Jyllands-Posten* has often pointed to their caricaturistic intent, there is hardly any real danger that any Danish or international Muslim might get the idea of using the twelve Danish drawings for rituals of idolatry. Moreover, the proscription against depiction having its motivation in the avoidance of idolatry, the motivation of the proscription is aimed at Muslims and thus cannot, based on its own purpose, claim to be valid for non-believers.

A further aspect is that the proscription of depiction is primarily claimed by Arab Sunnis and not to the same extent by Shi'ites and Turkish Sunnis—which is why there is a long tradition of depictions of Muhammad in the history of Islam, especially in the Turkish and Persian areas. The strong proscription against depiction is nowadays maintained especially by rather novel, fundamentalist currents such as Wahhabism and Salafism, which thus claim the right to hegemony not only over non-believers but also over other Islamic currents when they claim the proscription to hold for them as well. All in all, the argument from the proscription of depiction is rather weak, even internally to Islamic theology. The decisive argument for the right to depict Muhammad remains, of course, external and motivated in the principles of free speech in a democratic society; today it might be necessary to be reminded of the fact that these principles hold for agnostics and atheists as well.

A further argument is the status of Islam as a minority religion in Denmark, and the idea that a special consideration should be paid to the taboos of minority cultures. As the Cartoon Crisis exemplarily demonstrated, however, the world is now globalized to the extent that the Danish Muslims may not be seen as a minority in every respect. In a sense they constitute a majority, in so far as they are a subset of the 1.3 billion Muslims in the world, just as is often explicitly claimed by their Danish and international spokesmen. But in that case, the minority argument ceases to be valid for Danes (6 million) or EU citizens (ca. 0.45 billion), even for EU and the US taken as a whole (ca. 0.8 billion). This argument is mirrored in the fact that in most Muslim countries nothing remotely like freedom of religion exists for Christians, Jews, atheists, or other minorities, and that the state press of these countries regularly publish anti-Christian, anti-Western, and anti-Semitic cartoons which do not hesitate to use racial stereotypes. Strangely, one often hears the opposite argument from the very same persons or sources: Islamic taboos should be respected because Islam is a world religion. The shift in the argument from few to many illustrates very well that it is no argument whatsoever that a doctrine or a culture has few or many devotees. In neither of these cases may that doctrine be exempted from discussion.

Schledermann (2006) has pointed to a further argument. The imam Abu Laban, one of the leaders of the protest committee against the Danish cartoons, attacked PM Anders Fogh Rasmussen for having awarded a Liberty Prize to the Somali critic of Islam, Ayaan Hirsi Ali, in 2004, and he claimed that the struggle around the cartoons must be seen in that context. According to Laban, this award brought "the blood of Theo van Gogh to Denmark and demanded of the Muslim society to pay blood money for him" (Schledermann 111). This award was thus, according to Laban, aimed against Danish Muslims in order to create an anti-Muslim sentiment which led to the publishing of the cartoons and made him ask: "Why should we pay blood money for van Gogh?" As revenge for this incorrect act by the PM, Danish Muslims were entitled to an apology, if not revenge. As no apology was forthcoming, revenge had to be planned. As a result, the imam's trip to the Middle East was planned to incite international rage. In this conception of the drawings, maintained by one of the chief instigators of the crisis, the crucial point is not any insult to religious sensibility, but an intentional blow in an on-going fight. A Muslim kills van Gogh; against this crime PM Fogh hands out an award and urges *Jyllands-posten* to publish drawings, and against this move Abu Laban and his colleagues organize their campaign and the international boycotts. They claim that the award and the drawings assert they have done something which they haven't, and they feel compelled to react. Faced with this argument, however, it must still be said that murders of film producers and arson of embassies seem neither fair nor legal measures in a struggle against the legal publication of drawings, not to mention the overinterpretation of Hirsi Ali's award.

Another much-discussed element in the context is the *intention* of the drawings. Why were these cartoons drawn? As to the Fogh cartoon, it forms a part of the daily cartoon drawings of the daily *Politiken* and is, most often, motivated by actual political discussions and events which Fogh is claimed to be too primitive to understand. The drawings form a thematic series which has continued over many years with Stone Age Fogh as constant center; the total number of drawings probably amounts to hundreds. The Muhammad drawings, by contrast, were not part of the corresponding daily cartoon satire of *Jyllands-Posten*. They were motivated by the fact that the Danish author Kaare Bluitgen had tried, in vain, to find an illustrator for a book with a (sympathetic) description of Muhammad's life. The draughtsmen who were asked allegedly refused to contribute because of their fear for their lives in the wake of the murder of the Dutch film-maker and Islam-critic, Theo van Gogh, in 2004. The inability of Bluitgen to find an illustrator became an issue of public debate in Denmark, and the newspaper *Jyllands-Posten* wanted to investigate whether the same self-censorship could be found amongst all Danish draughtsmen. This is why they asked a number of Danish cartoonists to depict the prophet. The paper received positive answers from twelve cartoonists. They were not asked for caricatures but for drawings of Muhammad "as they saw him;" some of them then chose satirical cartoons, as Westergaard did with the bomb-in-turban cartoon. The text accompanying the twelve cartoons directly addressed freedom of speech, asking whether Bluitgen's problems signified a real fear among Danish draughtsmen and, thus, whether the limits of free speech had changed without it being publicly acknowledged. The text, authored by editor Flemming Rose, rhetorically pinpointed this idea: "Modern, secular society is rejected by some Muslims. They demand special treatment, when they insist on a special consideration for their religious feelings. This is incompatible with secular democracy and freedom of expression where you must be ready to take sarcasm, mockery, and ridicule."

Another Danish daily, the center-left *Politiken*, took a very critical stance against *Jyllands-Posten*'s cartoons. It is remarkable that this newspaper had recently published drawings satirizing the prophet and stereotyping Muslims without any protests. Thus, it seems that the programmatic investigation undertaken by a center-right paper was more crucial to the development of the protests than the actual character of the drawings themselves.[78] Probably, it was this programmatic investigation of the relation between free speech and cultural group rights, which prompted well-organized Danish and international Islamist networks to an answer on the same programmatic level in the shape of the international campaign against the cartoons. Is it possible that the campaign directly took up the challenge of secularism and attempted to set new limits to Danish (and Western) freedom of speech, such as actually seems to have been the outcome of the crisis?

In the wider context, the immigrant and integration debates of recent years also play a role. In Denmark, a number of much-discussed and problematic pieces of legislations have been passed in order to reduce immigration and prevent forced marriages. Other doubtful initiatives, such as the so-called "hunger legislation" reducing social support for recent immigrants by half, have led to easily understandable dissatisfaction among immigrants. A similar, also easily understandable anger is due to the crude and stereotypical characterizations published by some Danish right-wing politicians, peaking with the comparison of Muslims with "cancerous tumors" on the homepage of Louise Frevert, MP for the Danish People's Party, assertions which have an offensive and malignant character quite dissimilar to the cartoons. This background has probably led some observers to misunderstand the cartoons as coming from the same direction as those assertions, but as has been made clear, such an interpretation lacks any support in the cartoons themselves.

As the cartoon crisis unfolded internationally, it quickly grew beyond this context and came to address free speech directly and explicitly, insofar as the Danish and international Islamists involved at an early point focused their demands on pressing the Danish PM to go against the constitution by "taking to task" *Jyllands-Posten* and thus somehow to go against its right to publish the cartoons.[79] Many international actors (OIC, the Turkish government, the British House of Commons) argued for a strong restriction on free speech with reference to the cartoons, just as international actors such as EU and the UN contemplated the adoption of such regulations.[80] Finally, the case came to involve freedom of speech in its most basic and serious form, to the extent that both the draughtsmen and the publishers of the cartoons were made the targets of death threats, forcing them to live under police protection.[81]

If one investigates the Cartoon Crisis in detail, what *Jyllands-Posten* has been accused of appears rather far-fetched. Even down to the minutest details of their mode of functioning, the cartoons form part of a completely normal Danish and Western tradition for cartoon satire which goes back to the Enlightenment and the European cartoon traditions of the 17th century.[82] Even if individual Muslims feel insulted in their religious feelings by the cartoons, they have, just like the individual Danish Liberals who may feel insulted by the Fogh caveman cartoons, no clear reason to complain, neither against Danish legislation (paragraph 77 of the Danish Constitution) nor against the average "tone" of Western cartoon satire in general.

The fact that Islamist organizations and their representatives in Denmark, in close cooperation with the Egyptian foreign office and the Islamic Conference Organization OIC, took the opportunity to challenge *Jyllands-Posten* and used these cartoons as a pretext for a campaign for the restriction of Danish and Western freedom of expression by their encouragement of international outrage, is another story.

The Religious Pressure against Freedom of Speech

A central argument for many who have attacked the publication of the cartoons has been that they offended a Danish minority, and that the responsibility for the further development of the crisis lay with the Danish government, which did a poor job of managing the situation. Following this argument, the crisis has nothing to do with freedom of speech, which is supported by the fact that no influential Danish politician has demanded a change in the freedom of speech granted by article 77 of the Constitution. This argument has the interesting structure that it interprets the crisis as an internal Danish affair, involving Danish actors only: Danish victims (Muslims), Danish heroes (Danish imams, the daily *Politiken*), and Danish villains (*Jyllands-Posten*, the Fogh government, the Danish People's Party). This point-of-view does not overlook, of course, the burning of embassies, but this is seen as mere unavoidable side effects of exclusively Danish causes, effects following automatically and without any local responsibility, dependent as they were on Danish events. This point of view, however, is deeply provincial and reduces the extension of the case, so that the widespread and international struggle for and against freedom of speech associated with the crisis is conveniently kept out of sight. When there is a refusal to compare the crisis with the long series of related cases, from the Rushdie controversy to the attacks on Pope Benedict's address in Regensburg and so forth, then there may be success in representing it as a unique case of Danish stupidity with no relation to freedom of expression. To illustrate this connection, we have constructed a timeline, summing up essential events in what appears as a strongly enhanced international religious pressure against free speech during the last 25 years (see the Appendix). This timeline brings together large and small events and gives a comparative background for understanding the Danish case, a background which disappears completely if one puts on local spectacles and imagines that the case stops at the Danish border. A picture emerges of a widespread religious pressure against free speech, spearheaded to a large extent by Islamic organizations and Islamist threats and actions, but also with an intensive participation by Christian organizations, fundamentalist Christians and other religions, including Judaism and Hinduism.

This pressure against freedom of speech depends on many heterogeneous actors. On one side, it consists of organizations both national and international. Among the international actors are the OIC (Organization of the Islamic Conference, the association for coordinating international policies of the 57 Muslim countries—led by Saudi Arabia, Egypt, Pakistan, Iran, and Malaysia), the Vatican, the Russian Orthodox Church, The European Council for Fatwa and Research (led by al-Qaradawi and associated with the Muslim Brotherhood), Hizb-ut-Tahrir, EU, UN, The European Council, Al-Qaeda, and several others. As is evident, it is an array of highly diverse actors. Among national organizations are many religious associations in many countries, such as the Islamic Society of Faith in Denmark, the Muslim Council of Britain and the Anglican Church in England, Conseil Français du Culte Musulman in France, and many more. The pressure also involves leading national politicians such as the Turkish PM, Tayyip Erdogan (taking the crisis as the pretext for demanding the restriction of free speech in the whole of the EU), many politicians on different levels in many Muslim countries, the Labour Party of Tony Blair and Gordon Brown attempting to diminish British freedom of speech by prohibiting criticism of religions, Ayatollah Khomeini and the later generation of Iranian leaders continuing the Rushdie fatwa, the Dutch PM Jan Peter Balkenende, and the Slovenian leadership of the EU which tried to prevent the public showing of an Islam-critical movie, and more.

In addition to these political and organizational levels, one must consider the pressure from many ordinary people, whether in peaceful demonstrations and debates or via less peaceful death threats aimed against intellectuals, artists and others who are accused of having insulted something or other. Finally, the pressure also involves decidedly criminal actors such as van Gogh's murderer Mohamed Bouyeri, the assassins of Rushdie's translators and publishers, the Somali axeman Mohammed Geele who attempted to murder Kurt Westergaard, and the organizers of different terror attacks in many countries, successful or not, which legitimize themselves by reference to the defamation of religion as their motivation. It is difficult to draw sharp distinctions between these forces. The increasingly aggressive policy of the UN against "defamation of religions" is, for instance, the result of many years of pressure on behalf of the OIC; Tony Blair's curtailing of British freedom of speech was heavily supported by different British religious organizations (but was opposed by Mr. Bean). Correspondingly, it is not the case that the organizations mentioned have necessarily supported the pressure against free speech *en bloc*; the fact that it forms part of an organization's official policy does not mean there may not be forces in that organization which work in the opposite direction. Finally, there are the different clandestine actors who may be associated with different organizations, links which it may be difficult or impossible to chart. Even if such connections undoubtedly exist, it is no organized conspiracy against free speech. It is rather a partial agreement about ends and means by many different actors who may have only a weak connection or none at all.

In that sense, the sharp increase in pressure against freedom of speech, appearing in the years around 2000, forms a historical current *sui generis*, just like the Enlightenment of the 18th century, European fascism in the interwar period, or the 68 movement. Such "currents," when they are investigated more closely, are composed of many heterogeneous forces, state policies, the actions of organizations and individuals, without any overall coordination. It may just be observed that this pressure against free speech has grown considerably during the last two decades, and the many different actors involved have increased that pressure. It is in the context of this broad, international current that the Danish Cartoon Crisis must be seen; in a certain sense, it is but one small case among many. The many points of our timeline (see Appendix) serve to portray the details and existence of this pressure, but let us here take a closer look at some of the often overlooked individual cases.

The Organization of the Islamic Conference has played a large and not yet completely understood role in the establishment of the pressure against freedom of expression, both internally in Muslim countries, but especially within the UN system. OIC, with its main seat in Jedda, was founded in 1969 with Saudi financial support. Analysts often understand the OIC as supporting Saudi interests in particular and thus allow for the sparsely populated but affluent country to gain strong international influence and thus compete with other Muslim leadership candidate countries like Egypt and Iran. OIC was behind the 1990 publication of the so-called Cairo Declaration for Islamic human rights, which places all human rights under sharia. With particular regard to freedom of speech, the Cairo Declaration makes clear that it is delimited by sharia (see the column on "Islamic Rights"). Freedom of religion, in the sense of the individual's right to freely choose his religion, is thus also curtailed by sharia and its prohibition of apostasy. The OIC works continually to develop this Declaration to a more binding doctrine for all the member countries, a proper Muslim human rights charter. OIC seems, however, to have acted comparatively moderately on the international stage for many years, judging by the successive resolutions published after OIC summit meetings.

A decisive change, however, seems to have taken place between the summit meetings of 1997 and 2000; the resolution after the latter meeting listing a series of wholly new policies. The member countries should now support each other against NGOs who "libel" them for violations of human rights, and they should coordinate their actions in international organizations, also for preventing the "defamation of religions," especially Islam. Consequently, the OIC has since presented a series of still more radical proposals for the adoption of such rules against "defamations" in the UN system, and the President of the OIC regularly appears and demands the adoption of such rules, for example through letters to the UN General Secretary. In the newly founded Human Rights Council (which replaced the earlier HR Committee), the coordinated pressure of the OIC has had success. In March 2007, the Council passed a declaration which obliges the member countries to adopt legislation against "defamation of religions," and in March 2008, this declaration was sharpened by the decision to investigate all member nation legislations to establish their current position on this issue. In both cases, the resolutions were passed thanks to a majority of primarily Muslim and Third World countries against a minority of primarily Western countries. The ongoing pressure of the OIC enjoys media focus in the Muslim countries much more than in the West, which naturally does not obey these directives of the UNHRC. At the very least, this development implies a continuous delegitimation of the UN Human Rights Council such that strong Western countries cease to be interested in what the Council might adopt, but it is also evident that the policy of the Council supports the anti-free speech forces in countries where the issue is in the balance. In any case, the OIC's policy gives legitimacy to the anti-free speech polices of individual Muslim countries and Islamic organizations, networks and individuals, who partake in the pressure.

In the case against the Danish cartoons, the OIC played a central role which has not yet been investigated thoroughly.[83] On the second round trip of the Danish imams to the Middle East, an important destination was the Foreign Secretaries Meeting of the OIC in Mecca, December 7–8 2005, where the original agenda was the tension between Sunni and Shia Islam. This subject was pushed to the margin of the agenda by the Danish cartoons, however. The Danish imam delegation had been received by the foreign ministry of Egypt in Cairo, and when the Danish imams arrived they distributed, supported by the Egyptian foreign secretary Abdul Gheit, their dossier of genuine and false drawings to all participants. Also present were people like Sir Iqbal Sacranie, leader of the MCB (Muslim Council of Britain), and only a few weeks after that meeting, the state-supported boycotts of Danish goods began on the Arabian peninsula, an action originally proposed by the Danish imams. Those initiatives shortly culminated in the burning of Danish embassies in Syria and Lebanon, events tacitly supported by those states. All this took place a matter of weeks after foreign secretaries and high-ranking officials from the Islamic countries spent most of an OIC summit meeting discussing the cartoons. An obvious hypothesis is that they had discussed that the Danish cartoons served as a fine pretext to make an example in the ongoing international campaign against free speech.[84] The final communique of the OIC December conference broadcast the news to all the member countries and, as Klausen (2009) says, "ensured that the states joined the movement" (75).[85] The OIC frequently publishes declarations against Western freedom of speech, declarations of increasing radicality, which are simultaneously orchestrated to fit to the recurrent cases of protests in Muslim countries. A recent example is the bombing of the Danish embassy in Islamabad in 2008 which the OIC immediately criticized, only to broadcast, one week later, a radical demand for government restrictions on freedom of expression in the West, referring to the fact that the situation would otherwise "escalate"—something short of an explicit threat.

Simultaneous with the Cartoon Crisis, Tony Blair concluded his long drawn-out attempt to criminalize the criticism of religions. The proposal had been made several years before with the active support from the Muslim Council of Britain, the Anglican Church and other religious organizations, backed by large parts of the British left. It originally constituted parts of the British Terror Acts in the wake of 9/11. It is important to examine the details of this proposal. The original proposal did not only address threatening actions, but also "abusive" and "insulting" expressions aimed against religions, *no matter whether this offense was intentional or not.* [86] The potential punishment for this crime was no less than seven years imprisonment, a fine with no upper limit, or both. This implies that if a citizen puts forward a commentary which some religious person happens to find insulting, no matter what the intention of that citizen might have been, then this act may be punished very severely.

This very radical delimitation of free speech in England, the country where free speech originally developed in the 17th century, called for resistance. The House of Lords found the proposal problematic and attempted, on October 25 2005, to restrict the proposal to address intentional, threatening acts only, and directly demanded the addition of a clause protecting free speech.[87] Amendments by the House of Lords, however, are merely consultative, and the more radical law text was kept by the Labour government with its majority in the House of Commons. After a campaign against the proposal by the comedian Rowan Atkinson and British free speech supporters, the proposal was set for vote towards the end of January 2006, in the midst of the exploding Cartoon Crisis. During the final debate in the House of Commons, Deputy Secretary of State Paul Goggins made clear that after the expected passing of the law the next day, the publication of the Danish cartoons would be illegal in Britain, and Sir Iqbal Sacranie, the head of Muslim Council of Britain who had been a driving force behind the proposal, asserted that after the passing of the vote, the very use of the expression "Islamic terrorism" would be unlawful; such an expression would incite religious hatred by erroneously associating Islam with terrorism. Labour, at the time, had a comfortable 40-odd majority in the House, and everyone saw it as a matter of convenience to vote the radical proposal through the House of Commons.

On the very day, however, Blair failed. Convinced that the adoption of the proposal was unproblematic, he took early leave and left Parliament. The party "whip," whose task it is to ensure that all party members stick to the party line, had not done his work properly. A group of 21 Labour "backbenchers" had secretly agreed that the proposal was problematic, and they voted against it.⁸⁸ The proposal fell by a single vote. If Blair had not gone home early, there would have been equal votes, and his vote as PM would have been decisive.⁸⁹ This defeat for the protection of religion gave rise to rage amongst religious organizations in Great Britain, and it is an open question to what extent the contemporaneous campaign against the Danish cartoons, in many Muslim countries as well as England, was intended to pressure the British public to secure the passing of the act. In the spring of 2008, the Archbishop of Canterbury, head of the Anglican Church, reopened the case and demanded new legislation, supported by Muslim organizations. The issue has not left the British political agenda since.

But even the weakened version authored by the House of Lords, which was adopted instead and became valid from October 1, 2007, has created a new category of crime in England and has probably sharpened the interpretation of the whole of the Public Order Act in general, of which it is a part. The law was, for example, used by the London police force on May 20ᵗʰ 2008 at a demonstration against Scientology in front of the London headquarters of that organization. There a 15 year-old boy was ordered to remove his home-made poster declaring that the organization was not a religion, but a dangerous cult. The police addressed the boy: "You are not allowed to use that word," the word "cult." The boy was given 15 minutes to remove the poster, and a police officer read aloud the paragraphs of the Public Order Act determining that a person is guilty of a criminal offense if he "... displays any writing, sign or other visible representation which is threatening, abusive or insulting, thereby causing that or another person harassment, alarm or distress" (Ch. 64. 4A1.b). The boy, for his part, was well-prepared and cited a verdict from the British High Court from 1984 where Judge Latey had established that "Scientology is both immoral and socially obnoxious. [...] In my judgment it is corrupt, sinister and dangerous." When the boy thus refused to withdraw, the police presented him with a court summons and confiscated the poster as evidence. The case gave rise to considerable debate in Britain and, after human rights protests, the charge was later dropped. But there is no doubt that even the watered-down version of the "Racial and Religious Hatred Act," with its explicit attempt to protect free speech, is in the process of constituting a new class of crimes in England and is thus limiting free speech in its very country of birth.

Three years later, history repeated itself in Norway. Again, a governing Labour party, the Norwegian "Arbeiderparti," came very close to passing a law to protect religious sensibilities, thereby severely curtailing free speech. In 2009, Arbeiderpartiet led a coalition government including also the left-wing party Sosialistisk Venstreparti (Socialist Left Party) as well as Senterpartiet (The Center Party). Discussing a removal of the blasphemy law no longer in use, the Center Party proposed it be substituted by an extension to the law against racism that would also cover criticism of religions. Thus, the government proposal presented in December 2008–January 2009: "The government will extend the law against hate speech in such a way that it also involves qualified attacks on religions or world views." The Center Party put great effort into persuading the coalition partners to accept such a proposal, and in late January 2009, its leader Liv Signe Navarsete made the triumphant remark: "We have lost many issues concerning value politics in this government. I rejoice in the fact that we have won this case and forced the Labour Party to its knees." Labour expressed its acceptance of the proposal and, with a comfortable majority in Parliament, nothing seemed to be able to stop the proposal from passing. Now however a public debate ensued. Many academics and commentators, even the Norwegian church, came out against the proposal. A more important development, however, was the fact that local Center Party leaders began to air doubts. On February 3rd the Chairman of Parliament, former Labour PM Thorbjørn Jagland, came out in a highly unusual action; he published a commentary against the PM of his own party for accepting the proposal and using the party "whip" to ensure agreement in the Labour Group in Parliament. He wrote that in a case concerning Freedom of Speech, it would be a paradox to prevent the Labour Group from freely expressing its points of view on the issue. The day after this column, the Center Party suddenly withdrew the proposal: "We cannot live with the impression that we are out to curtail free speech", Navarsete now said, "We must recognize that the process and debate in no way reflect our point of view and our intentions." The confusion of the Center Party, however, was nothing as compared to how this pirouette left the major coalition partner, the Labour Party. PM Stoltenberg, who had been speaking warmly about the proposal a few days earlier, now had to back down at an emergency press conference. Here, he claimed the intention had been to extend freedom of speech rather than limit it, and the plan was now to make the proposal more "precise" before a renewed presentation in 2011.

Both the British and the Norwegian cases raise the question as to whether European Social Democrats may go as far as to actively work for drastic curtailments of freedom of expression. In both cases, they presented legislative proposals to dismantle some of the most basic parts of the Enlightenment heritage. In both cases, the pullback was possible only after far-reaching protests, and gave rise to internal splits in the parties. Norwegian commentators wondered about the strange carelessness with which the Labour Party first adopted the proposal and then rejected it, without sensing the importance of the basic principles of democracy with which they were tinkering. The pressure on free speech originating in the OIC and supported by Islamist movements and Islamist terror actions around the globe thus also receives support from substantial parts of the Western left, even at the governmental level. These parts of the Western left have, in a strange development, given up their old universalist principles, seemingly without even explicitly discussing it and almost without knowing it, in order to support culturalism instead.[90]

These examples of the workings of strong organizations and governments in order to curtail freedom of expression indicates why it is highly provincial to try to isolate the case of the cartoons as a unique and purely Danish event, and thus divorce it from comparison with the large cluster of parallel international cases. The Danish Cartoon Crisis is but one strand in a world-wide policy of pressure against free speech, that began many years ago and is still in the process of development.

So what of the whole discussion for and against "sarcasm, mockery, and ridicule" in relation to multiculturalism? Can the Muslim right not to be insulted or defamed be defended from a multicultural position? Seen from the point of view of the "hard," culturalist concept of culture, the case seems clear: culture has a right to be preserved in the larger society—but this also entails that it has the right to an unhindered own organic development, as it had in its former homeland. This implies that others must not criticize it, not to mention proselytizing among its members, and it entails that it has—by explicit or implicit means—the right to maintain the culture of its members within the host culture and its religion. From this point of view, there is no doubt: sarcasm, mockery and ridicule must yield, if immigrant culture should be protected to continue unchanged. It remains, however, an unsolved problem for hard multiculturalism that it has no set of concepts or criteria to determine how clashes of interest or principle between different cultures within one society should be regulated and decided, or compromises formed. In any case, they are not considered as issues which may be discussed publicly in verbal struggles. As the education director Dr. Yussof in Kota Bahru explains with direct reference to the Danish drawings: instead of just publishing them, there should have been a "civilized dialogue" behind closed doors between the believers and the publishers about the feasibility of publication. If it would not suit the faithful as those touched by the act (in this case the Muslim organizations of faith) then, in the name of civilized dialogue, publishers should be restrained from doing it. In that case, a sort of institution of clandestine arbitration is called for, functioning before such cases are allowed to enter the public scene (see the column "Who may criticize?" below).

But the other hard culturalism, the nationalist variant, might just as well argue about all varieties of insult: why should nationalist traditions be defamed? Does not the attack on sarcasm, mockery, and ridicule constitute an insult against the Danish or Western culture and its century-old tradition of political satire aimed at all parts of the political, social, and religious life and at groups operating there? Should not Danish culture be protected so that this cultural tradition can survive? This would, of course, be downright incompatible with (what some claim is) the legitimate interest of the Muslim culture. Hard multiculturalism has no principled answer to this argument (recall, for example, Kymlicka's inability to find criteria for "targeted" multiculturalism) and the only possible solution would probably be complete segregation, so that the individual cultures lose any contact with others and are thus completely protected against the strange behaviors, critical gazes and unkind comments from unbelievers, strangers and deviants. But would such a separation be possible without territorial segregation à la Lévi-Strauss? And would such a segregation not strongly approach the "ethno-pluralism" of the international extreme right, which celebrates the diversity of cultural traditions and the rights of different groups to continue those traditions unhindered in their own territory (Alain de Benoist)? Would such total protection be anything other than apartheid?

Softer and more sophisticated multiculturalists with liberal leanings (like Kymlicka) would, of course, never go in such a direction. As we saw, Kymlicka invoked the distinction between group rights for external protection and for internal restriction, where the former are deemed democratically legitimate, but not so the latter. But which status would the idea of protection of certain groups against insult have in these terms? The idea of freely giving up on freedom of speech in order to prevent offense to certain cultures is most often presented as though it is an act of the former character: it serves to protect those groups. But does it have that character in reality? Is there anything in the tradition of cartoon satire which prevents a religious group from continuing its worship, from "expressing its culture" or otherwise participating in society? Quite on the contrary, it could be argued, as does editor Flemming Rose, that being the object of cartoon satire puts a cultural group on equal footing with other groups in society which are natural and legitimate targets for ridicule, so that the cartoons should actually be viewed as a step towards integrating those groups in public debate on a par with other groups. The attempts at preventing offense rather belong to Kymlicka's latter category, that of internal restrictions. It is, in the first place, the believers themselves who are subject to the ban on depiction and thus give up part of their freedom of expression—but is the idea of preventing mockery of beliefs not also in order to prevent group members from getting the idea that they might leave the group and seek other beliefs and affiliations? Recently, such an idea was broadcast on Muslim TV screens all over the world when the popular TV preacher Muhammad al-Munajid from *Al-Jazeera* declared (March 30 2008) the following:

> Some of these heretics say: "Islam is not the private property of anyone." So what do they want? They say: "No sect has a monopoly on Islam." So what do they want? They say: "We want to issue rulings." Someone who is ignorant, who does not know any Arabic, or who has no knowledge of Islamic jurisprudence wants to issue rulings?! They say: "We reinterpret the texts." There is a very dangerous conspiracy against the religion of Islam in newspapers

and in what these people say. [...] These people are a mixture of Western, local, and imported ideologies, but they want to express their views with regard to religious rulings. This is the prerogative of religious scholars, not of ignorant people, the prerogative of knowledgeable people, not of fools or heretics. [...] The problem is that they want to open a debate on whether Islam is true or not, and on whether Judaism and Christianity are false or not. In other words, they want to open up everything for debate. Now they want to open up all issues for debate. That's it. It begins with freedom of thought, it continues with freedom of speech, and it ends up with freedom of belief.[91]

In Malaysia, we met exactly the same argument from the Dean from Kuala Terengganu. The reason why freedom of speech cannot be permitted, at least not in all subjects, is that freedom of speech leads to freedom of belief, and freedom of belief leads to conversion, to apostasy. This interpretation also better fits the intriguing fact that most of the protesting Islamists had never seen the Danish cartoons and consequently were unable to mobilize any personal insult over them. Not very many Danish Muslims have subscriptions to *Jyllands-Posten*, and the few who do could simply quit their subscription in order to avoid further insult.

So it is not the direct perception of the cartoons, which constitutes the insult, rather it is the very knowledge that such cartoons exist. But how could this be problematic? Because Muslims who are perhaps weak in faith (such persons exist in all groups of believers) might see them, maybe begin to giggle or even begin to reflect on the fact that there exist, in a free society, other possibilities, such as the freedom to become a non-practicing Muslim, to change one's faith, or even to adopt a stance critical of all religions, such as some of the cartoons suggested. In this sense, the argument against insult is not so much an external protection of the group as it is motivated by the prevention of the free choice of group members to leave the group.[92] This may, of course, also be called "protection of the group" in a broader sense, but taken in this broader sense, there is indeed a great deal of overlap between Kymlicka's two ideal categories. So, if the protection of the group against defamation both (1) constitutes a violation of the rights of other groups, and (2) provides internal suppression within the group, then such a group right would not be legitimate as measured in terms of Kymlicka's liberal multiculturalism.

This can easily be seen if the argument is generalized. Consider the case in which the same right not to be defamed or offended could be claimed by other religions, even other associations or social groups in general.[93] Public debate would quickly wither away to leave only the ritual exchange of courteous remarks behind, which is exactly as, for example, the Malaysian press appears to behave. Then the spokesmen for the nice "tone" in public debate would realize their ideal society; an ethos of "respectful" and "honorable" dialogue would reign in public life. This would be bought, however, at the price of a *de facto* prohibition against "defamation of religion," against criticism of religion, against social critique. We would then live in a society like that described by the Indian author Chirita in Malaysia: a society of lies and concealment, dissimulation and nauseating deference to those in religious and political power.

Political Columns

Culturalism: Culture as Political Ideology

The controversy over multiculturalism has changed the political fronts. The left defends respect for minority cultures, while the right stands guard over the national culture. But these two fronts merely constitute two variants of a culturalist ideology.

Culturalism is the idea that individuals are determined by their culture, that these cultures form closed, organic wholes, and that the individual is unable to leave his or her own culture but rather can only realize him or herself within it. Culturalism also maintains that cultures have a claim to special rights and protections, even if they violate individual rights at the same time.

The culturalism of today, in which culture becomes a political ideology, thrives on both the left and the right. Most well known is leftwing multiculturalism, which has a radical, anti-democratic variant as well as one that suggests that it is possible to harmonize multiculturalism and (social-) liberal views. However, multiculturalism can also exist in forms that belong to the far right, such as the French concepts of ethnopluralism, the idea that all cultures have the right to autonomy so long as each remains in its own territory. This approach results in political conclusions to the effect that immigrants must either allow themselves to be assimilated lock, stock and barrel, including everything from their religion down to their cuisine, or else return to their original native countries (assuming that such countries exist).

Culturalism has an entire range of categories in common with nationalism; indeed, nationalism in reality constitutes a sub-variant of culturalism, in which a single culture provides the basis for the state. Therefore, it does not come as a surprise that the present nationalist renaissance in European politics makes use of culturalist ideas to a great extent. On the local stage, the Danish People's Party is the obvious example with its re-adoption of Danish nationalist ideas from the 19th and early 20th centuries, including its radical anti-Enlightenment stance. Since the Mohammed cartoon controversy, the party has felt a strategic need to join the defenders of freedom of speech against Islamist machinations. Irrespective of what one can surmise to be the motives for this about turn, it has to be noted that it was possible only as a result of the party claiming freedom of speech as a "Danish value," as though it were a home-grown invention. This is naturally a culturalist falsification of history: freedom of speech is not a Danish invention. Its roots are of course found in international Enlightenment movements; freedom of speech is a high-quality foreign import. It is something that liberal and democratically-minded forces, by dint of great effort and at great cost to themselves, managed to force through in the face of Danish absolutism and the Danish State Church until that right was finally formalized in the June Constitution of 1849, the first democratic constitution in Denmark.

An immediate problem in Denmark (and also in international politics) is that there is culturalism on both sides of the political spectrum. On the left we hear culturalist battle cries calling for the recognition of the most anti-modern and unappetizing cultural practices; on the right we hear the battle cry of Danishness and the reawakening of a most anti-modern and unpalatable Danish nationalism. These two versions of culturalism are natural enemies, even though they base themselves on the same spurious system of ideas. For a hundred years, French and German nationalisms were each other's main opponents, yet frequently drew on exactly the same intellectual heritage. One culturalism is the automatic enemy of the other precisely because culturalisms are naturally particularisms, which is to say, they each select their chosen people, and not all people can be equally chosen. But this strident antiphony of particularisms, in which the reinforcement of the culturalism of the left frightens more voters to move towards the culturalism of the right and vice versa, ought not to persuade anyone into believing that culturalisms of the left and the right constitute the main antithesis in modern politics. On the contrary, the conflict is between Enlightenment and culturalism; between democracy, political liberalism, the rights of the individual, universalism and the Enlightenment on the one hand, and the unenlightened maintenance of culture, tradition and authenticity on the other, and the conservative opinion that the individual is linked by fate to a specific culture.

There are consequently two kinds of criticism of Islam that often sound as though they were related, but which must not be confused. One of them criticizes Islam because it is a foreign religion that is irreconcilable with Danish values and Danish traditions. This is the criticism of one culturalism expressed by another; it is Jesus Christ against Mohammed;

it is one mythological figure in fateful conflict with another. The other criticism, meanwhile, attacks Islamism, not because it is un-Danish, but because it is a totalitarian ideology related to the various forms of totalitarianism during the inter-war period in Europe. This criticism is an informed criticism of a political movement that is opposed to an open society and fundamental democratic principles. This criticism is not directed at Islam as such, but rather focuses on ideological, political and social barriers that cut off individuals from their rights. Whether these barriers have their background in cultural, political, religious or other dogmas is, ultimately, irrelevant.

There is scarcely a more important task in contemporary politics and political philosophy than giving full consideration to developing universal enlightenment, and with the greatest possible force, turning against both the prevailing right- and left-wing forms of culturalism and their enslavement of the individual in his or her "culture."

A glance at the criticisms directed by the left at the culturalism of the right provides a point of reference for how far it has strayed from its starting point in the Enlightenment. It also reveals how little the left actually knows about its political opponents in the battle that has developed over the last few decades, during which the question of culture has appeared on the agenda and gradually replaced a prior debate on divergent political utopias.

Let us take a look at the task facing left-wing culturalism and at the way in which the two culturalisms are blind to the similarities between them. In Denmark, it is remarkable that since the defeat of the left in the parliamentary elections of 2001, left-wing culturalism has not yet been able to produce an analysis of its ostensible opponent, the Danish People's Party. It seems that many years after its defeat, the left has not been able to move on. It continues to base its ideas on what it sees as the only thing applicable to the right: that it is "racist" and that the voters that the right has succeeded in mobilizing are either "racist" or suffer from other psychological defects such as "Islamophobia." Political analysis seems in some way to have been taken over by a rather slipshod social-psychological diagnostic. Naturally, this finds expression in repeated accusations of racism aimed at right-wing culturalism.

In his book *Islams and Modernities*, the Syrian philosopher Aziz Al-Azmeh points out that differentialism, which is a more generalized concept for racism, has undergone what he calls a "de-racialization." "Race" is no longer used as a valid form of identification, and all that is left is the culturalist argument. In Denmark, the Danish People's Party should be understood as being a culturalist party whose attitudes are an expression of a modern differentialism. No major political movement in Denmark or anywhere else in Europe bases its platform on racism. Such a position is no longer held by the elite and is not represented by any but radical losers without political significance.

But why is the left unable to diagnose culturalism in its political opponent and to launch an offensive against the opinions that the party really represents? Logically enough, this is due to the fact that they allow themselves to be blinded by the same cultural views as their homologous opponents: they are themselves culturalist. This naturally establishes limits to the extent to which they are able to analyze their opponents' position.

Both culturalisms express respect for cultural differences and espouse their belief in the protection of these identities. Right- and left-wing culturalists merely maintain these protective measures under various guises. Left-wing culturalists claim that various distinct cultures should be able to co-exist in the same territory or in the same state, where, formally or informally, different jurisdictions for individuals are applied, according to the cultural group into which those individuals were born. Right-wing culturalists maintain the same attitude towards preserving cultural identity, but each culture should be in its own territory, each culture in its own country.

An important and frequently overlooked effect of the growing importance of the two forms of culturalism on contemporary politics is that social groups that had previously organised themselves on the basis of "interests" are now increasingly organizing themselves on the basis of "culture." This naturally divides these groups politically.

British philosopher Brian Barry writes that:

> The proliferation of special interests fostered by multiculturalism is [...] conducive to a politics of 'divide and rule' that can only benefit those who benefit most from the status quo. There is no better way of heading off the nightmare of unified political action

> by the economically disadvantaged that might issue in common demands than to set different groups of the disadvantaged against one another. Diverting attention away from shared disadvantages such as unemployment, poverty, low-quality housing and inadequate public services is an obvious long-term anti-egalitarian objective. Anything that emphasizes the particularity of each group's problems at the expense of a focus on the problems they share with others is thus to be welcomed.[94]

If underprivileged groups can be persuaded to become more concerned with religion, culture and identity, they will be split, and the focus will be moved away from concrete political problems. The current configuration in Danish politics, in which many disadvantaged Danes support the culturalist right, while immigrants and multiculturalists support the left, is a striking example of this phenomenon. It probably constitutes one of the main structural reasons for the profound crisis in the Social Democratic Party, whose core voters are now distributed according to cultural affiliation rather than their own interests. The question poses itself as to how long the Social Democratic Party and the rest of the Left intend to allow themselves to be guided by the delusion of culturalism.

The Left's progressive involvement with the hardline concept of culture both in Denmark and internationally is one of the most important and least recognized political developments of the last thirty years. Culturalism, in its political and left-wing forms, is by no means a recent phenomenon. Its first appearance on the world stage came in 1947, when American anthropologists attempted to derail the UN Human Right's Charter. They refused to accept that it was possible to presume universal human rights, since this would suppress individual cultures. However, the Western left—whether in its Communist, Social Democratic or social liberal variants—was at that time so international in its views that culturalism remained below the surface. Meanwhile, in the 1980s and 90s a vacuum was created by the demise of Marxism and its role as a reference point for left-wing parties in the West. The profoundly conservative cultural ideas of culturalism subsequently and surreptitiously moved into this arena. The surprising thing is that this transformation took place largely without a blow being struck, although culturalism is in many respects diametrically opposed to Marxism. Whereas Marxism maintains that culture is a superstructure on social economic regularities, culturalism contends that the economy of a society depends on its culture and the value systems of that culture, or at least that the economy is indistinguishable from all other cultural features in the society in question.

In this way, culturalism constitutes a kind of anthropological counter-revolution that turns Marxism on its head. The argumentation of the left in the 1960s and 1970s was above all the economy, the class struggle, means of production, sociology, political systems and resources that were seen as crucial, and it was quite rare and peripheral for the term "culture" to appear. The reverse now applies, and culture attracts far more attention than economics and society, but there has never been any major confrontation in which one model was exchanged for another, as might be expected in ordinary political debate. There have been no furious confrontations between parties concerning the absolute importance of the economy or culture. The transition between opposites has been achieved through a gentle transformation, almost from one day to the next, often without the figures embodying the two attitudes being aware of what was taking place. This is perhaps due to the fact that both Marxism and culturalism have an even simpler and deeper pattern in common: the phenomenon of an oppressed group in relationship to the dominant majority. It is then possible to take the political side of the oppressed following the left-wing slogan of the 1970s: "An oppressed people is always right." This was understood quite literally, with implications that far surpassed the argument that an oppressed people have the right to be liberated from their oppression. They were now right with respect to all their cultural dogmas, regardless of whether what these dogmas maintain is just or true; what was important was that they were derived from the culture of an oppressed people, an argument purely *ad hominem*. It was thus possible to replace the working class with "the oppressed culture," even if the implication of this was that emancipation was to be replaced by disciplined culturalism, which maintains antiquated and pre-modern norms—which is to say, an absolute reversal, both in terms of philosophy and values, of what the left used to stand for.

In her book, *La tentation obscurantiste*, the French journalist Caroline Fourest presents an interesting hypothesis regarding the advance of what we call left-wing culturalism. She notes that the two great prototypical points of identification for the European left during and after World War II were the anti-totalitarian struggle on the one hand and decolonization and anti-imperialism on the other. For a long time they were able to co-exist without conflict but, following the important growth of Islamism in the Islamic countries and among Muslim immigrant groups, the left found itself divided according to which of the two principal causes was considered most important. If the anti-totalitarian struggle was considered crucial, people tended to turn against Islamism as yet another form of totalitarianism from the inter-war period, but if the anti-imperialist struggle was considered paramount, the tendency was to support Islamism as a legitimate challenge to Western imperialism, at first in the colonialist version and subsequently in the globalized version. This latter choice naturally opened up the left to culturalism. This turns out to be a twofold problem for the hardline, multi-cultural left wing: culture means too little and too much at once. On the one hand, it is very important in that it provides an individual with an identity and therefore the right to political care and protection—conservatism built into the culturalist concept of culture. On the other hand, the left has historically maintained that culture has no meaning, for it is economic and social conditions that are the critical determining factors. Yet at the same time, this Marxist doctrine is behind the multiculturalist idea that all cultures, irrespective of how anti-democratic and anti-liberal they are, can a priori co-exist in the same society. This duality is naturally a constant source of confusion for hardline left-wing multiculturalism. Culture is at once an immutable source of profound identity and at the same time a purely surface phenomenon based on economic determinants. It is naturally impossible for both to be true.

Islamophobia

One encounters the concept of "Islamophobia" with increasing frequency; it is used to stigmatize any criticism of Islamism and aspects of Islam that conflict with democracy, human rights and the constitutional state. The hardline, culturalist concept of culture throws a crucial light on the problems raised by the word, first deployed by the Islamic world organization, OIC, in its struggle against human rights, and more specifically the freedom of speech. The campaign against the cartoons published in the Danish newspaper, *Jyllands-Posten*, and the subsequent Mohammed crisis was an example of this struggle. The word "Islamophobia" is increasingly used by Islamic organizations and hardline multiculturalists in an attempt to limit criticism of Islamic movements. Both valid and unfounded criticisms of various forms of Islam are brushed aside by the argument that they constitute "Islamophobia," and are thus grouped with racism, anti-Semitism, homophobia, etc. In this way, the concept has also been able to infiltrate the Left, where it is seen used alongside "xenophobia" and the other terms listed above. The word, even semantically, with its clinical suffix "phobia," expresses a negative quality; it combines a critical analysis with the implication of mental illness. However, the crucial problem with the word "Islamophobia" is in fact that, unlike the other words that are similarly constructed, it applies to a set of opinions. Racism, homophobia and so on are words that speak to a disproportionate reaction to qualities intrinsic to an individual (the colour of their skin, their sexual orientation, etc.), but Islam is not a race. Islam is a set of beliefs exactly like other sets of beliefs such as Christianity, communism, liberalism, conservatism, Nazism, Hinduism and many other widely divergent intellectual doctrines of a religious, political or philosophical nature. This is not altered by the fact that certain Muslims, including Islamists, are adamant in their conviction that their set of beliefs is particularly prominent and transcends conventional debate, development and revision. As two Danish democratic mottos have it, democracy is based on the principle of "taking sides according to opinion" and "holding one view until you adopt another."

Philosophies are susceptible to open and on-going criticism and revision, and if you are resolutely convinced of your position, you are naturally welcome to attempt to uphold this true faith in an unaltered form, but you cannot compel others to participate in this by asking them to refrain from criticism. This is what the word "Islamophobia" attempts to do. In this, the left has devised a useful attitude towards Islamism through its uncritical adoption of the term, with its intentionally manipulative and disciplinary effect. This approach has also served to paralyze the left's own ability to reflect. Any criticism of culturalism is deflected and condemned as Islamophobia, and as such it is politically excluded.

The acceptance of the term Islamophobia is achieved precisely by invoking a hardline concept of culture, as if there were such a thing as *homo islamicus*. This is carried out in alliance with those various practices in Islam that specifically attempt to give the Muslim religion the quality of fate, requiring, in all circumstances, that male spouses in mixed marriages convert to Islam, while information regarding other choices is suppressed, and most importantly, with respect to the prohibition against apostasy. (Apostasy is always punished, either by a fine, "re-education," the confiscation of property and compulsory divorce from the husband or wife, by so-called "civil death" or even by real death.) For this reason, "Islamophobia" leaves a particularly strange taste in the mouth. The word transforms religion into race.

The reason why intellectual Islamism has succeeded in infiltrating international forums, the political left and liberal groups, is that is has been able to gain general acceptance of the cultural argument. This has been achieved through the popular anthropological concept of culture, culturalism. It is all the more harmful to the democratic debate, as it tends to de-politicize dogmas that are essentially political and as such are open to criticism—and insult.

Political opinions are one-sided by nature; liberalism, conservatism, social liberalism, social democracy, socialism and so on all compete against each other, although as a rule they are united at a more basic level, each in turn confronting fascism, communism, Islamism and other totalitarian "isms." But if a set of dogmas, a political movement, is defined as "culture," then there is a tendency for it to be immediately left in peace and for it to no longer be seen as a particular partisan and discussible point of view among others. According to this concept, cultures are organic, irreducible totalities in themselves. Hence, cultures not only have a right to existence and a claim to respect (and to have privileges conferred on them) they also have a claim to protection and to the right to continue living in an unchanging way. This was made topical in the case of the caricatures in *Jyllands-Posten*, which were accused of insulting a culture.

In the first section of this book, we asked Islamists in multicultural Malaysia why they believed it was inappropriate to criticize, mock or hurt people holding different opinions and how one might instead behave when dealing with a subject such as *Jyllands-Posten* wanted to address. A director of studies in an Islamic university explained that it is necessary to first enter into dialogue with the party you wish to criticize, before anything is printed. With the case in question, *Jyllands-Posten* ought to have called, for instance, Islamisk Trossamfund ("The Islamic Religious Community"—a Danish branch of The Muslim Brotherhood) to seek permission. The consequences for democratic discussion that this implies are quite remarkable: if this approach were systematically applied any exchange of views would be removed from the public sphere and relegated to a closed forum, in order to prioritize mediation between parties. The result of protecting cultures in this way would be to close down open public discussion, and to abandon free debate among citizens.

If one were to follow this logic, it would naturally have dramatic consequences for the way in which democracy functions. *Jyllands-Posten* caricatured scurrilous political ideas about using religion in the service of politics, as in Kurt Westergaard's famous cartoon of the prophet with a bomb in his turban, but the Islamists attempted to delegitimize *Jyllands-Posten* by accusing the newspaper of Islamophobia.

In all cases, whether in its reformist, revolutionary or terrorist variant, Islamism is in agreement that society should be organized according to the principles of sharia. When this is categorized as "culture", it becomes possible to reject any exterior criticism as "Islamophobia" or "racism" because the critics are not "respecting" a "culture." Nazism attempted something similar when it presented itself as the continuation of ancient Germanic culture; in those days, however, the critics were sharper than the left today, and they were able to see through the rhetoric. We are now in the process of witnessing how Islamist movements such as Deobandi, Wahhabism, Salafism and the Muslim Brotherhood (directly influenced by Italian fascism and the French fascist Alexis Carrel) are protected by the "cultural" argument: to wit, they are not recognized to be political programs, but are instead viewed as real "cultures" which *eo ipso* cannot be criticized. But as soon as cultures enter the political arena, they must, by definition, be as accountable to discussion and criticism as all other associations, groups, parties and movements that make political demands. In this regard, neither priests, imams or clerics of any faith have an ounce more right to respect than any other individual simply because they make use of divine rhetoric in their political demands.

Free Speech and "Those in Power"

During the aggressive debate pro and con the cartoons in *Jyllands-Posten*, the opponents intensively sought for arguments which might legitimize their spontaneous dislike of the publication of the cartoons, arguments to counterweigh the free speech proclamations which they, at the same time, felt obliged to make. You could have heard, for instance, that the decisive criminal aspect was that the cartoons had been published in a center-right newspaper; if the very same cartoons had appeared in a left-wing paper, they might have been alright. Another argument was that the cartoons targeted a minority group while free speech was meant to be used against "those in power" and not against minorities.

Let us investigate this argument. Legally understood, no such thing is implied by freedom of expression. It is not claimed by the First Amendment to the American Constitution or by Article 77 of the Danish Constitution that free speech is a right only admitted to people criticizing powerful groups or persons, while state censorship in all other cases may be freely undertaken. The first part of the argument seems to rest on the idea that the primary motivation of freedom of expression is to direct the attention of the public to cases of abuse of power. This is, indeed, a very important function in public debate. The argument, however, rests on the further premise that it is evident for everybody to see who are "the powers that be." The idea seems to be that "those in power" are easy to identify: they wear top hats, expensive suits, smoke cigars and drive big cars and populate large downtown offices and look, by and large, like George Grosz's cartoons of capitalists in the 1920s. But the problem in this populist idea is that, in a pluralist democracy, it might, in many cases, not be so easy to establish who "those in power" are and who abuse the powers with which they have been entrusted. This can only be *established* as a part of ongoing public debate. Is *Jyllands-Posten* a mighty power or is it, rather, a small paper in the crisis-ridden Danish press? Were the protesting imams powerless immigrants or were they members of a powerful international network? The power of persons and institutions may change dramatically from case to case, from context to context, and the powerful very often have an obvious interest in dissimulating by posing as powerless victims calling for support.

The reality of such issues may, in many cases, only be established in the course of continuous public investigation and debate, and to deny "the powerful" the possibility of expressing and defending themselves beforehand is not only contrary to free speech, but is also contrary to the basic juridical and journalistic intuition that an accused has a right to defend himself. It is impossible, hence, to be sure that your expression is, in fact, aimed against the majority or against "the powerful" only, for it is public debate which eventually can determine who, in a given case, is powerful. A further premise for this sentimental argument is that minorities, *eo ipso*, are not powerful. We saw Kymlicka realize, more realistically, that cultural minorities may easily exert a brutal power over and against their own members, just as they may get the idea of abusing multiculturalist policies to support such a display of power or attack other groups. Thus, the problem in the idea is that there are power relations everywhere in a democratic society, from the smallest to the largest groups, and there is nowhere in society positions which are *a priori* secured against the illegitimate use of power.

Another issue (see Amartya Sen, below) is that society does not fall into nice, separate groups, such as culturalism would have us imagine, groups which are easily identified as powerful or powerless. In a modern, pluralist society it is rather the case that each individual partakes in a manifold of different groups and power relations, and such different relations will display different degrees of power. The opponents of the Muhammad Cartoons thus vacillated between saying that a minority must not be mocked and saying that you should not attack a world religion with 1.3 billion believers, claims which entail a certain tension. Is the Danish Islamic Society of Faith a weak organization of a few Danish Muslims, or is it a part of a widespread, strong international network of Muslim Brothers with supporters in many countries? In a certain sense it is both of these things at the same time, and it was the strength of Muhamed Sifaoui's documentary that proved this to be the case: it showed that the allegedly small and purely Danish organization was a part of the international Muslim Brotherhood. This documentary, which revealed and even ridiculed a Danish minority organization, should—according to the multiculturalist power argument—have been abandoned and not shown on television.

The argument is phoney because, in democratic societies, by far the majority of organizations and groups are, in fact, natural minorities. The Danish Liberal Party, the leading force in the current government coalition, is supported by a minority among the population (in recent years receiving around 25% of the popular vote). Does that imply that there is no right to criticize it? Should there be a limitation to restrict criticism to the government as a whole which has, by definition, a majority of the voters behind it? Or is it illegitimate to attack the numerous religious minority groups in the West, such as Born Again Christians, Jehovah's Witnesses, Scientologists? Or to take a worse example: was it illegitimate, in 1920s Germany, to attack the growing Nazi Party which was still a minority? Should one have postponed criticism of that movement until it finally assumed power in 1933 and became "powerful?"

It is probable that some of the proponents of the argument proposing that it is in bad taste to attack Islamist extremist groups would mean something like this: We must not attack Islamists in the West, for they have no power; we must wait until they might assume power. At bottom the argument is, of course, motivated by culturalism: all cultural groups have a dignity and are worthy of respect. If one generalizes, in this way, Benedict's old doctrine to cover extreme political and religious currents, so that they have a right to protection as "cultures," then one may easily end up thinking that free speech may be used to attack the government only, because it is the only group in a democracy which *eo ipso* represents a majority.

Culture as a Refuge

Culturalism, the vulgar anthropological concept of culture, is so much more detrimental because it tends to depoliticize issues which are essentially political. Political positions are necessarily partial: liberalism, conservatism, social liberalism, social democracy, socialism, and so on. are turned against each other, even if they (as a rule) come together on a more fundamental level, turning against fascism, communism, Islamism and other totalitarianisms. But if a political current is categorized as a "culture," there is a remarkable tendency for it to become sacred and to no longer be seen as only one, partial and discussable, point-of-view among many.

Religiously motivated policies may exploit this to avoid criticism because the vulgar anthropological concept of culture has a certain affinity to religion. Many of the societies studied by classical anthropology did not know the different distinctions, separations and modularizations of later high cultures, such as, for example, the distinctions between religion, politics, science, art and technology. Here, rather one integrated world view was articulated, where religious convictions were often central (even if anthropology's tendency to gloss over contradictions within the individual culture studied was almost never without effect). This has given rise to an automatic reaction: the assertion that religion forms the basis of the culture of a society, and that other levels simply mirror religion, a sort of anthropological turning-around of the old Marxist idea of an economic base. If one accepts the culturalist concept of culture, then it often entails that religious assumptions are given a priviledged position to be protected as "culture", no matter what unsavory political programs and demands may be associated with that religion.

This problem is not only actual in the strongly anti-democratic positions of some religious currents, but can be found all the way down to tiny details of multiculturalist legislations.[95] Why should British Sikhs be exempted from the legal prescription of helmets for bikers? Could one not just as well say that there is no human right or basic need to be able to ride a motorcycle, and that this must be one of the secular goods that a believing Sikh would have to sacrifice on the altar of his religion and chose another means of transport not irreconcilable with that faith? Why do the demands of orthodox Jews and Muslims have a special weight when they demand ritual slaughter which is, presumably, more painful for the animals than ordinary slaughter? Why do the religious-cultural authorities here have the upper hand, while the claims of animal welfare activists are not heard? Could one not say that if faith bans the eating of meat which is not prepared in a certain gruesome way, then the believer would have to renounce such nourishment and turn to other items of food? Are such cases not examples where there is, in reality, no inequality? It is the free choice of such cultures to dispense with bike riding or the eating of meat provided according to normal practices. Such exemptions are, of course, compromises which must be argued pro and con in the specific cases, but it's remarkable that "religion" and "culture" automatically give such demands a special aura, contrary to demands from other lobbies.

The Other

The sneaking deification of political discourse via the culturalist notion of culture may sometimes be read off quite directly. Very often, one hears the claim among radical multiculturalists that the special tragedy of the West is that it is incapable of understanding "the Other" or even "the radical Other." We—the writers of this book—have never encountered "the radical Other," and we believe there is reason for serious doubt that such a creature exists at all. All cultures are created by human beings who, all over the planet, have many properties in common, even while it remains true that man has been able to create impressive cultural variety on that common basis. Thus one may easily encounter something other (other ways of eating, governing, exchanging, and dressing) but hardly ever anything "radically Other" as it is often expressed, in awe, with capital O. It is an interesting fact that this concept has been imported from the historiography of religions and theology. Its central source is the early twentieth-century German historian of religion Rudolf Otto and his doctrine that religion has its foundation in the meeting with "*das ganz Andere*," the "wholly Other," that is, the holy, the godly, the sacred.

Most of the actual users of the phrase hardly know of its roots in this esoteric corner of the twentieth-century history of religion. As such, the concept is interesting. In and around the history of religion, there developed special types of new faiths, building on the fact that gradually, public access to many of the central texts of the world religions was made possible in translations, so that comparative study could find similarities between them. The way was thus opened for a synthesis of religions where one was not subject to a single orthodoxy but rather constructed a cult of "the sacred" as such, torn loose from the particular traditions that had invoked it. Several leading figures in the history of religions cultivated variants of such a meta-religion (Rudolf Otto, Mircea Eliade for example), but the tendency also spread to the sensitive middle classes in the West, where the syncretism of many religious impulses was often considered finer and more sophisticated than dogmatic tradition. Thus, such meta-religions, shopping freely in Christianity, Islam, Eastern religions, mysticism, etc. became a powerful anti-modern current in the twentieth-century middle classes, nowadays often parading under the tempting slogan of a "New Age."

A good example of this meta-religious syncretism within the history of religion is provided by Mensching's history of religions (1948). He conceives of the whole of the development of the history of religion as one long struggle to leave behind its roots in the Enlightenment and its criticism of religion. Rudolf Otto is the one who decisively conquers the Enlightenment, who powerfully reinstates irrationalism in the history of religion (87) by focusing on the very object of religion: the sacred, defined by *mysterium tremendum et fascinosum*, the dreadful and fascinating mystery. The historian of religion must consequently be a believer himself, otherwise he does not understand the object of religion. At the same time, however, his faith must be oriented towards the sacred as such, beyond the narrow orthodoxies of individual religions. This is why both rationalism and the orthodoxies of particular faiths are, according to Mensching, opponents of the historian of religion. This religious tendency within the history of religion as a discipline is, of course, highly problematic and may, with its radical anti-modernity, at times approach fascism (as was famously the case with Mircea Eliade).

The "radically Other" is an arch-example of modern syncretism of religions and shows how religious the thoughtless idea about "respect" for "other cultures" in itself is. It appears that the recent history of the concept proceeds via Jacques Derrida, who uses the term to refer to the alleged presence of the sacred anytime we encounter *"le tout Autre"* which may mean, in French, both the Other as an instance and the Other as a person. Inspired by the "face ethics" of Emmanuel Lévinas, the concept of the sacred here seeps into sociality and politics. Should one, paralyzed by sacredness, respect any Other person, just because he differs a little from oneself? Should one not rather respect *"le Même,"* the Same, to the exact same degree? Is it not rather because other persons are moral subjects just like oneself that they are entitled to be treated decently? Here, culturalism and the cult of difference become charged with irrational, theological power.

Xenophobia and Xenophilia: Two Kinds of Difference Worship

An important insight relating to "Otherness" is that xenophobia and xenophilia—exaggerated fear of strangers and exaggerated celebration of strangers—are intimately related, even if each naturally takes the other as its opponent. Both of them rest on the culturalist notion of culture: the idea that the other constitutes a foreign, unchangeable and holistic essence, which may then be threatening to you or which you may love and defend unreservedly. In this way, both are outgrowths of the cult of the particular (one's own or the others' particularity), and they characteristically increase and decrease in the same historical periods, typically anti-Enlightenment periods where irrational and reactionary views of the world are otherwise blooming. Nobody has seen this better than the Syrian philosopher Aziz Al-Azmeh in his diagnosis of what he calls "differentialism," the celebration of differences.

> With economic deregulation came also correlative social and cultural deregulation, ideologized by communalist, anti-state paternalism on the part of western Non-Governmental Organizations and their local analogues, which became not only distributors of aid, but also loci for the production of culturalist knowledge and social practice in the name of Difference, a sort of gentrification of backwardness. Mass social and economic marginalization also led in the South to results analogous to those in the North. Among these is the strong appeal of the ultra-conservative hyper-nationalist populism with a chiliastic flavor which we call radical Islamism, or which in India is associated with movements like the RSS (Rashtriya Swayamsevak Sangh). Both political Islam and the RSS—and indeed also Revisionist Zionism so overwhelmingly central in Israel today—followed the rhythm of modern world history: in their emergence simultaneously with Fascism in the 1920s and 1930s under al-Banna, Golwalkar and Jabotinsky, and in their revival simultaneously with the retreat of modernism and with the spurning and denigration of the Enlightenment, and the correlative revival in the West of conservative ideologies, religious and secular—a revival officiated under a benign signature as well

> as a malignant one, the one xenophobic and the other xenophilic, both premised on a culturalist differentialism which has recently become hegemonic, and both of which, in two different spirits, speak of 'cultural specificity' which, towards the end of the twentieth century, came to perform the same conceptual functions as race had earlier performed. Racial, national and religious 'profiling' as practiced since September 11, most hysterically in the US where it is accentuated by the stridency of Republicanist Protestantism, is unthinkable without the differentialism I am talking about (Al-Azmeh 2003, 29).

Cultural differentialism—the celebration of cultural differences—now assumes the same role as the concept of race did earlier. Differentialism exists in its positive variant, xenophilia, or its negative variant, xenophobia. In both cases, the individual is caught up in the prison of culture. Al-Azmeh acutely diagnoses these tendencies in the European fascisms of the interwar period, among which he (as does Mehdi Mozaffari) counts Islamism, founded in 1928 with direct inspiration from contemporary European totalitarianisms. Mozaffari counts four such major movements —Italian fascism, bolshevism, nazism, and Islamism, in that order—all of them motivated by the urge to reinstate former imperial glory by different means, in the Islamist case the goal, of course, being the Caliphate. Al-Azmeh sees this differentialist tendency of the interwar period coming back today in different guises, in the American and Israeli right-wing movements, in current political Islam, as well as among the NGOs obsessed with teaching the natives their own "culture." Xenophilia, just like xenophobia, locks the individual into his culture as a mere, typical representative of it, and it thus constitutes, in his striking words, a "gentrification of backwardness". To be premodern becomes an ennobling quality in and of itself. The current left-wing cult of "real" Muslims as opposed to more modern Muslims clearly displays this tendency. In Denmark, the extreme left-wing party "Enhedslisten" (The Unity List), for instance, boasted about their nomination of a veiled woman for parliamentary elections by claiming they were the first Danish party to have a "real Muslim" running for office, thereby discarding the many already active Danish Muslim politicians with more modern and moderate world views as less real Muslims.

Al-Azmeh conceives Islamism as being very far from that return to a purified, original Islam, as it often portrays itself. Rather, Islamism must be seen as a current with deep roots in the European history of ideas. Here, Al-Azmeh makes an important distinction between reactionary versions of Islamist fundamentalism, turned towards the past. On the one hand: Saudi Wahhabism, Sudanese Mahdism, Afghan Talibans, etc. On the other hand: modern Islamism has completely different roots, closely related to political currents in the West and in other religions. They feed on the availability of a proto-fascist, populist right-wing terminology and should be seen as parallel to the Indian Hindu fascism of the RSS party. With their roots in the interwar period, they suffered a backlash in the decades after World War II while they gained new impetus from the 1980s onwards, with the Iranian revolution and a renewed capitalist crisis. "Cultural difference," as we know it from "hard" multiculturalism, is not only a current which colors and governs large parts of Western thought and policies regarding "cultural" issues; this differentialism is an active force contributing to shaping such non-Western culturalist currents from the inside. Thus, Islamism forms part of a large historical culturalist movement emphasizing and developing cultural differences. We offer a long quote to display the range and complexity of al-Azmeh's amazing analysis:

> Briefly stated, discourse on matters Islamic at present is characterized, broadly and in the form in which it enters the public sphere, by what we might call a neo-Renanism, the reference being, of course, to Ernest Renan's famous theories about the congenital incapacity of the Semitic mind to produce science and philosophy, but to excel nevertheless in the realm of poetry—a discourse based on taxonomic antitheses. We have a politilogical neo-Renanism which speaks, among other things, of the essential inappropriateness of democracy for countries characterized as Muslim because democracy goes against the grain; as a corollary, we have the proposition propounded in many circles that democracy for such countries is best achieved if they were to be ruled by groups which best correspond to the authentic nature of these societies, which is Islam. Correlatively, we also have a neo-Renanist pseudo-sociology, which takes the populist declamations of authenticity

for accurate descriptions of social reality and which denies the realities of secularism in Arab life on grounds of congenital incapacity, served up under the title of 'revivalism' and the trope of return. This discourse has as its Leitmotif a culturalist differentialism, that is to say, a culturalist ethnology which supposes 'cultural meaning', including the trope of return, to be determinant at once of action as of the interpretation of action. This is a matter to which I have given considerable thought and I have concluded not only that culturalism uses the same figures and tropes that had been previously employed in racialist discourses, but that like racialism it operates in a rather simple manner, which consists of selecting visible tokens of ethnographic distinctiveness, which could be the color of the skin, a certain manner of dress, or certain propositions concerning the organization of gender relations, then proceeding to give these the status of iconic markers or of stigmata of otherness—or correlatively of inwardness, as nodes of ideological interpellation as I indicated earlier. These are finally served up as totalizing criteria of ethnological classification broadly conceived, constituting Muslims by analogy with ethnotypes or what older American anthropology referred to as 'patterns of culture', though I must say that Ruth Benedict was far more conscious of her appropriate intellectual genealogy than present-day proponents of the post-modern version of this conception, citing few anthropologists but appealing rather to German vitalist thinkers like Dilthey and Spengler. This is really not unlike regarding, for instance, Lederhosen and skinheads as the iconic markers of Germanity, of cowboys and mobsters as markers of the North American identity, corresponding to its inner nature and constituting its cultural genetic capital, and proceeding to construct an ethnic type based on the associations of these images (Al-Azmeh 2003, p. 41–42).

In this surprising and extraordinary piece of Marxist analysis, Al-Azmeh clearly sees the consequences of the spread of culturalism from the West and to the self-images of "ethnic groups:" the close connection to the anthropological concept of culture, the tokenism where the ethnic group takes over the stereotypical, organic description as valid for itself and elevates it to the role of a guiding light; the vitalist conception of politics which is the consequence. The latter forms a very important addition to the understanding of such movements. If an "ethnic" group assumes the "hard" concept of culture as the adequate means for its own self-description, then it tends towards seeing its political options for action simply in terms of authenticity[96], decadence, and renaissance. The "culture" takes over the organic, anthropological idea of itself, and if it faces problems, they are no longer conceived of as specific issues regarding economy, legislation, sociology, democracy, rights, international politics and the many other factors which shape political relations and options in the real world. Rather, the group turns to its anthropological self-image and conceives of actual problems as the result of the loss of an original cultural authenticity and a state of decadence now prevailing because the original state is no longer sufficiently seriously cultivated by the group, or because of foreign cultural contamination. This originality may now be found again and re-established by means of a revitalization of cultural tradition, which may (just as in the case of European fascisms) easily use modern means, media, internet, weapon technology, etc. This is the formula for al-Azmeh's conception of the modern variants of Islamism, and this explains how they may, at the same time, see themselves as searching backwards to the assumedly authentic life lived by the first generations of Muslims, and, at the same time, keep their close ties to modern, totalitarian, Western political currents, maybe even without knowing it. In that sense, culturalism is not only a problem for the West and its misunderstanding of other cultures, it is also directly playing into the strongly conservative, even totalitarian currents which form in the image of culturalism, aimed against the West.

Faced with this challenge, culturalism must be given up, in its xenophobic as well as in its xenophilic variants. Whether you unconditionally love or hate "strangers" as exotic figures is equally problematic, for "the Other" is not completely determined by strange, frightening or attractive culture from head to toe. The others are human beings like us who, on some points, differ in their world view and way of living. When this world view assumes deplorable, antidemocratic, political tendencies, we have as much right and obligation to attack it, just as we would in the case of any other antidemocratic current.

Secularism is Fundamentalist!

Religious people of any denomination who are accused of holding a fundamentalist view in secular society find a way to counterattack more and more often. As a sort of payback, they claim that secularism is itself fundamentalist, due to the fact that secularists are not inclined to give in on the secular principles of society. To strike such an uncompromising attitude is indeed fundamentalist, they say.

It is a charming rhetorical strategy that the religious fundamentalists display. When any point of view is considered fundamentalist if it is held strongly enough, then a wonderful camouflage has been created. We are all fundamentalists to the extent we all seriously hold a point of view. All viewpoints then seem to be equally legitimate, so why should religious absolutism be worse than secularism? Abracadabra!

But there is a very basic difference between fundamentalism of any sort and secularism. Fundamentalism refers to a certain kind of religious practice which shows adoration for holy texts and worships them as the literal word of God. What is commanded has to be followed without any reservation, compromise, or interpretation. Nothing is open to negotiation. Fundamentalist sects can be found in both Christianity and Islam, and they seldom have a very long history. They have often been established to give new life to the old religion, which their founding fathers have considered both decadent and trivialized. The strategy is then to go back to the sources (the holy texts) and read them faithfully and literally—not unlike many currents in the Protestant Reformation. Wahabism and Salafism are two such sects in Islam which do not date back more than approximately two hundred years. Another sect, The Muslim Brotherhood, was founded in 1928. In Christianity many of the American fundamentalist sects are likewise not more than two hundred years old. Dispensationalism, for instance, was founded in the late 19th century. In this way fundamentalism can be seen as a regular form of reformism in the old religions, which insists on a literal reading of the holy text without the interpretative distance of scholarly tradition.

When examining holy texts, they can generally be described as very heterogeneous: they contain statements of different natures; they claim the existence of holy beings; they provide accounts of the history of creation of the World and the creation of Man and his ontological character.

They prescribe the right way to live according to God, giving specific commandments concerning prayer, faith, what to eat and drink and what is absolutely prohibited to eat and drink, how to dress and how to behave as a woman and a man respectively, how to treat the infidels. The texts might also contain a complete legal system and a criminal law. If you believe all these various aspects should be read literally and followed without any reservation or moderation, then you can be said to be a fundamentalist.

Secularism on the other hand can in no possible way be defined as a fundamentalism. First of all, there is no holy text in secularism. And neither is there any knowledge of any kind by revelation. Secularism does not concern the possible existence of God, demons or other beings of extrasensory nature. It does not have any opinion of whether gods exist or not. It doesn't propose any idea of the ontology of the World or Man and neither does it contain any commandments for the behavior of the members of a congregation. Secularism is exclusively a social-political doctrine for how to organize society so that various believers and non-believers can live peacefully together, and it is most successfully achieved if the political system is not built upon religious laws or commands. Neither should political discussions be based on arguments of a religious nature. Secularism can be said to be a minimum program for the cohabitation of people of various faiths and political opinions. Basically, it simply demands toleration of those who are different from oneself—toleration of their confession, of their way of life and of their culture—even if it may be contradictory to one's own.

Secularism is therefore closely related to the Enlightenment era tradition characterized by ideas about democracy and human rights (particularly ideas about religious freedom and freedom of expression). The very term 'secularism' originates with the Englishman G.J. Holyoake, who introduced it in the 1840s and later elaborated it in his books, *The Principles of Secularism* (1860) and *The Origin and Nature of Secularism* (1896). Holyoake assumed "... the practical sufficiency of natural morality apart from Atheism, Theism or the Bible" (1860, p. 17). Moreover, the success of secularism is based on empirical experience, as the religious tensions in democratic societies after the introduction of secularism have been significantly less violent than in the centuries before.

It is very important to understand that secularism does not worship any doctrine, or the existence or non-existence of any gods. This is simply not what secularism is about. It is exclusively concerned with the political organization of modern society. It does not imply any opinion whatsoever about whether the world is created or not created, whether the holy texts really are revealed by God or not, nor does it command people how to live. In this sense secularism can be defined as a meta-principle, as an idea of how people of all confessions and worshippers of all other principles can live together.

Therefore, it is wrong to identify secularism with fundamentalism. Even if one is fanatical about secularism, one will never become a fundamentalist.

Fifty-five Questions to the New Norm

As a result of the religious pressure on freedom of speech, a new norm of behavior is developing in the West. This new set of values is not yet an explicit, formal system of rules—even if some intellectuals and politicians do strive to change the formal free speech legislation in Western countries. But until further notice, this codex remains implicit: respect must be paid to cultures and religions. Expressions of all sorts which do not satisfy this must be avoided. Given this implicit norm, however, it is difficult to know where the exact limits are. When does a draughtsman, an author or a publisher violate this new norm? This new codex cannot yet be tested in a court. This places artists, writers, moviemakers, journalists, academics, and other public persons in a dire situation. It is difficult to ascertain beforehand whether some cultural group might exist somewhere in the world who might take offense because of something one might say, write, draw, paint, or show. To obtain a more precise understanding of the new norm, it would clarify matters to have answers to the following questions.

1. May caricatures of Jesus be drawn?
2. May TV and other media broadcast calls for the murder of illustrators and authors?
3. May Disney's *Aladdin* still be shown?

4. May critical research into the origin of the Koran still be practiced in universities?
5. May critical research into the origin of the Bible still be pursued?
6. May the Koran be displayed in Western media?
7. May groups like Jehovah's Witnesses and Scientology be the subject of cartoons?
8. Are political ideologies with a religious structure protected? Should Nazism be respected?
9. May the Arab press continue publishing anti-Semitic cartoons?
10. May Voltaire's books still be sold and translated (for instance his *Muhammad, or Fanaticism*)?
11. May the work of Jorge Luis Borges be sold publicly?
12. May Saramago's *The Gospel of Jesus* be similarly sold?
13. May Ayaan Hirsi Ali direct her movie about the life of Muhammad? Could public film support be given to such projects?
14. May *Life of Brian* be shown in public?
15. May journalists investigate the relation between the word and deed of priests, imams and other clerics?
16. May traditions for the oppression of women in Muslim and Christian currents be criticized?
17. May Human Rights Watch continue publishing annual reports about violation of rights in Muslim countries?
18. May cultural groups in the West construct strict rules against free speech, that would be binding on their own faith members?
19. Are religions with organized networks of boycotts and threats more entitled to respect than others?
20. Will the Western Foreign Secretaries maintain lists of actual boycotts and threats all over the world with which one can modulate one's expression in accordance?
21. May the cartoon *Iznogood* continue?
22. Should Christians, atheists, and democrats in Muslim countries keep silent?
23. Should Muslims in the West also keep silent?
24. If several different currents exist in a religion, which one of them should be obeyed? Should the ban on depiction in Sunni

Islam be obeyed, or rather the permission to depict in Shia Islam?
25. Will a public commission be devised which may give guidance in cases of doubt?
26. How big should a minority be in order to appear in a cartoon?
27. May sociological investigations of religious groups be undertaken?
28. How should it be established whether a culture claiming to be insulted is in fact so insulted?
29. May paintings depicting religious scenes be displayed in galleries and museums?
30. May the names of illustrators and authors who are subject to death threats be published? May the fatwas?
31. May depictions of deities of competing religions be banned? May they be destroyed (the Afghan Buddha statues, for example)?
32. Are larger religions more respectable than smaller ones? Or vice versa?
33. May historians of religion conduct research into the Born Again Christians and the American right?
34. May Marx's *Theses on Feuerbach*, Freud's *The Future of an Illusion*, and Durkheim's *The Basic Forms of Religious Life* be reprinted for public sale?
35. May the Turkish siege of Vienna be referred to? May the Crusades?
36. May the historical person Muhammad be referred to in non-positive terms?
37. May pictures of him be kept in private, if they are not published?
38. May Ibn Warraq's *Why I am not a Muslim* be published?
39. May breadfruits still be eaten or spoken about—as is well known, such fruits are taboo among the Yamis on the Batan islands where the mere reference to such fruits is considered deeply offensive?
40. May expressions like "Jesus Christ!", "Jesus Fucking Christ!", or "By the beard of the Prophet!" be used in public?
41. May traditional Jewish cakes be sold in public?

42. May the imprisonment of editors reprinting Muhammad cartoons be criticized?
43. If you happen to violate the new norm, should you give an apology? Or has the offended culture the right to revenge despite any apology?
44. What should be done about the Internet where offensive cartoons circulate freely?
45. How should the authority of the printed press be protected when it may no longer publish material which is easily accessible on the net?
46. Is the insult of individual cultural persons outlawed by the norm, or does it only apply to cultural groups?
47. May writers quote others who violate the norm if they themselves avoid violating it?
48. Is respect only required towards religious cultures, or are other cultures included as well?
49. How is it established who among the many spokesmen of a culture has the authority to feel insulted?
50. May one religion or culture mock another?
51. Can atheists or agnostics be offended?
52. Is reference to the Enlightenment allowed?
53. Does *Opus Dei* have the right to be written out of the Dan Brown movie *Da Vinci Code*?
54. May Salman Rushdie's *The Satanic Verses* be reprinted?
55. May one use the expression "Holy shit!"?

Enlightenment Versus Culturalism

Modern society is often attacked for being colorless, gray, disenchanted and incapable of satisfying the deeper passions of its citizens. It may, admittedly, satisfy lesser or greater parts of their needs, but it is unable to address the deepest levels of existence. You may recall Tocqueville's depressing predictions about democracy where each individual remains, like a mussel, closed around his own petty world of self-centered purposes, while all other larger-scale, grand issues wither away. You may recall Marx's equally depressing description of bourgeois society and its ice-cold waters of egocentric calculation. Many will, however, cling to the idea that liberal democracy has yet proved itself to be the lesser evil and thus push such mutterings aside, but the point is that this kind of criticism of modern society keep occurring and seem, again and again, to touch something deep in the hearts of many. It could not possibly be right that the vast, free and rich modern societies should be nothing more than one enormous, insipid mall, and life nothing but one sad circle with the shopping cart between home, work, and television. This is, in fact, the most serious criticism of liberal, democratic society which, in its welfare versions, has had a much easier time meeting the socialist criticism of the left which focuses on poverty. The last considerable wave of criticism from the left (the 68 movement) took place in the richest societies the globe had ever seen and, for the same reason, had the character of longing for one big social redemption rather than aiming for concrete, useful reforms.

In the vacuum after the demise of radical socialist critique, the longing for redemption again haunts the political scene. You may feel it does not belong there, but you must realize it is there; it is so in both right and left-wing versions. The surprising fact is that both now come dressed up in "culture." Try to recall how frequently, twenty or thirty years ago, the differences in behavior of different groups of human beings were described without any use of the c-word. Then, one spoke about different societies, different economies, about ideology, politics, resources, etc., but very rarely about "culture". Now the talk is of little else.

This slide is decisive. In this culturalist use of the word, "culture" is, as we have seen, closed worlds, unable to communicate and learn from each other, because it is assumed that all cultures consist of a "set of values" and none of them may pass judgment on the other. One must accept stoning, the cutting off of hands, the suppression of women and the persecution of deviants as colorful exotica on par with pickled bull's eyes, grasshoppers, dog soup and Swedish fermented herring or whatever else exotic people may fancy to celebrate as "values." No negotiation between such worlds is possible, closed around themselves as they remain, and the only relation which may hold between them is unconditional respect, or equally unconditional rejection.

This notion of culture exists in right-wing and left-wing versions. The version of the right can be found in nationalism, where the limit of the world is the border of the nation, and where the cohesion of the nation is presumed to depend upon how uniformly national you may shape its population. It was widespread in nineteenth-century nationalism and enjoys, for the time being, a renaissance on the European right, from where its ideas influence both centrist and even left-wing parties. A more comprehensive version of it can be found in the doctrine of the "Clash of Civilizations," where the cultural "worlds" have grown vast and cover continents, but where they still clash in inimical borderline zones. The left-wing version can be found in the multiculturalist idea that cultures can and must live together in the same territory without requiring any modification or a common set of basic principles, and where the individual "cultures" have the right to demand special treatment in the shape of special respect and privileges. The size of cultural "worlds" may dwindle to the size of neighborhoods or stairwells, but the culture is still something absolute which precedes and determines the individuals, who may only meet in total acceptance or total rejection, the civil war between neighborhoods.

The tragicomic thing in actual debate is that even if nationalism and multiculturalism see themselves as absolute opponents, they still share exactly the same notion of culture as a matter of homogeneous, closed worlds without mutual communication; they just have different requirements for the distribution of those worlds on the map. The right-wing version imagines few, large worlds, bound to territories, while the left-wing version imagines many, smaller worlds, mixed within territories—but in both cases just as segregated, and in both cases with the idea that the group (the "culture") is more important than the individual. But this is a fundamentally sham picture of cultures; in the real world, cultures are in constant development. They meet, break, hybridize, decline, evolve, change, meet problems, learn in an ongoing and steady trial-and-error process. To assume these homogeneous worlds as your cultural concept thus yields support for the most extreme conservative forces of "cultures", those who claim that cultures have an "authentic" original state to which they must return by homogenizing culture and its individuals. In this way they will all correspond to a supposedly pristine version of that culture, which is, more often than not, the most authoritarian version.

But nationalism and multiculturalism both share this particular demand that society should "respect" culture, that the grayish absence of passion in modern society should be compensated for by an authoritarian culture. Some of us, however, cannot imagine anything more boring than sitting chewing over one's own identity, no matter whether it be national, religious, Danish, American, Muslim, or Christian. To mirror oneself in the self-congratulating recognition that you are and will be your own glorious self, and will eternally remain being yourself, dozing in your own identity, is, to some of us, a vision of hell. Many, however, take delight in "indentity politics", the right wing or the left wing version.

Peace be upon them. Modern society should accommodate widely differing roads towards happiness of individuals, and if some of them go via eternal self-pollination, then so be it, with no complaint from the democrat and secularist, provided, that is, that the identity-lovers enter into a minimal contract with modern society that they recognize the right of others *not* to share their identity or the rules of behavior that comes with it, and which is very often of central concern to them. That they recognize not just the right to existence of other such "identities" but, even more importantly, the right to existence for those of us who do not care much about identity hygiene. Many identity politicians, however, are not willing to pay this price, and it is for this reason that it is gradually becoming apparent that the decisive opposition in current Western politics is not between nationalism and multiculturalism, nor between left and right, Christianity and Islam, the West and the rest, or whatever else. The central opposition is between enlightenment and culturalism. Not that issues of economic distribution or religious issues have ceased to matter at all, but they may be dealt with continuously within different spheres of modern society. Culturalism, on the contrary, is aimed directly against central tenets of modern society: freedom of expression, freedom of religion. As a tradition, enlightenment rests upon democracy and human rights and regards "culture," in this particular use of the word, as something which thrives best in private life, in the life and associations of civil society. But the celebrators of culturalism want their special culture to delimit and restrain enlightenment, which is seen as inferior because of the dull materialism of modern society. But modern society should not, in general, award special privileges to identities, cultures, or religions, for the privilege of one group is automatically the inequality or suppression of another, and religious and "cultural" persons are not in any way more worthy of respect than other persons simply because they refer to invisible leaders in their claims and demands.

To a certain degree, modern society may have a part in the blame. Maybe it has made the case too easy for the national-religious identity projects. Maybe it has painted modernity grayer than it deserves. For it is indeed correct that part of the foundation of modern society is that religious fantasies of redemption should be kept out of politics, or that, at the very least, they should not enjoy any privileged role in politics. But politics is not the whole of society, and modernity offers far more than the blasé criticism of civilization is capable of discovering.

What would the Enlightenment say to this criticism? What is it that is lost in this dull picture of modernity? What is it that makes life worth living, if it is not Yahweh, Allah or the routine circular track with ever-larger trolley carts? This is, of course, art, science, nature, love, friendship, curiosity, sport and much much more. Recall the German Enlightenment philosopher from the 1920s, Ernst Cassirer, who insisted that when any direct access to infinity is barred for man, one can only search for infinity by going to the finite in all directions. And recall his opponent, the somber Heidegger, the hero of many culturalists and celebrators of "authenticity," who took the consequence and converted to Nazism in order to sack the Jewish cosmopolitan professors from the University of Freiburg. All the facets of modern life disappear when you put on your culturalist spectacles, which may see only two things: the despicable market and democracy, and the promises of culture. When you see only hucksters and clerics in the world, you must prefer the latter, forced by the necessity of the vulgarity and sham of market society.

Liberal society is not without guilt in this sad situation. Indispensable as it has been to force religious and "cultural" passion out of politics, liberalism has, on the other hand tended to de-politicize the political, as Carl Schmitt's critical diagnosis goes. This in no way implies that one should accept Schmitt's different, cynical and dark, alternatives, but it means that the idea of liberalism to translate all political tensions to economic tensions, which may then be negotiated in the market, involves the danger of eroding the real victories of modern society. The splitting up of modern society into an array of domains, each with their logic and criteria, does not have the market as the only such domain. So, the passions of redemption do have their place elsewhere in modern society, far from being referred only to "identity," "culture," "religion" and their sad repetitions of themselves. They develop in the vast domain of art with roads to the depth of existence, whether they be provocative, beautiful, shaking, comforting, satirical, critical, passionate; they unfold in the enormous and passionate quest for truth in the sciences about everything from bosons to computational paleontology, from algebra to hypertext; they also unfold politics when it strives not for building paradise on Earth, but for making this life as good as possible for as many as possible.

This is why the ideas of extreme liberalism that art is but a commodity among others which should exist on market conditions only, that science is but the shortest way from research to profit, that politics consists just of structures for regulating behaviors by economic incitements, are destructive. They play the cards into the hands of the culturalists and fail to realize that a central long term goal for modern society is to add to art, science, technology, politics as autonomous values. Our own age must be seen not from the severe viewpoint of a god, but from our descendants. Should our time, the richest yet on the planet, be remembered only as a shallow party of consumption, after which only empty packaging and green house gases are left? Or should it be seen as an era in which new and glorious heights in art, science, and politics are reached? None of these areas provide any ticket to paradise, to be sure, but it is a basic contention of the enlightenment that no agreement as to the availability of such tickets exists, and that a focus on this life should take political precedence over that of an afterlife.

Here, it is important to remember another central idea of the Enlightenment: that of the perfectibility of man. This is routinely misunderstood by religions and "cultures" as a frightening *Ersatz* religion which vainly puts man in the place of god and hence constitutes a totalitarian desecration. Such claims may be found almost word for word from the Western right-wing and from al-Zawahiri, the new leader of Al-Qaeda, and from different traditions hostile to human rights and democracy. But this is wrong. The idea of the Enlightenment is not that man is perfect, but that he and his society can be improved. The flip side of this idea, of course, is that the individual living at any particular time is not yet perfect, and, for that reason you will be better off trying to acquire a gay self-irony, the better to bear one's own lack of perfection. Self-irony includes, among many things, taking one's own "identity" and "culture" less seriously, based on the insight that the individual is not exhausted by any "cultural" identity. But it remains perfectly possible for the individual as the fragile, imperfect, even in a certain sense sinful human being he is, possessed by his personal passions, ragings, and obsessions, kept on a low heat by the reactor bars of self-irony, to partake in the further development of art, science, politics, and civilization. This is where modern society offers a super-individual passion which has the advantage of being less fanatical than identity and culture in their ongoing acceleration.

Republicanism and Culturalism

Speaking about liberalism in this book, we have used the word as referring to democracy, rule of law and equal rights—that is, referring to political liberalism rather than economic liberalism. But is our criticism of culturalism closely associated with political liberalism in a narrow sense? It is evident that communitarianism and its attack on liberalism will have close affinities to "hard" multiculturalism, so our criticism will not be compatible with a communitarian viewpoint and its emphasis on pre-political value communities before democracy. But there is another, both classic and current criticism of liberalism which shares basic points with communitarianism, namely republicanism as it appears, for example, in Philip Pettit or Quentin Skinner. This basic idea goes that liberalism pulverizes the citizens into atomized, isolated individuals, struggling only for egocentric interests, just as the liberal state becomes a merely procedural apparatus for mediating the warring interests of individuals. Both communitarianists and republicans agree that this is "too little" (see both Marx's and Tocqueville's classical critiques of liberalism's dissolution of society into self-enclosed egotists) but the alternative of republicanism is completely different from that of the communitarianists. Supporters of republicanism (not to be confused with the term 'republicans' from The Republican Party) will claim that what is lacking in the picture of naked liberalism is political cooperation among the citizens of the republic. This is not, as in communitarianism, a set of pre-political cultural values which everyone celebrates; rather, it is values which are constantly developed through the ongoing process of citizens freely governing their republic in common. Supporters of republicanism will not agree, hence, with the liberals' idea that the first task of the state is to protect the individual against interference from the state as well as from other individuals, the famous "negative liberty," in the words of Isaiah Berlin. They will assert, rather, that the decisive freedom is that from "arbitrary domination." This may appear to be a very subtle distinction, but it is crucial. The supporter of republicanism will claim that freedom from interference may be found also in non-democrat, non-republican states (for example, the freedom of religion in the absolutist but tolerant Prussia of Frederick the Great), but if non-interference is simply the result of an individual, mild, but still absolutist ruler's whim, then the citizens are still subject to arbitrary domination; the politics of non-interference could change anytime. Furthermore, the supporter of republicanism would not, in all cases, object to interference as such. The common government of the state sometimes necessitates interference against citizens, but only insofar as it is the result of the open, political process with the right to complain, and with protection for minorities, so that the interference does not become arbitrary.

The crucial weapon against arbitrary domination is thus the republicanist collaboration of the citizens. This is only made possible by the continuous schooling of the citizens in civic virtues, the orientation towards and ability to participate in common work on the public issues of the republic. The notion of "civic virtue" may sound dated and corny, but variants of it may be found both on the political left where the idea of the unselfish "engagement" in public matters is central as well as in well-to-do people feeling obliged to spend parts of their fortune on science, arts, and other projects beneficial to the public. The concept of "civic virtue" derives from Machiavelli's "vertú" and is counterposed to his notion of "corruption," which not only comprises nepotism and untrustworthiness in state bureaucracy, but more generally the tendency that individuals may place their own interest higher than that of the republic during times of crises. To avoid the development of corruption in the state, the republican takes a strong interest in the division of power, both the classic tripartition of Montesquieu and the more general striving for state organs to function as control mechanisms vis-à-vis each other; thus state decisions are to be challenged by hearings, civic movements and the like, often summarized as the idea of a "contestative" democracy. At the same time, republicanism claims that even if the state should remain neutral in relation to the values of individual groups or "cultures," this does not imply that the state is neutral in all areas. State institutions may incarnate values that are developed within the confines of common republican government—for instance, state support for independent institutions of knowledge and research resting upon the recognition of the political value of the development and distribution of unbiased knowledge (something similar may hold for support to the arts, etc.). In the history of ideas, republicanism peaked during the eighteenth century, and the original bourgeois revolutions, the American and French revolutions of 1776 and 1789, were inspired by republicanism. During the nineteenth century, however, the sister ideology to republicanism, liberalism, gained the upper hand on the ideological level. Yet, many democracies continued to harbor and develop republican principles, perhaps without explicitly reflecting upon it in their liberal self-understanding.

We shall not go further into republicanism in this context but limit ourselves to the observation that our critique of culturalism and "hard" multiculturalism is equally compatible with republicanism and liberalism. The republican emphasis on the continuous articulation of common political values on a higher level than that of the single individual or single culture may even be said to be more antagonistic to "hard" multiculturalism than is naked liberalism. Radical laissez-faire liberals (e.g. Kukathas) may claim that the state must remain so liberal that it refrains from interfering against strongly anti-liberal cultural groups with "internal restrictions," based on the argument that such cultures have the freedom to develop as they like. The republican would not agree; he will claim instead that it is a duty of the state to act against groups suppressing their members (for instance, claiming a ban against apostasy) making it impossible for them to change religion or culture, if they so wish. Here, the republican will typically claim that it is a public task to prevent such "arbitrary domination" of individuals, and that this aim is more important than the ultra-liberal principle of non-interference. The republican will thus tend to be less permissive with regard to the development of suppressive subgroups within society.

The criticism of "hard" multiculturalism which we develop in this book is thus compatible with both liberal and republicanist interpretations of democracy.

Who Is Entitled To Disagree?

During the Cartoon Crisis, a new argument for what was appropriate to publish was presented in Denmark. It was suggested that the cartoons wouldn't have been so insulting had they been printed in another newspaper. *Jyllands-Posten* is known to be conservative.

A similar discussion took place in the Danish branch of the PEN. The organization published support for the cartoonists' right to express their points of view as they faced the accusations of religious insult. This provoked some to leave the PEN club. However, some later changed their minds and supported the right to publish satirical cartoons. That was in February 2007, when the French weekly, *Charlie Hebdo* (which republished the Danish cartoons and added some new ones), won the court case French Muslims conducted against it. The reason for this change in support of freedom of expression is remarkable. It was argued that *Charlie Hebdo,* which is a libertarian and left-wing weekly, represented a tradition for satire and blasphemy and therefore was in its right to do what it did when it published the cartoons. But this revolutionary pedigree was not part of *Jyllands-Posten's* legacy, and therefore it had no right to be satirical and print the cartoons.

One could perhaps find this motivation somewhat spurious, but a similar discussion took place on the German internet site, *Signandsight*, at the same time, in February 2007. The journalists, Ian Buruma and Timothy Garton Ash, argued with philosopher Pascal Bruckner over principles regarding free expression in a multicultural context. Who is allowed to say what and when?

It all began when Garton Ash criticized the Dutch Muslim dissident of Somali origin, Ayaan Hirsi Ali, for what he defined as her "Enlightenment fundamentalism." Indirectly quoting the murderer of Theo van Gogh, who stabbed a note on his victim's chest, complaining about the "fundamentalism of the infidels," Garton Ash implicitly equated one side's murder with the other side's argumentation style. Moreover, he hinted that the reason why she attracted so much attention from the media was because of her beauty, not her points of view. However, he later regretted the accusation of "Enlightenment fundamentalism" after a simple objection from Pascal Bruckner about what it means to be a fundamentalist and to act like one. The peaceful Ali should not be compared to or identified with the fundamentalist murderer of filmmaker Theo van Gogh. It is a question of the means one uses in the promotion of one's point of view: violence or writing.

Ian Buruma then intervened. He claimed that Hirsi Ali had no right to quote Voltaire since, in his time, he was up against the powerful Catholic Church, while she was criticizing a vulnerable minority in Europe (thus using the argument that freedom of expression must exclusively be used to criticize the powers that be). Bruckner replied that her criticism was aimed at tendencies within Islam as such and not only tendencies in European Islam, but to that Buruma stated his crucial argument: She was not allowed to criticize Islam as she was not a Muslim anymore. The critique ought to come from within Islam, and that was why Buruma preferred to listen to the so-called "reformism" of Tariq Ramadan.

Let us remember what the sociologist, Norani Othman, from Sisters-in-Islam in Malaysia, said about what she defined as ethnopolitical communitarianism in her own country. She underlined the importance of the principles that everybody has the right to intervene in anything in the public sphere and that no group or institution enjoys the privilege of rejecting criticism simply on the grounds that it is coming from outside its own ranks. The scholar, Farish A. Noor, pointed to the fact that such an attitude to freedom of expression is damaging to the free and open public sphere in a democratic society. What these Malaysians are saying is that it is not crucial *who* says what, or *where* they say it, but *what* they say. Some in the West seem to have a hard time understanding this principle. Instead, they seem to think it is more important who speaks where. But do the consistency of an argument and the truth of a statement really depend on who presents it?

The fact that Hirsi Ali was raised as a Muslim does not count for Ian Buruma. She was also a member of the Muslim Brotherhood and a devout believer before she discovered the diversity of this world by reading—nineteenth-century English novels that she stumbled upon in Nairobi, Kenya, where her family had taken refuge. After that, she rebelled against her Muslim traditions and escaped a forced marriage. After these events, she is considered to be no longer in a position to criticize Islam, as she is an apostate, a dissident. Moreover, Ian Buruma poses a further criterion to be met: the criticism not only has to come from within the Muslim community, but it must also not be too radical, for it must be suitable for the persuasion of already moderate Muslims.

It is difficult to follow the logic that an argument might be dismissed on the sole grounds that it is too radical. How would the world ever have been able to modernize, to promote science, democracy and human rights had this form of logic been predominant? Only the nobility would have been in a position to criticize feudalism, only the Jesuits would have been in a position to criticize the Inquisition, only communists would have been in a position to criticize the Soviet Union, only national socialists would have been in a position to criticize the Nazi Party? Only those who agree are allowed to disagree?

Two Levels of Values

A crucial and fatal property of the "hard" concept of culture is that all of the ingredients of a culture are taken to participate as equally important parts of the inseparable, organic unity which culture is assumed to constitute. Religious ideas, clan or caste structures, and kinship structures are all viewed at the same level as canned food and stockings, (as we saw in Benedict), and the formula for this idea, of course, is the suspect concept of "value." Any type of preference for any type of reason (ethical, political, aesthetical, epistemic, geographical, gastronomical etc.) may be subsumed under the concept of "value." If ever any values are understood to be more basic than others in culturalism, it will typically be religious values—but the overall tendency is that cultures comes as a package, take it or leave it; it is impossible to pick and chose from it at will.

This severely delimits the freedom of the individual to select his own menu of different cultural features, but it also makes impossible the comparison between cultures, because all such features are taken to be fully specific for the single culture. Culturalism therefore becomes systematically blind to the fact that most cultural and political systems of ideas are constructed in a way so that all values do *not* claim equal importance.

This goes not only for the fact that some values may determine others (as when certain Islamists claim that specific dress codes are dictated by religion), but it also goes for the fact that some "values" may have the role of *not* determining other values but rather of keeping open a space in which the individual may himself realize values according to his own wishes. It would probably be better to refer to such values as "principles" or "rights," and indeed, among the classic human rights several, such as the freedom of expression, of conscience, of religion, of assembly, of association, have this character. They establish a space of possibility for the individual and, at the same time, they oblige the state to protect this space of possibility. Which values individuals and groups now choose to put into these spaces remains open; which organizations, meetings, beliefs, and expressions one prefers to participate in or express remains a choice. These two levels of "values" constitute a very important distinction in different versions of liberal democracy and its doctrines. As Timothy Garton Ash expressed it (before he turned culturalist himself): "The belief in the value of tolerance is not like a belief in Jesus Christ, the prophet Muhammad, Ahura Mazda or, for that matter, the scientific wisdom of Darwin; it is the belief alone that makes it possible for other beliefs to coexist."[97]

In a multiculturalist context, we have already encountered such distinctions several times: in the controversy between Rawls and the communitarianists where Rawls claimed that all ideas about the good life are fallible and open to revision, which is why the individual has access to two levels: one at which he lives in and through his values, and one of making, on certain occasions, when one step backwards to judge and evaluate those values at a meta-level. Against this, the communitarianists claimed that certain values are so deeply embedded in a community that its individuals are *not* able to take this backward step and thus remain incapable of revising the idea of the good life in their community.[98]

We also encountered such a distinction in Kymlicka, at this point distancing himself clearly from the communitarianists. This also became clear in his idea that the single culture within multiculturalism should be protected and developed, *at the same time* as the culture and its members should develop a higher-level consciousness of forming part of a larger, multicultural whole, a consciousness supposed to include basically liberal principles for the mutual relations between such groups. In the Canadian case, one was expected both to remain within the frame of one's immigrant culture *and*, at the same time, to develop a special, Canadian pride in forming a part of the multiculturalist mosaic, a version not unlike a Habermasian *Verfassungspatriotismus*, a patriotism of the Constitution.

Interestingly, we saw a related two-level theory in Benedict: even if the individual was understood to constitute an inseparable part of his culture, the possibility of taking the backwards step played a role at several points in her doctrine. One was the double consciousness of the anthropological participant observer, where one identifies with and participates in the life and beliefs of the culture studied at the same time as one continues to observe objectively, as befits a social scientist. Another was in her own doctrine of tolerance, where she herself takes the step back from all specific cultural values and judges that toleration between the closed worlds of cultures is recommendable as a meta-principle. For her, the antagonism between these ideas and her own culturalist doctrine of the inseparability of culture and individual remained unresolved, but it is striking that even through-and-through culturalists seem unable to escape this double structure of values. Even communitarianists do not speak only on behalf of the one specific community to which they belong; when developing their theory they treat it as valid for completely different communities.

To us, there is no way to avoid this principle: the autonomy of the individual is closely connected to his ability to take the famous backward step and subject his own values (and those of his culture) to critical examination. Human rights is, to a large extent, motivated by the attempt to create a society which supports this individual possibility rather than banning or delimiting it, and the whole idea of a public sphere as a venue for debate in modern societies is constructed on the basis of this distinction. Such a distinction, however, tends to disappear once one dons the culturalist glasses. Here, by contrast, you find constant attempts to limit the public sphere and deconstruct the two levels of values, as we saw in the Malaysian idea that free debate about issues deemed sensible should be replaced by hearings in closed councils where religious leaders were awarded the right to determine beforehand which insults they might be willing to accept. We also saw it in the ongoing campaigning of the OIC and the UN Human Rights Council to ban the "defamation of religion."

This is why culturalism so easily clashes with human rights. Culturalism strives to make individuals forget they have the autonomy to step out of their culture, and instead subjects this autonomy to "culture," that is, to priesthoods, politicians, spokesmen, traditions, authenticity, in all cases authorities which will deny the individual the basic freedom of mind which can only unfold in a free, public sphere. Our advice, then: be skeptical anytime "cultures" as "systems of values" are put forward in an argument—here the two levels are, as a rule, fatally absent.

Freedom of Speech: Freedom from Whom?

Freedom of speech is seemingly simple. Everybody has the right to say what they want without any censorship by the state (within the ordinary codified restrictions such as libel, making threats, etc.), but it hides a problem. Jeremy Bentham famously called natural rights "nonsense upon stilts" and in this lies the insight that the right to do certain things does not come by itself, but is something somebody gives to somebody else. Freedom of speech is a right which the individual has due to democratic institutions; this implies that it forms a restriction which the state imposes on itself. The state might, in principle, censor away critical claims to smithereens, but decides to restrain itself and not indulge in such actions. It is this definition which conceives of freedom of speech (and the other central civil liberties among human rights) as a negative restriction on state action towards citizens, which has led many people to claim that freedom of speech was not threatened during the Cartoon Crisis. There might have been self-censorship on the part of certain cartoonists and editors, and there might have been death threats against some such persons, but all influential political forces never ceased to support freedom of expression. In Denmark, very few people, apart from a few romantics at the University of Copenhagen and the Islamic Society of Faith, craved restrictions on constitutional free speech. We have already seen how the international picture was bleaker, with strong currents working for the curtailment of Freedom of Expression in the UN, in the EU, in Britain, in Norway. But if we restrict our focus to the small state of Denmark, is it not correct that freedom of speech was not attacked?

The purely negative definition of free speech as the freedom from interference from the state is, in a certain sense, a liberal illusion. As argued by Carl Schmitt, there are certain basic matters that much of liberalism is oriented towards forgetting, centered around issues of sovereignty. Schmitt's basic contention is that a state must first of all be sovereign. The state must gain control over a territory with the use of instruments of violence such as the army and police. Only thereafter, a form of government may be chosen and a normal condition may prevail where peace is kept, ordinary legislation is enacted and the state may decide, for example, to constrain itself by declaring free speech for its citizens.

In cases where the sovereignty of the state is threatened, it may declare a state of emergency where greater or smaller parts of ordinary legislation are temporarily suspended, with the basic aim of ensuring the survival of the state. It is precisely civil liberties that are usually among the first legislations to be thus discarded in a state of emergency, in order for the state to deal more efficiently with the threat against it's security. Only thereafter may normal conditions be reinstated. The secret services of the state constitute, in a certain sense, a small element of a state of emergency apparatus, even during normal peace time, to the extent that they are exempt from ordinary legislation and budgetary control. They occupy a vague margin in which they operate which is not at all, or only weakly, controlled by parliament, the courts and the police. The drastic act of declaring a state of emergency must, of course, be administered with utmost care and only be sought in extremely serious circumstances, because very basic democratic and rule-of-law principles are suspended. The existence of secret services demonstrates that the state is also, even during normal conditions, able to act in a "state of emergency-like" way to a limited extent. Thus, there is a continuous scale from normalcy to emergency, rather than a sharp, categorical limit.

Emergency actions reveal an aspect of the state which ordinary liberal theory of democracy often hesitates to acknowledge, because it *a priori* conceives of the state as powerful, as endowed with a power the distribution, restriction, and control of which constitutes the basic democratic question. But even if the state is indeed a very powerful actor, it is not all-powerful. Its sovereignty may be contested, both by international and internal forces, and it is in fact constantly contested, to greater or lesser degrees. Sovereignty constitutes the constantly crumbling basis of the state, and, from a Schmittian point of view, the failure to realize this is the fatal blindness in liberalism. It is for this reason that it is not sufficient to assert that no influential force in Danish politics worked to restrict the legislation on free speech.

From the perspective of sovereignty, this becomes clear. It is a basic fact that for the moment, unlike ten years ago, Danish politicians, cartoonists, and editors must live under long-term constant police protection. This forms a radically new development. But that police protection is, of course, not a protection against the state; it is not a guarantee against the state suddenly dispatching a body of censors to curtail free speech. This police protection is aimed against attacks on certain citizens from *other* powers which try to force those citizens not to express themselves. Under normal conditions, one would say that such cases belong under normal criminal law; if my neighbor threatens me, it is an ordinary police and court matter. But in the case in question, these threats were not ordinary criminal acts between Danish citizens. They were threats which were supported by other states, by international political networks with connections to other states, or by internationally operating, state-like militia forces, such as al-Qaeda.

The forces threatening freedom of speech were thus not actors of the Danish state,[99] but they were indeed state-like actors, operating on Danish territory, which thus threatened Danish sovereignty in its own territory. The founding fathers of the Danish Constitution hardly predicted such a situation when they articulated the forerunner of the present Article 77 about free speech: that it should be possible that several competing sources of sovereignty operate simultaneously in Danish territory, such as is exemplified by the Danish police protection of citizens against attacks originating in other states or international networks. The present situation thus has certain similarities to the period 1933–45, where Denmark, as a small state close to Nazi Germany (in Bismarck's words, a "wart on Germany's forehead") had to accommodate to German pressure. This was particularly evident in the period of German occupation between 1940–45, but even as early as 1933, Danish foreign secretary P. Munch had to gather the leading press editors and, succumbing to German pressure, ask them not to publish any cartoons ridiculing Germany.

Former Danish foreign secretary (1982–1993), Uffe Ellemann, has famously said, that nobody "among us" challenges freedom of expression.¹⁰⁰ But one can only reach this conclusion through an extreme provincialism. Such a claim completely overlooks the fact that there are indeed many strong international forces working towards the restriction of free speech—and some of these forces are present within the borders of the state. To claim that free speech is not threatened, just because most Danish politicians still behave decently, is provincialism of a shattering proportions. Such provincialism prevents Ellemann and many others from realizing that the presence of those alternative sources of sovereignty which (albeit by other means than in 1933) put intense pressure on Danish free speech. A further difference from 1933 is that such powers have, since then, been able to prosper from the culturalist ideology to legitimize themselves. Thus, to the threats of violence is added another level of threat, in which culturalist politicians, editors, and writers in actuality support the threats by claiming there are "cultures" that have the right to be protected against certain offences, and which have the right to be spoken about exclusively in soft and careful tones.

Islamic Rights

The restriction on freedom of expression plays a central role in the different outlines of "Islamic rights" which have emerged during recent decades, for instance, the outline for an "Islamic constitution" (produced in 1979 by the Islamic Research Academy at the Al-Azhar University in Cairo, considered to be the highest authority of Sunni Islam), the Universal Islamic Declaration of Human Rights (written by representatives of Pakistan, Saudi Arabia, and Egypt and presented at UNESCO in 1981), and the Cairo Declaration about Islamic human rights (elaborated by OIC in 1990). Such restriction of free speech also forms an important point in the different programs of Islamization actually being implemented in many Muslim countries (Iran, Egypt, Saudi Arabia, Pakistan, Sudan, etc.), and which are also propagated internationally (Wahhabism promoted by Saudi Arabia, Salafism propagated by the Muslim Brotherhood and its offshoots, Deobandism by Pakistani organizations).

In our context, the interesting aspect is that these different Islamic initiatives for rights have the character of cultural protection measures.

As Ann Elizabeth Mayer, probably the most knowledgeable analyst of Islamic rights, says, they "legitimize their opposition to human rights by appealing to supposedly distinctive cultural traditions" (Mayer 2007, 203). Mayer's analysis of the background to these initiatives is worth summarizing. As always, it is imprecise and indeed wrong to blame "Islam" generally. Mayer emphasizes the rationalist Mu'talizit school from around 800 to 900 as an example of a current within the Islamic heritage which is open to human reason as an alternative source for legislation, in addition to revealed doctrine, but she asserts, at the same time, that currents of this sort have, as a rule, held a low profile in mainstream Islam. In our era, such voices are often marginalized or even criminalized by Islamization programs. As regards modern legislation, she observes how most Islamic countries introduced legislation during the 19th and 20th centuries, following Western influences, especially continental European law rather than Anglo-Saxon common law, and most often after initiatives from political circles within those countries rather than as a dictate from the West. As an example she mentions how England tried in vain to introduce common law in Egypt which preferred French law. During the recent thirty or forty years, the growing currents of Islamization conceive of this legislation as Western decadence and call for the "reintroduction" of Islamic law.

This call for a "reintroduction" has two problems, according to Mayer. First, the different Islamization movements share a tendency to discard the long historical development of Islamic jurisprudence over the centuries, and therefore try to "reintroduce" Islamic law based solely on the oldest sources: the Koran and the Hadith. Second, these sources are so few and so narrow that, in a wide range of modern juridical domains, it is impossible to derive legislation from them, which is why these countries must, in practice, rely on their existing Western-inspired legislations. The impossible compromise of the Islamization movements between these two incompatible sources of law consequently leads to the dissolution of the rule of law because, in many cases, contradictory sources of law may claim validity. This becomes particularly evident in the Islamic conceptualizations of rights. The international prominence of universal human rights constitutes one of the basic causes of the growth of these outlines of rights, and they mix, even down to the individual linguistic expressions, universalist human rights rhetoric with particularist ideas intended to protect a specifically Islamic culture—that is, culturalist ideas.

It is important here to underline Mayer's emphasis on the actual universalist character of the UN Declaration on Human Rights, both as to its validity, but also as to its origin. Middle Eastern and Muslim delegates played a central role in the elaboration of the Declaration in 1947–48, and it cannot be claimed to be a specifically "Western" product (Mayer recalls how the right to change religion, for instance, was proposed by a Lebanese delegate). Yet in the Islamic proposals for declarations of rights, universalist and particularist terminologies are mixed, without resolving, let alone even acknowledging the many clashes between the two.[101] For Mayer, the creation of a real Islamic Declaration on Human Rights might be possible, but this would require a vast amount of work, involving the use of historical Islamic jurisprudence as well as some fundamental reflection in the philosophy of law as to what a right could be, Islamically conceived, and how it may be universalized. Such a piece of work, parallel to the elaboration of the UN Declaration, is completely lacking in the existing, eclectic declarations. Rather, they have the character of adding particularist restrictions (or "precisions," as the proponents may claim) to the more general, universal human rights. This takes place, for instance, when sharia is quoted as the framework for the declarations. But sharia, as a divine law, is a very vague and imprecise set of norms. The Cairo Declaration, for example, claims that the whole of the Declaration is placed under sharia, without it being made clear precisely what that involves, as when Article 22 about free speech says that "Everyone shall have the right to express his opinion freely in such manner as would not be contrary to the principles of the Shari'ah." The different rights proposals differ in their explicitness on the touchy issue of freedom of religion. Here, Article 10 of the Cairo Declaration is quite outspoken: "Islam is the religion of true unspoiled nature. It is prohibited to exercise any form of pressure on man or to exploit his poverty or ignorance in order to force him to change his religion to another religion or to atheism."

While universal human rights in general constitute a protection of the individual against the state in which he lives, it remains completely unclear in the Islamic drafts just who is subject to the protection offered by the rights and who it is assumed to protect against. Protection of the individual, as in the UN Declaration, mix freely with protection of the Islamic community (the *Umma*) or the Islamic state (for example, mentioned in Articles 10 and 22). As Mayer points out, the particularist Islamic additions to universal rights have an especially ironical character because of their vagueness. How, in Article 10, are attempts to convert defined? It is not made precise. When is an utterance against sharia, in Article 22? That is not made explicit. But this implies—counter to universal rights setting a limit on the state's sphere of action regarding its citizens—that the Islamic rights drafts leave complete authority to states and priesthoods to make precise the content of the vague, culturalist references to sharia in general. To Mayer, this forms one of the decisive problems: Islamic rights are, in effect, directed against universal human rights, even if their form mimics the language and style of the latter; they leave it to the power structures of Islamic states to decide the range of particularist special rights, which these drafts, again and again, employ against universal rights. A core example is the ban on apostasy. In this way, these sketches constitute an interesting compromise between two sets of ideas, both of them originating in the West: universal human rights on the one hand and, on the other, the culturalist notion of culture, where "Islamic rights" employs the latter to relativize or undermine the former. This clash becomes obvious in the repeated adoption of the OIC resolution "Combating Defamation of Religion" in the UN Human Rights Committee and Council, sharpened incrementally from 1999 to the present day. Here, human rights jargon like "freedom of religion" is mixed with culturalist jargon like "Islamophobia" to yield a result which is juridically indigestible and politically dangerous. These resolutions oblige UN member countries to adopt legislation restricting freedom of speech so it may not be used to "defame" religion. The universal concept of "religion" is, in the resolution texts, always only exemplified by "Islam." In this clash, universal principles of freedom of religion are radically challenged by culturalist ideas about the protection of certain cultures.

Apostasy

Apostasy—leaving one's religion—appears as one of the central issues which must be addressed by any sort of multiculturalism. Kymlicka does not write much about it, although his idea that group rights with the aim of "internal restrictions" must not be admitted would contradict the right of religious or cultural groups to punish or prevent apostasy. What does enlightened democracy do with groups advocating punishment for apostasy? In Malaysia, we saw the Lina Joy case, where civil courts and the parallel structure of sharia courts clashed until the case was settled at the Supreme Court: while apostasy is a religious matter the decision eventually lies within the jurisdiction of the sharia court system, and this system will not, of course, allow Lina Joy to convert to Christianity, referring to the ban on apostasy. This ban is legitimized, as we saw from Dean Abdul Hakim bin Abdullah in Kuala Terengganu, with reference to the fact that it serves to "control Muslims." More precisely, it serves to protect organized religion against losing believers. Lina Joy is taken as a hostage and is unable to claim her universal right to freedom of religion, as she is, as a legal subject, placed within the domain of the sharia courts.

For this reason, apostasy appears as an especially sensitive central issue. The four traditional Islamic law schools all agree, with slight variations, that apostasy is a crime, and they even agree about its punishment: for men death, for women life-long imprisonment. The law generally speaks about three days' right to regret for men, while women in some cases may regret later. In addition to punishment, apostasy is also associated with the notion of "civil death;" an apostate immediately loses all civil rights, his or her marriage is dissolved, children are given to the family, any assets are confiscated. If an apostate and his or her spouse continue having sexual intercourse, this is now to be considered as adultery which is criminal and also, in some cases, associated with death penalty. Until the Islamization movements of the past 40 years, the ban on apostasy was slowly sliding into the background in many Islamic countries, but now, once again it occupies center stage, even if most of the "Islamic rights" drafts, as A.E. Mayer says, try to conceal their support for the ban on apostasy in foggy declarations about the freedom of religion and the simultaneous references to sharia (and its implied ban on apostasy). The ban is not, in fact, mentioned in the Koran, but is claimed to be derived from the Hadith, which has given cause for liberal Muslims[102] to try to relativize it and claim that it holds only for apostasy as associated with high treason; in Malaysia, we recall the different attitudes of the Islamic theologians bin Yussoff and Abdullah.

The apostasy rule, however, has very wide consequences. One is that the idea of "civil death" is not only juridical, but also an active, cultural concept. This implies that a person who is declared to be an apostate very often has his ties to family and friends radically cut off and in reality is expelled. Another is that the struggle against apostasy is intimately connected to Islamic marital law: an Islamic man may marry non-Islamic women, because it is, in all cases, the religion of the father which decides that of the children. The mother is a birth machine whose religious observation does not matter, because the important thing is the faith of the children. Conversely, Muslim women must not marry non-Muslim men, because the children, in that case, would be lost to Islam. This is also why men may divorce unilaterally, without the consent of their wife, while women do not have this right, but are forced to sue for divorce in long and complicated sharia court cases.

The asymmetry in inheritance law (women receive only half inheritance) is also motivated by this protection of Islam: the faith of the children follows the father, so he is considered primary caretaker. These basic standards of classic Islamic law are involved in different compromises with Western inspired legislation in most Muslim countries, but they continue without compromise in countries such as Saudi Arabia and Iran. The apostasy ban is thus intimately related to some of the discriminatory and anti-feminist aspects of much Islamic law. As Mayer says, the transformation of Islam into an ideology of state has led governments to make apostasy equivalent to high treason, and the concept has received new life after the tendency in pre-modern Islamic jurisprudence was to let it wither away (167). The apostasy ban has "... broad ramifications and potentially limits the rights in a much larger segment of the populations of Muslim countries than one might initially assume" (170). First, it may be used against a whole population which is born into a non-Muslim religion but whose ancestors are claimed to have been Muslims at some earlier point in history. This is the argument behind the comprehensive Iranian persecution and extermination of Baha'i believers; Mayer also mentions the Pakistani persecution of the Ahmadi minority, or Sudan's persecution of so-called Islamic Republicans. The apostasy ban is thus widely used to force Muslims to adopt a specific version of Islam, most often the version preferred by the strong, local Islamization movement (see, for example, Yap Swee Seng from the human rights organization

SUARAM about the persecution of Islamic heretics against Sunni Islam in Malaysia).

Mayer also addresses the connection between apostasy and discrimination of women: "The choice-of-law rules that are in force in most Muslim countries mean that religious affiliation decides which law is applicable to personal-status issues" (171). Exceptions are reformed states like Turkey and Tunisia, but "Elsewhere, *sharia* law still applies to personal-status questions where one or both of the parties is Muslim" (ibid.)—a rule we saw achieving institutional status in Malaysia. This implies that conversion from one religion to another in order to escape severe marital legislation has been common practice in the Middle East: if a Muslim woman could not have her divorce approved by the sharia court, she could convert to Christianity and suffer "civil death," and hence automatically get her divorce. For this reason, Mayer says (172), there is an intimate connection between the ban on conversion in "Islamic rights" and the maintaining of traditional legislation of personal status (family and inheritance law). In Malaysia, as we have seen, the issue is pressing and the subject of struggle; in post-Taliban Afghanistan, even the new legislation mandates the death penalty for apostasy. In Egypt, a debate has raged for many years about introducing the death penalty for apostasy, following the declaration, in 1980, making sharia the superior source of law.

The case of Abu Zaid, from 1994 to 1996, illustrates the extensive implications of the ban on apostasy very well. Abu Zaid was a professor at the University of Cairo; he was accused of apostasy and convicted as an apostate by a court. Subsequently, his marriage was dissolved, and he and his wife had to emigrate to Europe. The verdict referred to the articles of freedom of religion in the Egyptian constitution, which were interpreted in the Islamic tradition of law as referring to the freedom of the religion to impose the ban on apostasy. At the same time, Abu Zaid was subjected to forced divorce from his wife, his Muslim wife no longer having the right to be married to him, a non-Muslim husband. To Mayer, this case furthermore shows, that the old struggle between Sunni Islam and Mu'tazilism is still alive: Abu Zaid was famous for arguing that there were, from days of old, several competing interpretations of the Koran, and further arguing for the idea that Islam did not cover all legal areas so that human rights, for example, fell outside the bounds of what religion could decide upon.[103] The court case against Abu Zaid was probably motivated by his unorthodox Islamic beliefs, according to Mayer, and after the sentence he and his wife received death threats which induced them to flee. As Mayer concludes: "The outcome is a reminder that, in the climate of intolerance prevailing in many Muslim countries, it is not necessary for the state to impose a death penalty for an 'apostate' to be severely penalized" (175).

The case thus shows that a more rationalist Islam is still alive, even if most often as a persecuted minority viewpoint, and also that in countries influenced by the ongoing Islamization movements, apostasy legislation may also be used to suppress advocates of deviant interpretations of Islam. For a multiculturalist like Kymlicka, who wants to be liberal, the apostasy ban must be moved from the margins and to center stage when the issue is the "internal restrictions" of immigrant groups. As the Abu Zaid case goes to show, a climate of intolerance is more than sufficient, and a group needs not resort to explicit juridical apostasy verdicts in order to fulfill "civil death" in practice. The death threats, as we know them against Salman Rushdie, Hirsi Ali, the Danish MP Naser Khader and others can be understood as attempts to extend the apostasy ban across borders to include ex-Muslim citizens in non-Muslims countries.

The informal version of "civil death" is, of course, not the subject of legislation, but just as multiculturalism in general is also interested in informal discrimination and the fight against it in information campaigns, it must take the apostasy ban seriously, precisely because it serves the maintenance and discipline of the cultural group by means of the internal display of power. It is tightly connected to the issues of freedom of speech and conscience on the one hand and, maybe more surprisingly, to the issues of family politics on the other. When the Anglican Archbishop, Rowan Williams (2008), supported the introduction of elements of sharia in Great Britain and referred to family law in particular, it may not be as innocent as His Magnificence seems to assume. Precisely these aspects of sharia are oriented towards "internal restrictions" and constitute, as such, a group right which no liberal multiculturalism should accept, however "cultural" they might be.

Asian Values

We have met the notion of special "Asian values" in several contexts in this book, for example when a nationalist politician as the former Prime Minister Mohammad Mahathir advoated culturalist norms and compulsory regulations of civil life. In his justification for the ban on apostasy in Islam and its ramifications for marriage law and the family arrangement of marriage between believers, he actually finds support outside the Koran, indeed from a non-religious source: He maintains that such regulation is desirable specifically in Asia, where great importance is attributed to the cohesion of family and community, contrary to the West, where the freedom for the individual is held sacred. In Asia, Mahathir claims, the individual must submit to collective rules in order to protect and support the religious community and family.

The ban on apostasy is elsewhere justified exclusively with reference to the Koran, as we heard from the Muslim clerics, Dr. Yaacob bin Yussoff, from the Sultan Ismail Petra International College, Kota Bharu and from Dr. Abdul Hakim bin Abdullah at the Institute for Islamic Contemporary Studies, University of Terengganu. But the fact that the politician Mohammed Mahathir makes use of a culturalist argument rather than a religious one can be interpreted as suggesting that he intends to convince a foreign audience about the legitimate status of the ban on apostasy, evidently resisting an alleged Western influence. This may implicitly appeal to a sense of historical guilt through a defense against foreign colonialist influences and a protection of national culture. The culturalist concept of "Asian values" is apt, in this way, to reconcile various authoritarian traditions in Confucianism, communism, and Islam, in spite of the particular contradictions among these branches of belief. Indeed, the concept of "Asian values" makes possible a sort of ideological peaceful co-existence between them. We witnessed how this concept has been promoted thoughout South-East Asia to justify culturalist (specifically religious) dogmas in order to maintain and enforce segregated cultures within the confines of the nation. For politicians like Mohammed Mahathir, it is yet another weapon in the ideological arsenal against universalism and human rights.

Daniel A. Bell, in his book, *East Meets West—Human Rights and Democracy in East Asia,* offers an interpretation of what is concealed in this evasive concept. He discusses how "Asian values" are mobilized for further conservative and authoritarian initiatives and how they are granted priority over so-called Western human rights. In the West, human rights and democracy are perceived as being justified by their very existence. They don't need a higher and more supreme justification than their very praxis in everyday life, as they make it possible for people of various ideological and religious beliefs to live together in peace (see the column "Two Levels of Values"). However, the original justification in the preamble of The UN Declaration of The Human Rights from 1948 certainly bears a shrill, quasi-religious tone.

Bell points to the fact that in a South-East Asian context human rights and democracy are not regarded as self-evident. The promotion of the ideological concept of "Asian values" is driven by both Chinese and Confucian civilisation and by a post-colonial confrontation with what is seen as Western influence. Human rights and democracy are thereby subordinated to higher and more supreme objectives, such as the power position of the state, security of life and property, law and order and the welfare of the citizens. Since their independence and in their state-building period after World War II, the South-East Asian societies have been facing problems of post-colonial impacts and challenges that the western liberal societies have never understood in their "fundamentalist belief" in human rights, according to those who advocate "Asian values." No consideration has been given to so-called 'trade-off' arguments. In other words: would you prefer state security and not ethnic violence? Would you prefer the society to prosper and not end up in chaos? Then, for a limited period of time and within certain areas, you might have to accept security measures that could compromise democratic principles and human rights. Just think of the Internal Security Act (ISA), which was implemented after the wave of ethnic violence in Malaysia in 1969. This law gives the home minister (in fact the prime minister) the right to detain any citizen in custody for a period of up to two years, and after two years, custody can be prolonged for another period of two years by purely administrative measures. These and other authoritarian precautions of state security or religious nature all regulate the life of the individual in a very heavy-handed way. In a 'trade-off' argument, they compromise human rights and democracy in order to guarantee state security and social stability which, according to the "Asian values," are the supreme and absolute goals of politics.

There seems to be a contradiction, however, between the reference to a thousand year old tradition of civilizational values on one side and immediate and temporary emergency measures on the other. Any state may, for a limited period of time, face the need to compromise human rights and democracy in a situation of emergency, but justifying these measures with reference to so-called "Asian values" from days of old not only sounds hollow; it also makes one doubt whether these measures really are just of temporary nature. Here, it might be helpful to point to the fact that human rights and democracy are not (as the parallel with "Asian values" might suggest) old and traditional "European values," for also in Europe, people have had to struggle for the promotion of liberal principles against conservative, absolutist and clerical powers which claimed to defend a holy tradition, a tradition which might just as well be called "European values," or "ancient values," be they Asian or European. Both insist on the subjugation of the individual under religious, national and cultural authorities based on the prescription stemming from nonnegotiable cultural values inscribed deeply in the history of the area.

Christianity as the Mother of Enlightenment: A Culturalist Myth

In recent years, one often encounters the assertion that the Enlightenment grew out of Christianity. It may be claimed for example by Christians who are eager to distance themselves from some of the darkest aspects of their own faith in the past, and who may, in return, like to enjoy some of the honor for the results of Enlightenment. The argument may also be found in Enlightenment adherents who would like to give the Enlightenment more historical depth or who, in a friendly gesture, will gloss over the tensions between Christianity and Enlightenment. It may also be found, however, in opponents of Enlightenment who want to relativize the universalist claims of Enlightenment by asserting that Enlightenment is but a particular product of a special, Christian culture and thus forms just another piece of a despicable European culture. Such an argument may be found amongst conservatives, multiculturalists, Islamists, and many others, but all these variants share a culturalist myth: that the Enlightenment is an outcome of Christian culture.

Many points of objection may be raised. First, it may be said that processes of Enlightenment are in no way restricted to Europe. Many other cultures display intense periods of Enlightenment. One might point to the Mesopotamic cultures where trade, science, and urban culture developed; one can also think if the Islamic golden age around 800–1100, when Baghdad was the most enlightened city on the earth; one can identify several periods of Chinese history; one can, as Amartya Sen does, refer to 16th century Indian Enlightenment, where both rationalism and atheism were strong; one can point to the development of astronomy and mathematics in Mesoamerican cultures—and there are many more examples. But even if we focus on the strong European variant of Enlightenment during recent centuries, it is an imprecision bordering on fallacy to claim that it grew easily and without resistance out of Christianity.

It's sometimes argued that there are certain aspects of Christianity which are compatible with Enlightenment, such as the distinction between Caesar's and God's realms, the institutional divide between state and church (which Protestantism and the absolute monarchies, however, tend to dissolve in the foundation of state churches after the Reformation), the encouragement to love one's neighbor as a misty anticipation of individual rights. Finally there is (as in Judaism and Islam) monotheism, which tends to eliminate sacredness from this world which then becomes available to scientific investigation. But even if certain aspects of Christianity have been able to support Enlightenment, there are as many or more aspects which pull in the opposite direction: intolerance of anything but orthodox belief, persecution of heretics, inquisition, clerical hierarchy, the constant interference of the Church in politics and other secular matters, the claim for revealed knowledge over experience and the ensuing anti-scientific stance, vast wars of religion, and severe strictures against free speech. These many anti-Enlightenment aspects of Christianity also become apparent in the difficult struggles when the early Enlightenment had to fight against the powers of absolutism and churches in the early modern period. Both Catholic and Protestant Europe persecuted "heretical" and Enlightenment thinkers, punished them with long terms of imprisonment, burning their books, expulsion and banishment, even in some cases capital punishment. A famous example is the Calvinist execution of Michael Servetus in Geneva. In this case, Enlightenment in no way found support from Christianity, quite the opposite.[104]

The claim that Protestant Christianity should be particularly conducive to democracy and human rights encounters a problem when considering the 250 year period between the Reformation and the first establishment of governments oriented towards human rights during the bourgeois revolutions in the late eighteenth century. During this period, absolutism reigned in most of Catholic and Protestant Europe, and blasphemy legislation, for example, was as harsh in the Protestant parts as in the Catholic parts. Witch-hunts peaked, and in the Protestant parts of Europe, a general theological tendency celebrated the claim that political authority, the absolutist Prince, had been instated by God and should, for that reason, be unconditionally obeyed by his subjects. When tolerance and Enlightenment slowly gained ground in northwest Europe from the late seventeenth century onwards, beginning in the Netherlands and England, the initiative did not in any way originate in the churches but in fact appeared against their will. As is well known, the Catholic Church did not refrain from capital punishments against outspoken persons, such as in the famous cases of Bruno and Vanini.

The Calvinist church in the Netherlands led the persecution of Spinoza and the Spinozists with their call for tolerance, democracy and free speech. In 1668, Spinoza's friend, Adriaan Koerbagh, was sentenced to ten years imprisonment followed by banishment for the publication of the book *Bloemhof*, which criticized religious doctrine; he died in prison. The tendency was the same in the Lutheran churches, for example in Northern Germany, where the famous rationalist Christian Wolff was expelled and banished from the state of Prussia in 1723 for his prasise of Confucius, reason, and determinism. Luther's original call for liberty had primarily claimed the freedom of himself to deviate from Catholicism, not any general freedom of belief and expression at all (cf. Lockean toleration; see the column Tolerance and Respect). Victorious after the triumph of Reformation in Northern Germany, the later Luther became an ardent opponent of "blasphemy," a notion he contributed to spreading as he used it instead of "heresy," of which he had himself been accused. Anabaptists and other "blasphemists" were, according to Luther's 1536 position, liable to capital punishment; Jews, as blasphemists, should be driven out, have their homes and synagogues burned, their tongues cut out.[105] As an example, one needs only to be reminded of the article against blasphemy in Danish absolutist law ("Danish Law", Book 6, Chapter 1, Article 7) from 1683, the first complete legislation in Lutheran Denmark after the Reformation, which prescribed the following punishment for the mocking of God: the tongue of the perpetrator should be cut out while he was still alive, the hand should be cut off if he had used that for blasphemous acts, and finally the head should be chopped off. These limbs and organs should then be publicly displayed. Pakistan's present blasphemy law almost seems mild by comparison.

Even in our time, the tendency against free speech in Christian churches remains clear. The Vatican condemned *Jyllands-Posten*'s publication of the cartoons, as did the World Council of Churches, the Russian Orthodox Church and the Lutheran World Organization.

To gloss over these long and hard fights by talking about a "dialectic" relation between Christianity and Enlightenment is but a euphemism which conceals that the Church has been, until recently, a formidable and frightening anti-liberal antagonist. Finally, such a falsification of history overlooks the many influences on the European Enlightenment from non-Christian sources, from other cultures which the discoverers brought to Europe, from Islamic thinkers (Averroes, Avicenna, Ibn Khaldun, etc.), from India (the "Arab" numbers), from China (powder, paper, pasta), and not least from antiquity (from Greek antiquity: science, philosophy, criticism of religion, free thinking, democratic ideals; from Roman antiquity: Roman Law as a secular legislation, non-ethnic Roman citizenship, the republic, the Stoic concept of humanitas) and much, much more.

To call the Enlightenment a child of Christianity is nothing but a convenient fraud, and it forms yet another variant of culturalism, because it tries to make of Enlightenment a particular culture only, rooted solely in Europe. Whether one wants to celebrate or reject this supposedly particular culture, such an intellectual operation remains equally untenable.

The Invasion of the Word Snatchers: Culturalist Newspeak

In the mid-twentieth century, George Orwell introduced the term 'newspeak' as a characteristic of totalitarian propaganda. As communism could never compete with political liberalism in defining or realizing the basic human rights of man, it had to word snatch the meaning of the words freedom, peace, and democracy.

Culturalism shares the same characteristic with communism in its semantic body snatching of words. When the American Anthropologist Association criticized the human rights declaration from the United Nations in 1947 for its alleged violation of freedom, it had its own definition of this term in mind. The anthropologists didn't mean freedom for the individual to profess his faith and to worship his God (or no God at all) or the freedom to think and express his or her thoughts. They meant the freedom for the culture or the religion to its jurisdiction over the members, for man is inextricably bound to his culture and cannot live outside it, according to the culturalist AAA. Therefore, a culture has the right to protect itself from alien influence. That was the teaching.

What is the reason for this word snatching of terms defining the rights of man? The paradoxical answer is the victory of the human rights discourse. An oppositional ideology like culturalism, the latter day totalitarianism, is forced to express itself in liberal political terminology. The so-called "Islamic rights" of the Cairo declaration are dressed up in universalism even though they are an expression of a culturalist mindset. They claim to complement the UN Declaration of Human Rights, but freedom in the UN declaration is defined as the freedom for the individual and the rights for the individual vis-à-vis the State. In the Cairo declaration, freedom is defined as the freedom for the culture vis-à-vis the rebellious individual, and the authorities are the agent and law enforcer for the culture and the religion in Muslim countries. The meanings of rights and freedom are turned upside down. This invasion of newspeak has also spread to the West.

The term 'integration' once meant that immigrants would find their place in society; they would learn the language, work together with the natives, participate in public and political life, and get to know some friends among the natives. But that would not mean they would lose all the customs they had brought with them from their cultures of origin. 'Integration' therefore held a different meaning from that of 'Assimilation,' but it also held a meaning different from that of 'segregation', meaning living apart from the rest of society, as for instance people in the Jewish ghettos in medieval Europe lived physically apart in separate areas, abiding by their own rules and discriminated against by the authorities.

Now, more and more often, we are presented with the idea that true integration demands special institutions for immigrants, special religious facilities at work, leisure and transportation, permission for special religious dress codes, special prohibition laws against freedom of expression in the media regarding religious issues. The term 'integration' has been imperceptibly word-snatched. The meaning becomes the opposite of what it once was. Now it is the preservation of the religion and culture of the immigrant community, and the protection against influence from the surrounding society and rebellious individuals from within the immigrant community itself. And not before the immigrant community has its own institutions, its own laws and jurisdictions, (and thereby in fact constitutes a fully independent community within society), is it successfully integrated. But that was what we once called 'segregation' in South Africa and in the south of the United States, And 'segregation' was contrary to 'integration.' Now integration actually means—segregation and apartheid.

During the period of Enlightenment in the seventeeth and eighteenth centuries, religious freedom had an ambiguous meaning. It could define the freedom for other congregations and churches than the dominant one to profess their faith and worship their God. And it could mean that the individual had a right to choose his own confession and profess his religion. Sometimes it meant a freedom granted to an institution, sometimes a freedom granted an individual. Until the human rights declaration from 1789 (and its confirmation by the UN declaration of 1948) it did not become clear what religious freedom defined. It is expressed in the UN declaration, Article 18: "Everyone has the right to freedom of thought, conscience and religion; this right includes freedom to change his religion or belief, and freedom, either alone or in community with others and in public or private, to manifest his religion or belief in teaching, practice, worship and observance."

As we observed in the apostasy trials of Abu Zaid and Lina Joy, the meaning of the term religious freedom is now undergoing a change. It increasingly implies the authority of the particular religion to set up its own laws and, by means of a special police force and legal system, to enforce these laws upon the members of the religion. It doesn't matter if these laws collide with basic human rights or the common law for other individuals in a particular country. We learned that from Malaysia, and we can learn it from Canada and Great Britain, where Muslims promote this kind of religious freedom under the pretext of multiculturalism. Again, the meaning of a term is turned upside down. Freedom is slavery.

During the Cartoon Crisis and whenever totalitarian Islam collides with human rights, there is hardly an occasion on which a term is more abused than 'dialogue.' Over and over, we are told that contradictory principles and religious tensions can be resolved with dialogue. This claim is made by both well intentioned people with a liberal point of view and Islamists, Christian fundamentalists and culturalists of all kinds. But then: what is a dialogue? What does it mean? The most common conception used to be that dialogue is an open discussion where opponents present their own points of view, and seriously consider the others point of view. There is scope for the modification of opinion on the matter in question and an agreement may be reached, or, alternatively, a compromise. But the basic assumption is that all parties recognize the possibility of their own misjudgement of a matter and, no matter how convinced they are that they are right, they are nevertheless ready to revise their opinion if new data, new arguments and new proofs are presented to them.

But this is not what the term 'dialogue' means anymore. This is not what culturalists and fundamentalists think of when they use it. They have body-snatched the word. According to the culturalist understanding, culture must be seen as an organic whole, and every individual is inextricably bound to his own culture. Influence from other cultures is bad for the integrity of the culture, and revision of basic principles is therefore not possible. The Danish branch of the Muslim World League has expressed understanding of dialogue like this: "For a Muslim it is basically artificial to discuss Islam. Actually, everybody considers any discussion as an expression of a Western way of thinking."

But what meaning can dialogue then hold? It has now become the more or less courteous presentation of a point of view from various opponents, often articulated in an ambiguous terminology as we know from UN human rights council, OIC and the Durban I and II conferences. It is a mutual presentation of a compromise in terms that are themselves body-snatched, with their original meanings turned upside down. Dialogue is now a ceremonial expression of ambiguities, but no longer a reasonable and comprehensible exchange of ideas and opinions. Real communication and dialogue are no longer possible, when it is accepted that words can mean practically anything: racism is political critique, reform is growing intolerance towards religious dissidents, tolerance is our ignorance of violation of human rights, and respect is fear.

Tolerance and Respect Are Not the Same Thing

In discussions of culture, one often encounters the assertion that what is lacking in the West is "more respect and tolerance towards other cultures" and similar beautiful slogans. The problems inherent in the expression "other cultures" have been analyzed at length in this book, but what about "respect and tolerance?" Might they not be good ideas? Immediately, they sound like very fine and simple extensions of ordinary polite and urban attitudes. The problem is that it is not very clear what "respect" and "tolerance" exactly entail, and both words may be used in several different ways.

The concept of "tolerance" or "toleration" goes back to Renaissance humanism and the Enlightenment, and its origin pertains to the severe religious conflicts in Europe during those periods. A famous articulation of early Enlightenment toleration, and one that has become a classic in the liberal tradition, is John Locke's (1684) "A Letter on Toleration," which many refer to in discussions of free speech, tolerance and cultural issues.[106] Locke's toleration, however, has considerable limitations as compared to other conceptions of tolerance and freedom of thought, faith and expression. Israel (1999) lists three such limitations of Lockean toleration which are important to keep in mind in the present discussion. Locke's theory is founded on a theological basis, hugely influenced by the Dutch sect of so-called "remonstrants". The argument is that the pursuit of salvation is a matter of utmost importance, into which political power or churches different from one's own belief should not interfere. This is why freedom of worship is central in Locke's toleration concept, which does not address freedom of thought in a broader conception, not to mention freedom of expression. It is thus primarily a toleration of different branches of Protestant Christianity, even if the basic argument does not explicitly exclude, for instance, Jews or Muslims. The first limitation on Lockean tolerance, therefore, is that toleration is a privilege for organized but dissenting communities of faith. Individual preferences are not considered; similarly, deists, agnostics, freethinkers, and people not obsessed with their own salvation, are not included. The second limitation concerns Catholicism, which is not tolerated because it constitutes an alternative power structure to the state, and has as an aim the repression of non-Catholic Christians (Locke is writing when a Catholic is on the English throne and the Huguenots are about to be expelled from Catholic France). The third and most serious limitation is his emphatic rejection of toleration for atheists who, by not seeking salvation, exclude themselves completely from the community.

Few latter-day Lockeans draw such implications (at least not in open debate), but the structure of Lockean tolerance still plays a central role in many ideas on toleration. Namely the notion that the important thing is to allow freedom of religion in the sense that organized faiths are free to practice their worship without state interference, but this also implies that they are free to suppress, force, punish, expel, even kill internal dissenters. This is the *libertas ecclesiae* which Kymlicka suddenly invoked in defense of certain internal restrictions.

The great competing current in Enlightenment toleration is charted by Israel (2001, 2006) as leading from Spinoza and Bayle and a group of Dutch freethinkers (including van den Enden, Koerbagh and Meijer) to the radical faction of the French Enlightenment, (Boulainvilliers, d'Holbach, Diderot, etc.). In this Spinozist conception of toleration, the emphasis is on the individual's right to think freely and express his thoughts freely. The decisive distinction here is between actions, which the state has a legitimate interest in regulating by legislation and thought. Spinozist toleration, hence, does not accord any special importance to organized sects—and freedom of religion, in this conception, rather becomes a subset of the broader *Libertas philosophandi*—the right to philosophize. This right, in return, is closely connected to the public presentation of thoughts and thus to freedom of the press, quite unlike Lockean toleration. To Spinoza, the "real schismatics are those who condemn the writings of others and seditiously incite the quarrelsome multitude against the writers, and not the authors themselves who generally write only for scholars and appeal to reason alone; and that, finally, the real disturbers of peace are those who, in a free commonwealth, vainly seek to abolish freedom of judgment which cannot be suppressed."[107]

It is this conception of toleration which ends up in the famous quote attributed to Voltaire: "I disapprove of what you say, but I will defend to the death your right to say it."[108] In the broader context, the deist Voltaire belongs to the moderate current of Enlightenment, but his concept of toleration is rather that of the radical current. The important thing here is that toleration is an attitude which should be undertaken by those who may feel insulted or outraged and otherwise would seek to suppress what insults them to hear, but restrain themselves and endure the insult. At the same time, such tolerance does not in any way prevent the tolerant person from himself attacking what insulted him in equally harsh verbal ways. In this conception of tolerance, then, it is an act of omission to act.

This completely sets it apart from "respect," "recognition," "living interest for" and other such attitudes which may be recommended vis-à-vis other cultures. These acts are positive acts, not just acts of omission, and, unlike toleration, they imply a positive value judgment on the cultures and persons respected. Thus it is comparatively easy to demand toleration of other people; it is merely asking them to refrain from certain actions. Respect requires a specific act (the positive value judgment) which requires considerable knowledge of the object judged. This is why respect and recognition, in return, are difficult to require in other people, especially if they do not agree with the implied positive value judgment. How should I respect a culture which I do not at all find respectable? I could tolerate such a culture and speak of or to it in a polite, circumspect way. I could respect not the culture, but its right to enjoy basic human rights, but these acts in no way imply that I should necessarily respect that culture in itself or the horrible acts it may indulge in. If I am forced to pay respect to such cultures or persons, it will necessarily be in the form of a mimicked respect, a theatrical recognition, a sham interest. It will force me to facile lies and stiff gestures, and to say something I do not mean at all. It will oblige me to put up a petit-bourgeois show of staged emotions which are not really there. Life indeed does involve situations where such behavior may be necessary, but that is not the same thing as recommending it as a general attitude to other cultures or persons.

The issue becomes even more complicated with the fact that the word "respect" is ambiguous; it may also refer to the attitude one harbors towards cultures or persons on which you do *not* pass a positive value judgment, but which you merely fear because they are capable of harming you in some way or another. The behavior one displays faced with such threats is often indistinguishable from ones behavior when showing "real," positive respect; that is probably the reason why these two rather different attitudes are covered by the same word. But such respect is "mafia" respect—the respect enjoyed by leaders of state, bosses, officers, mobsters, bikers and other with access to means of power or violence—and from their point of view, respect out of fear is pleasantly difficult to distinguish from respect out of admiration. The fact that such respect is also directly sought in threatening and violent acts, perpetrated by certain "cultural," religious or political groups, from street violence to terrorism, should not lead us to "respect" them, in any sense other than the fearful sense of the word.

Such demands for "respect," "recognition," and other similar terms easily blend with the Lockean conception of toleration; here, toleration is something awarded to organized religions which (unlike atheists) deserve respect because they strive for the salvation of their members. But real, Spinozist, tolerance is irreconcilable with the demand for "respect" for other cultures. The only respect which they can rightfully demand is not the respect for any culture, but the respect for the human rights of their members, which implies respect for the rights of that culture's individuals to associate, worship, and express themselves. In short, to enjoy the liberties granted by human rights, not a respect for the contents of their beliefs.

With regard to cultures: tolerance is the non-performance of prohibiting or threatening acts against expressions which appear insulting to you. It is the act of he who would otherwise *be insulted*. Respect is the recognizing or fearful attitude which may lead you to refrain from expressing your own opinion freely. It is the act of he who might otherwise happen to *insult* someone. The two are oriented in opposite directions and one precludes the other.

Respect and tolerance are not the same thing.

Diversity as a Good

Diversity is, in itself, an undisputed good which ought to be praised and strived for. We encountered this premise in parts of the anthropological traditions discussed in the second part of this book. It is an axiom, a moral judgment, from Ruth Benedict in anthropology to Charles Taylor in political philosophy.

It is remarkable that this premise about the unconditional good in the preservation of any culture in its purest form, uncontaminated from any co-existence with other cultures, may assume this status as an unproblematic and undebateable norm in a globalized world where cultures spread and mix with intercontinental migrations. This idea does not attract much principled reflection or concrete criticism regarding its possible clash with human rights or with other co-existing cultures. What if two cultures in the same territory claim dogmas which are irreconcilable? An example might be a modern and a pre-modern culture, fighting about the status of principles of emancipation in domains like gender or freedom of conscience—which of them should prevail? Should the pre-modern culture with dogma restricting its members enjoy protection for reasons of diversity?

Such problems are not discussed by the culturalist anthropologists in the second section of this book. Their scientific authority, it could be said, lies elsewhere, in the meticulous description and comparison of cultures. The anthropologists do not have any special access to value judgments or moral judgments on the basis of their scientific insight. Here, they remain amateurs or engaged citizens, like everybody else engaged in such domains or even personally affected by them. This should not prevent such anthropologists from discussing their premise about the unconditioned good in the preservation of cultural diversity. However, that does not happen. They just assume it as a given presupposition.

The Norwegian social anthropologist, Thomas Hylland Eriksen, mocks this protectionism of all cultures in his portrayal of the spread of this assumption from anthropology and all the way into UNESCO, where it has become part of the more or less explicit ideology of the UN. An aggressive version has developed in the UN Human Rights Council and the predominance of OIC countries in the Council. Hylland Eriksen asks, much to the point, which choices must be made in the work of preserving cultures, if conflicts arise, and he makes the guess in his diagnosis that pre-modern cultures will generally get priority over more recently developed cultures. This implies, of course, that cultures which tend to have the most problems with human rights get priority over cultures with fewer such problems. Courageously, he compares this unspoken priority list of the anthropologists with the Darwinian distinction between natural selection of species and artificial selection, as is undertaken by human breeders of animals and plants. The former is seen, by the anthropologists, as nobler than the latter. Pre-modern cultures are understood as the result of natural selection and must, hence, have first priority, as compared to modern cultures which are continuously being discussed and develop as the result of the same context in which the anthropologists themselves live. Thus, one of Hylland Eriksen's conclusions is that the relation to the cultural past unilaterally assumes the character of preservation, which has no other criterion than time. The older, the better and more worthy of preservation—and in this judgment, modernity loses out. Modern society with its culture, its rights and gender equality must, in this anthropological priority list, lose to a romantic striving for preserving the living past in a global open air museum. Everything, from all periods, the older the better, should exist in its uncontaminated and pure form anywhere, at the same time. This seems to be the unspoken principle.

Thus, a clear discrepancy appears between the statements cited in this book from human rights activists and citizens with unequal rights in Malaysia and the anthropologists discussed in the second part. The former group is not very engaged in preserving those goods consisting of pre-modern features of Islam which curtail human rights. Such people are not, like the anthropologists, "participant observers," but rather "observant participants."

The idea that diversity is a good in itself has thus developed into a creed found in many places, also beyond multiculturalism. Kymlicka, however, is hesitant to accept the argument and strives for founding his multiculturalism on liberal principles instead. If you look closer, diversity is a strange argument indeed, related as it is to an aesthetic conception of cultures as animal species threatened by extinction. Within the aesthetic domain, diversity is naturally an unconditioned good; we would like to be free to enjoy the pleasure of as many different aesthetic experiences as possible. It rests, in itself, on the concept of free choice; the vaudeville, short novel, or long poem which does not appeal to me, can freely be left alone. Quite different is the case for diversity in domains where no such choice exists, and where diversity may unconditionally impose itself upon us: a diversity of maladies, of errors, of lies, of poverties, of death threats, of fascisms, of parasites, of defeats, of deaths, of tyrants. In such cases, it is much more difficult to appreciate the richness of diversity.

The strange thing is that the diversity argument about cultures is very often made by people who also claim the culture is something unconditioned, something definitely enculturated, which is not the subject of individual choice. Given such a notion of culture, it is hard to see why there should be any positive value in the mere diversity of religions, punishments, marriage types, oppressions, clan or caste structures, etc., for the particular individual caught up in his particular culture does not have the possibility of selecting or even understanding other such features than those of his own culture. The person who benefits from the diversity is not, then, the particular individual caught up in his culture, but the tourist, the anthropologist, the observer, the outsider, who has unlimited access to a whole array of cultures, but without any obligations, and exempt from taking any of them as his personal destiny as well as from its systems of sanctions and punishment. If you are thus elevated over the array of cultures, there might be an aesthetic pleasure in enjoying the diversity of choices on the shelves of the cultural supermarket, but this requires an aesthete who has seen these shelves filled by histories of religions, anthropology, and the travel industry all of which have provided translations, books, exhibitions, guided tours and other harmless representations of cultures. In such representations, those diverse cultures may appear aesthetically appealing in their colorful manifold, but it is very hard to see how this decadent pleasure may be extended also to cover the single "cultural" individual carrying the task of living in one culture alone and who remains obliged to be "inextricably bound" to his single cultural destiny.

Monoculturalism in Plural

The tendency of anthropology to construct "cultures" might be able to gain some useful corrections from its old sister discipline, sociology. To a classical sociologist like Georg Simmel, it is an important characteristic of modern urban culture (where most multiculturalists take for granted that the "vibrant" meeting between cultures should take place) that the old, sharp group definitions such as those of estate, vocation, nobility, clan, guild, and class wither away. As the identity of the individual is co-determined by its social connections, this has important implications. The individual ceases to have one identity only, tied to his social group as a nobleman, a peasant, a blacksmith, a casteless or an unmarried copy-holder's daughter. Instead, each individual assumes a bundle of different identities or roles, dependent upon the many different contexts of function which develop in a modern, differentiated society. One may have one identity as a father, as a spouse, as a son, as an uncle, as a friend, a second at work, a third at your extra job, a fourth in your neighborhood, a fifth in your region, a sixth in your country, a seventh in your religion, an eighth in your skin color, a ninth in your philatelists' club, a tenth in the football club you support, an eleventh in the political party you vote for, a twelfth in the rock group you are a fan of, a thirteenth in your favorite dishes, and so on. The economist Amartya Sen has, in his well-argued *Identity and Violence,* taken up this classical sociological insight and made it into an annihilating weapon against those brands of multiculturalism that build upon "identity politics." Sen takes pleasure, repeatedly, in making long lists of the identities one and the same individual may assume in a modern society:

> The same person can, for example, be a British citizen, of Malaysian origin, with Chinese racial characteristics, a stockbroker, a non-vegetarian, an asthmatic, a linguist, a bodybuilder, a poet, an opponent of abortion, a bird-watcher, an astrologer, and one who believes God created Darwin to test the gullible (24).

In reality, the "politics of identity" strive to exterminate this manifold of identities, coexisting in the head of any modern individual, in order to leave only one simple identity behind. This is, of course, made possible by culturalism, according to which all cultures are organic and are thus able to answer all questions of identity at once. Sen points to the fact that there are basically two different approaches to multiculturalism: one which takes diversity to be a good in itself, and one which focuses upon the free decisions of individuals and thus only celebrates diversity to the extent that it is the result of choices that are as free as possible. This is also why Sen points to the fundamental role of reason. Reason is not a particularly "Western" construction—quite the contrary. Sen points to how rationalism and atheism were sophistications of the Indian tradition, as in the example of the Great Mogul Akbar in the 16th century, who asserted that religion should be cultivated with reason and not be uncritically inherited with "blind faith" from the "swampy regions of tradition."

This, of course, requires reasoning, choice, and responsibility in the individual. Seen from this perspective, multiculturalist identity politics appear radically anti-modern; in one stroke, all these difficult choices which must be constantly reflected upon anew, even when the choice is to continue, are exterminated. The attraction of identity politics in this context should not be underestimated: if you chose a "culture," then all doubts, hesitations, regrets about wrong choices, overlooked possibilities and speculation about what to do in your short life cease to be important. Culture and religion have already been chosen for you. Thus, a utopia of "simple living" forms an important element in the tempting package offered by culturalist identity politics. Even if this siren song is easily understandable in times of confusion, it remains illusory. Individuals have never been mere passive products of their culture, and in a modern society it is a completely impossible and regressive utopia that they should be. It is easy to observe how societies trying to impose such an identity on their citizens, automatically grind to a standstill, the prime example being Saudi Arabia which, despite vast oil incomes, seems completely incapable of generating an ordinarily well-functioning economy. On the level of the cultural group, a similar process results. If a cultural group isolates itself in identity politics, it becomes disconnected from its connections to the energizing diversity of currents in modern society, and the danger hangs over its members that they will sink, mentally and socially, towards the bottom of society, with culture as a weight around their feet.

Segregated, hard multiculturalism, where cultures close around themselves and do not enter into hybridizations nor merges with wider society, perfectly suits the striking description of Amartya Sen: monoculturalism in plural.

Revealed by the Veil

The variety of Muslim headdresses for women has become a standard object of heated debate in the West during the last decade, and it is easy to find spokesmen for simple xenophile and xenophobic positions alike: "It is a mere 30 grams of textile," or "They should be banned everywhere." A liberal approach will naturally see headdresses as protected by ordinary freedom of expression. Among other possibilities, dress is a way of expressing oneself, and it is the free choice of the individual to decide how to dress and which messages are thereby communicated. Complications only arise in situations where the freedom of the individual is already constrained for other reasons.

This does not necessarily have anything to do with what the headdress means. Muslim female veils may have many motivations. Muslims may don the veil for reasons of custom, tradition, Muslim ideology, because the imam says so, in order to provoke Western society, for reasons of youth rebellion against the traditional Islam of their parents, and even further reasons. What makes the case difficult is the international dimension. Several states maintain, for the time being, severe regulations prescribing that women should wear veils—for instance Saudi Arabia, Sudan, or Iran; the latter even have state patrols throwing acid into the face of women considered improperly dressed. In other states, strong Islamization movements exert a growing pressure on ordinary women to wear headdresses; take Iraq for example, where it is estimated than no less than fifty unveiled women in Basra alone were killed during the months after the Western occupation forces left. Similar movements can be found, with different strengths, from the Maghreb countries to Pakistan. The Muslim Brotherhood has the imposition of the veil high on its list of priorities, in Europe as well, both in the charming Tariq Ramadan and the more openly hawkish al-Qaradawi. The Iranian exile author Chahdortt Djavann gives the following explanation of the role of the veil in such Islamist movements: "To wear the veil is the symbol of, the flag for, and the key to the Islamist system. It is around the veil that an Islamist society may create itself. The veil is the Islamists' best means of gaining terrain. With the veil, the women (…) are objects owned by Muslim men (…). When first she has been presented on the market, the veiled girl may only be bought by a Muslim man. To veil women is to display not only the sex market, but also the system which supports it. 'Here are the women we possess and which you cannot have unless you convert to Islam;' the Islamists addresses this message to all men who are able to understand it, if only because they circulate in the street and take the metro. The veil is the best instrument for the Islamist mission."[109] Nonetheless, the individual veil-wearing Muslim woman may however wear her headdress for different reasons than this Islamist strategy.

The veil thus forms the object of a broad internal struggle in Islam. In such a situation, the mere wearing of the famed thirty grams of textile risks being associated with such Islamist force; the veil as a signal cannot be completely dissociated from these enforcement policies, even if the individual wearer of a veil may have quite different and completely innocent motives. It is a little like the 1930s, when the Danish beer brand Carlsberg had to stop using the Aryan swastika on its beer label because a strong and highly disgusting political movement had, in practice, monopolized the use of that symbol. This association with radical Islamism cannot be eradicated and probably even forms the reason, in a subset of users, for the very attraction of the veil. Correspondingly, it has the effect that many democratically-inclined observers do not like the signals sent by the veil. This does not, of course, imply that such observers necessarily support a ban on the veil. Compromise with basic liberal principles should only be considered in urgent danger, and then only temporarily. Normally, we do not support bans on Nazi parties, Hizb-ut-Tahrir, and the like, not least for the reason that such sympathies are easier to monitor when openly expressed than if they are forced to seek clandestine outlets.

A similar argument must hold for the veil in politics. Elected representatives in parliaments, city councils and the like are private individuals who represent a segment of voters. They may naturally dress as they like, within normal decency norms. Other observers, like us, may strongly disagree with the signals sent by those dresses, but we must tolerate people wanting to dress differently. Tolerance, of course, does not imply we are obliged to like what we tolerate. A completely different argument, however, holds for persons employed in public and private jobs. If such employment in some way involves wearing a uniform, there is no argument for why the veil should not fall. Discussions about veil-wearing judges or police officers belong here. Judges or police do not appear in bathing clogs, hooligan face paint, bikinis, jogging suits or other spectacular items of fashion, just as they do not don a Ku Klux Klan hood, a Catholic priest's collar, or an orange Hare Krishna robe, even if they might have a strong sympathy for the points of view associated with those modes of dress.

This position is not changed by the culturalist argument that the Muslim veil signals identity in an especially deep and committed fashion, for any other such identity-signaling modes of dress will also be precluded in court or among police officers. The judge who happens to be a nudist must yield and conceal his secret parts while in court; the judge who is a Barcelona fan and loves to don his Zlatan jersey must not do so during court proceedings; the judge who is a punk and promenades his Mohawk hairstyle in the street must lay it down while the court case goes on; the judge who is a Hell's Angels member must take off his insignia jacket while assuming the bench. Correspondingly, the equally hypothetical, radical, female Muslim who might serve as a judge, must take off her veil in court—and just like the others, she is free to don it again when changing to private dress after the court is adjourned. The veil is, just like the biker jacket, a competing uniform, and the individual cannot serve two uniform tasks at the same time. To be a judge is to serve in a position which is elevated over the particular individual who at any time occupies it. The judge undertakes a public service, and his behavior is highly constrained by a specific set of rules, leaving his personal preferences behind during the process. This is what is signaled by the formal change in dress code.

This is particularly important in those sensitive positions which, like the police officer and the judge, have to do with the executive and judiciary powers of the state which, unlike the legislative power, are usually not representative. They have an obligation to equality before the law. When one enters into such a position, the neutrality of the uniform signals this blindness to personal preferences, just as signaled by the classical depiction of the blindfolded goddess of justice. This is one of the basic reasons for the uniformization of such functions in the first place.

Uniformization of police and military, for example, has the rationale that the respective persons and their rank are easy to recognize and understand. This signals, at the same time, that the uniformed person is not, or not only, a private individual, but functions as an instrument of the state and is, as such, subject to a series of characteristic constraints on his freedom and his behavior. Such a basic restriction is that of neutrality, in which personal preferences are bracketed. It is just natural that female Muslims in such units let go of their veil.

Other cases are less problematic. Private companies with a dress code may chose to employ veiled Muslims, or they may choose not to employ such persons. This forms part of a private contract, and if an employee refuses to remove the veil when such removal is required by the dress-code, she must seek another job. Here, the employer might argue from the position of his "culture," and if this does not fit with that of the employee, then there is just no basis for an agreement between the two. Correspondingly, Muslim employers are at liberty to claim a dress-code making the veil obligatory for employees; the woman who refuses to wear one will then have to find other employment.

A precarious field, of course, is those parts of public service where the employee incarnates state power to a lesser degree: veils in state schools or state supported schools. Here, arguments pro and con may be made, and the decision will rest upon which local habit develops and which problems show up. Western countries normally do not have strict dress codes for teachers who are not prevented from displaying, to a moderate degree, their points-of-view by sartorial means. The fact that small girls are sent to school veiled appears as a tasteless act, in the same way as in other cases where small children are used as marketing signals for the ideology of the parents. The case for a direct ban on veils in school can be made if, like in France, special problems arise. The French ban on veils in schools had its background in the increasing amount of serious bullying and violence against non-veiled Muslim girls, including some cases of rape and killing, undertaken by Islamist youths with the motive of forcing all Muslim girls to don the veil. If such things develop systematically in certain Muslim circles, a direct ban on veils in school may be a proper emergency action, as a state response to "internal restrictions" in such Muslim groups.

Spokesmen for a Culture

A widespread fallacy with a direct connection to culturalism is the idea that self-appointed leaders of a "culture" are, in fact, representative of that culture. During the Cartoon Crisis, the Danish grouplet called the Islamic Society of Faith, which was instrumental in the development of the crisis, tried, with some success, to play such a role, supported by its generic name which seems to indicate an association of all Danish Muslims. After the crisis, however, the true nature of that group was revealed: it is a Salafist organization, closely connected to the Muslim Brotherhood and thus representative only of a special branch of radical Islamism, not at all representing the many Danish Muslims of Turkish descent, of Bosnian background, nor the many non-practicing Muslims and many other groups and individuals. This did not prevent the group from making assertions on behalf of all Danish Muslims as such, or, in more ambitious cases, on behalf of all Muslims in the world. In many cases, media and state institutions seem to have taken such claims at face value and accepted, *de facto*, the spokesmen of that organization as Muslim representatives in political discussions and councils. This process rests on a culturalist prejudice: that cultures are indeed unitary and organic, so if anybody claims to be the spokesman of a culture, it goes without saying that they must be representative, because cultures are homogeneous and the individual is inextricably bound to his culture.[110] But there is no reason to assume that "cultures" are any less internally diverse than any other social groups. Given the lack of any vote, election or other procedure of selecting representative spokesmen, such "spokesmen" remain completely self-appointed and serve, in reality, merely as spokesmen for themselves.[111] To accept them as more than this runs the risk of treating individuals who hold extreme positions as spokesmen. In the case of the Danish Islamic Society of Faith, such spokesmen included its leading imam, Abu Laban, who had been banned from entering Egypt because he was considered a danger to that country's security, or one of its secondary imams, Ahmed Akkari, who publicly recommended the use of violence against unveiled girls and toyed with plans of assassinating a Danish MP. During the Cartoon Crisis, these imams played a central role, both in inciting Middle Eastern leaders to act, and in appearing before the Danish public as leaders of Danish Muslims.

By accepting such persons as representatives, culturalism comes to add to bias in public debate, where very extreme and marginal individuals may be taken for true representatives of a moderate majority, which they do not, in reality, represent at all. Their claim to represent an especially "pure" Islam may then mirror Western culturalists' celebration of authenticity; the result is an alliance which supports the most reactionary, romanticized, and anti-modern version of the "culture" in question, an alliance which may scare more modern and moderate voices within that culture into keeping quiet. This unholy alliance may also contribute to a picture of individuals who break with reactionary norms in their cultural background as inauthentic persons, traitors against their own culture. This also implies that any individual from a "culture" may be required to act "authentically;" the space for individual deviance is eliminated.

In his book on the development of British multiculturalism, *From Fatwa to Jihad*, the British columnist and neuroscientist, Kenan Malik, has pointed to the fact that the very policy of multiculturalism may be co-responsible for the careers of such spokesmen. British multiculturalism of the 1990s saw the possibility of easing what was perceived as racial tensions by making a support system for different ethnic groups. Spokesmen were appointed, and the application for financial support for community centers, facilities, events, etc. was made possible. Malik, a secularist of Indian descent, understandably wonders why those leaders were invariably religious. Why should a Caribbean immigrant in Britain feel represented by a priest, and why an Indian like himself by an imam? By means of this policy, Malik argues, different groups were artificially molded into religious cultures, fossilizing around clerics and competing against each other for the same funding, even ending up fighting against each other in culturalist clashes among immigrant groups. Malik remembers, not without sentimentalism, the solidarity *between* immigrant groups and their common political actions before, as he sees it, the British left was split into competing, conservative cultural groups headed by religious leaders.

Such things may also lead to puzzlement over why many Western countries have tax exemptions for religious groupings. Why is it that religious associations, very often led by some of their most conservative figures, should have this special right? It is an already existing culturalist group right. Why should such associations have more right to escape taxation than any other group, association, or club? Ornithologists, role players or strip clubs do not receive special treatment—why should other associations, simply because they claim to have invisible friends whose existence nobody else has access to verify? Here, more equal treatment between different groups might provide a more realist multiculturalism than this mystical bias giving advantage to religious flocks and their more or less dubious spokesmen.

The extent to which such spokesmen are real representatives was an issue that was highlighted by the Cartoon Crisis. On October 2nd 2005, a group of eleven Danish Muslim organizations created a committee to organize the campaign against *Jyllands-Posten*'s drawings, which had been published two days earlier. This committee quickly grew to comprise 28 organizations, but as the daily *Ekstra Bladet* investigated the list, it became clear that some of the organizations did not exist at all and others among them had never been asked whether they wanted to participate. The protests against the drawings were undertaken by actually existing organizations representing not more than 15,000 Danish Muslims, around one tenth of the Danish Muslim population. This did not prevent the spokesmen for the committee from speaking on behalf of all Danish Muslims, even on behalf of all the Muslims in the world: "With the exception of very few hypocrites, everybody supports us. You must remember this does not only hold for the 200.000 Muslims in Denmark, but 1.3 billion Muslims in the whole world,"[112] exclaimed the spokesman, Kassem Ahmed, from the Islamic Society of Faith.

The fact that "cultures" are often claimed to be represented by some of their most "cultural," conservative spokesmen also makes possible a biased conception of the possible threats against such a group, because all events are seen by such leaders as having a cultural background or cause. In modern society, all cultural groups and other collectivities are subject to strong forces of change when they try to rearticulate their traditional forms of life in a democracy, which is, in itself, in an ongoing process of development. The culturalist viewpoint has a tendency to be blind to general structural changes in economy, civil society and state policies which affect all groups in society. Seen from a strong culturalist point of view, such developments are easily misread as "racism" or "xenophobia," for which other cultural groups or the majority in the society are taken to be responsible (see Walker 1997, 224). Culturalist spokesmen and leaders of cultural groups, their personal careers dependent on the survival of culturalism, easily misrepresent such developments and take all misfortune as having cultural roots, as if all problems in the world were the result of cultural clashes and xenophobia.

The Dynamics of Extremism

In relation to the murder of the film director, Theo van Gogh, and the attempts on his female writer's life in the fall of 2004, it is remarkable that something exceptional was at stake for the perpetrators. That led many politicians, a writer and an editor to criticize not the perpetrators, but the victims—not least the writer, Ayaan Hirsi Ali. They called for empathy with the perpetrators. These people had feelings of a special, sensitive kind which must be respected. They had certain taboos and holy doctrines that they will not allow to be insulted under any circumstances, and if you don't respect this, you'll have to realize that they react violently no matter what the consequences. In a sense, they are a kind of martyr on behalf of their culture which they are prepared to defend by any means. They claim that you have to understand this, even if you don't share their religion.

An aspect that was never discussed in relation to the screening of the film *Submission*, however, was the fact that it was the perpetrators themselves who made it famous all over the world and, with their anger, threats and deadly violence, invested it with enormous credibility, even before people had had an opportunity to watch the film. The public was left with the impression that there must be something about the film's supposed statement that could generate such a dramatic chain of threats and violence and make people announce that they were within their right to violently defend their doctrines against criticism.

If the film itself is the prelude, then the scenario of threats and violence is the first act in a macabre social show which feed backs into a chain of reactions from anti-Muslim circles in the media. The result is the spread of an attitude of general suspicion about Muslims and Islam as a religion and a culture. But the first acts of threats and violence are conducive for this kind of radical political entertainment to begin, where exchange of verbal aggression develops into physical assaults. Everything runs according to the script for the radicalization of society. The next possible move is arson on mosques and Muslim shops, followed by arson of churches, which was what we saw in the Netherlands. In Western Europe, this is unfortunately not the last case of exchange of attitudes where acts of violence are substituted for points of view. Which was, in fact, the first side to cross the line is the most trivial question in this chain of mutual escalation. At this stage of extremism, it is crucial that reactions will permanently outdo or at least match the acts of the adversary so the dynamic can continue. Only imagination is the limit, justified all the time by the noblest of sentiments.

Thus, the reaction of passionate Islamists to artistic expressions breaks the boundaries of normal behavior in the public sphere. They no longer understand such expressions as part of a free public sphere and their own part as spectators or readers with an extensive but still constrained set of reactions at their disposal. They can keep silent, they can criticize, they can ignore, they can insult, or they can make their own film or write their own commentaries. These are the limits, granted the openness of a public sphere, but sometimes they seem not to be sufficient. Instead, they send out a crowd to trash a writer; many European writers have experienced such threats and actions, most recently the axeman trying to kill Kurt Westergaard on New Year's Day 2010.

But an early and little noticed example of this happened to a Norwegian journalist in the October 2003 because of a joke he wrote in the journal *Night & Day* in Oslo. He was not beaten up himself, but only because a colleague of his with the same name was mistaken for him. They share the name Bård Tøgersen. But what did the real Bård Tøgersen write to anger his Islamist audience so much as to attack his innocent namesake?

He had merely delivered a kind of parody of a lifestyle manual, instructions, apparently addressed to Norwegian boys, if they dreamt of having sex with a Muslim girl. It was, of course, a provocation, which anybody who was able to read Norwegian and endowed with a minimum sense of humour would realize. And, indeed, he managed to press the right buttons.

The manual makes a number of points that you will have to consider if you intend "to get in under the veil" as it was written. Tøgersen encourages Norwegian boys to keep their spirits high and go for the project. As he argues: we in the West are not supposed to look at the world in black and white and therefore the veil should not automatically lead us to believe that all Muslim girls are as pious as they may look. They are as individual as snowflakes. As types they wary widely all the way from the circumcised girls from North Africa to "the happy and horny Turkish girls." Nevertheless, Tøgersen focuses his attention on the Pakistani girls who apparently constitute the majority among Oslo Muslim girls.

Having defined his focus group, Tøgersen then lines up the number of points to be considered for success when the flirt is about to begin. The girl dreams of a romantic affair, in line with "Romeo and Juliet," and our hero has to prove he is able to save her from a patriarchal tyranny. Therefore, he ought to consider his dress code. He should not show up in folkloric costume, but instead style himself as a bohemian with an air of adventure; long hair, exotic tattoos and a skateboard will be part of the paraphernalia he cannot do without. He should certainly not imitate Muslim men who, according to Tøgersen, are too involved with weapons, crime, drugs, and hard sex. As an indication of this lamentable fact, he points to Pakistani newspaper stands stuffed with porn magazines of all kinds. Our hero ought to set a superior standard for himself and be more polite and sensitive. He should reject all kinds of stupid macho behavior.

But he should also pay tribute to the sensitive question of culture. In terms of gastronomy, he should absolutely avoid eating pork, which would appear too disgusting and alien for the girl, a thing which will only make her think of eating rats. Halal Kebab is recommended instead.

The cultural profile should also be considered for a successful flirting—it would be nice if you can namedrop some Bollywood hits. But if the conversation drifts into the political field, always take the side of Pakistan in the conflict with India over Kashmir. Speaking about politics, you should admit that the West also struggles with problems of its own. Take greed and over-consumption, to name but two. Add to this that Islam might have a lot to offer.

This manual is, of course, written for fun to a general public with a sense of humour and gifted with irony, to which it assumes the apparently pious ideal of the virtuous Muslim woman in veil is an object of discussion. But this icon also seems to be the heart of the cultural and political identity of Islamism. This might explain why the text outraged Muslim extremsts. The real Bård Tøgersen hit the bull's eye and made everybody laugh, except for the people who were the laughing stock; they announced themselves with threats, anger, and violence.

The Norwegian stunt is about defamation of the icon of the virtuous Muslim woman. Something similar seems to have been at stake in connection with the film *Submission* by Theo van Gogh, where quotations from the Koran dealing with draconian punishment of women are written on the skin of a naked female body. But here, the subject of the film (real submission and physical mutilation) is no laughing matter. It draws attention to parts of the canonical scripts of Islam, quotations that are interpreted literally in some Muslim circles, and it criticizes them. But the murder of the director generated reactions in the media that went far beyond the criticism in the film. We were told in several exegeses about a long and abhorrent tradition of violence and intimidation of people of faiths other than Islam. Muhammad, founder and role model, initiated this tradition by killing the poet Asma bint Marwan and her children in their bed. Her crime: insulting Muhammad and his teachings.

The same kind of argument, a sectarian exegesis, might just as well be applied to canonical scripts in both Christianity and Judaism. Calls for punishment against non-believers are to be found in the holy scriptures of all three religions, but the crucial aspect is, of course, whether there are believers who interpret such calls literally and are prepared to act accordingly. This is indeed true in radical parts of Islam today. There are such groups, mostly springing out of the radical revival movements of Islam, such as Deobandi, Salafism, Wahhabism, the Brotherhood and their many splinter groups, but it is obvious that this fact does not tell us anything about all living Muslims today who have to ignore many of the draconian rules of the Koran in order to be able to live in a modern, multiethnic and multicultural society. This operation is also known by the name "interpretation of religion."

The general stigmatization of Muslim culture and the degeneration of the political discussion into a demagogical exegesis of holy scriptures is a militant simplification used by right-wing nationalists after the murder of Theo van Gogh. Thus, it closely follows the script for radicalization. Extremists on both sides strengthen each other and do everything they can to take the rest of society hostage in their battles, and impose a dynamic on the discourse in the public sphere which only knows one direction: escalation of extremism. Both of them have the interest of exaggerating the force of the other in order to scare people to join their own ranks. Both of them indulge in endless repetitions of the scenario about the West versus Islam. In the process, the reflections of the individual become less and less important in favour of his or her ethnic affiliation. At the end, there is no more room for the individual point of view: everybody is reduced to his or her ethnic-religious identity. Dialogue is over, and only violence speaks between the ethnic cultures of society. That's the lesson we learned in Bosnia at the beginning of the nineties.

After the murder of Theo van Gogh, followed by the general stigmatization of Muslim scripture and tradition, it is not surprising to look for and actually find confirmation of the nationalist's allegations about Islam as a religion of hate. You just have to read what Islamists say about Islam and the West. Islamists readily confirm the nationalist stereotype of how Muslims behave in general, just as nationalists readily confirm the Islamist stereotype of how the West behaves in general. The chronology of statements is of no importance; it is no longer of any importance when who said what in this phase of escalation. Statements and text are now dynamic parts of a more general discourse of extremism where they mutually build hatred.

Let's take an example which apparently confirms the allegations about Islam as a religion of hate. April 18th 2004, the Portuguese newspaper *Publico* published an interview with Omar Bakri Muhammed, who is under suspicion of being affiliated with an Al-Qaeda cell and who is the leader of a radical Islamist group Al-Muhajiroun based in London. Out of eight persons arrested for participating in a terror operation in London, seven of them are followers of Omar Bakri Muhammad, which might indicate something about his teachings. The Imam Muhammed invites a Portuguese journalist to visit him in his home. He tells him about the thousands of books in his collection which are all about Islam, with the exception of one book of British law which he has received as a gift. It is simply pathetic, we are told, as it is prohibited to Muslims to follow laws created by man. Therefore, Omar Bakri Muhammad can only look forward to the day when the Islamic flag will fly from Downing Street. That's what he is obliged to work for, as the Prophet tells him, he cannot live among non-believers without trying to convert them. Omar Bakri Muhammed justifies the attacks on the Twin Towers in New York as retaliation for US policy towards Muslims all over the world. The fact that civilians lost their lives does not affect him, as he says: "We don't make a distinction between civilians and non-civilians, innocents and non-innocents. Only between Muslims and nonbelievers. And the life of a non-believer has no value. There's no sanctity in it… We are not hypocrites. We don't say: 'I'm sorry, it was a mistake.' We say: 'You deserved it.' We assume the purpose is to kill as many people as possible, to spread the terror, so that people in the West think: 'Look what happened to us!' … Terror is the language of the twenty-first century."

The ingenious aspect of the discourse of extremism is that stigmatizing statements can operate in both ways: nationalists will be confirmed by Islamists and vice versa. Readers of the interview with the Imam Omar Bakri Muhammed will find confirmation of the allegations made by nationalists about the hateful nature of Islam. In relation to the political murder of Theo van Gogh, the statements of the imam are granted an imperative trustworthiness. The exegeses of nationalist demagogues may evoke a response in many readers because they are uttered in a situation which calls for anger and justice, but the only thing they do is to escalate the conflict and take all Muslims as a symbolic hostage for retaliation, while the actual perpetrators are out of reach. Allegations from nationalists that condemns Islam in general terms invites confirmations from the homologous partners from among Islamist radicals, men like Omar Bakri Muhammed for example, who will always be a ready supplier of a foreboding narrative.

Such radical speech acts can also work in the reverse direction, so the Islamists supply the allegation and the nationalists supply the confirmation. Nationalist demagogical exegesises about the violent and abhorrent nature of Islam might serve as confirmation to the Muslim who initially has read the statements by Omar Bakri Muhammad. This mental operation may also take place against the backdrop of real events. A Muslim might experience disturbing news about how other Muslims are treated and find no credible answers from the political establishment, or the Western audience may learn troubling news about Islamist terror cells and find no answers but the empty reference to discrimination against Muslims as a whole.

In Bernhard-Henri Lévy's book about the murder of the Jewish-American journalist, Daniel Pearl, he outlines elements of the life of the alleged killer, the British-Pakistani Islamist Omar Sheikh. The writer traces the roots of his Islamism and follows him from being quite a normal citizen and talented student until he becomes engaged in radical circles in London and takes part in the struggle to defend the Bosnian Muslims at the beginning of the nineties. This genocide on European Muslims both tortured and anaesthetized the public at the time, as no state or international organization was able to react to it. Sheikh realized that what he had heard in radical, Islamist circles was absolutely correct: the West hates the Muslims and all talk of humanism is empty rhetoric only meant to glorify Western culture and nothing else; humanism is only reserved for Christians and non-religious Europeans. The democracies are worth nothing in the defence against Christian violence. The only things politicians can offer are whimpers and regrets, but nobody even dreamed of an armed intervention to rescue the Bosnian Muslims from genocide. The young Omar Sheikh watched this day after day on TV broadcasts from the besieged cities: negotiations are apparently going on, time passes slowly, nothing happens, the killings continue and the concentration camps are organized again to destroy a people. The young Omar Sheikh disappeared into the brigades of Islamist militia, first to Bosnia, later on to other destinations where faith called. The journey ends in madness and nihilism as he materializes again in Bernard-Henri Lévy's book as the main suspect in the killing of the American journalist in Pakistan. After the reading of Lévy's book and Omar Sheikh's road to Jihad, all the European politicians who were in power at the beginning of the nineties will have to face the question of why nobody reacted to the genocide. Why didn't they understand that they betrayed the lesson from the Nazi concentration camps: that this could never happen again? They did not act when Sarajevo was besieged, but that was not because the inhabitants were Muslims who were attacked by snipers. When Eastern Bosnia was stormed by paramilitary Christian legionaries and the civil Muslim population was massacred and cleansed from the homeland, it came to the politicians as a surprise. When they heard about the camps it was all too late. The genocide of the 7000 men and boys in Srebrenica was due to communication problems; the request for air support to the Dutch forces in charge of defending the town was delivered on the wrong form and was lost in UN bureaucracy... Let us stop this. We cannot take it anymore. The more we repeat all the sick excuses, the more these politicians sound exactly like people who want to distance themselves from Islamist violence as the murder of Theo van Gogh and at the same time express how complicated everything is when you also have to pay respect to the insulted feelings of the murderers.

Let us return to the current conflict about freedom of expression, as artists are blamed for blasphemy and insults against Islam. After the release of *Submission,* we have, time and time again, witnessed threats and violence against journalists, academics, newspapers, publishers and artists, most famously, of course, against the Danish cartoonists, but also against the Swedish conceptual artist Lars Vilks for his humorous provocations of the prophet Muhammad as a lost dog on a roundabout, which resulted in Islamists preventing him from lecturing at the University of Uppsala as well as attempting arson on his home in the spring of 2010. Most recently, we have witnessed threats against the American Comedy Central who produce the TV animation *South Park*. The occasion which spawned the anger in this case was an episode where the prophet appears disguised as a bear. That led the station to censor the episode as well as the following one which commented upon the events—and in some countries, the episode was taken off the air entirely. Consequently, it was a success for the violent mob that forced a TV station to change its policy and censor a cartoon. More recently the story has repeated itself in another dynamic of extremism: radical Christian circles take inspiration from the Islamists. On June 3rd 2010, a coalition of American Christians called "Coalition against Religious Intolerance" waged a campaign against the very same Comedy Central and their plan for a TV serial titled *JC* in which Jesus is a frustrated NYC boy trying to escape from his domineering father. They now demand that Jesus Christ must also be protected against caricature. The mitigating circumstances, however, are that they don't threaten with violence but instead prepare to mobilize an economic boycott among the advertisers. These Christians argue that they won't let their holy scripture be exposed to ridicule when the Muslims have succeeded with censorship against Comedy Central. The reasoning is consistent: why respect freedom of expression for your opponent when your religious competitor does not do it? Violence talks—why not money? As in the case of the Middle East campaign against the Danish cartoons, the scene is set for whoever dares take the next step from a boycott and to arson, violence, and murder.

Most recently, the spiral of radicalization has also led a right wing terrorist inspired by culturalist ideology to commit an attack in Oslo, July 22 2011. 77 victims were killed, 8 of them by a bomb attack in the government districts of Oslo, 69 of them young Labour Party members gunned down at a summer camp on the island of Utøya.

Before his actions, the terrorist Anders Breivik published a 1500-odd pages manifesto on the internet. This manuscript, largely consisting of internet copy-pastes, displays an eclecticism involving conservative nationalism, Christian fundamentalism, white suprematism, knights templar fantasies and nazism. All of it is mixed with the aim of providing a counter-ideology to Islam—Breivik characteristically confusing Islamist extremism with Islam as such. European leftists are branded as "cultural marxists" facilitating the spread of Islam on the continent—hence his attacks on the governing Labour Party of Norway and its youth branch as those allegedly responsible for the growing presence of Muslims and Islam in Europe. As such, this terror attack displays a further step in the escalation spiral between Islamism, nationalism, and multiculturalism. It is the first large-scale terror attack in Europe motivated by right wing culturalism against Islam, and, in particular, against the multiculturalism ascribed to the Norwegian Labour Party.

A couple of conspicuous details should be mentioned. In the immediate wake of the killings, the suspicion was aimed against Islamists, not only because of earlier attacks in Europe such as the bombings in London and Madrid committed by Islamist fanatics, but also because an Islamist grouplet, the Ansar al-Jihad al-Alami, was reported to assume responsibility. When Breivik was arrested, the media concluded instead it was a right wing attack. It is remarkable that two groups of terrorists with supposedly diametrically opposite motives can be assumed to commit the very same criminal act. But the question remains: are Islamists and right wing extreme nationalists really so different? Islamists are against modernity, liberal democracy, equal rights and seek to privilege a special group of people, the believers—just like Breivik and his likes are against modernity, liberal democracy and cultural and religious diversity. The bottom line is that the West has witnessed the emergence of a new extreme faction of right wing culturalism and anti-modernity in the shape of Islamism—so that there is now a throng on the extreme right in the West: more strange and violent groups and ideologies compete for attention than ever since WWII.

Another aspect in the dynamics of extremism was the claim marketed by multiculturalists after the Oslo events: the real culprit was not Breivik but European critics of Islam and Islamism. Immediately, to many multiculturalists, the events thus once again called for curtailing free speech. So both Islamist and nationalist terrorism demands one cure, according to many multiculturalists: further constraints on free speech. But as the editor of the German weekly *Die Zeit* Josef Joffe soberly remarked: "Who equalizes word and murder does more harm to the open society than does any Breivik."

A final bizarre and extraordinary detail in the Oslo tragedy is Breivik's thinly veiled adoration, in his manifesto, for his Islamist counterpart. He even goes so far as to propose a sort of collaboration or compromise so that Islamists will be granted sovereignty over the Middle East, once they leave Europe under the sovereignty of Breivik and his associates. In this hallucinated geo-political offer we recognize a political inspiration from ethno-pluralism.

Within the dynamics of extremism we now recognize not only a mutual inspiration to violence—but also to identification. Monoculturalists like Omar Bakri Muhammed and Anders Breivik both advocate violence in their quest for purity. Anders Breivik adds another turn of the screw by involving himself in terror against multiculturalists, because they favor, in his eyes, his homologue competitors on the Islamist right wing.

Thus, we witness again and again new repetitions of the dynamics of extremism. It's no longer just the culturalists on both sides—Nationalist and Islamist—who radicalize the discourse in the public sphere by going from exchange of speech to the exchange of violence. Different culturalist and religious pressure groups learn from each others' fear of freedom and the spiral of means invented to fight it. Even if they are struggling against each other, from a bird's eye view they appear strategically more and more united in accelerating the dynamics of extremism against the basic standards of the enlightenment.

The Disneyland of Culture

The spokesmen of culturalism claim that authentic life takes place within the confines of one culture, and that man has a universal need to have access to a single cultural framework of understanding. Remember the reference to Chief Ramon's Clay Cup in Ruth Benedicts' "Patterns of Culture". But what if that is not the case in the Modernity? What if locking oneself up in a traditional culture without contact with social and political currents, without connections to art, literature, science, news, debate outside of "culture" is, in fact, to lock oneself out from the real world and live a staged fantasy life? Jeremy Waldron answers that question: to submerge oneself in the traditions of a particularist community is like living in Disneyland and to mistake one's environment for being the true expression of real cultural existence. Even worse, he continues, it is demanding support for living in Disneyland, while also insisting that modern society guard and protect the borders of Disneyland. In the meantime one imagines that what goes on in Disneyland is all that is needed to live an adequate and fulfilling life (Waldron 1992, 763). If that is right, then the whole issue of "authenticity" may be quite the opposite of culturalist belief. Authentic living is participating in modern, international culture and the cosmopolitan development of civilization, while it is non-authentic to lock oneself up in a staged and dreamt-up past, which may anyway only survive on subsidies and special rights.

The idea of culture as a destiny is but a reactionary, romantic ideologization of culture which, for the time being, is besieging Western politics from both the left and the right, and which is taken up with relish by authenticity-seeking groups demanding special rights. But if one manages to break the spell of culturalism, a big step is taken. As the Norwegian social anthropologist, Thomas Hylland Eriksen, one of the strongest anti-culturalists in anthropology, has argued: instead of invoking "culture," when you speak about, say, local art, you could just say: "local art." The same goes for language, ideology, patriarchy, children's rights, gastronomy, ritual practices. He goes on to say you could simply use such terms instead of covering them in the cozy, but misrepresenting, carpet of culture (Eriksen 2001). Call things what they are, instead of wrapping them up in the mystifying and oppressing veil of culturalism. The fact that customs are ancient does not make them more dignified than recently established habits. The mere fact that we have always rubbed our hair with fox grease, eaten pork, beaten our women or eaten our enemies does not make it either more or less right to continue, and that old, yellowish documents claim that we should continue to do so every hour in order to prevent the destruction of the world or secure for ourselves good seats in paradise should count as a good reason for philological criticism of those documents rather than for their celebration.

Down with culture!

Appendix
The Religious Pressure against Free Speech: A Chronology

"If freedom of speech means anything at all, it is the freedom to say things that people do not want to hear."

George Orwell

This timeline records events featuring in the growing religious pressure against freedom of speech and freedom of religion during recent decades. It is a selection of highlights from a more extensive and detailed 300-page timeline which is updated regularly and may be found in a Danish version at www.fridebat.nu

1971
Protests outside Broadway Theatre in New York at the opening of *Jesus Christ Superstar*.

1979
Monty Python's *Life of Brian* gives rise to broad Christian protest. The movie is blacklisted in Norway and Ireland, which cancelled the prohibition one and eight years later respectively.

1981
The Dutch comedian Rudi Carell shows a sketch on German TV where veiled women throw their underwear at Ayatollah Khomeini. Iran dismisses two German diplomats, closes its Goethe Institute and issues death threats. Carrell apologizes and never again makes fun of Islam.

1986
Pakistan passes §295c of the penal code, criminalizing any direct or indirect criticism of Muhammad. The punishment is death or lifelong imprisonment.

9/26 1988
Salman Rushdie's *The Satanic Verses* is published in England.

10/20 1988
The Union of Muslim Organizations in Great Britain demands a ban on *The Satanic Verses*.

10/27 1988
Martin Scorsese's *The Last Temptation of Christ* is met with a Molotov cocktail attack from an extreme Catholic group at its opening in Paris.

October–November 1988
The Satanic Verses is banned in India, South Africa, Pakistan, Saudi Arabia, Egypt, Somalia, Bangladesh, Sudan, Malaysia, Indonesia, and Qatar.

12/2 1988
The first public burning of *The Satanic Verses* in Great Britain.

2/12 1988
Six dead and more than one hundred wounded are the victims when 10,000 attack the American Cultural Center in Islamabad in a protest against Rushdie.

2/12 1989
Ayatollah Khomeini makes public a fatwa against Rushdie on Radio Tehran, encouraging Muslims to kill everybody involved in the production of the book.

February 1989
Many Western intellectuals and politicians support Rushdie. Others, such as the British authors Roald Dahl, John Berger, John le Carre, Paul Johnson, and Hugh Trevor-Roper claim Rushdie should have refrained from provoking.

2/17 1989
Leading British Muslim (and later secretary general of Muslim Council of Britain), the Mawdudist Iqbal Sacranie, says that death is too easy a punishment for Rushdie.

March 1989
OIC encourages its member countries to prohibit *The Satanic Verses*.

5/27 1989
20,000 Muslims protest in London and burn Rushdie effigies.

7/31–8/5 1990
The 19th meeting of the OIC Foreign Secretaries adopt the "Cairo Declaration" on Islamic human rights, which claims all human rights are subordinate to the principle of sharia legislation.

July 1991
The Japanese Rushdie translator Hitoshi Igarashi is murdered with a knife, and Italian Rushdie translator Ettore Capriolo is severely wounded.

1992
The Egyptian author and human rights activist, Farag Foda, is killed by fundamentalist militia for his book *To Be or Not to Be*.

1993
Taslima Nasreen is charged with blasphemy in Bangladesh for the novel *The Opponent* and must go into exile.

7/2 1993
A mob of 2000 surrounds the Turkish festival of literature in the town of Sivas and demands that the Turkish Rushdie translator, Aziz Nezim, be handed over for summary execution. He escapes, and the mob burns down the building where 37 Turkish authors and locals die.

10/12 1993
Tariq Ramadan brings about the canceling of a planned production of Voltaire's *Muhammad, or Fanaticism*. The play was first censored in 1742 on the occasion of the visit of Turkish officials in Paris.

October 1993
The Norwegian Rushdie translator, William Nygaard, is shot and severely wounded.

1994
Egyptian Nobel Prize Winner, Naguib Mahfouz, is stabbed for his support for Rushdie, but survives.

1995
The book *Why I am not a Muslim* is published. The Pakistani-British author chooses to publish under the pseudonym of Ibn Warraq.

3/30 1997
The European Council for Research and Fatwa is founded, headed by Muslim Brotherhood spiritual leader Yusuf al-Qaradawi.

4/19 1999
The OIC presents a resolution against the "Defamation of Religion" at the UN Human Rights Commission which adopts it. The passing of ever more stringent resolutions on that subject becomes an annual event in the Commission (from 2006 The UN Human Rights Council).

11/11–11/14 2000
At the 9th "Islamic Summit" of the OIC, the "Doha declaration" is passed. Here, the OIC countries decide to stand together against all accusations of human rights violations and to work together in international fora to campaign for sharia.

February 2001
Preparatory seminar for the UN anti-racism conference in Durban.

Jews are not allowed to participate.

3/21 2001
The Taliban destroys the two giant Buddhas of Bamyan, Afghanistan.

8/31–9/7 2001
UN's Durban conference seems to be the first larger forum where "Islamophobia" is launched and claimed as a sort of racism.

9/12 2001
Immediately after 9-11, Muslim Council of Britain demands a political defense of British Muslims. This forms the beginning of Labour's attempt to criminalize criticism of religions.

3/19 2002
A court in Florida prohibits the screening of the movie, *The Profit*, which may be seen as critical of Scientology.

6/24 2002
On behalf of the European Council for Research and Fatwa, al-Qaradawi makes a fatwa calling for death penalty for apostasy.

9/16 2002
The French author Michel Houllebecq is charged with racial hatred in Paris by Muslim organizations. His characters often speak out against Islam, and he himself has claimed that Islam is the stupidest religion.

10/6–10 2002
The American Baptist preacher Jerry Falwell claims Muhammad was a violent man. Protests against him among Indian Muslims results in twenty dead and hundreds of wounded. The Iranian leader Mohsen Shabestari declares a fatwa calling for the murder of Falwell.

November 2002
Ayaan Hirsi Ali receives death threats in Holland and must have police protection.

1/25 2003
Hirsi Ali says: "According to Western yardsticks, Muhammad was a pervert. A tyrant."

February 2003
OIC and the ambassadors from Saudi Arabia, Malaysia, Pakistan, and Sudan complain to the leadership of Hirsi Ali's party, VVD.

7/23 2003
The Polish artist Danuta Nieznalska receives a fine and a six

months travel prohibition for exhibiting artwork with a photo of a penis on a cross.

12/30 2003
Al-Qaradawi declares a fatwa against the computer game Pokémon, which allegedly uses Jewish symbols and indoctrinates the theory of evolution.

2/10 2004
British bishops force the BBC not to air an animated cartoon where the Pope appears as a preacher on a pogo stick.

3/21 2004
Al-Qaradawi declares a fatwa recommending lashes or death penalty for homosexuality.

7/14 2004
Sir Iqbal Sacranie demands the Blair legislation against defamation of religion must criminalize every criticism of Muhammad.

11/2 2004
The moviemaker Theo van Gogh is murdered in the streets of Amsterdam by Mohammed Bouyeri, for having made the feminist movie *Submission*, together with Hirsi Ali. She is threatened for her "fundamentalism of the infidels" in a note Bouyeri leaves stabbed to van Gogh's breast. In the ensuing weeks, mosques and churches in Holland are attacked.

November 2004
The journalist Rohan Jayasekara, in an article in Index on Censorship, calls van Gogh a "free speech fundamentalist" who misused free speech.

11/12 2004
The comedian Rowan Atkinson launches a campaign against the Labour government's planned "Racial and Religious Hatred Act."

12/7 2004
"Racial and Religious Hatred Act" proposes a definition of defamation as a crime, according to which unintentional defamation is as serious as intentional. Punishments of up to seven years in prison and a fine without any upper limit are proposed.

12/15 2004
Former *Daily Telegraph* editor, Charles Moore, receives death threats after having supported Rowan Atkinson.

12/18 2004
The play *Disgrace* by the British

Sikh Gurpreet Bhatti is canceled after Sikh riots. The play depicts, amongst other things, rape and murder in a Sikh temple.

12/22 2004
Two Australian priests, Daniel Scot and Danny Nalliah, are convicted by a court in Victoria for having presented a Christian criticism of Islam.

January 2005
More than 60,000 Christians protest against the BBC TV film *Jerry Springer: The Opera* for its depiction of Jesus. A blasphemy case is filed but is rejected at Westminster City Court and later at the High Court.

1/18 2005
Churches Commission on Interfaith Relations declares its support for Blair's Defamation Law.

1/27 2005
The international Film Festival in Rotterdam removes, for security reasons, Theo van Gogh's *Submission* from the program where it appeared under the headline of "Freedom of Expression."

February 2005
The President of the Canadian Society of Muslims, Syed Ali, declares that Canadian freedom of religion involves the right of religions to punish believers who give up or betray their faith.

2/3 2005
An erotic painting with Koran quotes by the French-Arabian painter, Louiza Darabi, is removed from a museum in Gothenburg because it insulted the Muslim faith.

2/8 2005
The Austrian draughtsman Gerhard Haderer is sentenced to six months prison in Greece for blasphemy in his *Das Leben des Jesu*.

3/16 2005
A French court prohibits a billboard campaign by the clothes company Francois Girbaut because of a photo imitating Leonardo's *Last Supper*.

4/15 2005
In a sermon in the al-Aqsa mosque in Jerusalem, Sheikh Issam Amayra from Hizb-ut-Tahrir encourages Danish Muslims to seize power in Denmark and "establish the Caliphate Denmark." He suggests this should be done not with weapons, but by inflaming tensions between Muslims and infidels.

6/16 2005
The Iranian Christian Hamid Pourmand, who is charged with apostasy, escapes the death sentence. Instead, he is subjected to forced conversion to Islam as well as three years imprisonment and the confiscation of all assets of his family.

7/18 2005
Masked men attack and destroy the sacred shrine of the Malaysian faith, "Sky Kingdom." Fifty-eight believers are arrested and convicted for rejecting Islam.

7/20 2005
The British civil rights group for homosexuals, OutRage, announces it has received repeated Islamist death threats, after having defended gay victims of honor killings.

9/15 2005
Mayor of London Ken Livingstone defends his invitation of al-Qaradawi. He claims al-Qaradawi is the leading force for aligning Islam to Western values.

9/17 2005
The Danish daily *Politiken* reports that the author of children's books, Kaare Bluitgen, is unable to find illustrators for his book about Muhammad, because of the illustrators' fear of persecution.

9/19 2005
Burger King withdraws an ice cream cone from British restaurants because a spiral on the paper wrapping is claimed to resemble the Arabic sign for "Allah."

9/25 2005
Tate Gallery in London removes the sculpture *God is Great* by the conceptual artist, John Latham; it displays the Torah, the Bible and the Koran cast in glass.

9/30 2005
The Danish daily, *Jyllands-Posten*, publishes a page with twelve drawings of Muhammad under the headline "The Faces of Muhammad." The alleged reason is to investigate whether self-censorship would prevent Danish cartoonists from participating. In an accompanying text, editor Flemming Rose writes that in a secular democracy you must be ready to accept satire, mockery, and ridicule.

10/2 2005
A group of Danish imams from different radical Sunni currents form a group planning nineteen

protest actions against *Jyllands-Posten*'s drawings.

10/3 2005
The city council of Dudley, Britain, bans all depictions of pigs and swine in the workplace after a Muslim complaint. The ban also comprises a coffee mug with a Piglet picture.

10/12 2005
Danish PM Fogh Rasmussen receives a protest letter from diplomats from eleven Muslim countries led by Egyptian ambassador Mona Omar. They ask for a meeting and demand that *Jyllands-Posten* be "taken to task under the law of the land."

10/15 2005
OIC sends a protest letter to the Danish government, largely identical to that of the eleven ambassadors.

10/17 2005
The Egyptian newspaper, *El Fagr*, reprints a selection of the cartoons It is the first paper to do so without any public reaction.

10/21 2005
PM Fogh responds by letter and refuses to meet with the eleven ambassadors, referring to the fact that he cannot interfere with the freedom of press.

10/25 2005
The UK House of Lords rejects the "Racial and Religious Hatred Act," adding amendments to the proposal, and limiting it to intentionally threatening behavior.

The Egyptian government urges the Danish government to dissociate itself from the drawings and warns about a possible escalation of the issue.

10/29 2005
Egyptian ambassador Mona Omar urges the Danish government to disapprove of the drawings and of any insult to Islam. She threatens to spread the knowledge of the drawings to the Islamic world.

11/11 2005
Turkish PM Tayyip Erdogan visits Denmark and claims "Free speech is important, but what is holy for me is more imporant." He warns about chaos and unwanted events.

11/18 2005
Egyptian Foreign Minister Abdul Gheit threatens a general Muslim and Arab trade boycott of Denmark.

Danish PM Fogh gives a Freedom Award to Ayaan Hirsi Ali.

December 2005
Two delegations of Danish imams travel to the Middle East with a dossier including the twelve drawings. In the dossier, they add further pictures of a praying Muslim raped by a dog, a man with a pig mask claimed to portray the prophet—without making clear these additional images did not originate from the Danish press.

They meet leading Egyptian politicians and clerics, including the Grand Sheikh of the Al-Azhar University, Muhammed Tantawy. In other countries, they meet with Shiite and Sunni leaders such as Sheikh Fadlallah in Lebanon, Grand Mufti Hassoun in Syria, and al-Qaradawi in Qatar.

They give rise to Arab press claims that all Danish media are campaigning against Islam, that Denmark plans censorship of the Koran, that *Jyllands-Posten* is a state paper and that the Danish government plans a sequel to van Gogh's film.

12/2 2005
The Pakistani party, Jamaat-e-Islami, offers a $10,000 reward to the killer of the Danish cartoonists.

The Danish police recommend the cartoonists go underground.

12/6–7 2005
The OIC Mecca summit meeting decides to wage a campaign against criticism of Islam. The drawings are distributed at the meeting by Egyptian Foreign Minister Abdul Gheit. Iqbal Sacranie from the Muslim Council of Britain is also present. The meeting adopts a communique attacking the use of freedom of speech as a "pretext" to defame religions. It claims all governments must grant full respect for all religions.

12/16 2005
The UN General Assembly adopts a resolution against defamation of religions. OIC claims this document forms the legal basis for action against European newspapers.

1/10 2006
The Christian Norwegian periodical, *Magazinet*, reprints the drawings.

1/20 2006
Demands for trade boycott against Denmark circulates in the Saudi press as well as in sms and emails.

1/21 2006
Al-Qaradawi encourages all Muslims in the world to boycott Denmark and Norway.

1/27 2006
Saudi Arabia declares a boycott of Danish goods and calls its ambassador home.

1/29 2006
OIC demands the adoption of a UN resolution requiring sanctions against member countries defaming religions.

Boycott of Danish goods begin in Qatar.

30/1 2006
Jyllands-Posten publishes an apology for having offended Muslim feelings, but not for having printed the cartoons.

At the final reading of the "Racial and Religious Hatred Act" in the House of Commons, the Labour Deputy Home Secretary, Paul Goggins, makes clear that after the expected passing of the Act the next day, the printing of the Danish cartoons will be illegal in Great Britain. Sir Iqbal Sacranie, leader of MCB, says that after adoption of the law, the expression "Islamic terrorism" will be illegal in Great Britain.

1/31 2006
The Egyptian parliament urges the population to boycott Danish goods.

Bomb threats against *Jyllands-Posten* leads to the evacuation of its premises.

Hamas demands punishment of *Jyllands-Posten* and the cartoonists.

Bill Clinton condemns "these totally outrageous cartoons"

Al-Jazeera airs a Danish adherent of the Brotherhood claiming there is a Danish plan to burn the Koran.

Labour surprisingly loses the vote on the "Racial and Religious Hatred Act" in the House of Commons by one vote. Twenty-one Labour "backbenchers" secretly conspired to vote against it. Had PM Tony Blair not gone home early, the bill would have passed. The upshot is that the House of Lords' revised version of the Act is passed instead.

2/1 2006
Many continental papers in Europe reprint the drawings—*France Soir, Die Welt, Berliner Zeitung, De Volkskraant, La Stampa, El Mundo*, etc. Many other papers and journals reprint selections in the drawings in the following weeks. Very few British and American papers reprint the drawings.

2/2 2006
The Jordanian paper, *al-Shihan*, reprints the drawings, arguing it is a greater insult of Muhammad to blow up innocent passengers with a bomb than it is to make a drawing. The editor, Momani, is sacked and taken to court.

The Roman Catholic bishops of the Nordic countries condemn the drawings.

Turkish PM Erdogan demands the restriction of freedom of the press in Europe.

2/3 2006
Demonstrators in London demand the execution of all who insult Islam under slogans like "Be prepared for the real Holocaust!" and "To Hell with Free Speech."

South Africa bans the printing of the drawings.

The US Secretary of State declares, regarding the drawings, that the incitement to religious and ethnic hatred is unacceptable.

Al-Qaradawi declares February 3 to be an international "Day of Wrath" against the drawings.

2/4 2006
Demonstrations in Damascus and the burning of the Danish, Norwegian, Swedish, and French embassies.

2/5 2006
Demonstrations in Beirut and the burning of the Danish embassy.

An episode of *The Simpsons* is canceled. In the episode, Muhammad appears to Homer in a dream and converts him by promising him 770 donuts in paradise.

2/7 2006
Demonstrations in Tehran, attacks on the Danish embassy.

A common declaration from OIC, UN, and EU, represented by Ekmeleddin Ihsanoglu, Kofi Annan, and Javier Solana. Among other things, they claim:

"We fully support the right to freedom of expression. But we understand the deep hurt and the general indignation felt in the Muslim world. We think that press freedom implies responsibility and discretion and that it must respect the beliefs and dogmas of all religions."

2/8 2006
The French satirical weekly, *Charlie Hebdo*, reprints the drawings along with additional new cartoons—including a front page depicting Muhammad in a depressive mood, saying: "It is hard to be adored by idiots!" President Chirac condemns the magazine as "manifest provocations."

2/9 2006
The EU commissioner for justice, freedom, and security, Franco Frattini, makes a proposal for a common European press code of conduct to avoid insults.

2/10 2005
The German cartoonist, Klaus Stuttmann, has a satirical drawing in the *Tagesspiegel* showing the Iranian football team as suicide bombers. He receives death threats.

2/12 2006
Two newspapers in Algeria are closed, and their editors arrested, for reprinting the drawings. Three papers in Yemen are closed, and three journalists are arrested for reprinting the drawings.

2/16 2006
In Malaysia, the Chinese paper, *Guang Ming*, is closed for having reprinted one of the cartoons.

2/17 2006
Pakistani imam Maulana Qureshi offers a reward of one million dollars for the killing of the cartoonists.

2/18 2006
The Italian Minister for Institutional Reform, Roberto Calderoli, is forced to resign his position after political pressure resulting from him donning a T-shirt with the cartoon of Muhammad with a bomb in his turban.

More than fifteen people die in a riot against the cartoons in Nigeria.

2/19 2006
OIC makes five demands to the UN. One is to criminalize criticism of religions. The others are

a UN resolution prohibiting "defamation of all prophets and faiths", EU legislation against Islamophobia, an ethical code for European media, and a UN media norm restricting free speech with respect to religious symbols.

2/20 2006
The British holocaust denier, David Irving, is sentenced to three years imprisonment in Austria. Many Muslims attack the West for double standards with regard to freedom of expression.

2/12 2006
In Volgograd, the Russian paper, *Gorodskije Vesti*, prints one of the cartoons and is closed by the city mayor.

2/27 2006
The EU Foreign Ministers adopt a resolution emphasizing free speech at the same time as claiming freedom of expression must be used responsibly.

3/1 2006
Twelve intellectuals publish the manifesto "Together against the new totalitarianism," supporting the freedom of the press for *Charlie Hebdo*. It is signed by Hirsi Ali, Chahla Chafiq, Caroline Fourest, Bernard-Henri Lévy, Ishad Manji, Mehdi Mozaffari, Maryam Namazie, Taslima Nasreen, Salman Rushdie, Antoine Sfeir, Philippe Val, and Ibn Warraq.

3/19 2006
Danish and French TV broadcast the documentary "Caricatures—behind the Wrath" by Mohammed Sifaoui, documenting assassination proposals by one of the Danish imams, and establishing that the Danish Islamic Society of Faith is a branch of the Brotherhood.

3/20 2006
In the Springer building in Berlin, the Pakistani Amer Cheema is arrested, allegedly planning to stab the editor-in-chief of *Die Welt*, Roger Köppel.

3/31 2006
A gang of young Muslims with iron bars force a Parisian café to censor the exhibition "Neither god nor god" with atheist drawings. Cartoons critical of Islam are removed by the Brotherhood under threat of arson against the café.

4/11 2006
An EU group is working on a

lexicon of permitted expressions regarding terrorism. Among other things, they advise against the use of the expression "Islamic terrorism."

5/5 2006
Amer Cheema, who allegedly planned to kill the *Die Welt* editor, dies in prison, probably from suicide. This gives rise to riots in Pakistan.

6/12 2006
The blasphemy case against the author Oriana Fallaci begins in Bergamo, Italy. She is charged with having characterized Islam as a "lake which can never become clean."

7/12 2006
German police find two bombs in the Cologne railway station.. The Lebanese Youssef el-Hajdib and Jihad Hamad are arrested. They claim the bombs were against the cartoons. They are later convicted in a Beirut court.

9/6 2006
The Turkish-German lawyer, Seyran Ates, receives death threats and must go underground and give up her work.

9/12 2006
Pope Benedict XVI gives a speech in Regensburg, quoting Manuel II Palaeologos, one of the last Byzantine emperors who, in 1391, said that Islam had brought nothing new but "evil and inhumane things, like his order to spread his faith by the sword." Furthermore, the Pope compares an Islamic tradition for claiming God is not bound by rationality with the Christian claim that God cannot act against reason. Many Islamic countries protest and demand an apology from the Pope. OIC calls the talk a "smear campaign," and many leading Muslim clerics call for apologies or punishments, or even the murder of the Pope.

9/17 2006
The Pope apologizes personally and claims the Manuel quote did not cover his opinion, just that his talk was an invitation to respectful dialogue.

9/20 2006
The French philosopher, Robert Redeker, publishes a column in *Le Figaro* on the issue of how the free world should act in the face of Islamist threats. Among other things, he claims Islam is a creed celebrating "violence and hatred."

Tunisia and Egypt prohibit sale of the paper, and Redeker receives death threats. His photo and address are published on Islamist home pages. He must seek police protection and move to a new place every second day.

9/22 2006
The Pakistani politician, Hafiz Ahmed, demands the Pope be crucified.

9/25 2006
A staging of Mozart's opera *Idomeneo* is canceled in Berlin, because it contained the severed heads of Jesus, Buddha, Poseidon, and Muhammad.

10/4 2006
Nancy Kobrin's book *The Sheikh's New Clothes* on the psychology of suicide terrorists is canceled by Looseleaf Law Publication for security reasons.

10/5 2006
Timothy Garton Ash supports Ian Buruma's characterization of Hirsi Ali as an "Enlightenment Fundamentalist."

10/6 2006
Whitechapel Art Gallery, London, removes a number of erotic pictures by the surrealist Hans Bellmer for fear for "offending the feelings of Muslims."

11/13 2006
The UN report, "Alliance of Civilizations," demands the drafting of a code for good press behavior.

12/19 2006
After a Pakistani proposal, the UN General Assembly adopts a resolution obliging member states to introduce laws against defamation of religions.

12/30 2006
Park officials in the Grand Canyon are not allowed to tell the guests about the age of the canyon. If asked, they should answer "No comment," in order not to insult creationists.

3/22 2007
Charlie Hebdo is exonerated by the court in Paris.

3/30 2007
The UN Human Rights Council approves a resolution demanding legislation against religious hatred and intolerance. The Council invites the special rapporteur to report on all cases of insult of religions, especially Islamophobia.

3/31 2007
The sculpture *My Sweet Lord*, a life-size Jesus in chocolate, is removed from a Manhattan gallery after protests from the "Catholic League."

4/2 2007
Historical Association in Great Britain reports that schools refrain from teaching the Holocaust and the Crusades because of conflicts with Muslim beliefs.

5/30 2007
The Malaysian convert, Lina Joy, loses her case in the federal court of Malaysia (see section 1 of this book).

6/18 2007
Pakistani Minister for Religious Affairs, Mohammed ul-Haq, threatens suicide bombings if Great Britain does not withdraw its recent ennobling of Salman Rushdie.

6/20 2007
The victorious Hamas claims Muslim law in Gaza holds for Christian Arabs as well.

8/16 2007
The Swedish paper, *Nerikes Allehanda*, publishes a cartoon by the artist Lars Vilks, depicting Muhammad as a "roundabout dog."

8/30 2007
OIC condemns Vilks's drawings, demanding immediate punishment of Vilks and the newspaper, as well as an apology from the Swedish government.

9/10 2007
The Italian EU commissioner, Franco Frattini, plans electronic censorship of the Internet so that it is impossible to use certain search words.

9/27 2007
The German author, Günter Wallraff, receives death threats and is named "Islam enemy number one" after he proposes that German Muslims invite him to read Rushdie's *Satanic Verses* aloud in the Cologne mosque as a sign of their democratic convictions.

10/2 2007
A Buddha statue with a banana and two eggs as private parts, by the artist Colin Self, must be turned around after protests.

A terror bomb against Flemming Rose, editor of *Jyllands-Posten*, is revealed in a court case against Danish terrorists.

November–December 2007
After the departure of British and Danish forces from Basra, it is judged that 40–50 women have been murdered for not wearing a veil, or for wearing Western dress and makeup.

11/22 2007
The author Taslima Nasreen is forced to leave Calcutta after riots against her, which necessitated the deployment of the army.

12/24 2007
The UN General Assembly adopts a Pakistani/OIC resolution urging member states to criminalize the distribution of racist and xenophobic ideas.

1/6 2008
Dutch-Iranian artist, Sooreh Hera, goes underground after execution threats because of her photos of exiled Iranian gays with Muhammad masks. Her photos are removed from the museum of The Hague after threats. Her part of the exhibition is then moved to the museum of Gouda, whose director receives death threats.

The Pakistani-British bishop of Rochester, Michael Nazir-Ali, claims multiculturalism creates closed zones where radical Islamists keep out non-believers, and he compares these Islamists with the extreme right.

1/17 2008
British Home Secretary Jacqui Smith announces a dictionary of expressions to be avoided, including "War on terror" and "Islamic extremism." Instead of the latter, the expression "Anti-Islamic activity" is recommended.

1/18 2008
Aleksander Sdvizhkov, the editor of the White-Russian magazine, *Zgoda*, is sentenced to three years in a labor camp for reprinting the cartoons.

1/21 2008
The leader of the foreign commission of the Iranian parliament, Alaeddin Boroujerd, threatens the Netherlands with breaking off of diplomatic contacts and waves of violence, if they do not prevent the production of Geert Wilders's announced film, which criticizes the Koran.

1/28 2008
The book fair in Cairo censors a number of titles, including books by Milan Kundera, Mohamed Choukri, Ibrahim Badi, Hanan al-Sheikh and Elias Khoury, appar-

ently because the books describe sexual situations.

1/29 2008
The supreme Anglican leader, the Archbishop of Canterbury, Rowan Williams, demands a restriction on free speech. He claims that "thoughtless and cruel" expressions should be punished.

1/31 2008
Iran prohibits the feminist periodical, *Zanans*.

The Afghan Senate supports the death penalty for the twenty-three year old journalist, Perwiz Kambaksh, for blasphemy. He downloaded and distributed an article which critically discussed certain Koran verses about women.

The Egyptian convert, Muhammed Hegazy, is refused conversion by a Cairo court with reference to the fact that sharia is above the law.

2/4 2008
Ninety thousand Muslims sign a petition against Wikipedia for showing several depictions of Muhammad from the 13th to 16th centuries in the entry "Muhammad."

2/8 2008
The Archbishop of Canterbury Rowan Williams proposes the introduction of parts of sharia in Great Britain. This will be a "constructive accommodation."

2/10 2008
Turkish PM Erdogan claims, in a speech in Cologne, that assimilation is a crime against humanity.

2/12 2008
Danish police arrest three men, two Tunisians and a Danish-Moroccan, for planning the assassination of the cartoonist Kurt Westergaard.

2/13 2008
Many Danish papers reprint the drawings related to their coverage of the assassination plot against Westergaard.

2/14 2008
Riots in several Danish cities with burning cars, etc.

Iran files an official protest against the reprinting of the drawings.

Burning of Danish flags in demonstrations in Karachi and Tehran.

2/15 2008
The OIC protests against the reprinting of the cartoons in the Danish media and demands an official Danish declaration assuming moral responsibility and the prohibition of support for religious hatred.

2/19 2008
The coordination council of the Gulf States demands the legal prosecution of the cartoonists.

World Muslim League, Egypt, Pakistan and several others protest against the reprinting of the cartoons.

2/20 2008
The UN secretary general, Ban Ki-moon, claims that free speech should be used with responsibility, respecting all faiths.

The Arab League adopts a charter, according to which TV-networks in Arab countries may be closed, if they offend political or religious persons or Arab values. Al-Jazeera protests.

2/22 2008
Demonstrations against Denmark in Iraq, Sudan, Pakistan, Gaza, etc.

Al-Qaradawi and several other clerics call for boycott of Danish goods.

2/24 2008
Pakistan closes YouTube because of the access to the Danish cartoons.

A pink rabbit in a Hamas children's TV program campaigns for a boycott against Denmark.

2/27 2008
The German Minster of the Interior, Wolfgang Schäuble, urges European papers to reprint the drawings to show that Europe stands together against Islamist threats. His statement is contradicted by the Ministry the same day.

High-ranking representatives of the Vatican and the al-Azhar university condemn the reprinting of the cartoons,

The Dutch bank Fortis stops the distribution of the piggy bank "Knorbert," claiming it does not satisfy multicultural requirements.

The Dutch government summons Geert Wilders to a meeting and warns him against screening his film, *Fitna*.

2/28 2008
Norwegian and Swedish police arrest six persons suspected of planning terror attacks on the artist Lars Vilks, amongst others.

Protestors close an exhibition in Berlin by the Danish artist group Surrend. The exhibition depicted a Jewish kepi and the Ka'aba with the legends "Stupid hat" and "Stupid stone," among other things

3/2 2008
NATO leader Jaap de Hoop Scheffer expresses concern that Wilders' film may cause trouble for NATO forces in Afghanistan.

The Dutch government tries to prevent the screening of Wilders' film.

The group of OIC ambassadors at the UN urges the Secretary General to act against the Danish drawings and to demand that the governments involved should stop tolerating blasphemy.

3/5 2008
The spokesman for the organization "The messenger of God unites us," Zakaria al-Sheikh, claims he will sue the Danish papers that have printed the cartoons. He is supported by many Jordanian media.

The Dutch Organization of Employers demands action against Wilders' film.

3/7 2008
An Arab consumers' organization and the Pakistani chamber of commerce encourage a boycott of Danish goods.

3/19 2008
Taslima Nasreen leaves India to settle in Europe.

In a tape recording on the internet, Osama bin Laden threatens a severe punishment of the EU because of the cartoons.

3/22 2008
The American internet provider, Network Solutions, closes the homepage where Wilders had announced the screening of his film.

3/27 2008
The Dutch ex-Muslim from the Labour Party, Ehsan Jani, announces another Islam-critical movie with the title *The Life of Muhammad*. Muslim organizations demand a prohibition of the movie.

Wilders' movie *Fitna* is released on the web site liveleak.com.

The UN Human Rights Council adopts its annual resolution against defamation of religions, in a sharpened version demanding the High Commissioner to review existing legislation in the member countries regarding the criminalization of the defamation of religions.

3/28 2008
Three UN special rapporteurs make a joint declaration criticizing Wilders' film, *Fitna*, and call for governments to prevent the association of Muslims with violence and terrorism.

3/29 2008
liveleak.com removes *Fitna* from its site after threats against its employees.

UN Secretary General Ban Ki-moon demands a prohibition of *Fitna*.

The former president of Malaysia, Mahathir, demands a global boycott against the Netherlands.

Trailers for the Hollywood feature film *The Love Guru* give rise to protests from Hindu organizations.

3/31 2008
liveleak.com reintroduces *Fitna* on the site after upgrading security.

4/7 2008
A Dutch court exonerates Wilders from allegations of incitement to violence in comparing Islam to fascism and calling Muhammad a barbarian.

4/9 2008
A picture titled "Religion, Flesh, and Power" by the Austrian artist Alfred Hrdlicka is removed from an exhibition in Vienna as a result of Catholic protests. It depicts the Last Supper as a homoerotic orgy.

4/22 2008
Danish embassies in Afghanistan and Algeria close after threats.

5/13 2008
The British Film Institute promises protesting Hindus not to show the movie *The Love Guru*.

3/19 2008
The Dutch cartoonist, Gregorius Nekschot, is arrested for insulting Muslims and blacks in his drawings.

5/20 2008
A British teenager is arrested during a demonstration against Scientology. He carries a poster claiming that "Scientology is not a religion. It is a dangerous cult." The police claim he must not use the word "cult." After human rights protests, he is released and the case against him is dropped.

6/2 2008
A suicide bombing against the Danish embassy in Islamabad kills eight and wounds thirty.

6/3 2008
The Pakistani ambassador in Denmark claims *Jyllands-Posten* is responsible for the bombing.

6/4 2008
Al-Qaeda in Afghanistan assumes responsibility for the Islamabad bombing, referring to the fact that Denmark has not apologized for the drawings.

6/8 2008
Protestant, Catholic, Buddhist and Jewish clerics join Hindus protesting against the movie *The Love Guru*.

The Indonesian government demands forced conversion of all Ahmadiyya Muslims to orthodox Islam. If they object, they will be sentenced to five years in jail.

6/10 2008
Malaysian PM Badawi claims the right of British Muslims to live under sharia.

6/19 2008
A court in Viborg, Denmark, exonerates *Jyllands-Posten* from an allegation of libel in publishing the cartoons.

6/24 2008
The OIC claims that the exoneration of *Jyllands-Posten* will lead to Islamophobia.

6/30 2008
The chief prosecutor of Amsterdam, Leo de Wit, concludes that Geert Wilders will not be prosecuted for inciting hatred against Muslims in his film *Fitna*.

7/1 2008
Muslims protest against a free postcard distributed by the police in Tayside, Scotland, which depicts, among other things, a police dog. This is an unclean animal, and the police force apologizes.

7/2 2008
Iran's parliament discusses a proposal for criminalizing the

encouragement of corruption, prostitution, and apostasy on the Internet. Such crimes should be punished by the death sentence.

7/3 2008
Lord Chief Justice Phillips of Worth Matravers, the highest judge in Great Britain, supports the introduction of a separate sharia court system in Britain for financial and marital issues.

7/5 2008
Two British school children are punished with after-school detention because they did not want to say the Muslim declaration of faith in a religion class. Parents protest.

7/8 2008
Children who say "yuck" to foreign food may be racists and should be corrected by pedagogues, according to a British government declaration.

7/11 2008
A French burqa-wearing immigrant is refused French citizenship because her version of Islam is judged incompatible with secularist principles.

7/14 2008
The BBC TV serial *Bonekickers* shows a fanatical Christian decapitate a moderate Muslim which gives rise to Christian protests claiming the depiction of the opposite would have been censored.

7/17 2008
Polio is back in Pakistan's Swat region after the expulsion of vaccination doctors who Islamists claimed had injected Muslims with chemicals to make them infertile.

The French blogger Fernand Cortes de Conquilla is arrested and has his computer confiscated because his homepage, "Pilori," is critical of Islam and allegedly promotes "racial hatred."

Yemen plans a "moral police force" to exterminate all sin in the country, including female singers, intergender dancing, night clubs, fashion shows, pornography, churches, unaccompanied women travelers, gender-mixed education, satire and offenses against the Koran, Muhammad, and Muslim clerics.

7/25 2008
UN's nine-member expert committee for human rights expresses concerns that negative public attitudes to Muslim members of

society is still permitted. People expressing such attitudes should be punished in an appropriate way.

The Texas Board of Education has decided that all state schools should have mandatory Bible classes.

7/31 2008
A British poll shows 32% of Muslim students support religious killings; 40% want sharia in Great Britain.

8/6 2008
After Muslim threats, the American publisher Ballantine cancels the publication of Sherry Jones's novel, *The Jewel of Medina*, which treats Muhammed and his child wife Aisha.

8/9 2008
Catholics protest against the exhibition of artwork by Martin Kippenberger at a museum in Bolzano, Italy. It depicts a crucified frog with an egg in one hand and a mug of beer in the other. After a hunger strike by a conservative politician, the museum wrapped up the work in paper and removed it to the upper floor.

8/10 2008
Thirty-five thousand Christians demonstrate against the adoption of sharia in Papua New Guinea.

Muslim clerics demand action against the Turkish TV serial, *Noor*, depicting love problems in an upper class marriage. They claim it leads to divorces, because female TV watchers adore the male character Muhammad who is a considerate and romantic spouse.

8/12 2008
BBC cancels a big-budget docudrama, *The London Bombers*, about the background of July 7 bombers in Leeds. They explain the drama was Islamophobic and offensive.

8/13 2008
The Danish secret police, PET, publishes a linguistic guideline claiming expressions like "war on terror," "crusade," "jihad," "jihadist," "holy war," "fundamentalism," "holy warrior," "mujahedin," "martyr," "salafaism," "wahhabism" and "Islamism" should be avoided. Allowed expressions include "terrorist," "extremist," "militant," "violent," and "militant Islamism." PET claims the purpose is to

describe things as precisely and objectively as possible.

8/14 2008
The Malaysian government prohibits two books which might undermine Muslim faith. One is Norani Othman's *Muslim Women and the Challenge of Islamic Extremism* (see Section 1 of this book).

8/6 2008
The Malaysian conference, "Conversion to Islam," about problems in conversion to and from Islam is closed after one hour because of intrusion by Islamic demonstrators.

8/18 2008
Liberal Muslims in Lucknow, India, stage a wedding with a female imam and female witnesses. This gives rise to protests from clerics who declare the marriage invalid under Islamic law.

8/24 2008
The leader of Danish PEN, Anders Jerichow, claims it is only rarely dangerous to speak out about Islam or Muslims.

8/28 2008
The Pope speaks out against the crucified frog in Bolzano, claiming it offends Christian religious sensibilities.

8/30 2008
Pakistani parliamentarian Israr Zehri defends the execution by live burial of five women in Baluchistan for claiming the right to choose for themselves whom to marry.

9/4 2008
Editor Quentin Peel, from the *Financial Times*, claims that Denmark's reputation has not suffered from the Cartoon Crisis. On the contrary, he claims that many have felt sympathy for the country's clinging to principles of free speech.

9/5 2008
Al-Qaeda leader al-Yazid warns that the Islamabad bombing was only the beginning of a campaign against Denmark which may terminate in the complete extermination of the country from the surface of the Earth.

9/14 2008
On the internet forum, al-ekhlass, Islamists discuss how to kill as many Danes as possible by poisoning the water supply with

cyanide, hydrochloric acid or thallium.

The superior Saudi judge Ibn al-Luhaydan claims it is legal to kill owners of TV networks that broadcast immoral programs.

Paul McCartney receives threats of suicide bombings because of his planned concerts in Israel.

9/15 2008
Saudi judge al-Fozan calls for death sentences for TV astrologers, who are viewed as sorcerers.

9/17 2008
Saudi imam al-Munajid declares a fatwa against Mickey Mouse; according to Muslim law, mice and rats are the "soldiers of satan" and should be killed.

9/18 2008
The first official sharia court in England opens in the Hijaz College Islamic University in Nuneaton, Warwickshire after a decree from Justice Secretary Jack Straw. The court addresses commercial, civil and marital law, and its verdicts of the sharia courts will be enforceable by ordinary courts.

The home page of biologist Richard Dawkins is prohibited in Turkey after creationist complaints.

9/25 2008
A gay parade is attacked by Muslims in Sarajevo shouting "Kill the gays" and "God is great."

9/17 2008
British police arrest three men after an incendiary bomb attack against the director of the publishing house Gibson Square which was about to publish Sherry Jones' novel, *The Jewel of Medina*.

9/30 2008
China prohibits the performance of Western religious music.

10/12 2008
More than a thousand Christian families flee their homes in Mosul, Iraq, after Islamists kill eleven Christians in the area.

10/23 2008
After protests from Muslims, Sony withdraws millions of copies of the Playstation game "LittleBigPlanet" from the shops. The Mali singer Toumani Diabate sings a song in the game which contains two Koran verses.

10/27 2008
The Egyptian blogger Reda Abdel-Ramen is arrested for promoting

the idea that the Koran is the only source for Islam and that Sunni and Hadith play no role.

10/30 2008
Activists break the windows of the British art gallery SaLon displaying paintings by Muslim artist Sarah Maple which depict Muslim women with a naked breast, with a piglet in the arms, etc.

11/1 2008
The city council in Oxford, England, prohibits the use of the word "Christmas" in all public writings in order to avoid insulting believers of other faiths.

The British think tank "Centre for Social Cohesion" calls for addressing the security and freedom of speech of Muslim critics of Islam. In a report, 27 cases of threats against Muslim authors, politicians, activists, and artists are investigated.

A priest in Stettin, Poland, dissolves a role playing group, claiming this activity leads to Satanism.

11/28 2008
EU adopts "Council Framework Decision 2008/913/JHA," which obliges EU member states to harmonize their legislation against racism with a minimum and maximum penalty of one and three years imprisonment, respectively, and a range of other punishments. Crimes covered include the distribution of writing, pictures, or material which contain racist or xenophobic statements (including denials of genocide) as well as involving assistance to and encouragment to such acts. Racist and xeonphobic motivations should be seen as aggravating circumstances.

11/29 2008
A Danish priest demands that the local kindergarten refrain from using pixies during Christmas; he claims they represent devil worshipping.

11/30 2008
An Islamist group in Dhaka, Bangladesh, destroys a huge outdoor sculpture of a group of white storks. They claim the sculpture leads to idolatry.

12/3 2008
Thirteen are wounded when Islamists attack a Coptic service in an abandoned factory in Egypt.

12/4 2008
The European Human Rights Court refuses a complaint from

two Muslim girls who were expelled from their school in 1999 for refraining to take off their veil in gym classes. The court claims the girls were well-informed about the rules of the school.

12/9 2008
Words referring to Christianity are removed from Oxford University Press's children's dictionary ("abbey," "altar," "bishop," "chapel," and so forth). The editors refer to falling church attendance and multiculturalism.

The leader of the Society of Muslim Lawyers in England, Anjem Choudary, claims all Muslims should avoid participation in Christmas celebrations. They will follow the road to the "fires of Hell," if they celebrate the illusion that Allah has offspring.

12/12 2008
The dance girls of Lahore, Pakistan, strike in protest against "talibanization" which threatens to exterminate the old Mogul tradition of Mujra dancing. The dance has been prohibited by the high court of Lahore.

12/13 2008
An Australian urban complex exclusively for Muslims is planned in Riverdale. The local Muslim leaders claim Muslims should be isolated from mainstream society and thereby become good Australian citizens. The cleric Abdul Jalil Ahmad explains that South Africa constructed completely segregated societies in apartheid, and it functioned well.

12/15 2008
An investigation by the think tank Centre for Islamic Pluralism shows that women are discriminated against in the newly founded British sharia courts.

12/17 2008
The British woman Dorothy Glenn is warned by South Tyneside City Council to remove Christmas decorations from her house because it might be "offensive to the community."

Four freedom of expression experts warn against the UN resolutions addressing "defamation of religions." Frank la Rue (Guatemala), Miklos Haraszti (Hungary), Pansy Tlakula (South Africa), and Catalina Botero (Organization of American States) claim that "religions, like all beliefs, cannot be said to have a reputation of their own."

12/21 2008
A movie is shown in cultural centers in Jedda and Taif, (which are protected by the royal court), thus challenging the Saudi prohibition against movie theatres. The religious police protest strongly against this infringement of the law.

"Grandpa Frost," the Bosnian version of Santa Claus, is prohibited in Muslim schools in Bosnia.

12/27 2008
The Taliban in Northwest Pakistan warns that girls will be killed if they are not kept away from schools. According to estimates, the Taliban has already destroyed 252 schools in the area, predominantly mixed-gender schools.

12/30 2008
The Norwegian government plans to extend the legislation against Hate Speech to cover attacks on religions and world views. At the same time, the old blasphemy law should be abandoned.

1/1 2009
The Irsaeli left-wing daily, *Haaretz*, reveals a list of Jews suitable for assassinations made by Belgian Islamists. It includes authors, journalists, lawyers, and, among others, Bernard-Henri Lévy.

1/6 2009
General Ahmed Pasha, leader of the Pakistani secret police ISI, refuses to arrest Taliban leaders in Pakistan: "Shouldn't they be allowed to think and say what they please? They believe that jihad is their obligation. Isn't that freedom of opinion?"

1/7 2009
Daily Express reports that British jihadists have published a list on the net of prominent British Jews as targets for political action. Amy Winehouse and David Miliband are on the list.

1/16 2009
Somali politician Abdirahman Ahmed is executed for apostasy.

1/17 2009
The Dutch Muslim politician and al-Qaradawi disciple from the Labour Party, Ahmed Marcouch, proposes the founding of a new, purely Muslim city to the west of Amsterdam.

1/20 2009
The Dutch government passes a law to criminalize all expressions which offend religion or ideology.

1/21 2009
The Amsterdam appeal court sanctions the prosecution of Geert Wilders for his film *Fitna* and its "comparisons between Islam and Nazism."

1/22 2009
The Austrian politician Susanne Winter is sentenced at a court in Graz to pay a €24,000 fine for "humiliating a religion" by saying, among other things, that Muhammad was a pedophile.

The preparatory statement for the UN "Durban II" conference in Geneva calls for an international framework providing guidelines for state legislations against "negative stereotyping of religions" and "defamation of religions."

The Dutch Minister of Justice, Ernst Ballin, supports permission to enter the country for the Islamist preacher Khalid Yasin, who has demanded the death penalty for homosexuals and defended terror bombings. Critics ask why Wilders is prosecuted but not Yasin.

1/26 2009
Al-Rahma TV broadcasts a program in which the imam Amin al-Ansari shows footage of the Holocaust, saying, "This is what we hope will happen, but, Allah willing, at the hand of the Muslims."

The Norwegian Center party celebrates that it has forced the Labour Party to accept the criminalization of criticism of religions.

2/3 2009
The Norwegian government withdraws its proposal of a law against criticism of religions after threats of rebellion in the Labour parliamentary group.

2/8 2009
Riots prompted by the daily *The Statesman*'s reprinting of a column by Johann Hari claiming the right to criticize religions block access to central Calcutta for days.

2/9 2009
A wave of kidnappings and killings of actors, singers, and musicians occurs in Pakistan, motivated by Islamists because of the prohibition of such arts in the Koran.

2/12 2009
According to a poll, half of Danish Muslims want legislation against the criticism of religion in books and movies.

2/13 2009
Geert Wilders is refused entry in Great Britain to promote *Fitna*. British Home Secretary Jacqui Smith claims his presence presents a risk to general security. The Muslim British Peer, Lord Nazir Ahmed, takes credit for keeping Wilders out; he had warned his presence would "threaten community harmony and thereby public security in the UK."

The government of Pakistan accepts sharia law in the Swat valley of Northern Pakistan.

Al-Qaradawi celebrates Hitler and claims that the Holocaust was a divine punishment of the Jews. He claims that Allah has, throughout history, sent different people to punish the Jews for their corruption, and the last such punishment was organized by Hitler. He concludes, that if Allah wills it, the next such punishment will be at the hands of Muslims.

The Pakistani-Norwegian Bollywood actor Ghufoor Butt founds a Norwegian political party demanding hijab in the police force, segregated Muslim schools and hospitals, state salaries for imams, criminalization of both gay marriage and the defamation of religions.

2/20 2009
After pressure from the party grass roots, the Labour Party in Norway withdraws the proposal for hijab in the police forces.

Librarians in Leicester, England, move the Koran and other allegedly holy writings to the upper shelf after Muslim protests that they stood among ordinary volumes.

All girls' schools in the Swat Valley are closed by the Taliban.

2/22 2009
The Pope protests against an Israeli TV serial mocking Christianity. In the serial, Mary was depicted as a fifteen-year-old girl who was impregnated by a classmate, while Jesus was overweight and unable to walk on water. Israeli PM Ehud Olmert apologizes.

2/24 2009
The Lina Joy case forms precedent in Malaysian jurisprudence. All converts should seek the permission of sharia courts.

The Turkish state research council, TÜBITAK, removes a large paper on Darwin from its popular science journal.

3/16 2009
A gay pride demonstration in Moscow is prohibited by the city mayor Lushkov, claiming it is the "work of Satan."

3/17 2009
A threat of a boycott of the Durban II conference from the EU leads to the removal of the demands for the criminalization of the "defamation of religion" from the proposed final document.

3/20 2008
The framework decision of the EU about the fight against racism and xenophobia threatens freedom of speech. According to the decision, member countries are obliged to introduce legislation punishing such acts with up to three years in jail, but the decision does not make precise to what these terms refer.

3/26 2009
The annual resolution demanding legislation against the "defamation of religion" is passed in the UN Human Rights Council.

4/4 2009
The BBC indefinitely postpones the broadcast of an interview with Kurt Westergaard, fearing it would ignite Muslims around the world.

An attempt is made to cancel a public lecture by the biologist and atheist Richard Dawkins in Oklahoma. In the House of Representatives of the state, Republican Todd Thompson, claimed the lecture opposed the points of view shared by the majority of Oklahoma.

4/6 2009
French Foreign Minister Bernard Kouchner changes his point of view regarding Turkish EU membership to opposing it, based on Turkey's behavior at the recent NATO summit where the country tried to block former Danish PM Fogh as a NATO leader. He claims Turkey is developing towards a "less robust" secularism.

4/20 2009
Poland, New Zealand, Holland, Germany, Australia and Sweden boycott the UN Durban II conference, joining Israel, the USA and Italy.

4/24 2009
The final discussion at the Durban II conference concludes that there

is no opposition between free speech and the criminalization of hate speech. The UN high commissioner for human rights, Navi Pillay, declares: "The document reaffirms the centrality of freedom of expression and stresses its compatibility with the prohibitions of incitement to hatred, thereby reconciling these two fundamental principles of international human rights law."

German professor of Islamic studies, Sven Kalisch, doubts the historical existence of Muhammad and receives death threats. He must live under police protection, and his teaching is secret. Kalisch receives a prohibition from the Minister of Science Andreas Pinkwart against participating in the education of teachers of Islam, but he is permitted to continue his research.

OIC criticism leads to the removal of the computer game *Faith Fighter* from the producer Molleindustria. In the game, God, Jesus, Buddha, Muhammad, Ganesha etc. fight each other.

4/29 2009
The Irish Minister for Justice, Equality, and Reform, Dermot Ahern, proposes an amendment to the Defamation Bill of that country. All blasphemy cases must be initiated by the public prosecutor and address issues where the material is grossly abusive, where it outrages a substantial number of believers, and where there is intent to cause such outrage.

5/5 2009
Film director Ron Howard claims the Vatican tried to harass the production of the feature film *Angels and Demons*, based on Dan Brown's novel. The Vatican has allegedly prevented film scenes from being shot in Rome.

5/22 2009
Violent clashes between police and Muslim demonstrators in Athens caused by rumors about a copy of the Koran having been torn to pieces.

5/25 2009
A Turkish appeal court rejects the exoneration of author Orhan Pamuk. He has publicly addressed the Turkish genocide against Armenians during WW1. He now faces a demand for retribution of around 4 million dollars.

5/26 2009
The Turkish court case begins against Nedim Gursel for his

description of Muhammad and his family in the book *Allah's Daughters*, which allegedly insults religion and incites hatred.

6/4 2009
Italian police arrest a terror cell with North African background with plans for attacks in Northern Italy and Denmark, in revenge for Italian and Danish depictions of Muhammad.

6/8 2009
China demands that all computers sold in the country must contain software able to block access to certain websites with pornographic, political, or religious content.

6/14 2009
Islamists governing in Somalia prohibit any showing of films and DVDs, including in private homes.

6/19 2009
The TV journalist Roger Friedman claims he has been fired from Fox TV because of his criticism of Scientology. The Scientologist actors Tom Cruise and John Travolta are alleged to have pressured the TV channel to sack him.

6/21 2009
At least thirty-three journalists and bloggers are now imprisoned in Iran.

6/22 2009
Five thousand Catholic Poles demand a prohibition against showing Lars von Trier's *Antichrist* in Poland.

6/26 2009
Nedim Gürsel is exonerated from allegations of blasphemy in an Istanbul court.

6/30 2009
Al-Qaeda calls for attacks against France because of President Sarkozy's statements against the burqa.

7/10 2009
Ireland's new blasphemy law passes in parliament, requiring fines of up to €25,000 for blasphemous acts. Irish atheists attack the law, pointing out that religious disagreements will also be covered by the law.

7/13 2009
Thirteen women are arrested in a Khartoum restaurant in Sudan for wearing trousers. Ten of them plead guilty and have ten lashes

as punishment, but the remaining three do not, in order to make a public statement protesting such punishments.

8/3 2009
The German soccer club, Schalke 04, is hit by a Muslim protest wave because of its club song from 1924, "Blue and White, how I love you." The song contains a verse claiming Muhammad did not know anything about soccer: "Muhammad was a prophet/ who did not understand soccer/ yet among all the beauty of colors/ he chose Blue and White." Turkish media claim the song insults the prophet.

8/13 2009
Yale University Press removes the twelve *Jyllands-Posten* drawings from Professor Jytte Klausen's forthcoming book, *The Cartoons that Shook the World*. After having consulted twenty-four experts, the publisher removed all depictions of Muhammad from the book, including old Ottoman prints, depictions of Dante's *Inferno*, etc. "If we cannot see the drawings, how can we discuss them?" Klausen asks in an interview in the *Guardian*. The historian of religion, Reza Aslan, withdrew his positive blurb from the book's back cover after the decision of the press. The president of the American Association of University Professors, Cary Nelson, sharply criticizes the press for its decision in a statement of August 13. "'We do not negotiate with terrorists. We just accede to their anticipated demands.' That is effectively the new policy position at Yale University Press [...]."

8/18 2009
Indian artist Subodh Kerkar receives death threats for depictions of the Hindu elephant god Ganesha in unusual positions like that of Rodin's "The Thinker." Radical Hindus report Kerkar to the police.

8/19 2009
Muslim model Kartika Dari Dewi is convicted to six blows with a stick for having a beer in a bar in the Malaysian state Pahang. She is a Singapore citizen but declares herself ready to receive the punishment. She will be the first woman punished in the wake of recent religious legislation.

8/22 2009
The OIC warns a small Danish gallery in rural Jutland against exhibiting works by Kurt Wester-

gaard. The warning comes from OIC's Islamophobia supervision center in Jeddah.

Sweden rejects demands from Israel to condemn an article in the Swedish paper, *Aftonbladet,* claiming Israeli soldiers kill Palestinians in order to sell their organs. Sweden refuses to intervene in press freedom.

8/26 2009
British author Sebastian Faulks apologizes to Muslims after calling the Koran "the rantings of a schizophrenic" and deeming it without any "ethical dimension" in the *Sunday Times*. A day later he claims that Islam is equal to other religions and that he has the greatest respect for Islam.

8/28 2009
A Berlin exhibition at the publicly financed multicultural center *Werkstatt der Kulturen* is censored. Three out of ninety-six wall sheets in the exhibition *The Third World during WWII* tell about the grand mufti of Jerusalem al-Husseini who lived in Berlin and supported the Holocaust. These sheets are taken down on request from the director of the *Werkstatt*. The Berlin Commissioner for Integration Günter Piening defends the decision, claiming that in an immigrant neighborhood in Berlin, a "differentiated presentation of the involvement of the Arab world in World War II is necessary."

8/29 2009
Saudi lawyer Faisal Yamani demands an unconditional apology from Danish papers for reprinting Kurt Westergaard's cartoon in 2008. The demand is made on behalf of an unspecified number of descendants of Muhammad. If not met before September 1st, the papers and their editors face further legal steps.

9/25 2009
Former professor at the al-Azhar University in Cairo, Abdul Aziz Zakaria, claims converts from Islam should "be killed by the authorities."

10/1 2009
Muslim student organizations rage over Kurt Westergaard's visit at Yale University. His answer: "Muslims have to develop a sense of humor."

10/6 2009
The French Muslim soccer team Créteil Bébel refuses to play against Paris Foot Gay because

of the inclusion of several homosexuals on the team.

The publisher Droste in Germany withdraws a crime novel from its program out of fear of religious offense. The book deals with "honor killings" in immigrant families.

10/7 2009
The 32-year-old Saudi, Mazen Abdul-Jawad, is sentenced to a thousand blows with a stick and five years imprisonment for speaking out on TV about his sex life.

10/8 2009
After the USA joins the UN Human Rights Council, a resolution is passed, led by Egypt and the US, which urges the member states to condemn and criminalize "any advocacy of national, racial or religious hatred that constitutes incitement to discrimination, hostility or violence." The implication is that the US itself is obliged to restrict its famous First Amendment on free speech. Observers perceive this change in US policy as connected to Obama's charm campaign towards the Muslim world.

10/13 2009
The British tribunal for asylum and immigration rejects the prohibition of Geert Wilders entering the country.

10/16 2009
Geert Wilders's entry into Britain gives rise to demonstrations demanding that he be convicted under sharia with the shouts: "To hell with Wilders! To hell with freedom!"

10/27 2009
Two Chicago residents are arrested for planning a terror attack against *Jyllands-Posten* and other specific targets in Denmark under the code names Mickey Mouse Project and The Northern Project. The two suspects, David Headley and Tahawwur Rana, are American and Canadian citizen, respectively. The attacks involved the killing of editor Flemming Rose or cartoonist Kurt Westergaard. As part of the planning, Headley has twice visited Denmark to identify terror targets.

American Secretary of State Hillary Clinton condemns legislation against blasphemy in many countries. They are a bad means to protect freedom of religion, she claims.

11/12 2009
The Dutch film project about Hirsi Ali's life, *Dreamland*, is stopped in Kenya after protests from Kenyan Muslims.

11/20 2009
The arrest of the two Chicago men plotting against Danish targets leads to the arrests in Pakistan of a former officer and four accomplices. All of them are suspected of having participated in the terror attack in Mumbai, India, and of being monitored by the al-Qaeda leader Ilyas Kashmiri.

11/21 2009
Yale University rejects the claim that the removal of the Danish cartoons from Jytte Klausen's book was motivated by Muslim donations to the University.

11/25 2009
The Israeli soccer player Aviram Baruchyan is forced by fan protests to withdraw the statement that he would like to see an Arab player in his team, Beitar Jerusalem.

11/27 2009
When van Gogh's film *Submission* was shown at a Stockholm Free Speech exhibition, the film had been censored by the Stockholm imam, Abd Kielan.

BBC cancels plans for a ballet involving a humpback Pope raping nuns and eunuchs.

11/30 2009
After a referendum resulting in a majority for the prohibition of minarets in Switzerland, large Swiss firms fear a Muslim boycott. Muslim countries rage over the referendum.

12/1 2009
Sixteen American organizations send a protest note to Yale University, claiming it betrays freedom of expression by refusing to print drawings of Muhammed in Jytte Klausen's book.

12/11 2009
Catholic clerics in Vienna sue the cartoonist Manfred Deix for two drawings on the website NEWS.at which depict God and the EU-prohibition against crucifixes in schools, respectively.

12/18 2009
The journal *Index on Censorship* has censored a reprinting of the Danish cartoons in its own pages. The images should have appeared alongside an interview with Jytte Klausen on the censorship of her

book by Yale University Press.

12/21 2009
The UN General Assembly approves the annual resolution against the defamation of religions, but the majority appears to be shrinking year on year.

1/1 2010
A Somali man forces himself into the home of Kurt Westergaard and attempts to attack him with an axe. Westergaard finds refuge in his protection room and calls the police, who arrest the man.

1/2 2010
None of the major Danish papers reprints Westergaard's drawing, despite covering the murder attempt against him.

1/3 2010
Irish atheists publish a quote collection involving Mark Twain, Frank Zappa, Björk, Jesus, and Muhammad, hoping to be prosecuted according to the new Irish blasphemy act.

1/4 2010
Mullah Qureshi from Peshawar, who offered a one million dollar reward for the killing of Kurt Westergaard in 2006, regrets the assassin failed but praises him for his courage.

Liberal Muslims in Norway call for demonstrations to support Kurt Westergaard.

Eight European papers, including two Norwegian papers, reprint Westergaard's cartoon, covering the attack on him.

1/7 2010
Five Copts are killed in Egypt in a drive-by shooting after their Christmas service.

Public prosecutors in Minnesota refuse to prosecute a person for publicly posting anti-Muslim posters in the St.Cloud neighborhood of Minneapolis. They claim religious criticism is protected, even if it is offensive.

1/8 2010
Three churches in Kuala Lumpur are set on fire. Muslims are angered by Christians calling their god "Allah."

Norwegian politicians from the left and the center urge the media to reprint the Danish cartoons.

1/9 2010
The Somali axeman appears to be well-connected to extremist net-

works in Somalia and elsewhere.

1/16 2010
Norwegian flags are burnt in demonstrations in Lahore, Pakistan, protesting Norwegian reprints of the Danish cartoons.

1/28 2010
The Danish journalist from *Jyllands-Posten*, Puk Damgaard, is forced out of Pakistan after demands from two Pakistani journalists' organizations.

2/6 2010
A thousand Muslim taxi drivers block downtown Oslo in a protest against a Muhammad cartoon printed in the paper, *Dagbladet*.

2/13 2010
Two prominent Muslim fundamentalists in Cunit, Spain, are prosecuted for having persecuted a liberal Muslim woman for driving a car and not donning a veil.

2/15 2010
The comedy "Lick, but do not sink" by Ozen Yula is canceled in Istanbul after fundamentalist threats. The play describes an angel returning to earth in the shape of a pornography actress. The local mayor closes the theatre where the play should have been staged.

The deputy leader of the Italian National Research Council, Roberto de Mattei, demands the substitution of Genesis for Darwin in Italian education.

2/25 2010
A court in Karachi convicts the Christian Qamar David to a life sentence for having sent a blasphemous sms, offending Muslim feelings.

2/26 2010
The Danish daily *Politiken* agrees to a settlement with the Saudi lawyer Faisal Yamani. The paper apologizes for hurting Muslim feelings by reprinting Westergaard's cartoon in 2008 and Yamani abstains from further legal action. Observers argue that Yamani has an indirect threat in a possible "libel tourism" court case against Danish papers in London.

The Malaysian paper *The Star* publishes an apology for having criticized the sentencing of three women to beatings for adultery. Muslim organizations claim such criticism is an insult against Islam.

An art exhibition in Granada, Spain, is closed after Christian protests over the display of Jesus in bed with Mary Magdalene before he became gay.

International press organizations attack *Politiken*'s apology for reprinting Westergaard's cartoon.

The Iranian film director Jafar Panahi is arrested in Tehran. His films are banned in Iran, and he is known for supporting the opposition.

A pro-Israeli meeting at York University is canceled because of a security problem. An annual anti-Israel meeting is accepted without problems.

3/2 2010
Riots over a newspaper column by Taslima Nasreen arguing against the burqa in the Indian cities of Shimoga and Hassan cause two deaths and several casualties.

Nineteen women are arrested in Bangladesh for not donning the veil. Bangladeshi law does not require the wearing of veils, and observers claim it is the first time Bangladeshi police have shown interest in forcing women to be veiled.

3/5 2010
The OIC celebrates *Politiken*'s apology to the descendants of Muhammad and demands an apology from the other Danish papers sued by the descendants. The Saudi lawyer Yamani claims that *Politiken*'s apology involves a promise never again to depict Muhammad. It is revealed that the impetus for the case does not stem from Muhammad's descendants but from the law firm of Yamani himself, which has announced it is trying to locate descendents for whom a case could be conducted.

3/7 2010
The British Minister for Women and Equality, Harriet Harman, launches a legislative proposal according to which world views and philosophies should be protected on a par with religions. Vegans and anti-alcohol campaigners are mentioned as examples.

3/9 2010
Seven Irish Muslims are arrested for assassination plans against the Swedish artist Lars Vilks.

The secular British Muslim Shiria Khatun, Labour representative on the Tower Hamlets City Council, is forced by threats to abandon Western clothing and don a traditional robe.

The Egyptian journalists' organization supports a ban on atheist blogs.

3/10 2010
Swedish newspapers reprint Lars Vilks's drawing in support for him after the discovery of the Irish Muslim plot against him.

The secretary for the Swedish Academy, Peter Englund, supports Lars Vilks' freedom of expression. He concludes: "We can always discuss his artworks. But his right to make them—never."

3/12 2010
The man behind the Saudi law firm prosecuting Danish papers, Ahmed Yamani, is prosecuted himself in the US for providing financial support to al-Qaeda.

British pop star Elton John receives Christian death threats after claiming Jesus was homosexual.

3/14 2010
Malaysia demands that the Swedish government act against the Swedish media reprinting Vilks' Muhammad drawing.

The OIC publishes the Norwegian cartoon of Muhammad as a pig on its website.

Uzbek authorities arrest and convict thirteen Baptists for possessing Bibles without authorization.

3/17 2010
Facebook shuts down the page of a user ridiculing Islam after Muslim protests. Critics say Facebook's criteria for closing pages are neither public nor clear.

3/18 2010
David Headley pleads guilty on all charges of planning terrorism in Denmark. His plan was to decapitate hostages in *Jyllands-Posten* and throw out their heads to pressure Danish authorities. Headley also pleads guilty to participating in the Mumbai terror attack.

The American woman with the nickname "Jihad Jane" pleads not guilty at a court in Philadelphia. She is charged with planning to assassinate the Swedish artist Lars Vilks.

3/23 2010
Britain's Justice Secretary Jack Straw puts forward a proposal

for the revision of British libel legislation, which has drawn many cases to Britain in so-called "libel tourism."

3/24 2010
The rapper Akon is refused entry to Sri Lanka for allegedly having offended Buddha in his video "Sexy Bitch."

Indonesian critics of blasphemy laws are beaten by Islamists.

Muslim pressure closes a gay and lesbian conference in Java, Indonesia.

3/27 2010
The annual UNHRC resolution against defamation of religion is adopted. As always, the only religion mentioned is Islam.

3/29 2010
Atheist British author Philip Pullman receives death threats for his upcoming novel "The Good Man Jesus and the Scoundrel Christ."

4/1 2010
Muslim threats of violence stop the guest lecture of the Dutch author Benno Barnard, who is critical of Islam, at the University of Antwerp.

4/8 2010
Saudi mother to four, Hissa Hilal, receives death threats for her appearance on an Arab talent program. Participants compete in reading "natabi" poetry aloud. Hilal chose to attack the Muslim clergy for "spitting out fatwas harmful to Islam, society, and women alike." She attacked men for preventing women from education and jobs. She wears a niqab on the program only for protection against physical assaults.

4/9 2010
The German magazine *Titanic* is prosecuted for a front page where the crucified Jesus appears to be receiving a blow job from a Catholic cleric, as a commentary to the actual pedophilia scandals in the Catholic Church. The case is conducted by the public prosecutor in Frankfurt.

4/20 2010
Radical Muslims threaten the creators of the American animation series *South Park*, Trey Parker and Matt Stone, for having Muhammad appear in a bear costume.

4/23 2010
Parker and Stone claim the next *South Park* serial was censored

by the producers because it addressed the Muslim threats.

4/25 2010
The cartoonist from Seattle, Molly Norris, proposes May 20th as "Everybody Draw Mohammed Day" as a protest against the threats against *South Park*.

The animation serial *Simpsons* comment upon the *South Park* case by portraying Bart Simpson write repeatedly on the school blackboard: SOUTH PARK—WE'D STAND BESIDE YOU IF WE WEREN'T SO SCARED."

4/27 2010
After enormous internet response, Molly Norris withdraws her "Everybody Draw Mohammed Day" proposal.

5/3 2010
The Egyptian Music Association cancels a planned concert by Elton John because of his statements on religion. Its chairman, Mounir al-Wasimi, claims they cannot accept a gay who wants to ban religions and promotes free homosexuality. Elton John has attacked the lack of rights for homosexuals in the Middle East, saying that if you are a lesbian in the Middle East you might as well be dead.

5/7 2010
A lecture by Lars Vilks in Göteborg is canceled for financial reasons. The Swedish security police demands payment for protecting Vilks, which they usually do not when protecting soccer games, concerts, political meetings, etc.

5/11 2010
A Canadian-Iranian journalist for *Newsweek*, Maziar Bahari, is sentenced to thirteen and a half years' imprisonment and fifty lashes in Iran, allegedly for participating in the riots after the presidential elections in 2009.

The Swedish artist Lars Vilks is attacked by Muslims during a lecture at the University of Uppsala. He is immediately protected by police and is not hurt. Three participants are arrested for violence.

5/13 2010
The *Washington Post* publishes Westergaard's cartoon and is one of the first major American newspapers to do so. It appears in the electronic edition, in a short animated cartoon by the Pulitzer Prize winning cartoonist Ann Telnaes. A demonstrator holds a poster with Westergaard's drawing and the text Free Speech. Another person rages against the former

who hands him an empty poster and a pencil. The other person takes the empty poster and uses it to beat the demonstrator with the Westergaard drawing. It takes place under the headline "Cartoonist attacked while giving free speech lecture". (http://voices.washingtonpost.com/annteln-aes/2010/05/free_speech_doesnt_come_easily.html)

5/14 2010
Egyptian lawyers demand a ban on *Arabian Nights*. After a recent republication of the classic collection of tales, the organization Lawyers Without Chains finds it offends public decency. The organization refers to the Muslim concept of "hisba," which gives every Muslim the right to conduct a case against another in order to protect Muslim society. The Arabian network for human rights, ANHRI, claims an increasing use of "hisba" serves to curtail freedom of expression.

5/15 2010
An attempted arson against Lars Vilks's home in Sweden is discovered. Two Muslim Albanian brothers are arrested in Landskrona and charged with attempted murder.

5/17 2010
The Pakistani-American, Faisal Shahzad, who placed a non-detonated car bomb in Times Square, New York, now claims it was a protest against the Danish cartoons.

5/18 2010
An al-Qaeda terror action against the Danish and Dutch soccer teams at the upcoming World Cup in South Africa seems to have been prevented. Iraqi authorities have arrested the Saudi officer Abdulla al-Qahtani who, monitored by al-Zawahiri, planned to attack Danish and Dutch soccer players and fans during the match between the two teams on June 14th.

5/19 2010
A Facebook group for the occasion of the upcoming "Everybody Draw Muhammad Day" May 20th already has fifty thousand fans and two hundred drawings. Pakistan closes access to Facebook, and demonstrations support the government.

5/20 2010
Pakistan also closes YouTube and announces that the closure will last until May 31st. Scandinavian flags are burned in the streets of Karachi.

5/21 2010
The Facebook group "Everybody Draw Mohammed Day" is closed. The organizers receive death threats. New Facebook groups for and against are organized.

5/24 2010
The South African daily *Mail & Guardian* receives Muslim protests after printing a Muhammad drawing related to "Everybody Draw Muhamad Day." The drawing by the cartoonist Zapiro depicts Muhammad on the shrink's couch in the clouds, exclaiming: "*Other* prophets have followers with a sense of humor!"

5/6 2010
Mail & Guardian apologize for the publication of a Muhammad cartoon, according to a press briefing from United Muslim Forum of South Africa.

5/31 2010
Pakistan re-opens Facebook after the closing of the Mohammad drawing page, and after having received an apology from Facebook officials. Pakistan's Minister for Information and Technology, Najibullah Malik, claims Facebook has promised no such thing will take place in the future. Officials of Facebook make no comment.

Earlier, they claimed "Everybody Draw Mohammed Day" did not transgress the rules of conduct of Facebook.

6/3 2010
A religious activist group named "Coalition Against Religious Intolerance" demands that the American television network Comedy Central give up its plans for a new animated cartoon about Jesus, titled *JC*. The group warns advertisers not to support the project. It also attacks Comedy Central for hypocrisy becaue of its recent censorship of two "South Park" episodes thematizing Islam.

6/15 2010
Two men are killed in Suga Holaha, Somalia, for watching the Soccer World Championships. "Soccer is a heritage from primitive infidels and we can not accept people watching it," claims Sheikh Mohamed Abdi Aros, a spokesman for Hizbul Islam.

6/17 2010
The Pakistani public prosecuter prepares a case against Facebook founder Mark Zuckerberg for allowing the fansite "Everybody Draw Muhammad Day." According to paragraph 295-C of the Pakistani penal code, Zuckerberg risks

the death penalty for blasphemy. The case also involves the anonymous German woman called "Andy" who made the fansite.

6/24 2010
Indonesian police arrest three people for planning terror attacks against the Danish embassy in Jakarta because of the cartoons.

7/1 2010
Al-Qaeda's internet magazine *Inspire* publishes a death list of nine Western persons for having offended the prophet.

7/9 2010
The American professor Kenneth Howell is sacked from the University of Illinois for hate speech. In a course on Catholicism, he had said that "the Church believes that homosexual acts are contrary to human nature..."

7/13 2010
Two Russian gallerists, Jury Samadurov and Andrei Jerefeyev, are given large fines for organizing an exhibition called "Prohibited Art" at the Sakharov center, which included portrayals of Jesus as Mickey Mouse and as Lenin.

7/15 2010
Two Albanian brothers are convicted for arson against the Swedish artist Lars Vilks who drew Muhammed as a roundabout dog.

Pakistan prohibits the Indian movie *Without You, bin Laden*. Pakistan fears becoming the object of suicide attacks if the movie is shown.

7/16 2010
An ad campaign for vegetarianism is prohibited in Canada because it shows a lightly dressed Pamela Anderson with cut markings like an animal for slaughter.

7/21 2010
Muslim leaders in Malaysia call for a boycott of the British soccer club Manchester United along with a series of national teams because their jerseys display infidel symbols such as crosses, devils and alcohol ads.

7/22 2010
Zachary Chesser, a 20 year old Muslim from Virginia, is arrested for supporting al-Shabaab in Somalia. In April, he issued death threats to the creators and illustrators of South Park.

7/25 2010
A hospital in the Dutch city of Leerdam removes three paintings

of happy piglets. A patient, not himself a Muslim, had demanded that Muslims should not face the paintings. The paintings are replaced with cow paintings.

7/27 2010
The BBC TV host Jeremy Clarkson receives Muslim death threats for relating an anecdote about a Burka-clad woman he saw at Piccadilly, stumbling and falling over to reveal her red g-string and stockings.

The American Senate passes a law to protect American journalists and authors against "libel tourism" by preventing federal courts from enforcing foreign judgments inconsistent with the First Amendment.

7/29 2010
Apple removes erotic books from the bestseller lists of the Apple Book Store, including the number one bestseller, *Blonde and Wet* by Carl East.

8/18 2010
Hizbollah's TV network al-Manar stops broadcasting a series about Jesus called "al-Masih," following protests from Christian Libanese.

8/19 2010
A Dutch Muslim group is fined for publishing a drawing presenting the Holocaust as a lie.

9/3 2010
In a radio speech, Australian imam Feiz Muhammad demands the decapitation of the Dutch politician Geert Wilders and all who discuss Islam in his manner.

9/6 2010
The Muhammad cartoonist Kurt Westergaard receives the M100 Media Award in Germany in the presence of Chancellor Angela Merkel. The Frankfurter Allgemeine newspaper attacks her presence, claiming that it could have high foreign policy costs.

9/9 2010
Imam Feisal Abdul Rauf warns about an incipient Muhammad crisis, triggered by American resistance against the building of a mosque close to Ground Zero in New York. He implies that attacks on American embassies may result.

9/10 2010
After the premature detonation of a bomb, a Chechen bomber named Lors Doukayev is arrested

in Copenhagen with a map indicating the location of the newspaper *Jyllands-Posten*.

9/16 2010
Molly Norris, the American illustrator who had called for "Everybody Draw Muhammad Day," goes underground and changes her name after receiving death threats.

A court case begins against the Swedish politician Carl Herslow for making a poster depicting Muhammad with his nine-year-old wife, Aisha.

9/21 2010
Three art galleries in Istanbul are attacked by fifty people screaming "Allahu Akbar" and assaulting visitors for drinking alcohol.

9/23 2010
British police arrest six people for filming the burning of a Koran and putting it on YouTube.

9/25 2010
A Swedish anti-immigration politician is stabbed by ten Middle-Eastern men outside his home.

9/27 2010
The Iraqi Kurd Shawan Bujak confesses to planning a large terror attack on the Danish paper *Jyllands-Posten* with the help of two other men based in Norway.

10/30 2010
The Norwegian publishing house Kagge gives up a planned biography on Muhammad by the journalist Halvor Tjønn, suggesting that he publish it elsewhere.

10/1 2010
The OIC strongly condemns the Danish publication of Flemming Rose's book about the cartoon crisis, *The Tyranny of Silence*.

10/3 2010
Hizbollah condemns Rose's *The Tyranny of Silence*.

10/5 2010
A Strasbourg court accuses a French blogger of airing a video on the internet, in which he wears a devil's mask while tearing pages out of the Koran, making paper airplanes from them and aiming them against a Twin Towers model.

10/6 2010
The Norwegian paper *Adresseavisen* shreds ninety thousand copies because of a drawing

depicting Kurt Westergaard with one of his drawings in his hands.

10/8 2010
Censorshop against TV and internet prevent the Chinese public from hearing about the awarding of the Nobel Peace Price to the activist Liu Xiaobo.

Kurt Westergaard receives the German "Leipzig Media Award" in the presence of editors-in-chief from all over Europe.

The collage "Misadventures of the Romantic Cannibals" by Stanford professor Enrique Chagoya is removed from the Loveland Museum, Colorado, because it shows Biblical scenes where the people have been replaced with comics characters.

10/21 2010
The National Public Radio commentator Juan Williams is sacked for admitting to be nervous when seeing people in Muslim clothing on planes. His firing was demanded by the OIC-financed "Council on American-Islamic Relations."

10/30 2010
Syrian terror suspects are arrested in Gothenburg, Sweden, for planning attacks against Danish targets in the city.

11/4 2010
After pressure from British and American politicians, YouTube removes videos with the Islamist Anwar al-Awlaki calling for jihad waged by children.

11/6 2010
The Islamist website www.revolutionmuslim.com publishes a death list of British parliamentarians voting for the Iraq war in 2003. The site gives detailed instructions about how to find these politicians in their constituencies and about the proper use of knives.

11/11 2010
The Pakistani Christian woman Asia Bibi is sentenced to death for blasphemy against Muhammad. She fetched water for fellow field workers who refused to drink it because they deemed it impure, after which she was attacked by a mob.

11/15 2010
Egyptian blogger Kareem Amer is not released from prison after serving four years for libel against President Mubarak and for offending Islam. Instead, he is

tortured.

11/16 2010
A 26-year-old Palestinian is to receive a life sentence for spreading atheist and anti-Islamic content on Facebook. Conservative Muslims demand that he be executed.

11/16 2010
The British toy store Early Learning Center removes a plastic pig from their playing farm for young kids to avoid offending Jews and Muslims.

12/8 2010
With a 79–70 vote, the UN General Assembly decides to remove homosexuals from a list of threatened groups in a resolution against summary executions. The majority of the list consists of Muslim and Third World countries.

12/11 2010
A suicide bomber wounds two in central Stockholm, Sweden— a telegram claims the reason is the Muhammad drawing of Lars Vilks. Later investigations show that the intended target was Swedish newspapers.

The Austrian garden owner Helmut G. is convicted for offending his Muslim neighbor by yodeling while lawnmowing.

12/21 2010
Iranian film director Jafar Panahi is sentenced to six years imprisonment and a twenty year ban against filmmaking for having distributed propaganda aginst the Iranian regime.

According to documents from Wikileaks, the Arab League decided in 2007 to prohibit all films by Steven Spielberg because he donated some of the surplus from *Schindler's List* to Israel's fight against Hizbollah.

12/22 2010
British Labour parlamentarian James Fitzpatrick demands the removal of a Muslim poster campaign against Christmas that asserts that the belief in God's son leads to venereal disease, debt, rape, violence and more.

12/27 2010
According to Wikileaks documents, the Syrian government supported the 2006 attacks against the Danish and Norwegian embassies.

12/28 2010
According to Wikileaks documents,

the American ambassador to Denmark, James P. Cain, repeatedly contacted the prime minister and *Jyllands-Posten* concerning the rumour that the paper intended to republish the cartoons on the anniversary date 9/30/2006. Whether he exerted pressure is unclear.

12/29 2010
Five people are arrested in Copenhagen and Stockholm under suspicion of planning a terrorist attack against the Copenhagen offices of *Jyllands-Posten*. They seem to be connected to Ilyas Kashmiri's al-Qaeda network in the UK.

1/1 2011
The new media legislation in Hungary involves a five person state council to judge media which publish news stories that hurt human dignity and offend nationalities, religions and minorities.

In Alexandria, Egypt, 21 people are killed and 97 are wounded in a suicide attack on a Coptic church.

1/2 2011
A Swedish hockey referee is barred from participating in matches after he put a caricature of Muhammed on his Facebook profile.

1/4 2011
Punjabi governor Salman Taseer is assassinated because of his support for the loosening of Pakistan's blasphemy legislation.

The sentencing of the Afghan Shoaib Assadullah is postponed. He faces execution or twenty years of imprisonment (if he embraces Islam) for disseminating Bibles.

1/5 2011
A new version of Mark Twain's *Huckleberry Finn* subsitutes the word "slave" for "nigger," provoking controversy among literature-lovers and English teachers.

1/6 2011
More than five hundred Pakistani imams pronounce their support for the assassin of governor Taseer and for protecting Muhammad against blasphemy.

1/13 2011
Ibsen's classic play "Hedda Gabler" is prohibited in Iran because it depicts two people kissing.

1/14 2011
Canada prohibits broadcasting Dire Straits' 80s hit "Money for Nothing" because it contains the

word "faggot" three times.

1/20 2011
UK denies an entry permit to the priest Terry Jones, who threatened to burn the Koran in 2010.

1/24 2011
Jafar Kazemi and Mohammed Hajaghaei are hanged outside of Tehran for "enmity against God" because they disseminated flyers during the 2009 demonstrations.

1/27 2011
Egypt closes down all internet traffic to prevent riots inspired by the Tunisian revolution.

1/29 2011
In a Philadelphia court, Colleen LaRose (aka "Jihad Jane") admits planning to kill the Swedish artist Lars Vilks.

2/4 2011
The axeman who assaulted Kurt Westergaard, Mohammed Geele, is convicted to nine years of imprisonment in Aarhus, Denmark.

Muslim mobs set fire to three churches in Indonesia as a protest against the leniency of a five years prison sentence to a Christian for blasphemy against Islam; they demand the death penalty.

2/15 2011
The Austrian Elisabeth Sabaditsch-Wolf is convicted of offending religion because she exlaimed, about Muhammad's nine-year-old wife, "If that is not pedophilia, what is it?"

2/19 2011
Gadaffi closes down the internet in Libya after clashes between demonstrators and government forces.

3/2 2011
Pakistan's minister for minorities, Shabaz Bahatti, is killed in Islamabad. He was the only Christian minister in the country and had attacked the blasphemy legislation and defended a Christian woman sentenced to death for blasphemy.

3/17 2011
Two critical journalists, Ahmet Sik and Nedim Sener, are arrested in Turkey. They are alleged to have connections to the "Ergenekon" case against critics of the Islamist government.

3/26 2011
The UN Human Rights Council adopts the annual resolution proposed by the OIC countries, this time, however, without the demand for criminalization of the

"defamation of religion." Observers claim this shift is due to the democracy movement in the Arab world. Other observers point to a shift in OIC strategy toward embracing and trying to expand existing hate speech legislations.

The UK government presents a proposal to change libel legislation which has lead to "libel tourism" to Britain.

3/30 2011
The Turkish literature Nobel Prize Winner Orhan Pamuk is given a large fine by an Istanbul court for referring to the Turkish genocide against Armenians and Kurds.

Eleven people, including eight UN personnel, are killed in Afghanistan in a protest against a Koran burning in the US.

Libyan insurgents fight for a new state with freedom of religion. A spokesman for the opposition says religious freedom is unnecessary, since Libya is 100% Muslim.

4/2 2011
Ten people are killed and more than eighty are wounded in a Kandahar protest against the Koran burning by the American vicar Wayne Sapp.

4/7 2011
Chinese artist Ai Weiwei is arrested in Beijing Airport without any public charge. The party paper "Global Times" claims he is an activist and loner who "will have to pay the price for his choice."

4/11 2011
The blogger Maikel Nabil Sanad is sentenced to three years imprisonment in Egypt for publishing critical reports about the military. This is the first court case against a blogger under post-Mubarak military rule.

4/17 2011
So-called "Taliban thugs" of Eastern London put pressure on homosexuals and unveiled girls by means of threats and posters.

4/25 2011
A court in Amman, Jordan, opens a case against Muhammad illustrator Kurt Westergaard.

4/26 2011
Kurt Westergaard sets up a foundation for free speech with funds raised from the sale of signed drawings. The prize will be given to artists who express themselves despite violent attacks, court cases and death threats.

5/10 2011
The OIC demands that the Norwegian publication of Flemming Rose's *Tyranny of Silence* be prohibited.

5/11 2011
An orthodox Jewish paper in Brooklyn, *Di Tseitung,* removes Hilary Clinton and Audrey Tomason from a news photograph, allegedly because Jewish demands of "decency" prohibit the depiction of women.

5/13 2011
According to an interrogation report of David Headley, the Pakistani-American accused of terrorism, an officer from the Pakistani intelligence service, ISI, participated in the planning of the 2008 terror attack in Mumbai as well as in the planning of a terrorist attack against *Jyllands-Posten*.

Bibliography

Ahmad, Salbiah 2007 *Critical Thoughts on Islam, Rights and Freedom in Malaysia*, Petaling Jaya: Silverfishbooks

Al-Azm, Sadiq 2003 "Det universelle vs. det partikulære" ["Universal Versus Particular"], KRITIK162/163, 2003

Al-Azmeh, Aziz 1996 *Islams and Modernities*, 2nd ed. London: Verso 1996

────── 2003 "Postmodern Obscurantism and 'The Muslim Question'", JSRI nr. 5, summer 2003, http://www.jsri.ro/old/html%20version/index/no_5/aziaalazmeh-articol.htm

────── (no year) Conversation with Aziz Al-Azmeh on Islamism and Modernism Part I), *Iran Bulletin,* http://www.iran-bulletin.org/interview/AZMEH_1.html

Alliance of Civilizations, FN-rapport, 2006, http://www.unaoc.org/

American Anthropological Association 1947, "Statement on Human Rights. Submitted to the Commission on Human Rights, United Nations, by the Executive Board, American Anthropological Association", *American Anthropologist* vol. 49, no. 4, Oct.–Dec. 1947, 539-543

Amin, Mohamed & Caldwell, Malcolm (ed.)1977 *Malaya. The Making of a Neo-Colony.* Nottingham: Spokesman Books

Andaya, Barbara Watson & Andaya, Leonard Y. 1982 *A History of Malaysia.* Hong Kong: Palgrave Macmillan

Andersen, Lars Erslev 2006 *Den tabte uskyld. Verdensorden—Værdikamp—Islamisme,* ["The Lost Innocence: World Order—Value Struggle—Islamism"], Odense: Syddansk Universitetsforlag

"Arabisk mad på Krogerup Højskole" ["Arabian Food at Krogerup High School"] *Frederiksborg Amts Avis,* 17/2 2006, 2. sekt. s. 2(Anonymous newspaper article)

Baber, H.E. 2007 *Multicultural Mystique. The Liberal Case Against Diversity,* N.Y.: Prometheus Books

Bader, Veit 1999 "Religious Pluralism: Secularism or Priority for Democracy?", in *Political Theory* vol. 27, no. 5, 597–633

Baldwin, J.M. 1902 *Development and Evolution,* New York: MacMillan Company

Barry, Brian 2001 *Culture and Equality,* Cambridge: Polity Press

Barnard, Alan 2000 *History and Theory in Anthropology*, Cambridge: Cambridge University Press
Bauman, Zygmunt 2001 *Community: Seeking Safety in an Insecure World*. Cambridge: Polity
―― 2003 *Wasted Lives: Modernity and Its Outcasts*. Cambridge: Polity
Bell, Daniel A. 2000 *East Meets West. Human Rights and Democracy in East Asia*, Princeton: Princeton U.P.
Benedict, R. 1934 *Patterns of Culture*, Boston and N.Y.: Houghton Mifflin Company
―― 1959 *Patterns of Culture*, Boston and N.Y.: Houghton Mifflin Company
Benhabib, Seyla 1999 "The Liberal Imagination and the Four Dogmas of Multiculturalism", in *The Yale Journal of Criticism*, 12.2, 401–13
―― 2005 *Philosophy and Social Criticism*, vol. 31, no. 7, 753–71
Benoist, Alain de 1986 *Europe, Tiers monde, même combat*, Paris: Robert Laffont
Berlin and Kay 1969 *Basic Color Terms*, Berkeley: University of California Press
Bhabha, Homi 1994 *The Location of Culture*, London: Routledge
Bouchard, Gerard, and Charles Taylor 2008 *Building the Future. A Time for Reconciliation*, report from Consultation Commission on Accommodation Practices Related to Cultural Differences, http://www.accommodements.qc.ca/index-en.html
Bredsdorff, Thomas and Lasse Horne Kjældgaard 2008 *Tolerance—eller hvordan man lærer at leve med dem, man hader*, ["Tolerance—Or How to Learn to Live with Those You Hate"] Copenhagen: Gyldendal
Brown, Donald E. 1991 *Human Universals* New York: McGraw-Hill
Bruckner, Pascal 2007 "Enlightenment fundamentalism or racism of the anti-racists", the online magazine *Perlentaucher*, 24/1 2007
Bundgaard, Peer, 2006 "Sharia er vores menneskerettigheder" ["Sharia is our human rights"], *Politiken* 1/3 2006
Cairo Declaration on Human Rights in Islam, Aug. 5, 1990, http://www1.umn.edu/humanrts/instree/cairodeclaration.html
Canadian Multiculturalism Act http://laws-lois.justice.gc.ca/eng/acts/c-18.7/page-1.html#h-1
Cassirer, Ernst 1946 *The Myth of the State*, New Haven: Yale U.P.

Clapham, Andrew 2006 *Human Rights Obligations of Non-State Actors*, Oxford: Oxford UP

Crone, Patricia 2003 „Til Paradis i lænker. *Jihad* i historisk perspektiv" ["To Paradise in Chains. Jihad in a Historical Perspective"], i KRITIK 162–63

Darnell, Regna 2008 "North American Traditions in Anthropology", in H. Kuklick *A New History of Anthropology*, Malden: Blackwell 2008, 35–51

Deacon, T. 1997 *The Symbolic Species,* N.Y.: W.W.Norton

Derrida, Jacques 1999 *Donner la mort*, Paris: Galilee (1992)

Ellemann-Jensen, Uffe "Cui Bono", *Berlingske Tidende*, 20/3 2008

Eriksen, Jens-Martin and Frederik Stjernfelt 2003 *Hadets anatomi*, ("Anatomy of Hatred. Travels in Bosnia and Serbia"), Copenhagen: L&R

―――― 2004 *Krigens scenografi*, ("Scenography of War. New Travels in Bosnia and Serbia"), Copenhagen: L&R

Eriksen, T. Hylland 2001 "Between Universalism and Relativism: A Critique of the UNESCO Concepts of Culture", in Jane Cowan, Maire-Bénédicte Dembour and Richard Wilson, eds. *Culture and Rights: Anthropological Perspectives,* 127–48, Cambridge: Cambridge University Press

Eriksen, Thomas Hylland and Finn Sivert Nielsen 2001 *A History of Anthropology*, London: Pluto Press

The Executive Board, American Anthropological Association 1947 "Statement on Human Rights", *American Anthropologist*, New Series, vol. 49, no. 4, 539–543 (primary author: Melville Herskovits)

Fink, Hans 1989 "Et hyperkomplekst begreb" ["A Hyper-Complex Concept"], in *Kulturbegrebets kulturhistorie*, Århus: Aarhus Universitetsforlag.

Finkielkraut, Alain 1987 *La defaite de la pensée*, Paris: Gallimard

Forster, M.N. 2006 "Herder and the Birth of Modern Anthropology", preprint version, http://www.culcom.uio.no/aktivitet/Herder/Forster-Herder.pdf

Fourest, Caroline 2004 *Frére Tariq. Discours, stratégie et méthode de Tariq Ramadan*, Paris: Grasset

Garton Ash, Timothy 2005 "In Praise of Blasphemy", *Guardian* 13/1 2001.

Gellner, Ernest 2006 *Nations and Nationalism*, Oxford: Blackwell (2. ed.)

Geertz, Clifford 1984 "Anti Anti-Relativism", *American Anthropologist*, vol. 86, no. 2, 263–78

Goodall, Kay E. 2007 "Incitement to Religious Hatred: All Talk and No Substance?", in *Modern Law Review*, vol. 70, no. 1, 89–113

Gross, Paul and Norman Levitt 1994 *Higher Superstition*, Baltimore: Johns Hopkins University Press

Groupe μ 1992 *Traité du signe visuel*, Paris: Seuil

Gunew, Sneja "Multicultural Differences: Canada, USA, Australia", http://faculty.arts.ubc.ca/sgunew/MCMULTI.HTM

Habermas, Jürgen 1974 *Borgerlig offentlighet*, Oslo: Fremad

Hansen, John and Kim Hundewadt 2006 *Provoen og profeten. Muhammedkrisen bag kulisserne* ["The Provocateur and the Prophet: The Muhammad Crisis Behind the Curtain"], Copenhagen: Jyllands-Postens Forlag

Hansen, Mogens Herman 2007 *Republikanisme* ["Republicanism"] Copenhagen: Videnskabernes Selskab

Harrison, Lawrence 2006 *The Central Liberal Truth*, Oxford: Oxford University Press

Harrison, Lawrence and Samuel Huntington (eds.) 2000 *Culture Matters: How Values Shape Human Progress*, N.Y.: Basic Books

Heath, Joseph and Andrew Potter 2004 *Nation of Rebels. Why Counterculture became Consumer Culture*, N.Y.: Harper Paperbacks

Herder, J.G. 1990 *Auch eine Philosophie der Geschichte zur Bildung der Menschheit*, Ditzingen: Reclam (1774)

——— 1995 *Ideen zur Philosophie der Geschichte der Menschheit* I–IV, Bodenheim : Syndikat Buchgesellschaft (1784-91)

Herskovits, M. 1958 "Some Further Comments on Cultural Relativism", *American Anthropologist*, vol. 60, no. 2, 266–73

Heyer, V. 1948 "In Reply to Elgin Williams", *American Anthropologist*, vol. 50, no. 1, 163–66

Hirsi Ali, Ayaan 2007 *Infidel*, New York: Free Press

Hobsbawm, E. and T. Ranger 1983 *The Invention of Traditions*, Cambridge: Cambridge University Press

Holyoake, G. J. 1860 *The Principles of Secularism* http://www.gutenberg.org/ebooks/36797

—— 1896 *The Origin and Nature of Secularism*, London: Watts & Co.
Ismail, Rose 1995 *Hudud in Malaysia*. Petaling Jaya: Longman Malaysia
Israel, Jonathan, 1999 "Locke, Spinoza, and the Philosophical Debate Concerning Toleration in the Early Enlightenment (c. 1650–c.1750)", *Mededelingen van de Afdeling Letterkunde, Nieuwe Reeks*, Deel 62 no. 6, Koninklijke Nederlandse Akademie van Wetenschappen, Amsterdam
—— 2001 *Radical Enlightenment*, Oxford: Oxford UP
—— 2006 *Enlightenment Contested*, Oxford: Oxford UP
—— 2011 *Democratic Enlightenment*, Oxford: Oxford UP
James, William 1909 *A Pluralistic Universe*, http://www.gutenberg.org/ebooks/11984
Joppke, Christian 2001 "Multicultural Citizenship: A Critique", in *Arch. Europ. Sociol.*, vol. XLII, no. 2, 431–47
Joseph, Nathan and Alex, Nicholas "The Uniform: A Sociological Perspective", *The American Journal of Sociology*, vol. 77, no. 4, Jan. 1972, 719–30
Jussawalla, Feroza 2001 "Are Cultural Rights Bad for Multicultural Societies?", *South Atlantic Quarterly* vol. 100, no. 4, 967–80
Kallen, Horace 1988 *Culture and Democracy in the United States*, New Brunswick: Transaction Publishers (1924)
Kaur, Amarjit 1993 *Historical Dictionary of Malaysia*, New Jersey & London: Scarecrow Press
Klausen, Jytte 2009 *The Cartoons that Shook the World*, New Haven: Yale University Press
Kukathas, Chandran 1998 "Liberalism and Multiculturalism: The Politics of Indifference", in *Political Theory* Oct. 1998, 686–99
Kymlicka, Will 1995 *Multicultural Citizenship: A Liberal Theory of Minority Rights*, Oxford: Oxford UP
—— 2007 *Multicultural Odysseys: Navigating the New International Politics of Diversity*, Oxford: Oxford UP
—— 2007a "Disentangling the Debate", in Stein 2007, 137–56
Kymlicka, Will and Baogang He 2005 *Multiculturalism in Asia*. Oxford University Press
Lentin, A, "Replacing 'Race', Historicizing 'Culture' In Multiculturalism", *Patterns of Prejudice*, Vol. 39, No. 4, 2005

Lévi-Strauss, C. 1972 "Race et histoire" (1952), in *Anthropologie structurale deux*, Paris: Plon
—— 1979 "Race et culture" (1971), in Bellour, R. and Clement C. (eds.) *Claude Levi-Strauss*, Paris: Gallimard
Lévy, Bernard-Henri 2003 *Who Killed Daniel Pearl?* New York: Melville House
Levy, Leonard Williams 1993 *Blasphemy*, N.Y.: Knopf
Lægaard, Sune 2005 "On the Prospects for a Liberal Theory of Recognition", *Res Publica* 11, 325–48
—— 2007 "The Cartoon Controversy as a Case of Multicultural Recognition", *Contemporary Politics*, 13:2, 147–64
Mahathir, Mohamad 1970 *The Malay Dilemma,* Kuala Lumpur: Marshall Cavendish Corp/Ccb
—— 2004 *Achieving True Globalisation*, Kuala Lumpur: Pelanduk Pubns Sdn Bhd
—— 2006 *Islam, Knowledge and Other Affairs*, Petaling Jaya: MPH Pub
Malik, Kenan *From Fatwa to Jihad. The Rushdie Affair and its Legacy*, London 2009: Atlantic Books
Mayer, Ann Elizabeth 2007 *Islam and Human Rights*, Oxford: Westview
McDonald, Leighton 1996 "Regrouping in Defence of Minority Rights: Kymlicka's *Multicultural Citizenship*", in *Osgoode Hall Law Journal*, vol. 34, no. 2, 292–319
Mead, Margaret 1949 "Ruth Fulton Benedict 1887–1948" *American Anthropologist*, vol. 51, no.3, 457–68
—— 1959 "Preface", in Benedict 1959
Mensching, Gustav 1948 *Geschichte der Religionswissenschaft*, Bonn: Universitätsverlag Bonn
Mozaffari, Mehdi 2006 "Islamisme og totalitarisme" ["Islamism and Totalitarianism"], KRITIK 180
Musa, M. Bakri 1999 *The Malay Dilemma Revisited*. New York: iUniverse
Nissam-Sabat, C. "On Clifford Geertz and His 'Anti Anti-Relativism'", in *American Anthropologist*, vol. 89, no. 4, 935–39
Naipaul, V.S. 1998 *Beyond Belief. Islamic Excursions among the Converted Peoples*. London

Noor, Farish A.2005 *From Majapahit to Putrajaya*. Kuala Lumpur: Silverfishbooks

Okin, Susan Moller (ed.) 1999 *Is Multiculturalism Bad for Women?* Princeton: Princeton University Press

Othman, Norani (ed.) 1994 *Sharia Law and the Modern Nation-State*, Kuala Lumpur: Sisters-in-Islam Forum

——— 2005 *Muslim Women and the Challenge of Islamic Extremism*, Kuala Lumpur: Sisters-in-Islam

Otto, Rudolf 1991 *Das Heilige* ["The Sacred"], München: C.H.Beck (1917)

——— *Aufsätze, das Numinose betreffend*, ["Papers on the Numinous"], Stuttgart: Perthes 1923

Pensky, Max 2004 "Comments on Seyla Benhabib, *The Claims of Culture*", *Constellations*, vol. 11, no. 2, 258–65

Pettit, Philip 1999 *Republicanism: A Theory of Freedom and Government*, Oxford: Oxford University Press

Phillips, Anne 2007 *Multiculturalism Without Culture*, Princeton: Princeton University Press

Politiken (anonymous editorial) „Frisind", 16/4 06 (Easter Sunday)

Rahman, Abdul Muin Abdul 1999 *Witnesses in Islamic Law of Evidence*, Kelana Jaya: Pelanduk Publications

Redhead, Mark 2003 "Charles Taylor's Deeply Diverse Response to Canadian Fragmentation: A Project Often Commented On but Seldom Explored", in *Canadian Journal of Political Science*, vol. 36. no. 1, 61–83

Renteln, A.D. 1988 "Relativism and the Search for Human Rights", *American Anthropologist*, vol. 90, no. 1, 56–72

Rose, Flemming 2005 "Muhammeds ansigter" ["The Faces of Muhammad"], *Jyllands-Posten*, 30/9 2005

Schledermann, Helmuth 2007 *Gensidig tålsomhed*, ["Mutual Patience"], Aarhus: Hovedland

Schmidt, P.F. 1955 "Some Criticisms of Cultural Relativism", in *The Journal of Philosophy*, vol. 52, no. 25, 780–91

Schuster, A. 2006 "Does Liberalism Need Multiculturalism? A Critique of Liberal Multiculturalism", in *Essays in Philosophy*, vol. 7, no. 1, January 2006

Sen, Amartya 2006 *Identity and Violence. The Illusion of Destiny*, London: Allen Lane
Sifaoui, Mohammed 2006 March 23rd "Drawings of Wrath", documentary, France 2
Soong, Kua Kia 2002 *Malaysian Critical Issues*. Petaling Jaya: SIRD
Stein, Janice Gross et al. 2007 *Uneasy Partners. Multiculturalism and Rights in Canada,* Ontario: Wilfried Laurier University Press
Steward, J. 1948 "Comments on the Statement of Human Rights" in *American Anthropologist* vol. 50 no. 2, 351–52
Stjernfelt, Frederik 2007 *Diagrammatology. An Investigation on the Borderlines of Phenomenology, Ontology, and Semiotics*, Dordrecht: Springer
Stjernfelt, Frederik and Søren Ulrik Thomsen *Kritik af den negative opbyggelighed* ["A Critique of Negativism"], Copenhagen 2005
Sunada, Erika 2000 "Revisiting Horace M. Kallen's Cultural Pluralism: A Comparative Analysis", *Journal of American and Canadian Studies*, vol. 18, 51-76
Taheri, Amir 2006 "Hykleri. Der er ikke noget billedforbud i islam. Satire er også o.k.", ["Hypocrisy. There is no prohibition of images in Islam. Satire is also OK"], *Politiken* 15/2 2006
Taylor, Charles 1994 "The Politics of Recognition", in *Multiculturalism. Examining the Politics of Recognition*, Ewing NJ: Princeton UP
Turnbull, C. Mary 1999 *A Short History of Malaysia, Singapore and Brunei*, Singapore: Graham Brash
UNESCO 1995 "Our Creative Diversity. Report of the World Commission on Culture and Development", http://unesdoc.unesco.org/images/0010/001016/101651e.pdf
Verma, Vidhu 2002 *Malaysia. State and Civil Society in Transition*, Selangor: SIRD
Vermeulen, Hans and Boris Slijper 2000 "Multiculturalism and Culturalism", paper at the conference *Democracy Beyond the Nation-State*, www2.fmg.uva.nl/imes/books/vermeulenslijper2000.pdf
Waldron, Jeremy 1992 "Minority Cultures and the Cosmopolitan Alternative", in *University of Michigan Journal of Law Reform*, vol. 25, no. 3&4, 751–93
Walker, Brian 1997 "Contested Territories: A Critique of Kymlicka", in *Canadian Journal of Political Science*, vol. 30, no. 2, 211–34

Washburn, W.E. 1987 "Cultural Relativism, Human Rights, and the AAA", *American Anthropologist*, vol. 89, no. 4, 939–43
Williams, Rowan, 2008 BBC Interview Feb. 7th, http://www.archbishopofcanterbury.org/1573
Wolin, Richard 2004 *The Seduction of Unreason. The Intellectual Romance with Fascism from Nietzsche to Postmodernists*, Princeton: Princeton University Press
Young, Iris Marion 1989 "Polity and Group Difference: A Critique of the Ideal of Universal Citizenship", *Ethics*, vol. 99, no. 2, 250–74
—— 1997 "A Multicultural Continuum: A Critique of Will Kymlicka's Ethnic-Nation Dichotomy", in *Constellations*, vol. 4, no. 1, 48–53.

Endnotes

1. A topical example of this can be found in the *Malaysia Sun*, April 3rd 2008. The Islamic Institute of Understanding Malaysia (IKIM) and the Sharia department of the Malaysian government organized a seminar which explored the possibilities of holding non-Muslims responsible for violating law in the same way as are Muslims, when they break the law of *Khalwat* which prohibits so-called "close proximity", i.e. holding hands, kissing, etc. A spokesman for the seminar admits that there are currently no legal possibilities for sentencing non-Muslims who commit *Khalwat* with Muslims. A new law is therefore being considered which makes it possible to punish non-Muslims in the same way as Muslims— but in the common courts. In reality, these courts will therefore have to adopt and implement aspects of Sharia law and apply them to non-Muslims. At the same time, it is proposed that the punishment for *Khalwat* be quadrupled.

2. The Archbishop's proposal is not very detailed. He finds that the introduction of sharia in Great Britain "seems inevitable" and speaks for "constructive accomodation to certain aspects of Muslim Law" (Williams, 2008). The already existing possibility for orthodox Jews to use certain aspects of Jewish law in Great Britain is given as argument. It is hard to judge what scope the Archbishop imagines this accommodation should have. Marital law is mentioned as the only example; here, the Archbishop opts for free choice for the individual of which legal system to follow, with the possibility of appeal to ordinary courts. His main argument, however, is that the idea of equality before the law must be given up: "An approach to law which simply said 'there is one law for all' I think that is a bit dangerous" (Williams 2008).

3. It is often argued that this development in anthropology separates biology and culture, but that is not correct. Human biology is, of course, decisive for the possibility for the human race, unlike most other animal species, to develop a comprehensive scope of different languages and cultures learned ontogenetically. To that extent, the ability to form culture constitutes a decisive part of human biology. What Boas separated is cultural variation and biological variation: the former does not have its roots in racial traits of the latter. It is also important to keep this argument separate from the issue of human universals. The claim

that cultural variation does not depend on biological variation is not the same as the claim that there are no universal biological features which characterize man, even if cultural relativism very often minimizes or even denies this. Finally, it is also important to keep this issue apart from the issue of cultural universals (in language, behavior, etc.), the issue of which non-biological features may be universal across cultures.

4.   In the main works of Herder's philosophy of history, *Auch eine Philosophie der Geschichte* (1774) and the large *Ideen zur Philosophie der Geschichte der Menschheit* (1784–91), he turns against the superficial faith in progress of the Enlightenment and presents the idea that historical epochs possess a closed, organic character which each their own claims, and hence they cannot be judged with external measurement criteria. The same thing goes for the actors in this history: the nations. They carry their own value systems within themselves and must be judged on their own criteria, not on those of the observer: "Each nation has its center of happiness within itself, just as every sphere has its center of gravity" (Herder 1990, 35). Herder can thus be counted as one of the founders of historicism. It is well-known how Herder politically became one of the central sources for nationalism, just as his significance for nationalist and historicist currents in the humanities and the social sciences is crucial.

5.   Forster 2006. Also the founding father of British anthropology, Bronislaw Malinowski, was influenced by Herder through his teacher Wundt.

6.   Herder even to a large extent shared the set of basic ideas identified by Jonathan Israel as "radical Enlightenment" (Israel 2011)—so there is a tragic irony in the fact that one of his main historical influences turned out to concern the counter-Enlightenment currents of nationalism and culturalism.

7.   Quoted from Forster 2006.

8.   The anthropology of Boas thus inherits what Thomas Hylland Eriksen calls "the Herderian archipelago vision" of culture—the idea that cultures form isolated islands in an ocean, clearly separated from one another (Eriksen 2001). It should also be kept in mind that "nation" around 1800 not only referred to national states but could also be used to refer to stateless people—the "Polish nation," the "Norwegian nation," the "Serbian nation," etc., even if those groups did not yet form national states.

9. Eriksen and Nielsen 2001, 62
10. Barnard 2000, 102
11. Mead 1959, vii
12. Brown 1991, 65
13. Darnell 2008, 44
14. The Executive Board, apart from President Herskovits, consisted of Clyde Kluckhohn, Charles F. Vogelin, Cora Du Bois, William W. Howells, Ralph L. Beals, and W.W. Hill; the Vice President was Frederick R. Eggan.
15. The "cultures" of the anthropologist are most often, in these discussions, mentioned without any specification, which makes their portrayal as tolerant pacifists easier. In the same volume of AA, however, there are anthropologists who more directly display the behaviors that cultural relativist tolerance is supposed to tolerate. Virginia Heyer writes a defense of Benedictian cultural relativism aimed against a certain Mr. Williams who had ventured the idea that marital violence must be invariably criticizable across cultures. She writes, sharply and correctly, that, "Cultural relativity, in its starkest abstraction, states the relativity of the part to the whole." (164) Williams is now taught, on the basis of this radical holism, that, "Violence in a marital situation will always be relative to the position of women in a society" (164). Heyer herself finds that "non-violence is more humane and more easily controllable than violence, but it does not follow that it would be possible or even constructive in every society. The Plains man treated his wife's adultery with expected dignity, by cutting off the fleshy part of her nose. Since Plains ethics demanded that a wife be faithful, no willingness to overlook adultery could be expected in the ordinary pattern. A meeker or more considerate response brought a man into disgrace before his tribe, dissipating the ideal in him" (164–65). This is plain talk: the Plains man has his full right to amputate his wife's nose, expected dignity and all.
16. This indirect and weak criticism of fascism was not even a part of Herskovits's first draft, but was added after criticism from one of the Board members, W.W. Howells, who feared that "perverted humans" otherwise would be able to say that the anthropologists claim that Franco is as good as anybody else (Washburn 1987, 942). The anthropological tolerance towards such perverted critics is not easily felt.

17. For example the idea, which for a period spread in parts of anthropology, that cannibalism had never existed and was only an ideological anthropological construction, both among neighboring tribes to the alleged cannibals, and among ethnocentric Western anthropologists.

18. Renteln 1988 investigates in more depth some of the aspects of relativism.

19. Berlin and Kay (1969) showed that a ranking exists across languages and cultures of the centrality of color categories (so that a language with only two color terms always has "white" and "black", with three terms always "white," "black," and "red," etc.) as well as a cross-cultural agreement of the place of focal colors in the color spectrum (pure white, pure black, pure red, etc....). This does not preclude, of course, that cognitive effects of linguistic categorization can be found. Thus, it has recently been shown that the Russian distinction between light blue and dark blue as two autonomous color terms makes this categorization more cognitively efficient than the languages which categorizes this distinction as sub variants as one and the same basic blue.

20. Today, this error can be found in scholars who attribute very categorical features to "Islam," such that this religion is assumed to be incompatible with democracy, or that this religion is constitutively peaceful and hence incompatible with terrorism. Both supporters and opponents may thus find weapons in the "organic" concept of culture which implies the attractive economy of thought that complicated social structures with competing subgroups can be reduced to one organic entity to be supported or attacked. Both are, of course, equally problematic.

21. In his defense of relativism, Herskovits (1958) underlines that its core is not the relativity of value systems, but the determinism of "enculturation," which not only refers to values but also to perception and thought, thus containing both ethical and epistemological relativism.

22. A priori: when people in most cultures believe that 2+2=4, it is probably not because it is a cultural heritage, but because 2+2=4. Biological: when human beings in all culture prefers food made up of proteins, carbohydrates and fats, rather than of sand, stones, or mud, it is because of universal features of animal biology. When all human cultures have languages, this is based on specifically human biological capacities not enjoyed by our closest kin, the great apes. When all known languages have demonstratives, it is not because of culture, but because of the need

of pointing out the object you are talking about. Economical: when the scarcity of a good makes its value rise while the abundance of the same good may make its value fall, it is an economical regularity which does not form an inherited value of a culture. Sociological: when two-person groups are more stable than three-person groups, this has sociological reasons which do not stem from specific cultural evaluations. And so forth.

23. Herskovits actually admits this in his (surprisingly weak) apology for relativism (1958) when he concludes that "there is no living in terms of unilateral tolerance, and when there is the appeal to power, one cannot but translate enculturated belief into action" (272). Tolerance must hence hold for all parties; if not, strife is inevitable.

24. The Lévi-Strauss and Finkielkraut quotes are translated by the authors.

25. Baldwin 1902, see also Deacon 1997.

26. Here, Finkielkraut refers to Hélè Béji's *Désenchantement national*.

27. The first chapter of Finkielkraut's book sketches this opposition between two conceptions of nation by relating the strife about Alsace/Elsass in the Franco-Prussian War 1870–1. Here, the Germans annexed Elsass based on the idea that, because the inhabitants spoke German and lived according to German customs, the area rightly belonged to Germany. The French counter-argument was that if the inhabitants were asked, they preferred French citizenship. This case clearly displays the two competing conceptions of nationality and also goes to show the radical anti-individualism of the "hard" conception of culture. If a group has a certain "cultural" characteristic, then it does not matter what the persons in the group actually prefer. This case changed the mind of Ernest Renan, formerly a French culturalist, who articulated his famous slogan about the nation as a "daily referendum."

28. It is strange to observe how culturalism has been able to blind many intelligent persons to accept this idea of "diversity" as an unproblematic basic criterion. One can compare this to how it would play out in other domains; a large diversity of illnesses, of enemies, of crimes, of violent punishments, of suffering, of plagues, of natural disasters, of errors, of lies would hardly be considered success criteria without further ado (See the column on Diversity below).

29. Something similar holds for the Cairo Declaration and other "Islamic rights" and their mixture of universalist and particularist principles, see below.

30. In the USA, the debate on multiculturalism has been considerably less connected to concrete policies and has flowed, to a large extent, into the campus radicalism debates on "political correctness." In concrete politics, US multiculturalism has especially emerged in the contested legislations on "affirmative action" in university admission where individuals from underprivileged groups have easier access than others. Other concrete effects have been aimed at education curricula, especially in universities. Multiculturalists have attacked existing curricula for being biased and too focused upon DWEM (Dead, White, European Males) and demanded a broader representation of other races, cultures, women, etc. in the required reading.

31. Even if the notion of "multiculturalism," as well as specific political actions connected to the term, dates from the 70s, there are clear earlier anticipations to be found in the history of ideas. In a paper from 1915, the German-Jewish-American philosopher, Horace Kallen, argues against the "melting-pot" conception of America and argues for a policy of conservation of immigrant cultures based on his own experience in the Jewish minority in the USA. Around 1907 he had coined the notion "cultural pluralism" that he later argued for in the book, *Culture and Democracy in the United States* (1924), but his efforts had scant results before they were rediscovered and re-circulated in the debates of the 80s and 90s (Sunada 2000). A related idea can also be found in the early American pragmatism of William James's *A Pluralistic Universe* (1909). It is, however, not automatically the case that ideas of "cultural pluralism" have a left wing character, such as is often assumed. Kallen's idea about society as a "democracy of nationalities" was defined on a racial basis and thus implied that "nationalities" were constituted by biological race which was why they could not possibly mix or integrate (Barry 2001, 85). In our context, it is interesting to remark that structurally analogous arguments against assimilation and against the "melting-pot" idea can be found in extremist right wing European groups. An example is the French philosopher Alain de Benoist with the concepts "ethno-pluralism" and the "right to difference." As Vermeulen and Slijper say, "culturalism may even make multiculturalism look very much like the ideology

of the new right" (2000, 7). It is a right wing position which no longer claims the racial foundation of differences but has inherited the idea of the cultural basis of differences from cultural relativism and, on this basis, argues against liberalism and universalism. This position claims that European peoples and cultures should demand the same territorial autonomy and segregation as do many political currents in the Third World (cf. the book *Europe, Tiers monde, même combat*, 1986). The position of de Benoist is thus a right wing Apartheid position on a culturalist basis. Interestingly, de Benoist expresses direct support for the multiculturalist ideas of a "politics of recognition" in Charles Taylor (cf. Vermeulen and Slijper 2000, 8).

32. It is interesting that the adoption of Australian and Canadian multiculturalism was not the result of social movements raising cultural demands (apart from *les québecois* in the Canadian case). As Vermeulen and Slijper say (2000, 12): "It was a small, but effective lobby of ethnic leaders, social scientists and politicians that was involved in the establishment of multiculturalism." The same point is made by Barry (2001, 94), who describes how the Canadian legislation has been created in a narrow collaboration between government departments, law faculties and private organizations with demands for rights, in contrast to the fact that a Canadian opinion poll in 1993 demonstrated an almost 75% majority against multiculturalism (ibid. 292).

33. In the *Charter of Rights and Freedoms*, where the basic civil rights are expressed as follows:

> "2. Everyone has the following fundamental freedoms:
> (a) freedom of conscience and religion;
> (b) freedom of thought, belief, opinion and expression, including freedom of the press and other media of communication;
> (c) freedom of peaceful assembly; and
> (d) freedom of association."

34. Some multiculturalists may favor changes of behavior and culture over legislation measures, (cf. the Hegelian Charles Taylor, favoring change of morality over change of law).

35. Their concept of "community" has been the target for a criticism which may also be aimed at the culturalist notion of culture: how *large*

is such a community? Is it neighborhoods and villages with face-to-face acquaintance among the members of the community, or is it on the scale of cities, nations, countries, or continents? (Waldron 755)

36. Cf. Bhabha 1994, ch. 8.

37. The titles of campus radicalism books and papers are orgies of ing-forms, take for instance *Unthinking Eurocentrism, Re-Imagining Multicultural Britain, Challenging the Liberal Nation-State*...

38. This forms a main point in Gross and Levitt's (1994) attack on campus radicalism, waged from a traditional left wing viewpoint centered on reform rather than polite expressions.

39. Cf. Joppke (2001, 433); yet Young attacks Will Kymlicka for limiting "differentiated citizenship" to minorities and immigrant groups only; to her, many more groups, which need not be territorially defined, should have right to self-government, and a group can have self-government rights regarding some things but not others (1997, 53). She leaves the question of how this fine-grained and ever-changing allocation of rights should proceed in practice unanswered.

40. It can be argued that Taylor's idea that bad press for one's cultural group gives corresponding low self-esteem is not empirically confirmed. Quite to the contrary, empirical investigations seem to show that negative attitudes towards a culture need not be internalized in the members of that group which, in a reaction of spite, may see their self-image strengthened.

41. To Taylor himself, it meant rather equivocal statements as his 1989 claim that those who defended Rushdie's freedom of speech were doing nothing but "endorsing the superiority of some cultures over others" (quoted from Jussawalla 2001, 977).

42. As argued sharply by Waldrop 1992, 760.

43. Schuster 2006 argues clearly, "Taylor would hardly approve of actual policies that discriminate between cultures according to our judgment of their different worth. Yet if studying cultures has no impact on public policy (and thereby on public recognition) why do it in the first place?" In an interesting paper, the Danish philosopher Sune Lægaard (2005) discussed the possibility of a liberal theory of recognition. Even if you recognize "the social basis of self-respect" as a primary good, Lægaard comes to the conclusion that the recognition of the "social basis" of different individuals must, in the last resort, build on the

equal dignity *of individuals*, a recognition which will hardly satisfy the demands of "identity politics" and "difference politics" (348).

44. This is clear even if Taylor's paper does not go into concrete and hard examples of the problem: should recognition also be given to cultures where stoning, cannibalism, totalitarianism are central practices?

45. It is a problem whether this concept of "societal culture" covers minority cultures and immigrant cultures which hardly possess this full range of societal institutions (cf. Benhabib 1999, Schuster 2006). Correspondingly, it can be pointed out that the concept fits badly Kymlicka's, among others, descriptions of "culture," which may change between notions based on territory and on society, on objective and subjective notions, on linguistic or ideological notions (Vermeulen and Slijper 2000).

46. Kymlicka's culturalism is sharply diagnosed by Benhabib (1999), where she counts four central dogmas in multiculturalism: its cultural holism, and the implications flowing from it; the exaggeration of the socialization of individuals; the radical perspectivism; and the suspicion against anything universal. These dogmas make a crucial ability of imagination in democratic politics impossible: the faculty of individuals and groups to take account of the point of view of others, to see a case with others' eyes. Kymlicka overlooks the fact that in sufficiently complex societies, there is hardly any single culture which covers the whole spectrum of human activity.

47. You could say polemically: did Nazi Germany give the individuals of this "societal culture" all the "options" they could chose between? Or did they receive options from elsewhere which this culture, quite to the contrary, tried to prevent from being available? Similar questions could be asked today regarding the cultures of Iran, Pakistan, Saudi Arabia, etc.

48. As Walker (1997, 221–22) says, it would not be correct to say that a Québécois uses his membership of the French-speaking group of Canadians as the actual "context of choice" for his options. He does not act reflecting upon what a typical Montrealer would do; he acts exactly like other modern individuals, with reference to a long series of different institutions, media, organizations, education, religions, of which most are transnational. Québec—the favorite example of Canadian multiculturalism—is already cosmopolitan and hardly fits the picture of a "culture."

49. A strong objection here is that Kymlicka's distinction between these two types of group is much too narrow because of his focus on the culturalist notion of "ethnicity." There are many other groups in society which might also demand special treatment—what about the classic peasants' culture in most Western societies which has come close to extermination during the recent generations, as Walker asks (217–18)? Or what about communities oriented around neighborhoods, fishing towns, subcultures, etc.? Kymlicka wants to delimit his investigation and rule out such groups by means of his "societal cultures" notion, but that concept is so narrow that most of his two groups (national minorities and immigrants) do not really qualify either.

50. Joppke (2001, 435) reasonably asks why such very concrete policies should have the name "rights," would it not be better to call them "contingent policies?"

51. As Barry remarks, Kymlicka constructs something of a myth about the repression of liberal society in order for this equation to fit, as when he laments over the fact that it was only accepted during the 1970s in Canada, Australia, and USA that "...immigrants should be free to maintain some of their old customs regarding food, dress, religion, and recreation, and to associate with each other for those purposes." (quoted from Barry 2001, 317). As Barry adds, it is not his impression that the Italian immigrants in the US have ever been prevented from eating pasta, being Catholics, or playing boccia.

52. As observed by MacDonald 1997, 302–03.

53. MacDonald (1997) also remarks how the culture as a "context for choice" stands in opposition to the specific cultural practices of that culture. The liberalist side of Kymlicka, which does not want culture to be defined only by shared values, must naturally prefer the former.

54. Brian Barry (2001, 118ff) rejects this distinction between tolerance and autonomy as a feigned opposition. The task of the liberal state is not to propagate autonomy, only to make political institutions which make autonomy possible if people so wish.

55. Joppke (2001) also presents a couple of examples which may throw some light upon Kymlicka's principal discussion: "Successfully invoked by immigrant defendants in California, New York, Georgia, and Minnesota, the cultural defense strategy has led some courts to reinterpret rape among Hmong refugees as part of their traditional court-

ship customs; to consider wife-beating and -killing among Chinese as conditioned by 'traditional Chinese values about adultery and loss of manhood'... and to exonerate a Japanese mother who had drowned her three children from manslaughter charges because in Japanese culture mother-child suicide is an accepted way for a betrayed wife to escape shame" (443). In Europe, there have been many similar cases: a German court acquitted a Muslim man from the charge of beating his wife, referring to the permission in sharia law for a husband to punish his spouse (the man was convicted at a higher court, however). In such arguments, individual responsibility and equality before the law is pushed back in favor of summary reference to the traditions of "culture."

56. In Malaysia, we also encountered the argument that the ban on apostasy should protect the individual (presumably against the implication of apostasy that the road to Paradise is blocked). This illustrates very well how Kymlicka's distinction between internal restriction and external protection withers if you involve the self-understanding of the "cultures".

57. A Danish example is the "Islamisk Trossamfund" (Islamic Society of Faith), which in its very name presupposes to represent Danish Muslims in general. Its leaders have acted in different public councils and associations as such representatives. During the Cartoon crisis, however, it became known, through Muhamed Sifaoui's documentary, *Drawings of Wrath*, that the association is, in reality, Salafists (in practice, a Danish section of the radical Muslim Brotherhood) and as such in no way representative of Danish Muslims in general.

58. The routine rejection of many Islamic organizations of any criticism, including criticism based on democratic and liberal principles, as "Islamophobia" constitutes a typical example of such a discussion stopper.

59. Here, he emphasizes that the Ontario sharia proposal was not made in the context of the Multiculturalism Act, but the Arbitration Act; he thinks the proposal would have been rejected even more quickly if the former had been the case. A large chapter on "the European experiment" does not at all address different European policies regarding immigrants, but only changing strategies to spread the multiculturalist faith in Europe, especially in the ex-communist states with minority issues.

60. Later, when he considers the strategies for the continued global expansion of multiculturalism, he admits that there is "virtually no enthusiasm in Asia or the Arab/Muslim world to develop regional norms on minority rights" (308). OIC has, he mentions, an elaborated policy for Muslim minorities in non-Muslim states, (that is, states outside of the OIC) while the organization has absolutely no policy for minorities in the member states of the organization itself.

61. As Schuster (2006) says, Kymlicka's compromise position between liberalism and multiculturalism always tends to "return" to liberalism.

62. Ibbitson's only real argument for ignoring the tension between anti-liberal religions and democratic principles is that those who worry about that tension do not have sufficiently clear proposals for action: "The biggest problem with the argument against toleration of cultures and religions that conflict with Charter rights, or that bring one Charter right into conflict with another, is that we really don't know what is being proposed by the people who make this argument" (67). The argument of the paper is basically that if you do not have a precise cure for a problem then you should keep your mouth shut. Compared to the fact that Kymlicka completely lacks an answer to the challenge of articulating explicit, useful criteria for the application for his (and Canada's) multiculturalism, it does not seem to be a strong argument.

63. As to family, the argument must be that grown-ups freely consent to enter marriage (and may so leave it again) and thus willingly accept the inequality it may involve, whilst, as minors, children cannot decide to leave it (here, public authority is assumed to step in if suspicion of offense to the children's right is presented). It is harder to see why religious organizations should be exempted from legislation pertaining to other associations or assemblies. Kymlicka's argument uses rights lingo in referring to the rights of assembly and association, but these rights are usually not taken as license to break the law.

64. Actually, he repeats Ibbitson's sleeping-dog argument in a slightly milder version: "there have been lots of public debates in Canada recently about potential conflicts between religion and equality rights. But too often these debates have been initiated by right-wing commentators as thinly disguised strategies for attacking immigrants, particularly Muslims, often accompanied by apocalyptic predictions about how Canada's

experiment in multiculturalism is on the verge of collapsing. Such commentators raise these issues in order to discredit multiculturalism" (148). Problematizing multiculturalism is thus seen as just as defaming as the attack on immigrants—that is, something that decent people do not do.

65. Referring to Nancy Rosenblum.

66. Whilst it is right to say that the confidence in liberal gravity is greater in Canada than in Europe for the time being, Kymlicka also gives a piece to solve the puzzle of why that is: the immigration policy of Canada. Given the fact that Canada scores better than most other countries on parameters such as immigrant participation in society, confidence, positive feelings of belonging, etc., this is often believed to be due to multiculturalist policies, but "some of this is undoubtedly due to the fact that we cherrypick our immigrants, selecting the most skilled" (150). One can add the Canadian system of quotas for immigrants from different cultures, so that the single immigrant group remains fairly small. Very often (also in *Uneasy Partners*) these facts are not mentioned by multiculturalism supporters. Would the (fairly weak) Canadian multiculturalism have had the positive effects mentioned if it was not for the—anti-liberal—policy of the selection of the best immigrant material? Are the internal liberal triumphs not bought at the price of an anti-liberal border policy, where the weakest immigration applicants, contrary to the case in most European countries—are rejected in favor of those with high education and work skills?

67. The question here, as Waldron says, is whether the protection of cultures or religious sects has a right to support from state policies. If a certain church vanishes because nobody is any longer attracted by its theology or ritual, then it has the same character of a dress mode or a hobby which disappears—it is not something anybody really needs. (1992, 762). The problem with the whole complex of metaphors involving broken cups and mosaics is that they create images of homogeneity of the past which has given place to heterogeneity of the present. But as Vermeulen and Slijper say: "Whereas the ideology of monoculturalism has neglected or even denied the cultural diversity of the past, the ideology of multiculturalism exaggerates the cultural diversity of the present" (2000, 11).

68. Metonymy, in general, is the figure that represents something by means of something else associated with it for other reasons than simi-

larity. The special metonymy using a part or aspect of the object as sign for the object is technically called a synechdoche.

69. As an expert witness in the French court case where the weekly *Charlie Hebdo* was charged with having reprinted this and others of the twelve drawings.

70. For more about the different meanings of *jihad*, holy war, and the different means for the expansion of Islam, see Crone 2003.

71. We can add that such an interpretation corresponds with Westergaard's own claims about his drawing. There is, of course, no a priori guarantee that he has not happened to draw something running counter to his own explicit intentions, but it should be kept in mind anyway, not least because many critics of the drawing have been very interested in establishing the *intention* or *motivation* behind it. In such readings, it almost appears that it is the intention rather than the drawing itself which is decisive for whether it should be published. Very often such arguments have referred to the text by Flemming Rose accompanying the twelve cartoons, a text talking about "hån, spot og latterliggørelse"— sarcasm, mockery, and ridicule (see below). The quote from Rose's text is very often cut in a way that makes it appear that these three acts should target Muslims in particular. A fair quote of the text, however, shows that it claims that *all* citizens, including Muslims, in a democratic free speech society must get used to being the object of sarcasm, mockery, and ridicule.

72. The expression refers to a classic scene in Romantic Danish literature, namely Oehlenschläger's play from 1805, *Alladin eller den forunderlige Lampe* (Aladdin or the Wonderful Lamp), where Aladdin receives an orange (to be precise: a "Pomerants," a bitter orange), in his turban as a sign of his luck.

73. Peer Bundgaard 2006 comes closest when he claims the cartoon does not display the prophet himself but rather a perverted idea about him, legitimizing murder.

74. As far as can be judged from various expert statements, the depiction ban has a weak theological foundation in Islam, (see below).

75. The following analysis of the *shahâda* is due to the historian of religion and Koran semiotician Thomas Hoffmann. Thanks to him for other good advice as well.

76. Even the detailed and information-rich account of the Cartoon Crisis in Klausen 2009 claims some of the drawings in Jyllands-Posten were "malignant representations of stereotypes in the manner of European anti-semitism" (20). Apart from Westergaard's drawing, she refers to three other drawings among the twelve. She does not make clear, however, why they should be stereotyping, as they represent only one particular person. She only speaks about "a semitic nose" and "lurid and racialist iconography," but fails to argue convincingly that semitic noses form part of any widespread stereotype of Muslims.

Talking about stereotypes, it is strange Klausen claims to be so sensitive. Some pages later, she claims: "Americans think it is the decent thing to say sorry when bad things happen. The English might even apologize for things they have not done just to make people feel better. Muslims think that an apology is a way of showing respect for the other party. (...) Danes, however, take the narrower view that an "apology" is only for cases when you intentionally do something you know is wrong" (31–32). This is homegrown speed anthropology, or, as it were, misleading stereotypes of the four "cultures" mentioned.

77. See Amir Taheri (2006), according to whom the depiction ban in Islam is far from absolute. It is not dictated by the Koran, and the extent to which it is claimed, it is rather due to old, iconoclastic Christian traditions in the area into which Islam expanded. The actual argumentation for a proscription against depiction of Muhammad is thus not due to Islam as such, but only Islamist organizations with a political agenda, such as the Muslim Brotherhood, Salafists, Hamas, Islamic Jihad, al-Qaeda, and the like. In stronger versions of Islam, the image ban may be expanded to cover all living beings, the argument being that man should not be lead to think he can create life. This wider image ban lay behind the Taleban's infamous destruction of the giant Buddhas in Afghanistan.

78. On top of this may come personal motivations among the protesters. Two of the leading imams of the Danish protest committee, Ahmed Akkari and Raed Hlayel, had both, shortly before, been severely criticized in *Jyllands-Posten*, the former for encouraging violence against unveiled girls, and the latter for calling women "instruments of Satan" in his Friday prayers.

79. The ambassadors from eleven Muslim countries wrote a letter to PM Fogh demanding he should take *Jyllands-Posten* "to task under

law of the land." Much ink was spilled after the crisis in discussing the exact implication of that demand—whether it implied a punishment of the newspaper or merely a critique of what they had done. We shall not go into that discussion here.

80. In addition to this comes the imprisonment and court cases against more than ten journalists and editors in the Middle East, as well as death threats and plots against cartoonists and editors in Denmark, who must live under police protection for an indeterminate period. To claim, as many observers do, that such cases have nothing to do with freedom of expression, seems very strange. (see also the manifesto of twelve international intellectuals, spearheaded by Rushdie, prompted by the Cartoon Crisis—a manifesto which may be signed at http:/www.petitionspot.com/petitions/manifesto).

81. According to Klausen (2009, 57), a source in the Danish police claims that two hundred out of many thousand death threats were perceived as credible and investigated, and a dozen plots were graded as serious. Three major court cases have lead to convictions of "home grown" Danish wannabe terrorists, and after Klausen's book, Westergaard was attacked by an axeman in his home.

82. It would take us too far to cover the whole tradition of satirical drawing here. Suffice it to mention that such drawings are known already from Antiquity, and that they enjoy an upsurge in early Enlightenment, with Jacques Callot in France and Romeyn de Hooghe in Holland in the 17th century, with William Hogarth, Mary Darly, and James Gilray in England in the 18th century, to be sophisticated in Thomas Rowlandson and Honoré Daumier in the 19th century. Thus, the modern tradition for satirical cartoons is closely related to the Enlightenment and to the growth of a public sphere of debate, with newspapers and periodicals, in Western societies. The right wing culturalist argument that satirical cartoons constitute a special "Danish value" is thus preposterous.

83. We cannot go into a detailed analysis of the minutiae of the crisis here. The most information-rich accounts are Hansen and Hundewadt (2006) and Klausen (2009). Immediately after the publication on Sept. 30th 2005, four Danish imams from different currents of Sunni radicalism organized a meeting and outlined an action plan with nineteen points, which already included a Middle Eastern boycott of Danish products etc. They contacted a large range of international Muslim and Middle Eastern

organizations. It seems like the escalation of the crises during the fall and winter of 2005 was especially driven by the Egyptian foreign ministry and later the OIC. The Egyptians also involved the League of Arab States (LAS), based in Cairo and led by Amr Moussa (Klausen 2009, 64). The LAS and the OIC sent protest letters to the UN, the EU, the OSCE and the OECD. The Danish imam group undertook two Middle East journeys in the early winter, meeting with a series of high-ranking clerics and politicians. Turkey, whose Ekmeleddin Ihsanoglu headed the OIC, also seems to have supported the escalation. Much has been made of Danish PM Anders Fogh's refusal to meet with eleven Muslim ambassadors in the fall of 2005, but much points to the fact that Egypt was determined to escalation, and that such a meeting would have had little if any effect. With the crisis up and running in early 2006, various Islamist currents (such as al-Qaradawi and the Brotherhood), jumped the bandwagon, and the attacks on Danish embassies seem to have been tolerated if not instigated by Syria and Iran.

Much speculation has circulated about Egypt's motives for spearheading the escalation. One theory, supported by Klausen (2009, 174) is the Egyptian government did it to send a signal to the West about not interfering in Egyptian politics, especially not to condemn Egypt's cracking down on the Muslim Brotherhood. In short, the protest should show that calling for democracy in the Middle East will release anti-Western mobs in the streets.

84. Klausen (2009, 38) directly claims a decision was made at this meeting "to escalate the conflict."

85. Klausen (2009, 78) observes that the Cartoon crisis was what prompted OIC's foundation of their "Islamophobia Observatory" in Jedda. Taking anti-Islamophobia as a common cause in that fraction-ridden organization was already, however, initiated around 2000. Klausen goes some way towards sympathizing with these initiatives for equality reasons. Her perception here is misinformed, however, on some points. One is that she maintains that Muslims in Europe claimed "the same right and protection against prejudice that everybody else enjoys in European democracies" (62), just like she claims Christian sensibilities are, by and large, respected in Denmark. Neither is true; there is no general "protection against prejudice" in European nor Danish law, and the Danish blasphemy paragraph is a "sleeping" paragraph not preventing mock-

ery of things Christian. Again and again, she even speaks as if Holocaust denial were criminal in Denmark (88, 182). Another point is when she quotes the leader of the Arab League Amr Moussa for demanding equal rights: "Christians are not being defamed here" (80) without in any way correcting him. As is well known, the Christian Copts of Egypt suffer severe repression, which is tolerated by the state. Moreover, this is *real* repression, involving murder, arson, violence, forced conversion etc., not just the drawing of cartoons. Klausen does not address this.

86. The text of the proposal went: "A person who uses threatening, abusive or insulting words or behavior, or displays any written material which is threatening, abusive or insulting, is guilty of an offence if (a) he intends thereby to stir up racial or religious hatred, or (b) having regard to all the circumstances racial or religious hatred is likely to be stirred up thereby." The House of Lords sought to soften the text to the following: "A person who uses threatening words or behavior, or displays any written material which is threatening, is guilty of an offence if he intends thereby to stir up racial or religious hatred" (http://pejar.blogspot.com/2008/01/incitement-to-hatred-here-we-go-again.html).

87. The text of that paragraph was: "29J Protection of Freedom of Expression. Nothing in this Part shall be read or given effect in a way which prohibits or restricts discussion, criticism or expressions of antipathy, dislike, ridicule, insult or abuse of particular religions or the beliefs or practices of their adherents, or of any other belief system or the beliefs or practices of its adherents, or proselytizing or urging adherents of a different religion or belief system to cease practicing their religion or belief system" (http://www.opsi.gov.uk/acts/acts2006/ukpga_20060001_en_1).

88. The twenty-one Labour "backbenchers" voting against the law were Joe Benton (Bootle), Ronnie Campbell (Blyth Valley), Colin Challen (Morley & Rothwell), Frank Cook (Stockton North), Jeremy Corbyn (Islington North), Bill Etherington (Sunderland North), Mark Fisher (Stoke-on-Trent Central), Paul Flynn (Newport West), Ian Gibson (Norwich North), John Grogan (Selby), Kate Hoey (Vauxhall), Kelvin Hopkins (Luton North), John McDonnell (Hayes & Harlington), Andrew Mackinlay (Thurrock), Robert Marshall-Andrews (Medway), Gordon Prentice (Pendle), Geraldine Smith (Morecambe & Lunesdale), David Taylor (Leicestershire North West), Rudi Vis (Finchley & Golders

Green), Robert Wareing (Liverpool West Derby), Tony Wright (Cannock Chase).

89. Given the strange circumstances around this vote, one could speculate whether Blair might have left Parliament purposely. Perhaps he did not want the law to pass, after all, and set up a situation in which the law failed to pass without him being held responsible?

90. It might be added that the government led by the Republican party in Ireland, Fianna Fail, passed a Defamation Act involving a severe blasphemy legislation on July 23rd 2009, effective January 1st 2010. The Act increases the fine for blasphemy to € 25.000 and has been attacked by atheists and human rights activists. For the time being, a referendum about the Act is being discussed.

91. http://www.freerepublic.com/focus/f-news/1999750/posts

92. The protection against defamation which we discuss here, and which has been recommended by many under the heading of "Freedom of Speech—BUT," does not, of course, have the character of legislative proposals. Such proposals, however, are widespread in the international pressure against free speech, in UN, in the British, Norwegian, or Irish governments, etc. There have been relatively few in Denmark who have demanded a change in the free speech article of the Constitution. The protection against offense which is discussed here is an informal protection which should be the result of a free agreement among participants in public debate to perform self-censorship. But multiculturalism can hardly imagine delimiting the group rights under discussion to pertain to explicit, formal legislation only. The very point of departure of multiculturalism was that ordinary, formal liberal democracy was insufficient to protect cultural groups because informal suppression took place. Thus, multicultism was concerned with informal protection from the outset, (for example the emphasis on such protection in Taylor and much of Kymlicka, referring to "morality" and "ethos"), but then it ought to be sensitive to informal discrimination, also when it is undertaken by cultural groups themselves against their own members.

93. One immediate consequence, of course, would be that the cultures themselves would have to cut out of their religions and narratives all criticisms of other cultures. It is well-known that both Islam and Christianity contain, within their doctrine, history, and holy books, sub-

stantial attacks against each other, not to mention attacks on polytheists and non-believers. All this should, of course, immediately cease.

94. Brian Barry, *Culture and Equality*, 2001, 11–12.

95. The discussion of both aspects has profited from Barry 2001 (44; 321).

96. That the celebration of cultural "authenticity" is completely alien to traditional, universalist Islam is sharply argued by Al-Azmehs friend Sadiq al-Azm. It is a Heideggerian conception which has been tactically assumed by Islamist groups only during the 1990s, because they discovered that arguing with "authenticity" and related concepts pays off, in relation to the West. In such a world view, there is no autonomous present, no actual moment of potential action which makes possible rational approaches and reflection where political decisions may be made operational. The cultural individuals are not even subjects with their own ability and will to think and act. All human expressions are always already part of the historical and cyclical corpus of kin, culture, and religion. Such a self-image easily plays into the minds of western cultural romanticists on both sides of the political spectrum, eager to understand non-western groups in such terms, in politics, aid associations, academia and tourist industry.

97. Garton Ash 2005

98. Even Taylor retains a version of the two levels when he distinguishes between "(1) the goods of a culture that makes conceivable actions, feelings, valued ways of life, and (2) goods that essentially incorporate common understanding of their value" (quoted after Redhead 2003, 65), where the latter provides the condition of possibility for the cohesion of a politics aimed at radical cultural diversity.

99. The requirement of human rights of non-state actors forms a whole, separate issue in contemporary international law studies, (Clapham 2006). Here the case *Marsh v Alabama* from the American Supreme Court in 1946 is related. In the private corporation town of Chickasaw, owned by Gulf Shipbuilding Corporation, a Jehovah's Witness had been seen distributing pamphlets outside of the post office. He had been arrested by the sheriff of the corporation and later convicted for violating the corporation's regulations. The Supreme Court found that the constitutional freedom of expression of the Witness had been violated by the corporation and concluded that "when we balance the

Constitutional rights of property owners against those of the people to enjoy freedom of press and religion, as we must here, we remain mindful of the fact that the latter occupy a preferred position" (488).

100. Ellemann 2008.

101. The Cairo Declaration thus claims to "complement" the original UN Declaration. This is not quite true when it is the basis of the Cairo Declaration that none of it may conflict with sharia, whose ban on apostasy is, of course, contrary to freedom of religion.

102. As an example, take the Lebanese Subhi Mahmassani, Mayer 168.

103. We cannot go deeply into the extensive discussion of more and less moderate interpretations of Islam (see Schledermann 2007); we must confine ourselves to remark that it is often overlooked that "moderate" may mean several different things. On the one hand, "moderate" may refer to an interpretation which, in some way or other, seeks to articulate an Islam which is compatible with the principles of democracy and rule of law. Such modern interpretations seem, for the time being, to constitute a minority, both as compared to traditional Islam, to classic Islamists (e.g. Wahhabism) and to modern Islamism (e.g. the Brotherhood and its offshoots). This does not necessarily mean, however, that moderation is weak in Islam. "Moderate" may also mean something quite distinct from the character of a theological doctrine, namely the behavior in ordinary believers. Exactly as many western countries have large population of "non-practicing Christians," many Muslim countries have many "non-practicing Muslims" who might pray now and then and pay an occasional visit to the mosque but who take no interest in the various theological doctrines and the differences between them, which they may hardly even know about. Just like with "non-practicing Christians", their number is difficult to judge, but it is a source of error to judge a religion only on the strength of its different theological positions and overlook the inertia of ordinary believers. The non-doctrinal moderation of such Muslims probably constitutes a larger group for the time being than those embracing explicitly moderate or liberal theological-political positions. Think of a classic Bosnian-Muslim joke: "Even when I am most pissed, I would never get the idea to show up in a mosque" (Eriksen and Stjernfelt 2004, 195).

104. The fight of early Enlightenment adherents against absolutist as well as Christian power structures has been meticulously charted in Jonathan Israel (2001, 2006). It is true that certain exiled groups of believers played a special role, such as Portuguese Jews in Holland (Uriel da Costa, Spinoza), or expelled French Huguenots in Holland, England, and Berlin, but this was not because of the theology of those groups, but because living in exile gave individuals in those groups a unique social setting with unforeseen liberties.

105. Cf. Levy 1995, 58ff

106. A Danish variant of Lockean tolerance is propagated by Thomas Bredsdorff and Lasse Horne Kjældgaard in the book *Tolerance* (2008). In the Danish version of the present volume, we argue against their claim that tolerance requires a "living interest" in what you tolerate, as if anybody was able to cultivate a "living interests" in all religious groups in the world. This leads them to assume an antagonistic relation between free speech and tolerance, because the latter is taken to imply that you refrain from attacking what you tolerate, due to your living identification with those persons. Such a definition of toleration as equal to self-restraint (as opposed to toleration as permissivity regarding the opinions of others) is rare to find, even in moderate Enlightenment, and provides a further narrowing of the already narrow Lockean toleration conception. This twisted notion of toleration is probably influenced by culturalist ideas of "respect" for the "dignity" of other cultures, and it is then set up as an antagonistic force to free speech which it should serve to restrain. It goes without saying that this concept of toleration serves as Bredsdorff and Kjældgaards' basis for a harsh attack on the Muhammad drawings and their publication. Such a notion of "tolerance", where the protection of religious sensibility plays center stage, comes closer to Counter-Enlightenment than to any strand of the Enlightenment.

107. Spinoza *Tractatus Theologico-Politicus*, quoted from Israel 1999, 18.

108. The real source of the quote is the English novelist E.B.Hall (writing under the pen name of S.G. Tallentyre) *The Friends of Voltaire* (1906). The quote does sum up, though, Voltaire's general stance.

109. In *Que pense Allah de l'Europe?* , éd. Gallimard, 2004, quoted from http://rappel.over-blog.net/, our translation.

110. As Walker says (1997, 224): "North American culturalists tend to adopt the point of view of ethnic activists for whom an ingroup versus outgroup narrative gives relatively straightforward answers to the question of where cultures are most vulnerable and which deserve protections. But the context for cultural protection in conditions of advanced modernity is considerably more complex than this."

111. In many cases, cultural and national "spokesmen" are persons who are not born into that culture or who only marginally belong to it but who have only learned of it late in life (Vermeulen og Slijper 2000, 12), and then adopt it deliberately in a textbook-like, doctrinaire and inflexible way. As to nationalists, we know such cases as the Austrian Hitler as a German nationalist, the Montenegrinian Karadzic as a Bosnian Serb, the second-generation Serbian Muslim Izetbegovic as a Bosniak. In modern Islamist movements, many leaders are the children of traditional Muslims who only as teenagers take up radical Islamism in a protest against the parental generation, an obvious example being Osama bin Laden, the former disco teenager.

112. This quote and the information preceding it are cited from Hansen and Hundewadt 2006, 81f.

Name Index

Abdel-Ramen, Reda 350
Abdul-Jawad, Mazen 360
Abdullah, Abdul Hakim bin 60-64, 284f, 288
Abdullah, Ahmad Badawi 69
Ahern, Dermot 356
Ahmad, Abdul Jalil 352
Ahmed, Abdirahman 353
Ahmed, Hafiz 338
Ahmed, Kassem 312
Ahmed, Nazir 354
Akbar, Great Mogul 305
Akkari, Ahmed 310, 402
Akon 366
Al-Ansari, Amin 353
Al-Awlaki, Anwar 373
Al-Azm, Sadiq 407
Al-Azmeh, Aziz 239, 253-257, 407
Ali, Ayaan Hirsi 261, 272f, 287, 312
Al-Banna, Hassan 207, 253
Al-Fozan 349
Al-Husseini, Haj Amin 359
Al-Luhaydan, Ibn 349
Al-Munajid, Muhammad 231, 349
Al-Qahtani, Abdulla 369
Al-Qaradawi, Yusuf 222, 306, 327ff, 331, 333, 335, 343, 353f, 404
Al-Sheikh, Hanan 341
Al-Sheikh, Zakaria 344
Al-Yazid, 349
Al-Zawahiri, Ayman 268, 369
Ali, Ayaan Hirsi 217f, 261, 272ff, 287, 312f, 328f, 332, 337, 339, 361
Ali, Syed Mumtaz 157, 325
Als, Roald 208

Amayra, Issam 330
Amer, Karem 374
Andersen, Lars Erslev vii
Anderson, Pamela 371
Annan, Kofi 335
Arjomand, Homa 157
Aros, Mohamed Abdi 370
Ash, Timothy Garton 339, 407, 272f, 275
Aslan, Reza 358
Assadullah, Shoaib 375
Ates, Seyran 338
Atkinson, Rowan ("Mr. Bean") 223, 226, 329
Averroes (Ibn Rushd) 293
Avicenna (Ibn Sina) 293
Badawi, Abdullah Ahmad 346
Badi, Ibrahim 341
Bahari, Maziar 368
Bahatti, Shabaz 376
Baldwin, James Mark 144, 392
Balkenende, Jan Peter 222
Ballin, Ernst 353
Barnard, Alan 390
Barnard, Benno 366
Barnett, H.G. 121, 126
Barry, Brian 166f, 179, 181, 240, 393f, 397, 407
Baruchyan, Aviram 361
Bauman, Zygmunt 23ff
Bayle, Pierre 298
Beals, Ralph L. 390
Béji, Hélè 392
Bell, Daniel A. 289
Bellmer, Hans 339
Benedict XVI, pope 221, 338, 348, 355

Benedict, Ruth 105-117, 121, 123-130, 132, 134f, 139, 142, 150, 249, 256, 274, 276, 301, 323, 390
Benhabib, Seyla 396
Benoist, Alain de 231, 393f
Bentham, Jeremy 277
Benton, Joe 405
Berger, John 326
Berlin, Brent 134, 391
Berlin, Isaiah 270
Bhabha, Homi 161f, 395
Bhatti, Gurpreet 329
Bibi, Asia 374
Bin Laden, Osama 344, 370, 410
Bismarck, Otto von 279
Björk 362
Blair, Tony 222, 225ff, 330, 334
Bluitgen, Kaare 206, 218f, 331
Boas, Franz 103f, 106, 108, 122, 125, 129, 150, 388f
Borges, Jorge Luis 261
Boroujerd, Alaeddin 341
Botero, Catalina 352
Bouchard, Gerard 191f
Boulainvilliers, Henri de 298
Bouyeri, Mohamed 222, 329
Boyd, Marion 157
Bredsdorff, Thomas 409
Breivik, Anders 321f
Brown, Dan 263, 357
Brown, Donald E. 105, 108, 390
Brown, Gordon 222
Bruckner, Pascal 272f
Bruno, Giordano 292
Bujak, Shawan 372
Bundgaard, Peer vii, 401
Buruma, Ian 272ff, 339

Bush, George W. 213
Butt, Ghuforr 354
Cain, James P. 375
Calderoli, Roberto 336
Callot, Jacques 403
Campbell, Ronnie 405
Capriolo, Ettore 326
Carrel, Alexis 246
Carell, Rudi 325
Carpenter, Edward, 115
Cassirer, Ernst 267
Césaire, Aimé 148
Chafiq, Chahla 337
Chagoya, Enrique 373
Challen, Collin 405
Cheema, Amer 337
Chesser, Zachary 371
Chirac, Jacques 336
Chirita (Malaysian author) 16-22 , 233
Choudary, Anjem 351
Choukri, Mohamed 341
Clapham, Andrew 407
Clarkson, Jeremy 371
Clinton, Bill 334
Clinton, Hilary 361, 378
Conquilla, Fernand Cortes de 347
Cook, Frank 405
Corbyn, Jeremy 405
Costa, Uriel da 409
Crone, Patricia 401
Cruise, Tom 257
Cummings, Dale 213
Dahl, Roald 326
Damgaard, Puk 363
Dante Alighieri 358
Darabi, Louiza 330
Darly, Mary 403

Darnell, Regna 390
Darwin, Charles 275, 355, 363
Daumier, Honoré 403
David, Qamar 364
Dawkins, Richard 349, 356
Dawson, Benjamin 14, 78-96, 97, 142, 178
Dea, Patrick 213
Deacon, Terrence 392
Deix, Manfred 362
Derrida, Jacques 161, 252
Dewi, Kartika Dari 359
D'Holbach, Paul Henri Thiry Baron 298
Diabate, Toumani 350
Diderot, Denis 298
Dilthey, Wilhelm 104, 109, 256
Disney, Walt 261
Djavann, Chahortt 306
Doukaev, Lors 372
Du Bois, Cora 390
Durkheim, Émile 262
Dworkin, Ronald 172
East, Carl 371
Eggan, Frederick R. 390
El-Hadjib, Youssef 338
Eliade, Mircea 251f
Ellemann-Jensen, Uffe 280, 408
Enden, Franciscus van den 298
Englund, Peter 365
Erdogan, Tayyip 222, 332, 335, 342
Eriksen, J-M vii
Eriksen, Thomas Hylland 149ff, 301f, 323f, 389f
Etherington, Bill 405
Fadlallah, sheikh 333
Fallaci, Oriana 337
Falwell, Jerry 328

Fanon, Frantz 148, 167
Faulks, Sebastian 359
Feuerbach, Ludwig 262
Finkielkraut, Alain 147-151, 184, 392
Fisher, Mark 405
Fitzpatrick, James 375
Flynn, Paul 405
Foda, Farag 326
Forster, Michael 104, 389
Forsyth, Neil vii
Fourest, Caroline 242, 337
Franco, Francisco 390
Frattini, Franco 336, 340
Frederick the Great 270
Freud, Sigmund 262
Frevert, Louise 220
Friedman, Roger 357
Fukuyama, Francis 164, 168
Fuller, Jake 213
G., Helmut 374
Gadaffi, Muammar 376
Gan, Steven 5, 24, 30, 39-49, 78
Geele, Mohammed 222, 376
Geertz, Clifford 125-128, 133
Gheit, Abdul 332f
Gibson, Ian 405
Gilray, James 403
Girbaut, François 330
Glenn, Dorothy 352
Goethe, Johann Wolfgang von 120
Goggins, Paul 226, 334
Gogh, Theo van 217f, 222, 272f, 313, 316f, 320, 329f, 333, 361
Gowalkar, Madhav 253
Griffiths, Tom vii
Grogan, John 405
Gross, Paul 395

Grosz, George 247
Gürsel, Nedim 357f
Habermas, Jürgen 276
Haderer, Gerhard 330
Hajaghaei, Mohammed 376
Hall, E.B. 409
Hamad, Jihad 338
Hansen, John 403, 410
Haraszti, Miklos 352
Hari, Johann 354
Harman, Harriet 365
Hassoun, grand mufti 333
Hauge, Hans vii
Headley, David 361, 365, 378
Hegazy, Muhammed 342
Hegel, G.W.F. 8, 164, 191
Heidegger, Martin 267
Hera, Sooreh 341
Herder, Johann Gottfried von 104f, 122, 147, 165, 167, 389
Herskovits, Melville 116-127, 131, 135, 137, 390ff
Herslow, Carl 372
Heyer, Virginia 390
Hilal, Hissa 366
Hill, W.W. 390
Hitchens, Christopher 216
Hitler, Adolf 354, 401
Hlayel, Raed 402
Hoey, Kate 405
Hoffmann, Thomas vii, 401
Hogarth, William 403
Holyoake, G.J. 259
Hooghe, Romeyn de 403
Hopkins, Kelvin 405
Houllebecq, Michel 328
Howard, Ron 357

Howell, Kenneth 370
Howells, William W. 390
Hrdlicka, Alfred 345
Humboldt, Wilhelm von 104
Hundewadt, Kim 403, 410
Ibbitson, John 193f, 197, 399
Ibrahim, Abdullah 41
Ibsen, Henrik 376
Igarashi, Hitoshi 326
Ihsanoglu, Ekmeleddin 335, 404
Irving, David 36
Israel, Jonathan 297, 389, 409
Izetbegovic, Alija 410
Jabotinski, Ze'ev 253
Jagland, Thorbjørn 228
James, William 393
Jani, Ehsan 344
Jayasekara, Rohan 329
Jerefeyev, Andrei 370
Jerichow, Anders 348
"Jihad Jane" (Collen LaRose) 366, 376
Joffe, Josef 322
John, Elton 365, 367
Johnson, Paul 326
Jones, Sherry 347, 350
Jones, Terry 376
Jong-Il, Kim 213
Joppke, Christian 163, 395, 397
Joy, Lina 72, 78f, 94, 97ff, 284, 296, 339, 355
Jussawalla, Feroza 395
Kabilan, K. 30-39
Kalisch, Sven 356
Kallen, Horace 393
Kambaksh, Perwiz 341
Kant, Immanuel 8, 120, 191
Karadzic, Radovan 410

Kashmiri, Ilyas 361, 375
Kay, John 134, 391
Kazemi, Jafar 376
Kerkar, Subodh 359
Khader, Naser 287
Khaldun, Ibn 293
Khaleel, 213
Khamenei, ayatollah 213
Khatun, Shiria 365
Khomeini, ayatollah 222, 325f
Khoury, Elias 341
Kielan, Abd 361
Ki-moon, Ban 342, 344
Kippenberger, Martin 347
Kjældgaard, Lasse Horne vii, 409
Kjærsgaard, Pia 202
Klausen, Jytte 225, 358, 361f, 402ff
Kluckhohn, Clyde 390
Kobrin, Nancy 339
Koerbagh, Adriaan 292, 298
Koestler, Arthur 194
Kojève, Alexandre 164
Köppel, Roger 337
Kouchner, Bernard 356
Krois, John Michael vii
Kukathas, Chandran 179f
Kundera, Milan 341
Kymlicka, Will vii, 8, 164, 168, 171-198, 230ff, 248, 275, 284, 287, 298, 302, 395-400, 406
Laban, Abu 217, 310
Lægaard, Sune vii, 395
Laplace, Pierre-Simon 144
Latham, John 331
Le Carré, John 326
Lenin, Vladimir Ilyich 120, 370
Lévinas, Emmanuel 252

Lévi-Strauss, Claude v, 124, 139-147, 149, 230, 392
Levitt, Norman 395
Lévy, Bernard-Henri 319, 337, 353
Levy, Leonard 409
Livingstone, Ken 331
Locke, John 297f, 409
Lushkov, Yuri 355
Luther, Martin 292f
McCartney, Paul 349
MacDonald, Leighton 397
McDonnell, John 405
McGuinty, Dalton 157
Machiavelli, Niccolo 270
Mackinlay, Andrew 405
Mafouz, Nahguib 327
Mahathir, Mohammed bin 23-30, 33, 36, 47f, 69, 80, 89ff, 94, 288, 345
Mahmassani, Subhi 408
Maistre, Joseph de 148
Malik, Kenan 311
Malik, Najibullah 369
Malinowski, Bronislaw 104, 389
Manji, Ishad 337
Manuel II Paleologos 338
Maple, Sarah 350
Marcouch, Ahmed 353
Margalit, Avishai 172
Marshall-Andrews, Robert 405
Marx, Karl 148, 204, 262, 269
Matravers, Philip of Worth 346
Mattei, Roberto de 363
Mayer, Ann Elizabeth 281ff, 284-287, 408
Mawdudi, Abdul Ala 207
Mead, Margaret 105, 107, 138, 390
Meijer, Lodewijk 298

Menching, Gustav 252
Merkel, Angela 372
Miliband, David 353
Mill, John Stuart 172
Momani, Jihad 335
Montesquieu, C.-L. de 271
Moore, Charles 329
Moussa, Amr 404f
Mozaffari, Mehdi vii, 205, 254, 337
Mozart, Wolfgang Amadeus 338
Mubarak, Hosni 377
Muhammad, Feiz 371
Muhammed, Omar Bakri 317ff, 322
Munch, Peter Rochegune 279f
Naipaul, V.S. 75
Nalliah, Danny 330
Namazie, Maryam 337
Nasreen, Taslima 327, 337, 340, 344, 364
Navarsete, Liv Signe 228
Nazir-Ali, Michael 341
Nekschot, Gregorius 213, 345
Nelson, Cary 358
Nezim, Aziz 327
Nielsen, Finn Sivert 390
Nielsen, Morten Ebbe Juul vii
Nietzsche, Friedrich 112
Nieznalska, Danuta 328
Nilsson-Mäki, Kjell 213
Nisim-Sabat, C. 127f
Norris, Molly 367
Noor, Farish A. 77, 273
Nygaard, William 327
Obama, Barack 360
Oehlenschläger, Adam 401
Okin, Susan Muller 193
Olmert, Ehud 355
Omar, Mona 332

Orwell, George 294, 325
Othman, Norani 72-78, 273, 348
Otto, Rudolf 251f
Pamuk, Orhan 357, 377
Panahi, Jafar 364, 374
Parker, Trey 367
Pascal, Blaise 140
Pasha, Ahmed 353
Pearl, Daniel 319
Peel, Quentin 349
Pettit, Philip 269
Piening, Günter 359
Pillay, Navi 356
Pin, Ayah 65f
Pinkwart, Andreas 356
Prentice, Gordon 405
Pourmand, Hamid 330
Pullman, Philip 366
Qureshi, Maulana 336, 362
Qutb, Sayyed 207
Raahauge, Kirsten Marie vii
Ramadan, Tariq 306, 327
Ramon, Chief 107, 109, 123, 323
Rana, Tahawwur 361
Rasmussen, Anders Fogh v, 208-220, 332, 356, 402, 404
Rawls, John 160f, 172, 275
Raz, Joseph 172
Redeker, Robert 338
Redhead, Mark 407
Reid, Lord 80
Renan, Ernest 255, 392
Renteln, A.D. 131, 136, 391
Rodin, Auguste 359
Roosevelt, Elanor 8
Rose, Flemming 219, 231, 331, 340, 361, 372, 378, 401

Rosenblum, Nancy 400
Rousseau, Jean-Jacques 165, 167
Rue, Frank la 352
Rushdie, Salman 149, 166, 215, 221f, 263, 287, 325ff, 337, 340, 395, 403
Sabaditsch-Wolf, Elisabeth 376
Sacranie, Iqbal 225f, 326, 329, 333f
Said, Edward 161
Samadurov, Jury 370
Sanad, Maikel Naibel 377
Sandel, Michael 160, 172
Sapir, Edward 104, 133f
Sapp, Wayne 377
Saramago, José 261
Schäuble, Wolfgang 343
Schledermann, Helmuth 217f, 408
Schmidt. P.F. 118, 130f
Schmitt, Carl 267, 278
Schuster, A. 395f, 399
Scorsese, Martin 325
Scot, Daniel 330
Sdvizhkov, Aleksander 341
Seidenfaden, Tøger 208f
Self, Colin 340
Sen, Amartya 186, 248, 291, 304ff
Sener, Nedim 377
Seng, Yap Swee 64-72, 286
Servetus, Michael 292
Sfeir, Antoine 337
Shahzad, Faisal 368
Sheikh, Omar 319
Sifaoui, Mohammed 337, 398
Sik, Ahmet 377
Simmel, Georg 304
Skinner, Quentin 269
Slijper, Boris 393f, 400, 410
Smith, Barry 132
Smith, Geraldine 405
Smith, Jacqui 341, 354
Solana, Javier 335
Spencer, Herbert 140
Spengler, Oswald 109, 114, 256
Spielberg, Steven 374
Spivak, Gayatri 161f
Spinoza, Baruch de 292, 298, 409
Stein, Janice Gross 193ff
Steward, Julian 120f, 126
Stjernfelt, Agnete vii
Stjernfelt, Frederik vii
Stone, Matt 367
Stoltenberg, Jens 228
Straw, Jack 349, 366
Stuttmann, Klaus 336
Taheri, Amer 402
Tallentyre, S.G. 409
Tantawy, Muhammed 333
Taseer, Salman 375f
Taylor, Charles v, 8, 139, 160f, 164-171, 191ff, 195, 198, 301, 394ff, 406
Taylor, David 405
Telnaes, Ann 368
Tjønn, Halvor 372
Tlakula, Pansy 352
Thompson, Todd 356
Thomsen, Søren Ulrik vii
Tøgersen, Bård 314f
Tomason, Audrey 378
Tocqueville, Alexis de 269
Travolta, John 357
Trevor-Roper, Hugh 326
Trier, Lars von 358
Trudeau, Pierre 153
Twain, Mark 362, 375
Tylor, Edward B. 140

Ul-Haq, Mohammed 340
Val, Philippe 337
Vanini, Lucilio 292
Vermeulen, Hans 393f, 400, 410
Vilks, Lars 320, 340, 343, 365-368, 370, 374, 376
Vis, Rudi 405
Vogelin, Charles F. 390
Voltaire, François de 261, 299, 327, 409
Waldron, Jeremy, 323, 395, 400
Walker, Brian 312, 396f, 410
Wallraff, Günter 340
Walzer, Michael 160
Wareing, Robert 406
Warraq, Ibn 262, 327, 337
Washburn, W.E. 128f, 390
Washington, George 204
Weiwei, Ai 377
Westergaard, Kurt 202f, 213f, 219, 222, 246, 314, 342, 356, 359f, 362, 364, 368, 372f, 376, 378, 402f
Whorf, Benjamin Lee 133f
Wilders, Geert 341, 343ff, 353f, 360f, 371
Williams, Juan 373
Williams, Rowan, 103, 287, 341f, 388
Winehouse, Amy 353
Winter, Susanne 353
Wit, Leo de 346
Wolff, Christian 292
Wright, Tony 406
Wundt, Wilhelm 104, 389
Xiaobo, Liu 373
Yamani, Faisal 360, 364f
Yasin, Khalid 353
Young, Iris 161, 163, 395
Yula, Ozen 363
Yussoff, Yaacob bin 50-59, 230, 285, 288

Yuzuk, Paul 153
Zaid, Abu 286f, 296
Zakaria, Abdul Aziz 360
Zapiro 369
Zappa, Frank 362
Zehri, Israr 349
Zlatan (Zlatan Ibrahimovic) 308
Zuckerberg, Mark 370

Also from Telos Press

Timothy W. Luke and Ben Agger
A Journal of No Illusions
Telos, Paul Piccone, and the Americanization of Critical Theory

Carl Schmitt
Hamlet or Hecuba:
The Intrusion of the Time into the Play

Victor Zaslavsky
Class Cleansing: The Massacre at Katyn

Ernst Jünger
On Pain

Paul Piccone
Confronting the Crisis: Writings of Paul Piccone

Matthias Küntzel
Jihad and Jew-Hatred: Islamism, Nazism, and the Roots of 9/11

Carl Schmitt
Theory of the Partisan

Carl Schmitt
The Nomos *of the Earth in the International Law of the* Jus Publicum Europaeum

Jean-Claude Paye
Global War on Liberty